STUDENT TEXTBOOK - ELE...

AMERICA'S STRUGGLE TO BECOME A NATION

Understanding the
Foundations of Freedom

RICK & MARILYN BOYER

First printing: November 2015

Master Books®, P.O. Box 726, Green Forest, AR 72638
Master Books® is a division of the New Leaf Publishing Group, Inc.

ISBN: 978-0-89051-910-3
ISBN: 978-1-61458-459-9 (ebook)
Library of Congress Catalog Number: 2015916603

Cover design by Diana Bogardus.
Interior design by Terry White.
A special thanks to Christina Boyer for supplying the journal entry suggestions and many of the projects in the Teacher's Guide for use with this book.

Scripture quotations taken from the King James Version of the Bible.

Please consider requesting that a copy of this volume be purchased by your local library system.

Printed in the United States

Please visit our website for other great titles:
www.masterbooks.com

For information regarding author interviews,
please contact the publicity department at (870) 438-5288.

Righteousness exalteth a nation: but sin is a reproach to any people (Proverbs 14: 34).

Master Books®
A Division of New Leaf Publishing Group
www.masterbooks.com

Contents

HOW TO USE THIS BOOK:

This book is designed to be used in coordination with *America's Struggle to Become a Nation Teacher Guide* also available from Master Books.

This curriculum is divided into 34 chapters in all, one for each week of the school year. Each chapter is divided into 3 reading sections.

There are at least two ways you can use it, depending on what fits your schedule best.

SUGGESTED PLAN: FIVE DAYS PER WEEK

Students will read a chapter per week. Each chapter is divided into three sections. On Monday, Tuesday, and Wednesday they will read one section. Projects supplied in *America's Struggle to Become a Nation Teacher Guide* will be done on Thursday. On Friday, student will complete the test questions provided in Teacher Guide.

ALTERNATIVE PLAN: FOUR DAYS PER WEEK

Students will read selections on any three days of the week you choose. They will then answer 1/3 of the questions supplied in *America's Struggle to Become a Nation Teacher Guide* each day when they finish reading. (Chapters are divided into 3 sections to make it easy to see where to read.) On the fourth day they can do the projects that are located in the Teacher Guide.

Additional recommended resources are provided in *America's Struggle to Become a Nation Teacher Guide*. Our aim is for your kids to learn to love American history! We suggest audio recordings that kids can listen to while they play or travel or at nighttime as well as books for reading fun. Publisher's Note: Since the audio selections do concern a time of war, we recommend that all audios be previewed by an adult to determine the age-appropriateness of the material.

The Grand Union flag (left) is considered the first American flag, prior to the Stars and Stripes (right).

WHO IS UNCLE RICK?

Hi! I'm Uncle Rick, the family storyteller. I love to tell boys and girls exciting true stories about America's history. I also like to record wonderful old books about America. God's hand is so plain in the history of our country!

In the Founders of Freedom history series, you'll often see me dressed in my Founding era outfit. That's because, whatever period of American history I'm teaching about, I always want to call our attention back to the godly principles of America's founding.

I hope you love America as much as I do. God has blessed our nation with freedom, prosperity, and peace. He has made America the leading nation of the world. Millions of people have come here from other countries seeking a better life. Many millions more hope to come someday.

The people who built America gave us a nation founded on the principles of Scripture. It is that wonderful heritage that gave us liberty in the beginning and has kept us free for over two hundred years. I hope that you will enjoy learning about our country's history with me. The freedom and justice that we enjoy today are God's gift to us. Let us treasure and protect that gift so that we can pass it on to future generations.

(You can listen to my audiobooks at UncleRickAudios.com.)

Yankee Doodle, 1776, three patriots, two playing dru and one playing a fife leading troops into battle

CHAPTER I

WHY A WAR OF INDEPENDENCE?

A HERITAGE OF FREEDOM

If we want to understand a big event in history, one of the most important questions to ask is, "Why did it happen?" If we know that something happened but don't know why it happened, it shows that we do not understand the event very well.

As Americans, we need to understand why the United States came into existence. Why did 13 small colonies of Englishmen decide that they did not want to be Englishmen anymore? Why were they willing to have a war that they knew would kill many people, cause homes to be destroyed, and make some people enemies of their own neighbors? War is always a terrible thing. Surely the colonists knew that.

Did the Founders consider themselves to be in rebellion?

The First Prayer in Congress September 7, 1774 by Jacob Duché in Carpenters Hall, Philadelphia, by T.H. Matheson 1848 (PD-US).

The Founders clearly believed that they were not in rebellion to God's ordained institution of civil government; they were only resisting tyranny and not the institution itself. In fact, Rev. Jacob Duché (a supporter of the British) argued from the Bible in favor of the American position, explaining:

> Inasmuch as all rulers are in fact the servants of the public and appointed for no other purpose than to be "a terror to evil-doers and a praise to them that do well" (cf. Romans 13:3), whenever this Divine order is inverted — whenever these rulers abuse their sacred trust by unrighteous

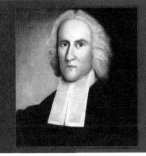

Jonathan Edwards, a Puritan preacher from Massachusetts, preached in Enfield, Connecticut, on July 8, 1741. His sermon, "Sinners in the Hands of an Angry God," is probably the most famous sermon ever preached in America. Edwards was no great orator. He read his sermon from a script and was so nearsighted that he had to hold a candle next to his page in order to read it. Yet the Spirit of God moved so powerfully on this occasion that people were clinging to the pews and columns of the church as if in danger of sliding suddenly into hell. Many cried to the preacher, "What must I do to be saved?"

Rev. Dr. John Witherspoon

attempts to injure, oppress, and enslave those very persons from whom alone, under God, their power is derived — does not humanity, does not reason, does not Scripture, call upon the man, the citizen, the Christian of such a community to "stand fast in that liberty wherewith Christ . . . hath made them free!" (Galatians 5:1). The Apostle enjoins us to "submit to every ordinance of man for the Lord's sake," but surely a submission to the unrighteous ordinances of unrighteous men, cannot be "for the Lord's sake," for "He loveth righteousness and His countenance beholds the things that are just."

Since the Englishmen in England and the Englishmen in America had so much in common, it might seem surprising that there was ever a war between the two groups. After all, they shared the same language. They shared the same rulers. They shared the Christian faith. They shared the same history, at least up until the time the colonies had been established.

But in fact, the main reason the American colonists gained their independence was *because* they were Englishmen. The English people had a long history of struggling to be free. It was a part of their traditions. Englishmen knew about Magna Carta (Latin for "The Great Charter") in 1215. The Magna Carta had greatly weakened the power of the king. Much of English law was based on it.

The Rev. Dr. John Witherspoon (also a signer of the Declaration) also affirmed:

> On the part of America, there was not the most distant thought of subverting the government or of hurting the interest of the people of Great Britain, but of defending their own privileges from unjust encroachment; there was not the least desire of withdrawing their allegiance from the common sovereign [King George III] till it became absolutely necessary — and indeed, it was his own choice.[2]

Significantly, as Dr. Witherspoon had correctly noted, it was Great Britain who had terminated the entreaties; in fact, during the last two years of America's appeals, her peaceful pleas were directly met by armed military force. King George III dispatched 25,000 British troops to invade his own colonies, enter the homes of his own citizens to take their private possessions and

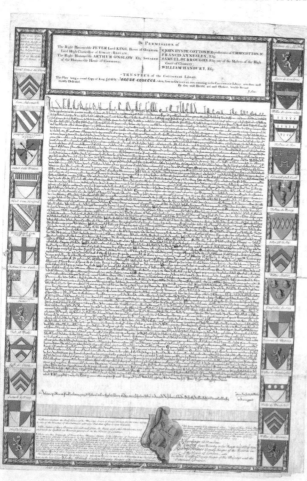

A 1733 engraving of the Magna Carta of 1215 by John Pine (PD-US).

goods, and imprison them without trials — all in violation of his own British Common Law, English Bill of Rights, and Magna Carta (centuries-old documents that formed the basis of the covenant between British rulers and citizens). Only when those governmental covenants had been broken by their rulers and America had been directly attacked did the Americans respond in self-defense.[3]

So it was that in the 1700s when King George III and Parliament insisted on doing things that violated the rights of Englishmen, there was strong reaction. In fact, there were many people in England who agreed that the colonists were not being treated fairly.

By the time battles were finally fought between the British army and the colonists at Lexington and Concord, a strong spirit of independence and self-reliance had grown up in America. These people were descended from those who had left Europe and risked the dangers and hardships of travel in those days to make a new life for themselves and their families in North America. Their parents or grandparents or great-grandparents had faced the hazards of a wilderness far from home and all the comforts of civilization.

Theologian Jonathan Edwards

The people in the young American colonies had grown sturdy and confident in overcoming great obstacles. They had cleared land for farms, built homes, grown their own food, made their own clothes, and protected their own settlements from hostile Indians. They had received very little help from the king in doing all this, so they felt far more independent of him than did their brethren in England.

This did not mean that the colonists did not love England and their king. The people of New World still loved their mother country. They considered themselves Englishmen first. The earliest settlers told their children stories of their homeland with all its rich history and heroes. But their experience of living without much help from the government back home had a lasting impact on their way of thinking.

British Parliament meets in the Palace of Westminster. Photo by DAVID ILIFF, 2007 (CC-BY-SA 3.0).

GEORGE WHITEFIELD

English-born George Whitefield was the foremost voice of the Great Awakening in America. He made several trips to America in the years before the Revolutionary War, preaching from Georgia all the way up to Maine. Many of the pulpits in the towns were closed to him because of his unusual way of ministering. Establishment ministers complained that he preached outside God's house and was harsh to sinners. Indeed, he did preach outdoors, especially after the churches refused to allow him in their pulpits. He had a tremendously clear and loud voice with which he could make himself heard by the huge crowds who turned out to hear him. He preached with a unique power, often leaving many people on their faces on the ground under deep conviction. He was a personal friend of Benjamin Franklin, who was pleasantly amazed at the positive effect Whitefield had on religious life in his town of Philadelphia. Franklin estimated that Whitefield could be heard by a crowd of thirty thousand. The evangelist often attracted crowds that large and even larger. When word went out that Whitefield was coming to a town to preach, the roads for miles around would sometimes be covered with clouds of dust rising high into the air as thousands of people left their fields and hurried down the roads to the meeting place.

The preachers of the Great Awakening did not all agree on every point of doctrine or teaching, but they all understood that salvation is by faith alone and through grace alone. It is not by good works, but by believing in Christ that our sins are forgiven and we are made new creatures.

"For God so loved the world that he gave his only begotten Son, that whosoever believeth in him should not perish, but have everlasting life."
—John 3:16.

Another reason for the independent spirit of the generation of 1776 was the Great Awakening. This was a mighty revival God sent to both England and America in the 1700s. John Wesley and George Whitefield were among the early leaders of this revival, from which the Methodist Church was born. Wesley's ministry took place mostly in England and his effect on the country was very strong. Whitefield made several voyages to America during the middle of the century and preached, often drawing crowds of many thousands. He and other prominent preachers such as Jonathan Edwards, Samuel Davies, and Jonathan Mayhew were often opposed by leaders of the Church of England, but they continued to preach and thousands were converted to Christ.

Many of them joined or formed churches not connected to the Church of England (also called the Anglican Church in England and the Episcopal Church in America). These independent churches did not take orders from a denomination. They ran their own affairs without interference from a national church.

It is important to understand also that many of the early colonists had come to America because of religious persecution by the Church of England. The Pilgrims, though they were loyal to their king, had suffered much at the hands of the king's church. Men who preached without a license from the church were jailed. People who worshiped in independent churches were sometimes jailed also, and others had their property seized or paid heavy fines. Boston was founded by Puritans, Christians who had not left the national church but wanted reforms in the church to make it conform to what the Bible teaches. Puritans were often persecuted as well, and they and the Pilgrims (who were among those called Separatists) got used to running their own local churches, as they believe the Bible directed. Religious freedom was the most important freedom of all to them.

John Wesley, artist and date unknown (PD-US).

Part of the message of the gospel is that all men are born sinners. This meant that, by nature, a king is no better than a

Embarkation of the Pilgrims, by Robert Walter Weir, 1857 (PD-Art).

11

Samuel Adams

peasant. All men stand in need of salvation through Christ. This truth also served to reduce the awe in which Americans held the throne of England. They certainly believed that the king and Parliament were to be obeyed, as long as they acted in obedience to God. But when the English government began to do things that English law did not give them authority to do, the colonists were not afraid to protest.

In fact, Samuel Adams (the "Father of the American Revolution" and a signer of the Declaration of Independence) specifically recommended a study of the Scriptures in order to understand the basis of America's struggle against a tyrannical king, explaining that:

> The Rights of the Colonists as Christians. . . . may be best understood by reading and carefully studying the institutes of the great Law Giver and Head of the Christian Church, which are to be found clearly written and promulgated in the New Testament.[4]

In 1638, the Rev. Glover brought a printing press across the sea from England. He died on the voyage, but his widow wasted no time in setting up a printing business with the help of Harvard College. Harvard's first president, Henry Dunster, took an interest in the press, which issued a publication called a "broadside," titled *The Freeman's Oath*, an Almanac (only eight pages long) and the famous *Bay Psalms Book*, a hymnbook with only lyrics and no musical notes.

The confidence of the Americans was also supported by the fact that they were a productive people. By the time of independence, the colonies were producing timber, tobacco, and other crops that England wanted. In 1760 alone, they had sent over five million dollars' worth of products to England. That was a very large amount of money in those days. So the colonists had another reasons to feel that their voice should be heard in the British government.

AN ARGUMENT WITH A PROUD KING

In fact, the colonies had developed greatly in the years since the first English colony, Jamestown, was established a century and a half before. In 1639 the first printing press in America had gone to work. Books and newspapers began to spread. Six colleges had been started and town schools had sprung up to educate children. The first six colleges in America were Harvard (1638), William and Mary (1692), Yale (1700), Princeton (originally called the College of New Jersey, in 1746), and King's in 1754.

The church pulpits were occupied by men who preached with wisdom and power. So the communities of young America were advancing by their success in trade, the strength of their churches, the harmony of their communities, and the spread of information through their newspapers and books. They were developing an established culture of their own that was not dependent on how everybody thought in England.

One important issue in the war was "taxation without representation." The people in England voted for men to represent their home districts in making laws for the nation. This was similar to what we Americans have in Congress. Just as the president of the United States has to share power with Congress, so the king had to share power with Parliament. He could not do whatever he wanted to do just because he was king. Together, the king and Parliament made laws, including laws about taxes.

> Harvard University, like most of the early American colleges, was started in order to train preachers. Number two in its rules for students was this:
>
> "Let every Student be plainly instructed, and earnestly pressed to consider well, the main end of his life and studies is, to know God and Jesus Christ which is eternal! John 17:3 and therefore to lay Christ in the bottome, as the only foundation of all sound knowledge and Learning. And seeing the Lord only giveth Wisdom, Let every one seriously set himself by prayer in secret to seeke it of him" —Proverbs 2,3

But the colonists in America did not have representatives in Parliament. They had colonial governments made up of men elected by the people. The colonies required the people to pay taxes, but there was no great objection to that, because the colonists had the chance to vote on their representatives. They believed that the laws of England gave them the right to vote for those who taxed them, just as Englishmen in England did.

But most people were not willing to go to war just over taxes. That was one reason for the disagreements that led to war, but there was much more to the problem.

The French and Indian War (1754–1763) had much to do with the founding of America for two important reasons. First, it had shown the American settlers that they could organize, prepare, and deploy forces to defend their colonies. In addition, it had driven the British government far in debt. That meant that the government needed money, and when governments need money they get it through taxes.

George Washington on horse, soldiers fighting during the battle of the Monongahela, 1854 (PD-US).

Death of General Wolfe (French and Indian War)

In the argument over this, the English government had some truth on their side. They reminded the colonies that they had provided a navy to protect American shipping from the French. The colonies replied that this was true, but England required them to trade only with England. So it was partly for England's benefit that the shipping was defended.

The king had sent thousands of his soldiers to help the colonists fight the French and their Indian allies. That had been very expensive.

The colonies freely admitted this. But they responded that they, too, had paid a high financial price by providing their own militiamen. As Benjamin Franklin said, they had "raised, paid, and clothed nearly twenty-five thousand men — a number equal to those sent from Great Britain, and far beyond their proportion. They went deeply into debt in doing this; and all their estates and taxes are mortgaged for many years to come in discharging that debt."[5] Parliament had admitted that this was true as well.

> Proverbs 16:18 says, "Pride *goeth* before destruction, and an haughty spirit before a fall." King George had much power and struggled with pride. Pride can get in the way of our making wise decisions.

But their own financial burdens were heavy on the minds of the British leaders now. They were not as open as they should have been to the claims of the colonies. King George and his advisers made up their minds that the colonies would be taxed and they would pay those taxes. They probably never thought that there would be active resistance. They lived in England. People in England depended on their king and had great respect for the throne. It was commonly accepted that the noblemen were better and wiser than the common people.

> John Hancock was a great patriot. He was a wealthy merchant and owned much property in the city of Boston. When the British were in control of Boston, it was thought that the only way to get rid of them might be to burn the entire city. When the possibility was mentioned to Hancock, he said, "Burn Boston and make John Hancock a beggar, if the public good requires it!"[6]

The colonists were not unwilling to pay taxes. But they believed that English law gave them the right to tax themselves through the elected leaders of their colonies. If the king had asked the colonial legislatures to collect some taxes to help pay the debt from the war, it is possible that peace would have continued.

But George III was young and headstrong. When he first became the king, his mother had said to him, "George, be king!"

and he intended to follow her advice. Young George was very impressed with his new authority, and he used it to fill high places in his government with men who would go along with whatever he said. He did not have a high respect for frontier colonists far away on another continent. He would bend those "commoners" to his royal will.

Probably, there were few men at the time who thought that a long struggle was just around the corner. Some of those who protested most loudly about the "right to tax" were just as loud in their claims of love and loyalty to the mother country. But as events went on and the British government got more and more aggressive in its effort to establish more control over the colonies, violence seemed more and more likely.

Taxation without representation was an important issue in the War of Independence, but far from the only one. The Declaration of Independence lists 27 causes for separation. Taxation without representation is only the 17th on the list.

Once the fighting started, then many of the colonists began to see that they must defend their freedom or lose it. War was on its way.

> *In circumstances dark as these, it becomes us, as Men and Christians, to reflect that, whilst every prudent Measure should be taken to ward off the impending Judgements. . . . All confidence must be withheld from the Means we use; and reposed only on that GOD who rules in the Armies of Heaven, and without whose Blessing the best human Counsels are but Foolishness — and all created Power Vanity.*
>
> John Hancock[7]

Unjust Laws

The bitter feelings toward the English government had started over a hundred years before the first battle. In 1651, just 31 years after the Pilgrims landed, Parliament had passed the first of the Navigation Acts. This act said that the American colonies could not trade with any nation besides England. They could not receive ships of any foreign nations in their harbors.

This meant that colonial businessmen had to accept whatever price the English merchants wanted to pay. They could not offer their goods to merchants in France or Spain for instance, to see if they could get a better price.

This law struck the colonies of New England especially hard. New Englanders were seafaring folk. Sometimes whole communities would work together through the winter to cut timber, saw boards, and build a schooner. Then in the spring, the ship would be loaded with more timber, along with animal skins and whatever other goods could be produced. A crew would be made up from the men and boys of the town and the ship would sail off, perhaps to the West Indies or some other port. There the cargo would be sold or traded for other goods and the ship would sail for home. The return cargo, whether of rum or molasses or some other product, would then be sold and

Portrait of George III of the United Kingdom by William Pether after Thomas Frye, c.1710 (PD-Art).

Capture of the *Cyane* and *Levant* by the *Constitution*.

divided among those who had taken part in the project. These voyages could be very profitable, and fortunes were made.

Virginia also, with its tobacco and other crops, suffered from this first navigation act. But the act had little effect because it was weakly enforced. The king appointed revenue officers, but they were lax about the law and many could be persuaded to look the other way for a handful of silver. So the trade went on.

England had also passed laws on manufacturing. The Iron Act of 1750 encouraged the colonies in the production of iron, but forbade the manufacture of finished iron products. So it was legal to make iron in the colonies, but illegal to use it to make tools such as pickaxes or plows. The colonists had to sell their iron to England and buy their plows from England. There were also laws forbidding one colony to sell certain products to the other colonies. The strict control that England wanted to hold over the business of the colonies had a negative effect on colonial development and was very much resented. Because they were so unpopular, the manufacturing laws as a whole were also only weakly enforced.

When people live together in communities and nations, government is necessary to protect the rights of each citizen. But when governments try to control more of community life than they should, people lose freedom. America's history is an account of a nation constantly struggling to maintain the right balance of freedom and responsibility.

But when the king started trying to enforce them a hundred years after they had been passed, trouble was brewing. The colonies suddenly realized how much control the government intended to exercise. The mother country was claiming the right to tax the colonies in any way she pleased, and the people of the colonies had very little to say about it. This was not a wise way in which to govern people who had conquered a wilderness.

In 1764, the fuse was clearly lit. That was the year in which the Stamp Act was passed. Perhaps the king and Parliament wanted to see just how the act would be received before really enforcing it, because they waited a year before they tried. The act said that official government stamps must be placed on paper used for certain business transactions. The stamped paper was required for newspapers, almanacs, lawsuits, even marriage licenses. Of course the stamps could only be purchased from the British government.

Significantly, as Dr. Witherspoon had correctly noted, it was Great Britain who had terminated the entreaties; in fact, during the last two years of America's appeals, her peaceful pleas were directly met by armed military force. King George III dispatched 25,000 British troops to invade his own colonies, enter the homes of his own citizens to take their private possessions and goods, and imprison them without trials — all in violation of his own British Common Law, English Bill of Rights, and Magna Carta (centuries-old documents that formed the basis of the covenant between British rulers and citizens). Only when those governmental covenants had been broken by their rulers and America had been directly attacked did the Americans respond in self-defense.[8]

The colonists were unhappy when the government decided to start enforcing the Navigation Acts. They were even more upset when the Stamp Act was passed. But the next event made smoldering sparks of resentment burst into flame: the king sent soldiers to enforce these unpopular laws. The insult was even greater because the colonists knew that the despised soldiers would be paid with money collected for the Stamp Act. The Americans were paying the soldiers sent to oppress them!

Coalbrookdale by Night. Blast furnaces light the iron making town of Coalbrookdale, Philipp Jakob Loutherbourg, 1801 (PD-US).

The Boston Tea Party

CHAPTER 2

TROUBLE OVER TAXES

FUROR OVER THE STAMP ACT

As quickly as word of the Stamp Act spread through the land, it appeared that the people had been waiting for just such news to bind them together with their neighbors and with the people of the other colonies. All through the colonies the men prepared for trouble, although few of them were thinking of independence from the mother country. England was still their country. They were concerned about the law and the few government officials who had taken the action.

Patrick Henry speaking before the Virginia Assembly.

Mass meetings were held to discuss what action to take. In Virginia, Patrick Henry was lighting fires with his eloquence. Far to the north in Massachusetts, James Otis was doing the same thing. The speakers themselves seemed on fire and the audiences were like dry grass, ready to burst forth in flames. Wouldn't it be wonderful if their speeches could have been recorded so we could listen to them today? But some of them were written down, as was Patrick Henry's "Give me liberty or give me death" speech. Reading their words still inspire our hearts today.

Sons of Liberty flag

The Sons of Liberty started out as an informal group of men in Boston who opposed the British taxes. The movement soon spread throughout the colonies. The Sons of Liberty claimed responsibility for the Boston Tea Party and the seizure of the *Gaspee*. Prominent patriots involved in the Sons of Liberty included John Hancock, John Adams, Samuel Adams, Paul Revere, Patrick Henry, and Christopher Gadsden. The groups of Sons of Liberty in various colonies created networks of communication with groups in other colonies. Some of these later evolved into Committees of Correspondence.

". . . Besides, sir, we shall not fight our battles alone. There is a just God who presides over the destinies of nations, and who will raise up friends to fight our battles for us. The battle, sir, is not to the strong alone; it is to the vigilant, the active, the brave. Besides, sir, we have no election. If we were base enough to desire it, it is now too late to retire from the contest. There is no retreat, but in submission and slavery! Our chains are forged, their clanking may be heard on the plains of Boston! The war is inevitable — and let it come! I repeat it, sir, let it come!

"It is in vain, sir, to extenuate the matter. Gentlemen may cry, peace, peace — but there is no peace. The war is actually begun. The next gale that sweeps from the north will bring to our ears the clash of resounding arms! Our brethren are already in the field! Why stand we here idle? What is it that gentlemen wish? What would they have? Is life so dear, or peace so sweet, as to be purchased at the price of chains and slavery? Forbid it, Almighty God! I know not what course others may take; but as for me, give me liberty, or give me death!"[9]

In colony after colony, the assemblies met and voted to declare that Parliament had no right to tax the colonists and no right to send soldiers to enforce taxes. The Sons of Liberty was formed, and units of it spread everywhere to help with resistance. But the action that most angered the king and Parliament was what happened to the stamps when they were sent to the colonies. They were seized and burned by groups of furious colonists.

The officers hired to sell the stamps quickly resigned. There was so much public fervor over the Stamp Act that they did not dare stay in their offices. So, when the day came that the act was to go into effect (November 1,1765), it fell flat. There were no stamps to sell and no officers to sell them.

Young Patrick Henry had introduced some resolutions in the Virginia assembly that declared that the people of Virginia were free-born men and would defend their freedom to the death. This alarmed some of the loyalist members of the assembly. Some shouted to him to stop speaking. Others cried, "Treason!" but he was too fired up with excitement to pay any attention to them. Many of the men in the assembly felt as strongly for resistance as Henry did.

In Massachusetts, James Otis suggested that a message be sent to all the colonies inviting them to send representatives to a meeting to discuss what should be done about the act. The meeting was held in New York in October 1765. Virginia did not send delegates because the king's appointed governor had broken up their colonial assembly so that none could be selected. New Hampshire, North Carolina, and Georgia likewise did not send representatives, but 9 of the 13 colonies had men there.

The meeting passed a resolution stating the rights of the colonists and drafted a petition to the king and Parliament to seek recognition of those rights. There was a force of soldiers in New York at the time, in addition to a British fleet on the water nearby. But even this did not stop the colonists from consulting together and stating their case to the British government. The language used was mild compared to what the people of the colonies were saying among themselves, but still it would have been a good idea for the king and Parliament to think carefully about what the colonists might be thinking in private.

William Pitt, 1st Earl of Chatham after Richard Brompton, 1772 (PD-Art).

The English leaders were quite surprised at the strong reaction to the Stamp Act and similar measures. They had not thought the colonies would be so offended. Even in England, there was pressure to repeal the act. America had many friends in England. After all, many Englishmen had relatives and friends who lived in the colonies. The English merchants too, pleaded for repeal of the act. They wanted to sell their wares in America and that was not going well when the king insisted on his stamps while the colonists refused to buy anything that required a stamp.

The Stamp Act was repealed in less than a year. However, there was no real settlement of the trouble, because Parliament still insisted that the government had the right to tax the colonies if they wanted to. There was little protest from the colonies because for the moment their troubles seemed to be over.

William Pitt was an important member of the British Parliament who stood with the Americans on the issue of taxation without representation. Even though this put him at odds with King George and many powerful members of Parliament, Pitt stood firm. There were many people in England who were sympathetic toward their American countrymen and believed they should have the same rights as all Englishmen.

But there was still considerable friction between some of the colonies and their royal governors. Trouble was hiding just beneath the surface even though most colonists still considered themselves loyal subjects of the king.

They still continued to ask for representation in Parliament. They said that if they could just have a voice in the government's policies toward the colonies, there would be peace in the national family. Some of the British leaders favored granting this request also. They said it was simply fair to put the Englishmen in the colonies on an equal footing with the Englishmen in England. But the young king was hardheaded and stubborn. He said he would never honor such a request. He intended to show that it was unwise to oppose the will of their "divinely appointed" ruler.

> The colonists tried repeatedly to appeal to the king and Parliament in a proper manner. Even after the bloodshed that would come at Lexington and Concord, the Americans sent the Olive Branch Petition in hopes of patching up relations with their mother country.

How might history have been different if the colonists' request had been granted? We will never know. But it seems likely that things would have been very different had King George shown his subjects in America more respect.

MORE TROUBLE —THEN VIOLENCE

After the repeal of the Stamp Act, things quieted down in the colonies for a time. But the season was brief. In 1767, an act was passed that upset Americans even more than the Stamp Act had. A tax was to be placed on tea and several other items that were shipped to the colonies, including glass, lead, and paint. Apart from the other items, tea was a very popular drink in America, so this tax would affect most people in the colonies. Revenue commissioners were to be sent to the colonies to collect the taxes, with redcoat soldiers to help them if it was needed. Anyone who refused to pay the tax was to be punished. Freedom was at stake!

Ben Franklin is often quoted as having said, "Rebellion to tyrants is obedience to God." This statement was suggested by him as a motto to place on the Great Seal of the United States when he served on the first committee created to produce the seal. He described his idea of the scene do be depicted: "Moses standing on the Shore, and extending his Hand over the Sea, thereby causing the same to overwhelm Pharoah who is sitting in an open Chariot, a Crown on his Head & a Sword in his Hand. Rays from a Pillar of Fire in the Clouds reaching to Moses, to express that he acts by Command of the Deity."[10]

Thomas Jefferson, who also served on the first committee, suggested: "The children of Israel in the wilderness, led by a cloud by day and a pillar of fire by night."[11]

In other words, these two Founding Fathers, both often described as irreligious men in modern history books, thought of a Bible account in describing what the colonies were doing in resisting King George.

22   Brewing raspberry leaves.

There was a quick reaction to this new law. People realized right away that the king was not mainly trying to raise money. This was an attempt to show the colonists that he would keep on trying to establish his right to tax them until they submitted. He was determined to bring them to their knees. The word "tyranny" began to be heard in private and public discussions.

Now talk about sending representatives to Parliament began to die out. There began to be rumblings of independence. John Adams of Massachusetts and some of the other bolder men began to think that their problems could not be solved as long as they were a part of the mother country.

Proverbs 29:1 says, "He, that being often reproved hardeneth his neck, shall suddenly be destroyed, and that without remedy." This verse likens the stubborn man to a horse that stiffens his neck when the rider pulls back on the reins trying to stop or turn him. It says that the stubborn man will suddenly be destroyed "without remedy." That means he will experience a serious loss from which he will never quite recover. With King George, that loss was his American colonies.

One thing many people agreed on was that they would change their tea-drinking habits. Some ladies began to experiment with other things, such as raspberry leaves, to brew a beverage to replace tea. Others found sources from which to buy tea shipped from Holland rather than England. The king would get no tax money from that tea.

To be sure, not all the colonists agreed. There were the Whigs, who believed in limited powers for the king. Then there were the Tories, who said that the king was always right and should be obeyed in all things. And there were others who did not belong to either camp, caring little for politics or having more moderate views than the two main parties. The Whigs were more numerous, so there was a strong sentiment of resistance throughout the whole nation.

Snowball fight.

John Hancock was a very wealthy man who liked expensive houses, clothes, horses, and carriages. But he was very generous with his money, giving large amounts for the care of the poor each winter and doing other good works with his riches as well. When Boston elected him to political office, Sam Adams commented that they had done a wise thing because they had "made that young man's fortune their own."

People who were loyal to King George and wanted to remain English citizens rather than fighting for independence were called Tories or Loyalists. In Parliament, there was a formal party called the Tory party, which often took a stand opposite to the opinions of the Whig party.

For several years things had been getting worse. In Boston, British revenue agents had seized the *Liberty*, a sloop belonging to Boston merchant and political leader John Hancock. They believed he had failed to pay fees for some merchandise he had unloaded from the ship. Hancock was very popular in Boston, as he had used his fortune to help in many charitable projects, public and private. Soon a mob formed and chased the officers until they took refuge on a frigate anchored out in the harbor. This happened in spite of the fact that there were British soldiers stationed in the town, under the command of General Gage.

The Liberty Tree: In Boston and in most of the other colonies, there was a tree (or sometimes a pole) designated as the Liberty Tree. The Sons of Liberty would hold meetings at this tree when some matter of importance needed to be discussed and notices of meetings and other significant news were often posted on its trunk.

But the Bostonians were not easily frightened and there was often quarreling and even street fights. Sometimes even the boys joined in, throwing snowballs at the soldiers. This got far out of hand on March 5, 1770, and an incident took place that has gone down in history as the Boston Massacre.

There had been a confrontation between some British soldiers and some unruly citizens. Soon snowballs, ice chunks, and sticks began to fly. The soldiers, vastly outnumbered, finally fired

Colonists meeting under the Liberty Tree.

their muskets. Three civilians were killed and several wounded. Later, two of the wounded died, bringing the death toll to five. That seems a small number to earn the title of *massacre*, but the newspapers of New England chose to portray the incident in that light.

John Adams, although very opposed to the presence of the soldiers, honorably accepted the job of defending them in court. None of the soldiers were convicted of murder, and there was only mild punishment for any of them. Still, the mood of the colony was already hostile to the redcoats, and the Boston Massacre only fed the flames.

In 1772, a boat named the *Gaspee* was collecting the revenue payments from ships that had been entering Providence. It was captured and burned by Rhode Island men. In New York, there had been fights as well. The soldiers who had been sent to help the revenue officers had been involved in altercations with New Yorkers. All over the colonies the spirit of resistance was growing bolder.

The burning of the *Gaspee*.

The British government began to refer to the colonists as "rebels," and ordered those who had burned the *Gaspee* to be sent to England for trial. But catching those men was the first order of business, and that proved impossible to do. Threats and agents were not working. Parliament decided to try a new plan.

THE BOSTON TEA PARTY

Indeed, it was a sensible idea on the surface. The problem was clear: the East India Company, the business that shipped most of the tea to America, was in trouble because people were refusing to buy and drink tea, or else they were getting it from Dutch shippers. Their warehouses bulged while their income was very low. Now the East India Company added their pleas to those of the colonists for the removal of the tax. So Parliament did two things. First, it took off the taxes on all the items besides tea. Then they arranged with the English tea merchants to sell the tea to the colonies at a lower price than before. The tax was still

The Yankees objected. "Yankee" was a term the people of England often called the colonists. The king was trying to get the colonies to admit that he had a *right* to tax them if he wanted to. He had thought that what they really cared about was cost. He found out that what they really cared about was a principle. So people in Philadelphia, New York, and some other places refused to allow tea to be unloaded from the ships that brought it. Some of them went back to England with the same cargo they had brought.

Faneuil Hall

in place, but the total price paid by the colonists was lower. Now, Parliament thought, those rebellious Yankees would happily drink their beloved tea again. After all, why would they object to a tax if it did not raise the price?

Boston tried to do what the people in Philadelphia and New York had done, but there were so many redcoat soldiers there that the citizens had to back off. The officers would not allow the ships to leave Boston Harbor. Shortly after the tea arrived in the hold of the *Dartmouth* and two other ships, patriot leaders, including Paul Revere, John Hancock, and Samuel Adams, held a meeting at Faneuil Hall for the public to discuss the issue. Such a crowd turned out that the meeting had to be moved to the Old South Meeting House to hold the thousands of people. The group decided to demand that the tea be sent back to England with the tax unpaid. They told the captain of the *Dartmouth* to ask Governor Hutchinson for permission to sail out of Boston and back to England.

The Tea Party has been thought of by some as a sort of riot, but this is not true. The "Indians" walked in a quiet, orderly group down to the wharf. They separated into three groups and boarded the ships. They did no violence to any ship's captain or crewman. They did not damage any of the ship's contents or equipment except the tea. One padlock, which belonged to the captain of one of the ships, was broken. The next day, money was sent to pay the captain for the loss of this hardware, along with a note of apology. Crewmen later testified that no damage had been done except to the tea, and in fact the "Indians" had even swept the decks before leaving.

Hutchinson would not agree. Other measures were taken to try to settle the matter peacefully, but no compromise was reached. Another huge meeting was held at Old South a few weeks later on December 16. The patriot leaders informed the people that Hutchinson had been appealed to and refused to cooperate. It was then decided that the only thing left to do was destroy the tea.

That night a large group of men dressed as Mohawk Indians to hide their identity and marched down to Griffin's Wharf, where the tea ships were moored. Their faces were blackened with grease, oil, or coal dust. It was later said by one of them that they could only tell each other apart by their voices. They boarded the tea ships and went to work.

Three hundred forty chests of tea were broken open and dumped in the harbor. The total value of the tea was equal to over a million dollars in today's money. Of course this made a great impression on people on both sides of the Atlantic. The other colonies were encouraged by Boston's courageous stand against what they considered an illegal tax. King George was outraged. He declared, "The die is now cast. The colonies must either submit or triumph."

Even among the patriots there was the opinion that the tea should be paid for. Even Benjamin Franklin said so. After all, their squabble was with the British government, not the East India Company. In fact, a wealthy merchant named Robert Murray from New York offered to pay for the cargo. His offer was refused.

THE GREENWICH TEA PARTY

Boston was not the only town to hold a "Tea Party" in response to the tea tax. A shipload of tea that was intended to be transported overland to Philadelphia in 1774 was seized by a crowd of colonists on the night of December 22. A group of 40, dressed as Indians, piled up the tea and set it on fire. One man who participated in the party was Richard Howell, who would become the third governor of the state of New Jersey. His granddaughter Varina Howell would one day become the bride of Jefferson Davis, the future president of the Confederacy.

The BLOODY MASSACRE perpetrated in King — Street BOSTON on March 5th 1770, by a party of the 29th REGT.

Engrav'd Printed & Sold by PAUL REVERE Boston

BUTCHER'S HALL

Unhappy BOSTON! see thy Sons deplore,
Thy hallow'd Walks besmear'd with guiltless Gore:
While faithless P—n and his savage Bands,
With murd'rous Rancour stretch their bloody Hands,
Like fierce Barbarians grinning o'er their Prey,
Approve the Carnage, and enjoy the Day.

If scalding drops from Rage from Anguish Wrung
If speechless Sorrows lab'ring for a Tongue.
Or if a weeping World can ought appease
The plaintive Ghosts of Victims such as these;
The Patriot's copious Tears for each are shed,
A glorious Tribute which embalms the Dead.

But know, Fate summons to that awful Goal,
Where JUSTICE strips the Murd'rer of his Soul.
Should venal C—ts the scandal of the Land,
Snatch the relentless Villain from her Hand,
Keen Execrations on this Plate inscrib'd,
Shall reach a JUDGE who never can be brib'd.

The unhappy Sufferers were Messrs. SAML. GRAY SAML. MAVERICK, JAMS. CALDWELL, CRISPUS
Killed. Six wounded two of them (CHRIST. MONK & JOHN CLARK) Morta...

CHAPTER 3

THE FIRST BATTLES

THE FIRST CONTINENTAL CONGRESS

In 1774, the British Parliament hastened the beginning of the War of Independence by passing four laws called the Coercive Acts or Intolerable Acts. The effect of these acts was so negative on the mood of the colonies that people who had hoped for a peaceful resolution of the earlier problems began to give up hope. Parliament was unaware of the true state of feelings in America. They were also eager to do the king's bidding. So they grew angry, as the king did when the Americans resisted the new laws about taxes on tea and other regulations. It is never wise to pass laws in anger. Anger drives out good judgment. So it was that the Intolerable Acts were passed. Parliament would soon see results very different than those they had hoped for.

Image of George III later in life.

 The first of these acts was the Boston Port Bill. It prohibited any vessel from entering or leaving Boston Harbor. The British confidently expected that this act would cause the people of New England to give up their rebellion. After all, they were sea-going people whose trade by sea had been increasing for generations. They depended very heavily on shipping for the economy of the colonies. Surely they would submit.

They did not submit. They only got more upset. Their freedom was being violated.

The second act was the Massachusetts Bill, which changed the charter of the colony so that they could no longer elect their own rulers. Instead, the colonial officers would be agents selected by the King George. The effect of this law was to alert not only

The Bible tells us that an angry man is foolish. Proverbs 15:18 says, "A wrathful man stirreth up strife: but he that is slow to anger appeaseth strife." Indeed, when Parliament got angry and passed laws to punish the colonies, they were not acting wisely. They only got more resistance.

Massachusetts but all the other colonies as well. After all, they reasoned, if King George would do that to Massachusetts he would not mind doing it everywhere if he got away with it there.

The third act was the Transportation Bill. This bill was aimed at any American who should "commit murder" in resisting the king's officers as they enforced his laws. A person charged with this offense would not get a fair trial in the colony where the offense occurred, but rather would be sent across the Atlantic to England for trial. The Americans were well satisfied that the results of such a trial would not be favorable to an American defendant, so this act increased the bitter feelings of every independent man in the colonies.

In the early days of America, the people were often called to prayer and fasting. Sometimes it was the preachers who called the people to fast and pray. Many times it was the Congress or a state legislature. Most of the early American presidents also designated days of prayer and fasting, especially in times of national emergency.

The fourth act was the Quebec Bill. This act made all of the country east of the Mississippi and north of the Ohio River part of Canada instead of the colonies that already claimed it. It affected regions in the modern states of Indiana, Illinois, Michigan, Wisconsin, Ohio, and Minnesota. So now that territory belonged to Quebec, a colony in Canada, instead of the American colonies. This did not make the American colonists happy. They had furnished men and money to take this very land from France in the French and Indian war. Now the king was claiming that it belonged to Quebec. Louder and louder grew the rumblings of resistance all through colonial America.

People grew more agitated than at any previous time. There was so much unrest in the colonial assemblies that some of them were broken up by their British governors. But this did nothing to quiet the people. Many of them observed the day the port of Boston was closed as a day of fasting and prayer. People everywhere were talking about how unfair and illegal recent acts of the king and Parliament were. Soon there was talk from north to south of meeting in a Continental Congress to see what could be done to stop the increasing tyranny.

On September 5, 1775, the First Continental Congress assembled at Philadelphia. All of the colonies sent delegates except Georgia. The people of Georgia were mostly in favor of the meeting, but their colonial governor had succeeded in preventing them from appointing delegates.

It was an impressive gathering of men who came together in Philadelphia that day. Even some of the British leaders in Parliament admitted as much. Some of them proclaimed that some of the papers and debates produced by the Congress were superb. Virginia's Peyton Randolph was elected president of the Congress. Other members have gone down in history as great founders of our nation as well. They included George Washington, John and Samuel Adams, John Hancock, Alexander Hamilton, Benjamin Franklin, and many others.

Benjamin Franklin was asked to go to England to submit the plan of Congress to Parliament. But he was refused permission to speak there. He sailed back home, his long trip wasted. Hardheaded Parliament, instead of giving the appeals a hearing, went even further in punishing the colonies. Now they voted to forbid New England fishermen to fish near the coast of Newfoundland. They also voted to increase the number of redcoat soldiers in Boston to 10,000. They blamed General Gage for not having done better in controlling the rowdy men of Massachusetts, so they sent General William Howe to replace him. Howe would now be the commander-in-chief of all British forces in North America.

Washington discussing the Revolution with Samuel and John Adams.

WAR CLOUDS GATHER

General Howe, like several other British army officers, had been elected to Parliament. His positions in the House of Commons showed that he was not in favor of being too harsh with the colonies. He told his constituents that he had no desire to make war on the Americans. He wanted to see peace between them and the mother country. In fact, all through the long war that was about to begin he was willing to make a compromise with the Americans to bring them back into the national fold with more concessions than either the king or Parliament were willing to offer. But

Very early in the First Continental Congress it was suggested that a minister be called to lead the group in prayer. Some members objected because denominational feelings were very strong and it was feared that bringing in a minister would lead to denominational wrangling among the members. But, as John Adams wrote to his wife Abigail, Samuel Adams stood and said that he "could hear a Prayer from a Gentleman of Piety and Virtue, who was at the same Time a Friend to his Country."[12] He suggested the Reverend Jacob Duche who lived in Philadelphia. Duche willingly responded and not only read a written prayer, but then went on in extemporaneous prayer and read Psalm 35. The prayer meeting/Bible study lasted three hours.

Richard, Lord Howe

when he was appointed to be commander-in-chief he could not decline, even though he had a friendly attitude toward the Americans. He was a soldier, and his king had commanded him to do a job. If war came, he must lead the British forces.

At the same time, the king appointed Howe's brother, Richard Howe to be admiral of the British fleet in America. So two brothers came across the Atlantic. Sir William believed he would be able to settle the trouble without war.

But soon, events would rapidly show the good-hearted warrior that he had been mistaken.

Meanwhile, in America, Gage had his hands full. The sentiment for resistance was growing ever stronger. Massachusetts had been the scene of much of the early trouble, and it was feared that in that colony would be the first outbreak of armed conflict. Men were meeting on village greens to drill as soldiers. The public speeches all contained an element of tension. Guns and powder had been collected and it was believed that 20,000 "minute men" were prepared to march at a minute's notice if they were needed. These men were mostly farmers and sons of farmers. They were sturdy men who had for years faced the hardships of weather, predators, and constant labor. They knew how to use guns as well. They were, in fact, better marksmen than the red-coated regulars of the king. They did not have uniforms, and they were not familiar with the routines of army drill. When they drilled as companies, any British soldier who saw them was likely to smile in glee.

But General Gage was not grinning. He had not been in Massachusetts long before he came to realize the mood of the local people. He considered his 10,000 men on the one hand, and the numbers and temper of the colonial militiamen on the other. He declared that he could not handle an emergency without more soldiers.

The British are Coming!

At this, Lord North (Britain's prime minister) and the king's other advisors laughed heartily. They did not believe for a minute that the farmer boys in homespun could stand before the well-trained, well-equipped soldiers of George III. But Gage was worried. He began to build fortifications on Boston neck, a narrow expanse of land that connected Boston to the mainland. As he heard further reports of what the country people were doing, he sent out spies into the countryside to try to find out just what was going on.

In April of 1775, he heard through his spies that military stores were being collected and stored at Concord, a small village about 20 miles from Boston. He ordered a force of 700 soldiers to march on Concord and destroy the powder and supplies found there. With that order, the Revolutionary War really began.

THE SHOT HEARD 'ROUND THE WORLD

The force was to march quietly through the night. Gage hoped that the Minutemen might not discern his intentions until it was too late to gather their men in force. But the patriot spies were just as active as his own, and their people were aware of what was going on before the march ever began. Paul Revere, William Dawes, and other riders were soon spreading the word in all directions. Revere and Dawes headed for Lexington, then Concord. They started on different routes to make it more likely that at least one of them would get through the scattered British outposts of the region and give the warning. Along the way, they knocked on the doors of patriot homesteads and soon other horsemen were riding north and south to arouse other militia men.

Signal fires soon blazed on hilltops, trumpets and cannon shots were heard, bells were rung. When dawn broke on a beautiful April morning, redcoat troops arrived at Lexington, a small village between Boston and Concord. They had missed capturing two known patriot leaders, John Hancock and Samuel Adams, who had been spending the night with a friend in the village. Awakened by Revere, the two had fled well ahead of the regulars. Now the redcoats found themselves facing a small force of armed militia already gathered.

A Minuteman

The militiamen were vastly outnumbered, so it would have been suicide to fight. The British commander, Major Pitcairn, rudely ordered them to lay down their arms and disperse. The patriot commander, Captain Parker, ordered his men to hold their fire and disperse but not to lay down their arms. But as they turned to disperse, someone fired a shot and the redcoats let go a volley that killed several militiamen. The rest ran for their lives. But

The Minutemen were not just militia members. They trained much more often than the militia. Two or three times a week was not unusual. Because of this, they were paid, usually one shilling per drill. They were expected to keep their weapons and equipment close by at all times and be ready to march "at a minute's notice."

the regulars would see most of them later in the day, along with hundreds of their comrades.

The British marched on to Concord. The countryside was buzzing like a swarm of bees, but as yet only a small force of militiamen had gathered at the village. Like those at Lexington, these were quickly dispersed. The redcoats began to search for and destroy war supplies, but it was slow work. The patriots had been warned days in advance that such a move might be made, and so had moved most of their material. Now the British could find only a few cannons to spike and some barrels of flour to dump on the ground. Around noon, the soldiers prepared to head back to Boston.

> ## The colonists acted in self-defense:
>
> Illustrative of this belief was the famous command to the Lexington Minutemen, "Don't fire unless fired upon!" Yet, having been fired upon without having broken any law, the Americans believed they had a Biblical right to self-defense. In fact, the Rev. Peter Powers, in a famous sermon he preached in front of the Vermont Legislature in 1778,[13] specifically noted that America had "taken up arms in its own defense" — that she had not initiated the conflict but was only defending herself after being attacked.

But it would not be that easy. By now the alarm had spread through the countryside and the militiamen were gathering. It seemed that the whole world was suddenly up in arms. At first, the redcoats marched along in good order. But then muskets and rifles began to pop here and there. Then the firing increased. From behind barns, walls, and trees, hidden farmers sighted in on red coats. Soldiers began to fall while their comrades looked in vain for a clear target among the trees. The patriots were fighting Indian style, never presenting much of a target. But their marksmanship was deadly. The redcoats encountered ambush after ambush as they marched along the narrow road.

Soon the regulars were no longer marching but running for their lives. Finally they reached Lexington once again and there met blessed reinforcements. The new troops formed a hollow square and the exhausted raiders of Concord fell to the ground for a brief rest. Then the men formed up and the march to Boston continued.

Here is a poem written by Ralph Waldo Emerson for the occasion of the completion of the monument, which is near where the old bridge stood.

Canal Boat and Freight House of Merrimack Boating Company (Concord Bridge).

CONCORD HYMN

by Ralph Waldo Emerson
Sung at the Completion of the Battle Monument, July 4, 1837

By the rude bridge that arched the flood,
Their flag to April's breeze unfurled,
Here once the embattled farmers stood
And fired the shot heard round the world.

The foe long since in silence slept;
Alike the conqueror silent sleeps;
And Time the ruined bridge has swept
Down the dark stream which seaward creeps.

On this green bank, by this soft stream,
We set today a votive stone;
That memory may their deed redeem,
When, like our sires, our sons are gone.

Spirit, that made those heroes dare
To die, and leave their children free,
Bid Time and Nature gently spare
The shaft we raise to them and thee.

PATRIOTS' DAY

American militia companies used country paths get ahead of the enemy and ambush them. A British ensign later wrote: "all the hills on each side of us were covered with rebels." The regulars encountered ambushes at Merriam's Corner, then at Brooks Hill, and a nameless turn in the road that became known as the Bloody Curve. As they reached a boulder-dotted pasture belonging to Tabitha Nelson near Lexington, Captain Parker and his reassembled Lexington militia were waiting in the brush on a hillside to the east. Some of Parker's men were wearing blood-stiffened bandages from wounds they had received in the unequal contest at dawn and all of them were eager for a chance to avenge their murdered neighbors. Waiting until the regulars were right in front of his position, Parker gave the order to fire. The redcoats were shocked and several of their number went down. The officer leading them fell from his horse with a bullet in his thigh. Then they charged the hillside with bayonets and the farmers were forced to retreat. But in the few minutes they had held up the enemy, more patriots had arrived to help.

The battles of Lexington and Concord are still celebrated in Massachusetts on the third day of April each year. The holiday is known as Patriots' Day.

Battle of Lexington

The new leader:
George Washington

CHAPTER 4

THE CHOICE OF A LEADER

AMERICA GETS AN ARMY

The Massachusetts men had taken a bold stand. With no help from the other colonies, they had attacked and driven away an organized, well-equipped invading force of the world's most powerful army. But they were not alone for long. As word quickly spread of the fights at Lexington and Concord, angry militiamen from the other colonies began to start for Boston in support of their Massachusetts brethren.

Tough old Israel Putnam, veteran of many battles in the French and Indian War, left his plow and oxen standing in the field for his children to deal with. He ran to his house, sent a messenger to summon the militia to follow him, then jumped on his horse and galloped away. He took only 18 hours to travel the 100 miles from his Connecticut farm to Cambridge, where the Minutemen were assembled. At about the same time, John Stark arrived from New Hampshire with the first company of men from that colony. Captain Benedict Arnold of New Haven, Connecticut, had led 60 men to join the little patriot army. So from towns and villages, forests and farms, the irate colonists came. Soon, General Gage and his redcoats found themselves bottled up in Boston by a rough and poorly equipped army of some 16,000 men.

War news from Lexington.

Boldness is facing confrontation with the assurance that God will bless the outcome if I'm standing firm for truth. Proverbs 28:1: "The wicked flee when no man pursueth: but the righteous are bold as a lion."

General Thomas Gage

No one seemed to know exactly what the next steps should be. It was agreed that the British should be held in Boston, but what then? There was no clear chain of command to make such decisions.

But a few days later, on May 10, two important events took place. These would be important in deciding the outcome of the war and the future of America. They were the assembling of the Second Continental Congress and the capture of Fort Ticonderoga. The Congress would set the direction of the colonies for the immediate future. The fall of Ticonderoga would encourage the citizen-soldiers and provide some much-needed equipment of war. The first issue for Congress was the creation of an army and choice of a commander for the army.

You must remember that at this early time there was no Continental Army. There were only several colonial militias made up of many local groups without strong organization and communication between them. An army must be built somehow. But there was a huge question as to what authority the Congress had in creating one. They did not have the power to tax the colonies for military equipment and supplies. They could not draft soldiers. Just what could they do?

Most of the outstanding men of the First Continental Congress had returned. Ben Franklin was back from his disappointing errand in England and he and the Adams cousins (John and Samuel) of Boston were already convinced that the only way forward was to declare independence. The president of the first Congress, Peyton Randolph, could not attend. Virginia sent Thomas Jefferson in his place. As business got under way, John Hancock of Massachusetts was chosen president of Congress.

He declared himself ready "to arm the army, appoint a commander, vote supplies, and proceed to business."[14]

Hancock's patriotism was unquestioned. He had already lost much of his property to the British and Tories in Boston because of his bold stands for justice. The Tories had a thorough hatred of him, which made his colleagues in Congress respect him all the more.

The discussion quickly turned to the subject of the army. John Adams made the motion to adopt the army in its infancy as the legal army of "these United Colonies of North America." His cousin, Samuel Adams, seconded the motion and debate began. John Adams unleashed all his passion and eloquence.

Some of the less bold members expressed hesitations and objections. Adams heard them out, then rose to speak again. There was a warmth in his tone that he could not conceal, nor did he wish to. He declared,

> Gentlemen, if this congress will not adopt this army, before ten moons have set, New England will adopt it, and she will undertake the struggle alone! Yes, with a strong arm and a clear conscience she will front the foe single-handed![15]

There was more debate, but it became clear that Adams' oratory had won the day. A time was set for the vote and the army was adopted by Congress. The Continental Army was born.

Artemus Ward lecturing.

WHO WILL LEAD THE ARMY?

Obviously, the next question was who was to be the supreme leader for the army. John Adams had discussed the question with his cousin Samuel at length. John proposed George Washington of Virginia. At first, Samuel resisted. But John had compelling reasons for his choice. As Samuel listened, he elaborated.

The colonies were spread out for hundreds of miles up and down the Atlantic coast. Everything possible must be done to unite them in heart and spirit. At that moment, the entire American army was in New England, and made up of New England men. Their commander at present was Artemis Ward, another New Englander. Already some of the men from the middle and southern colonies were complaining that the northern faction was taking prominence. The choice of a southerner for a commander-in-chief would unite all sections.

Integrity is speaking truth in all situations. Learning integrity fits you for future use. Colossians 3:9 says, "Lie not to one another, seeing that ye have put off the old man with his deeds." The best time to learn to tell the truth is now!

Samuel listened carefully, but expressed concern that the devotion of the soldiers to Artemas Ward might cause dissension should Washington be chosen. After all, Ward was not unqualified. Ward was a cultured man, a Harvard graduate, a successful leader in the French and Indian War, highly respected by all who knew him.

Adams willingly agreed with all the praise for Ward. Still, he ruggedly clung to his preference for Washington. He reminded

John Adams

Samuel of the Virginia colonel's many services to the colony, his sharp mind and solid judgment, broad experience, and especially, the great confidence the entire country had in his integrity and courage. He waxed eloquent about the advantages of having a Virginian at the head of the army for the sake of uniting northern and southern patriots. Again, he won the day. Sam agreed to move for an adjournment as soon as the nomination was made, in order to give time for the members to consult with each other privately before any public debate.

On the appointed day, John Adams stood to speak. First, he praised General Ward. He used such glowing language that the most dedicated Massachusetts man could not have praised Ward more highly. Then, Adams added: "But this is not the man I have chosen!"

It was a powerful dramatic touch, and it garnered the rapt attention of every man in the room. All eyes were on John Adams. At his right was seated George Washington in his uniform of a Virginia colonel. Like all the other delegates, he was staring intently at John Adams, eager to hear the name of his proposed candidate.

More calmly then, Adams went on to list the qualifications needed in the new commander. Growing more and more eloquent as he neared the end of his speech, he closed by declaring:

Humility — Acknowledging that any good I have achieved is a gift from God, and my life is to used as an instrument in His hand (see Micah 6:8).

"Gentlemen, I know these qualifications are high, but we all know they are needful at this crisis in this chief. Does anyone say that they are not to be obtained in this country? In reply, I have to say they are; they reside in one of our own body, and he is the man whom I now nominate: George Washington of Virginia!"[16]

Washington was thoroughly astounded to hear his own name put forth for this high responsibility. Humble as he was, he never expected for a second that he was the man Adams had in mind as he listed the virtues a supreme commander must have. Washington leaped to his feet as though from an electric shock. He rushed into an adjoining room as all the delegates sat astonished and silent. Quickly, Samuel Adams broke the silence with a call for an adjournment. The motion passed and the delegates were dismissed.

No doubt there were many private conversations between the delegates on this critical subject. Most of them we will never know of, as they were not written down. But the record shows that on June 15, 1775, George Washington was unanimously elected to be commander-in-chief of the American army.

John Stark

A HUMBLE WARRIOR

President of Congress John Hancock made the formal declaration of the result of the vote. Washington stood to answer:

> Mr. President, though I am truly sensible of the high honor done me in this appointment, yet, I feel great distress from a consciousness that my abilities and military experience may not be equal to the extensive and important trust. However, as the congress desires it, I will enter upon the momentous duty, and exert every power I possess in their service, and for the support of their glorious cause. I beg they will accept my most cordial thanks for this distinguished testimony of their approbation.[17]

He went on to say that if some unlucky event should occur in the future to tarnish his reputation as a general, he begged that every gentleman in the room would remember that he had said in the beginning he did not feel qualified for the great task ahead of him. He also said that he would not ask to be paid for his services. No amount of money could have ever induced him to leave the comforts of home and family to be commander of an army. So, he did not wish to profit from the calling. He would keep an exact amount of his expenses and trust that the Congress would repay him for those.

General George Washington (center) and the Committee of Congress at Valley Forge, Pennsylvania, 1778

Minutemen

The next day, he wrote home to his beloved Martha, whom he had nicknamed Patsy, telling her of the appointment: "I have used every endeavour in my power to avoid it, not only from my unwillingness to part with you and the family, but from the consciousness of its being a trust too great for my capacity; and that I should enjoy more real happiness in one month with you at home than I have the most distant prospect of finding abroad, if my stay were to be seven times seven years."[18]

Everyone who heard of the general's speech to Congress was touched by his modesty and sincerity. In less than a week, a committee of congressmen had written for him a commission as commander-in-chief, which was later preserved in a glass case in the nation's capitol.

On June 21, 1775, General Washington left Philadelphia for the American army's camp at Cambridge. All along the way he met with crowds of enthusiastic admirers — and the largest and most excited crowd was the band of ragged warriors he met at the camp on July 2.

JOHN PETER GABRIEL MUHLENBERG
THE PASTOR-RECRUITER

Storytime with Uncle Rick

America's Struggle

John Peter Gabriel Muhlenberg was a Lutheran pastor when the Revolutionary War began. He had much earlier made up his mind that if war came, he would throw in his lot with the Americans over the British. On the Sunday of Muhlenberg's last sermon, he chose Ecclesiastes, 3 as his text. He concluded his sermon by reading verse 8 "A time to love and a time to hate; a time of war and a time of peace." Briefly, he finished by commenting that "now is not a time of peace, but a time of war." Then he swept his black clerical robe to reveal the uniform of a colonel in the Continental army. He then stepped to the back of the church and began to sign up volunteers from among the men of his church as recruits for the American army. A day or two later, he marched away, leading 300 men to war. They became the 8th Virginia Regiment.

THE RISING, 1776!
by Thomas Buchanan Read

Out of the North the wild news came,
Far flashing on its wings of flame,
Swift as the boreal light which flies
At midnight through the startled skies.
And there was tumult in the air,

The fife's shrill note, the drum's loud beat,
And through the wide land everywhere

The answering tread of hurrying feet;
While the first oath of Freedom's gun,
Came on the blast from Lexington;
And Concord, roused, no longer tame,
Forgot her old baptismal name,
Made bare her patriot arm of power, –
And swelled the discord of the hour.

Within its shade of elm and oak
The church of Berkeley Manor stood;

There Sunday found the rural folk,
And some esteemed of gentle blood.
In vain their feet with loitering tread
Passed 'mid the graves where rank is naught;
All could not read the lesson taught
In that republic of the dead.

How sweet the hour of Sabbath talk,
The vale with peace and sunshine full
Where all the happy people walk,
Decked in their homespun flax and wool!
Where youth's gay hats with blossoms bloom;
And every maid with simple art,
Wears on her breast, like her own heart,
A bud whose depths are all perfume;
While every garment's gentle stir
Is breathing rose and lavender.

The pastor came; his snowy locks
Hallowed his brow of thought and care;
And calmly, as shepherds lead their flocks,
He led into the house of prayer.

The pastor rose; the prayer was strong;
The psalm was warrior David's song;
The text, a few short words of might—
"The Lord of hosts shall arm the right!"

He spoke of wrongs too long endured,
Of sacred rights to be secured;
Then from his patriot tongue of flame
The startling words for Freedom came.
The stirring sentences he spake
Compelled the heart to glow or quake,
And, rising on his theme's broad wing,
And grasping in his nervous hand
The imaginary battle brand,
In face of death he dared to fling
Defiance to a tyrant king.

Even as he spoke, his frame, renewed
In eloquence of attitude,
Rose, as it seemed, a shoulder higher;
Then swept his kindling glance of fire
From startled pew to breathless choir;
When suddenly his mantle wide
His hands impatient flung aside,
And, lo! he met their wondering eyes
Complete in all a warrior's guise.

A moment there was awful pause—
When Berkeley cried, "Cease, traitor! cease!
God's temple i? the house of peace!"
The other shouted, "Nay, not so,
When God is with our righteous cause;
His holiest places then are ours,
His temples are our forts and towers,
That frown upon the tyrant foe;
In this, the dawn of Freedom's day,

"Come out with me, in Freedom's name,
For her to live, for her to die?"
A hundred hands flung up reply,
A hundred voices answered, "I!"[19]

Benedict Arnold

CHAPTER 5

ARNOLD AND ALLEN

CAPTURE OF TICONDEROGA

On the very day when Congress gathered in Philadelphia, another historical event took place far to the north on the shores of beautiful Lake Champlain. The shores of the lake, along with nearby Lake George, had been the scene of bloody battles in the French and Indian War.

In 1755 the French had built a fort on a bluff that overlooks the narrow passageway between Lake George and Lake Champlain. Because this waterway was a main thoroughfare of the region, it was desirable to be able to use cannons to control fighting forces passing through. The fort was named *Cheonderoga*, an Indian word meaning "sounding waters." Eventually, it became known as Ticonderoga.

In the summer of 1758, during the French and Indian War, British General Ambercrombie had tried to capture the fort from the French. But his redcoats and colonials had fought in vain. He retreated with the loss of 2,000 men.

However, the fort fell about a year later to General Amherst, who attacked it with 11,000 men. Amherst did not repeat the mistake of Ambercrombie. Rather than try to force the fort in an assault, he was wise enough to lay siege to Ticonderoga and wait for hunger to do peacefully what bullets had failed to accomplish. It was not long before the French gave up the fort and retreated to Crown Point. Amherst had accomplished a victory without a shot being fired.

Ethan Allen at Ticonderoga.

Allen wrote, "Ever since I arrived at the state of manhood, and acquainted myself with the general history of mankind, I have felt a sincere passion for liberty . . . so that the first systematical and bloody attempt, at Lexington, to enslave America, thoroughly electrified my mind, and fully determined me to take part with my country. And, while I was wishing for an opportunity to signalize myself in its behalf, directions were privately sent to me from the then colony (now State) of Connecticut, to raise the Green Mountain Boys, and, if possible, with them to surprise and take the fortress of Ticonderoga."[20]

Jeffrey Amherst, 1st Baron Amherst, governor of British North America by Joshua Reynolds, 1766 (PD-Art).

In 1775, "Fort Ty," as it was known, was still held by the British. Captain Delaplace was in charge of a little garrison of 48 men and evidently expected no trouble in the immediate future. It must have been a very boring life for the young captain and his wife; far out in the wilderness with no society but 48 soldiers and a smattering of women and children. But the Delaplaces were soon to find out that Fort Ty could indeed have some excitement of its own.

When Benedict Arnold had arrived at the camp at Cambridge, he had quickly suggested an attempt to capture Ticonderoga. He argued that the fort held valuable war supplies badly needed by the young colonial army. It contained a considerable amount of ammunition and many guns that would come in handy in a number of possible places. Further, the fort's location would make it very useful in case of an invasion of Canada. You must remember that the Quebec Act involved a dispute over whether vast tracts of western territory belonged to the American colonies or to Quebec. It may be that Arnold was already thinking of leading an invasion of Canada himself, since he was a man of such energy and drive that he was compelled to be doing something challenging at all times.

In any event, the Massachusetts Provincial Congress gave Arnold a colonel's commission and authorized him to raise a force of 400 men in the western part of the colony. He was to take command of them and lead them in the conquest of Fort Ticonderoga.

Delighted and confident, Arnold sallied forth. But he soon found that there was a flaw in his plan: someone else was bent on doing the same thing. In Vermont there was a group of men known as the Green Mountain Boys. Along with their leader, the mighty Ethan Allen, these men had formed a militia group to resist the claims of New York on much of Vermont's colonial territory. Allen and his "boys" had already received authority from Connecticut to take Ticonderoga. When Arnold heard this, he changed his plans. Massachusetts had supplied Arnold with money, horses, and ammunition, but as soon as he learned of Ethan Allen's march he gave up trying to raise a force of his own. He hurried to find and join Allen's band.

This led to a conflict. Both Arnold and Allen were bold, aggressive men. Allen was strong of body and fared well in the good-natured tussles and wrestling matches of camp life. His men were very proud of their tough leader. Arnold was capable and eager to lead. Both men could not be the boss of the expedition.

General Ethan Allen

The problem was largely solved as soon as Arnold had time to learn how dedicated Allen's men were to their captain. No outsider was going to displace Ethan. So apparently Arnold decided that he was willing for the moment to be a member of the band rather than the leader of it. He pushed ahead with the rest of the troop. On the night of May 9, the force arrived on the opposite shore from Fort Ticonderoga.

Allen's job was made easier by the fact that he had a contact in the region. He knew a farmer there and quickly approached that man for help. The farmer's son, Nathan Beman, knew the lake and the fort as well. He had been inside Ticonderoga many times. Nathan became their guide.

This is Allen's account of the challenge he issued to his men just before the attack: "Friends and fellow soldiers, you have, for a number of years past, been a scourge and terror to arbitrary power. Your valor has been famed abroad, and acknowledged, as appears by the advice and orders to me, from the General Assembly of Connecticut, to surprise and take the garrison now before us. I now propose to advance before you, and, in person, conduct you through the wicket gate; for we must this morning either quit our pretensions to valor, or possess ourselves of this fortress in a few minutes; and, inasmuch as it is a desperate attempt, which none but the bravest of men dare undertake, I do not urge it on any contrary to his will. You that will undertake voluntarily, poise your firelocks."[21]

Only a few boats could be located along the shore of the lake, and these were soon busy ferrying men across. But with all their efforts, only Allen, Arnold, and 83 men had been landed on the Ticonderoga shore by daylight.

It was enough for Ethan Allen. He gathered his men, gave them a rousing challenge, and led them in three ranks quietly toward the fort.

THE FORT IS TAKEN

They ran into a sentinel who tried to fire his musket at Allen, but it misfired and the man was taken prisoner. The next sentinel tried to stab one of the leaders with his bayonet, but Allen silenced him with a stroke of his sword.

The men sneaked into the fort, lined up in front of the barracks, and then gave a united shout of triumph that must have made the forest ring for a long distance in all directions. Of course this awakened the British soldiers, and they all came stumbling out of the barracks.

Fort Ticonderoga, Ticonderoga, New York, photo by Mwanner, 2009 (CC BY-SA 3.0).

Ethan Allen's Capture of Fort Ticonderoga

Instantly they found themselves prisoners. With young Nathan leading, Ethan Allen quickly approached the house of Captain Delaplace. He gave three loud raps on the door with the hilt of his sword, at the same time shouting for Delaplace to come forth and surrender.

It was not a gentle invitation, but it was quickly accepted. A British officer opened the door and demanded to know the reason for the disturbance. But he quickly recognized the famous leader of the Green Mountain Boys.

Allen pointed with his sword at his men, gathered behind him and demanded the surrender of the fort.

"By what authority do you demand it?" asked the officer angrily.

"In the name of the great Jehovah and the Continental Congress!" roared Ethan Allen.[22]

Captain Delaplace may not have even known that there was such a body as the Continental Congress and very likely was unaware that the group was gathering for a second session. But there was no doubt about the identity of the man before him and the intent of the force supporting him. The fort was quickly surrendered, and the garrison was sent to Hartford.

Proverbs 11:2 says, "When pride cometh, then cometh shame: but with the lowly is wisdom." Benedict Arnold had many good qualities, but his downfall was his pride. Because he reacted with pride instead of humility when he was not fairly rewarded for his bravery in battle, he would one day betray his country by turning traitor. It would result in lifelong shame for him and his family.

So it was that for a second time the fort was captured without the firing of a shot. It was a rich prize for a struggling young army. The fort contained 2 mortars, 120 cannons, 1 howitzer, 3 cartloads of flints, a good quantity of boat-building material, some gun carriages, and a good supply of provisions and gunpowder. The Green Mountain Boys were ecstatic at their success. During the day, the remainder of their force crossed the lake to join them. On May 12, Crown Point also fell to the Boys.

Once the fort was surrendered, Arnold tried to assume command of Ticonderoga. But his claims were ignored. The men told him that they were being paid by Connecticut for this mission, and that, anyway, they would follow orders only from Ethan Allen.

Arnold had only a few men, but he was determined to do something significant. So a few days later when some more men joined him, he traveled across Lake Champlain and captured St. Johns in Canada, along with a sloop of war anchored there. For the moment, the colonial forces were in control of Lake Champlain, an ideal waterway into the heart of Quebec. An invasion of Canada would not be far behind.

Lake Champlain at sunset (CC BY 2.5).

These events caused a variety of reactions in the colonies. Some people were amazed at the news, some elated, and some frightened. The more timid among them declared that England would be enraged and would visit terrible revenge on the colonies. This fear was not without reason. Great Britain was powerful. The colonies were weak. Worse yet, the colonies were not yet strongly united, as the clash between Ethan Allen and Benedict Arnold showed — one leader sent by Connecticut, one sent by Massachusetts. Could the colonies forge a relationship that would stand against the might of the British Empire?

In Congress, there was the same assortment of reactions as in the general public. The bolder members were delighted to hear of the capture of Ticonderoga and its goodly supply of important weapons and war materials. The more timid ones were afraid such an action was going much too far. This was rebellion. This was open war. This was not what the colonies wanted, they said. They wanted their rights as Englishmen, but they certainly did not want to have a war with the mother country and even separate from her.

After much discussion, a compromise was reached. Congress recommended that the colonies would keep the supplies from Ticonderoga for now. They would be removed to the southern shore of Lake George and a strong post established in that location. They also recommended that the materials be carefully inventoried.

> In order that they might be safely returned when the restoration of harmony between Great Britain and the colonies, so earnestly desired by the latter, shall render it prudent and consistent with the overruling law of self-preservation.[23]

49

ETHAN ALLEN'S MEN:
THE GREEN MOUNTAIN BOYS

THE GREEN MOUNTAIN BOYS

by William Cullen Bryant

Here halt we our march, and pitch our tent
On the rugged forest-ground,
And light our fire with the branches rent
By winds from the beeches round.
Wild storms have torn this ancient wood,
But a wilder is at hand,
With hail of iron and rain of blood,
To sweep and waste the land.

How the dark wood rings with our voices shrill,
That startle the sleeping bird!
To-morrow eve must the voice be still,
And the step must fall unheard.
The Briton lies by the blue Champlain,
In Ticonderoga's towers,
And ere the sun rise twice again,
Must they and the lake be ours.

Fill up the bowl from the brook that glides
Where the fire-flies light the brake;
A ruddier juice the Briton hides
In his fortress by the lake.
Build high the fire, till the panther leap
From his lofty perch in flight,
And we'll strengthen our weary arms with sleep
For the deeds of tomorrow night.

Forward! He shouted.

AMERICA'S MOST FAMOUS TRAITOR

Benedict Arnold was born in Norwich, Connecticut, in 1741.
His father's name was Benedict also. His mother was a wealthy
widow, Hannah Waterman King, before her marriage to the
elder Arnold. The family prospered at first, but eventually some
business deals failed and financial pressures made life hard for
the family. Arnold's father turned to drink for comfort, making
the problems in the family worse.

Young Benedict Arnold attended school at Canterbury. He was there, away from home, when some of his siblings caught the yellow fever and died.

Because money was scarce in the family, Arnold was withdrawn from school. Without the confinement of the school regimen and without strong parental control, Arnold got into his share of boyish trouble. He was energetic and bold, willing to try new challenges, even those of the sort that might be disapproved of by authorities. His mother was at a loss in trying to rein in her precocious boy.

She finally found a place for Benedict that provided him with some measure of control and discipline. He was taken in as an apprentice by his cousins, Joshua and Daniel Lathrop. They were the owners of a successful apothecary (medicine) business. He worked with his cousins for years, gaining a solid education in the family trade. He left them for limited times to join the army during the French and Indian War, but returned.

Benedict Arnold

Arnold's parents died in 1759 and 1761. After leaving his cousins' employ, Arnold decided to try going into business for himself. He established an apothecary shop in New Haven, traveling to Europe to purchase supplies. He was assisted in the store by his sister Hannah, his only surviving sibling.

Arnold married Margaret Mansfield in 1767 and had three sons. He served in the militia as a captain. When word came of the battles at Lexington and Concord, Arnold led his troop off to the action near Boston.

In the years ahead, Arnold would show himself to be a bold and courageous leader of men. Unfortunately, he would also show himself to be a traitor.

The Battle of Bunker Hill

THE BATTLE OF BUNKER HILL

FORTIFYING THE HILL

In the year 1775, the city of Boston was far different than what you see today. Of course it was much smaller, both in land and in population. The entire city was located on the peninsula in the middle of Boston Harbor. On the mainland surrounding the peninsula were several hills. It was on these hills that the patriot army stood. They were farmers, these New England men. A few were also were fishermen, tradesmen, and merchants, but for the most part they were men of the plow. Now, poorly equipped and poorly organized but determined to protect their homes, they kept the British army bottled up within the town.

Sturdy men from other towns and colonies were rushing to join them. From many places powder and shot were being collected. Some of the most exciting adventures of the entire war were taking place already as Tories took every opportunity to interfere with men hurrying to join the patriot army and interrupt the delivery of powder and lead.

The people were now generally becoming very agitated. Mass meetings took place, and though the leaders of the meetings were often entirely honorable in their conduct, sometimes it seemed not enough care was taken to prevent some in the community from hostile actions toward their neighbors. It is always this way in war. Conditions are desperate, and some people are driven

The evening before the Battle of Bunker Hill.

"Don't shoot until you can see the whites of their eyes!"

This famous phrase has been accredited to several sources, including Colonel Prescott. Usually, it is attributed to General Israel Putnam. There are similar quotes known to historians from earlier, European wars. One soldier who was in the Battle of Bunker Hill said of Putnam "I distinctly heard him say, 'Men, you are all marksmen — don't one of you fire until you see the white of their eyes.'"[26]

Going to church.

to do desperate things. Also, there are always those wicked characters who take advantage of the unsettled conditions of war to rob and molest others.

"Tar and feathers" referred to the practice of covering a criminal with hot tar and feathers to make him not only humiliated but in great pain. This was one of the excesses to which people sometimes went, carried away with the stress and bitterness of war. The people of the colonies were indeed suffering from stress as well as oppression. Sometimes a few of them resorted to methods that were not justified even in this. Of course there were always a number of brutes in a community who used any possible excuse to justify abusing others.

New Jersey took the money in the colonial treasury to equip the New Jersey militia. In South Carolina, patriot leaders urged people to carry their guns with them any time they left their homes, even if they were going to church. In North Carolina's Mecklenburg County, the people published the Mecklenburg Declaration of Independence, stating that the address of the king and Parliament in February had "annulled and vacated all civil and military commissions granted by the Crown and suspended the constitutions of the colonies"[24] and that these rights now belonged to the people of the colonies.

In other words, they were saying that there was now no British colonial government in the colony and that the citizens of the colony had the right to create their own government as a republic. This has been called the Mecklenburg Declaration of Independence. It has been called the first act of its kind. Unfortunately for students of history, no copies of the original paper exist and its origins are somewhat hazy.

Alertness means "being keenly aware of what is taking place around me so I can be prepared with a right response."[25] First Peter 5:8 says, "Be sober, be vigilant; because your adversary the devil, as a roaring lion, walketh about, seeking whom he may devour." The patriots were alert to what was going on in Boston, and when additional troops arrived to help the British, they quickly moved to take action by building fortifications on Breed's Hill.

General Gage and his army found themselves prisoners in Boston, at least from the direction of the mainland. But reinforcements under Howe, Clinton, and Burgoyne arrived on May 25 by ship. The Americans had no navy to oppose the British landing, so the redcoat force in Boston grew to about 10,000 men.

This greatly reassured General Gage. Now confident that he would quickly crush the rebellion, he now issued a proclamation of pardon. He promised that if any patriot who had taken up arms against the government would lay down his arms and promise loyalty to King George, he would be forgiven of his transgressions. However, he made exceptions of John Hancock and Sam Adams. These two villains, he reasoned, were so evil that they could expect no pardon in this world or the next. Gage also went further and threatened to hang any man caught with arms still on his person.

The effect was not fear in the colonists, but determination. The little army determined that they must take action before the British could get organized and carry out the threat. So 1,200 men were sent to occupy Bunker Hill, just outside the town. This was one of several nearby hills, and if it was fortified, the guns could be aimed directly down at the ships in the harbor.

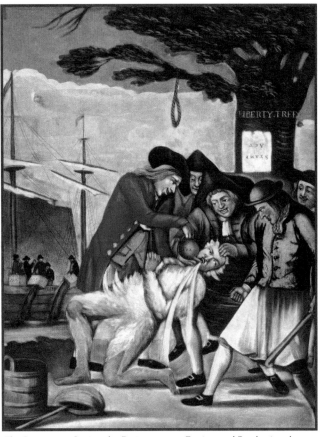

The Bostonians Paying the Excise-man, or Tarring and Feathering, by Philip Dawe, 1774 (PD-Art)

The Battle Begins

This was a very serious move. Colonel Prescott, in command of the men selected for the job was a veteran of the French and Indian War. His first move was to march his men to Cambridge Common where they formed up and heard Dr. Samuel Langdon, president of Harvard College, offer a prayer for them all. Then they started for Bunker Hill.

When they arrived, they found that nearby Breed's Hill offered a better command of both the harbor and the town. So they went a little farther and began to build fortifications. It was nearly midnight when they arrived. Steadily and as quietly as possible they plied their picks and shovels. These were farmers, men of the rocky New England soil. The tools in their hands were as familiar as their own reflections in the mirror. The fortifications went up as quickly and neatly as they could have been built by any men in the world. When daybreak eased across the sky on the morning of June 17, the British on the ships saw what had happened during the night.

The sight that met their sleepy eyes was astounding. In one night the patriots had built an elaborate earthwork on the brow of Breed's Hill. It had taken only a few hours and it had been done within a distance at which the workers could hear the British sentries call.

55

The Death of General Warren at the Battle of Bunker's Hill, June 17, 1775, by John Trumbull, 1786 (PD-US).

The startled sailors were quickly summoned to their battle stations. Soon the crashing of mighty cannons awoke the rest of the population of Boston and the area around. The roofs of the houses were decked with people watching the bombardment. Meanwhile, the militiamen were still building. The cannonballs were falling short and rolling back down the hill, or else striking the dirt wall of the entrenchments and sinking harmlessly out of sight. They were joined by more men and more leaders.

A Boston physician named Doctor Warren had just been made a major general. He was there, but not to command. Instead he carried a rifle like a private. Colonel Stark was there, fearless and determined. Tough old Israel Putnam was there too, hero of the French and Indian War and a veteran of the renowned Rogers Rangers. These men gave the patriots courage and inspired them even in the menial labor of picking and shoveling.

We know that the Bible says that pride goes before destruction and a haughty spirit before a fall (Proverbs 16:18). This was what happened to the British who thought they would easily drive the American "peasants" from Breed's Hill.

General Gage was as furious as he was amazed when he saw what the despised "rebels" had accomplished while he lay sleeping. How could this have happened? During the morning, while the guns of the fleet sent round after round of cannon fire against the slope of the hill, he was taking counsel with the British officers who had only recently arrived. They agreed that the militiamen must not be allowed to place their cannon on Breed's Hill. But, since they were all convinced that farmers could not possibly stand against His Majesty's loyal troops, they did not view the situation as much of a problem. A simple bayonet charge would drive the pests from their entrenchments and the hill would be vacant. But all the time they were discussing the fortifications, the farmers were strengthening them.

Dr. Joseph Warren

Dr. Joseph Warren was an ardent patriot and a leader of the spy ring in Boston that sent Paul Revere and William Dawes galloping to warn the patriots of Lexington and Concord of the coming British expedition. He had been appointed a major general by the Continental Congress, but when asked to take command of Breed's Hill by Putnam and Prescott he declined, saying that both of them had more military experience. Instead, he asked where the action was expected to be the hottest and took up a rifle in that part of the line.

Warren was among the last men to leave the hill when the gunpowder ran out, bravely lingering to help protect the retreat of the patriots. He was killed instantly when he was struck in the head by a musket ball. Nearly a year after the battle, his brothers and friend Paul Revere dug up his body, mutilated by the British, and moved it to a formal cemetery.

Dr. Joseph Warren

The body was identified by Revere, who recognized a false tooth he had himself placed in Warren's mouth. Warren was repeatedly heard to say of the British: "These fellows say we won't fight! By Heaven, I hope I shall die up to my knees in blood!"

Warren was a widower with four children. When he was killed, his children were refugees from Boston and staying with his fiancée, Mercy Scollay, in Worcester. She continued to take care of them, getting support for their education from Samuel Adams, John Hancock, Benedict Arnold, Mercy Otis Warren, and others.

Reportedly, General Gage said that Warren's death was equal to the death of 500 men. It encouraged the patriots because it was viewed by many Americans as an act of martyrdom.

First Blood on the Hill

When the sun was in the middle of the sky, a line of boats was seen crossing the river, loaded with red-coated soldiers. After they had all landed, 3,000 strong, they formed in two divisions. One division would move along the line of a rail fence that climbed the hill. The other would move directly toward the entrenchments. Now picks and shovels were put aside, muskets were retrieved and their loads checked. The bright red coats and shining bayonets must have presented a noble sight, as well as sending a chill up the spines of the poorly equipped farmers on the hill. Yet not a man left his place.

Battle of Bunker Hill

Grim, determined, and desperate, they gripped their muskets and watched the oncoming scarlet lines. Talking died away as they watched the enemy move steadily forward, up the hill. The people of Boston stood and stared. They were quiet as well. The stillness encouraged Gage's men, who did not believe the "peasants" in the earthworks would even stay long enough to engage His Majesty's troops.

But the patriots had been warned by their leaders to hold their fire until the enemy was too close to miss.

Hardly breathing, they waited. Nearer and nearer the enemy came, step by steady step. Then they were only fifty yards away. Then the waiting farmers heard the order for which they had been waiting: "Fire!"

Hundreds of dirty, calloused fingers squeezed triggers, and thick little clouds of silver smoke flashed from priming pans. Then the muskets roared and a sheet of orange flame belched forth. Then to the crashing of muskets was added the shouts of fighting men and the screams of the wounded. The front line of the redcoats seemed almost blotted out as men and officers went down in a tangled, writhing mass.

The British soldiers returned fire as best they could, but they were so shocked by the havoc caused by the patriot muskets that they quickly turned and ran down the hill in panic rather than reloading. What a shout burst forth from the throats of the tired farmers then! They wanted to leap over the earth wall in front of them and chase the redcoats right into the harbor. With difficulty, their officers held them back and they quickly plied their powder horns and pushed new lead balls down their barrels. Grins broke through grimy faces that had not smiled in several hours.

The British ships now began to shell little Charlestown, across the river from Boston. If they had hoped that this would frighten the militiamen, they were wrong. It only made them more determined as they thought of the burning houses at the next advance of the redcoats.

The advance came, and once again neat rows of soldiers steadily marched up the hill. Soon they were near the top and stepping around the bodies of their dead comrades. Here and there a wounded man staggered through their lines and down the hill behind them. This time the scarlet line was barely 30 paces away when again the muskets crashed again and the red line crumbled. There was a brief and vicious struggle, then the redcoats again broke and fled. Hundreds of them lay dead and wounded on the hillside. Behind their embankment, only a handful of farmers had been wounded or killed.

But they were nearly out of gun powder. Israel Putnam mounted his horse and galloped toward Cambridge to get reinforcements and powder; but the air was filled with flying lead from the ships' guns and it was almost certain death to cross Charlestown Neck. There would not be time for help to come.

Most of the red-coated soldiers had had enough of the patriots' marksmanship. But their officers re-formed their lines and once again ordered them forward. Pale and sick-looking, the soldiers started up the hill once more.

Israel Putnam mounted his horse.

On the other side of the redoubt, there was barely enough powder for even one more volley. Militiamen heard encouraging words from their officers, urging them to fire their remaining ammunition and then meet bayonets with musket butts. Then the redcoats were in range once again, and a weaker but still effective volley cut dozens down. Then the remaining regulars were on top of the redoubt and the battle became a tangled mass of shouting, struggling, panting men. But the patriots were out of powder and had few bayonets. Slowly, they gave way. But it was an orderly retreat, not a panicked rout.

Most of the American casualties came as they were retreating across the valley and over Bunker Hill. With no powder with which to blunt the volleys of the British, the farmers could do little to protect their rear. Few of them had been hurt while fighting on Breeds' Hill, but now they were in the open and exposed with no earthworks to protect them.

Still, they sustained less than 500 in killed and wounded while the British casualties numbered over 1,000. It had been a victory for the redcoats in terms of taking the hill, but a disaster in terms of men lost.

The Battle of Bunker Hill was over. The British had learned a lesson. Never again would they make frontal assaults on earthworks defended by the patriot farmers. Their respect for the marksmanship of the Americans would remain as well. Now the Battle of Bunker Hill would be added to the fights at Lexington and Concord as evidence that American men, led by officers schooled in the bloody years of the French and Indian War, could face with courage and effectiveness the best troops of King George's scarlet legions.

General George Washington

CHAPTER 7

LIFE IN THE NEW ARMY

THE GENERAL TAKES COMMAND

The news about the Battle of Bunker Hill shot through the colonies like a bolt of electricity. Despite the death of the beloved Dr. Warren, the enthusiasm of the Americans was boundless. The British had nearly been defeated. The patriots had shown that they were made of strong material.

General Washington had left Philadelphia for Cambridge on June 21 with a company of light cavalry accompanying him. All along the way he had been greeted with loud cheers and celebrations. He arrived in New York four days later, which coincidentally was on the very same day that the new royal governor, Tryon, arrived from England. There was much greater enthusiasm for Washington than for the governor. News of the fight at Bunker Hill reached Washington at New York, and added greatly to his encouragement. Now he knew that the patriots would indeed fight.

General Philip Schuyler

While at New York, Washington had a conference with General Philip Schuyler. Schuyler would soon distinguish himself by taking an active and effective part in the struggle. After conferring with Schuyler, Washington traveled on to Cambridge, arriving there on the afternoon of July 2.

On the following morning at 9 o'clock, the troops stood in parade on Cambridge Common. General Washington walked from his quarters to face his troops. With several of his officers, the general

Washington's rules of conduct for soldiers:

The General hopes and trusts that every officer and man will endeavor to live and act as becomes a Christian soldier defending the dearest rights and liberties of his country. [27]

While we are zealously performing the duties of good citizens and soldiers, we certainly ought not to be inattentive to the higher duties of religion. To the distinguished character of Patriot, it should be our highest glory to add the more distinguished character of Christian. [28]

President George Washington being received in New York, April 23, 1789.

stood before his men and made a short speech. Then he drew his sword and formally assumed the command of the Continental Army amid the cheers of the soldiers. It was a great day for the commander and an even greater day for America.

Washington immediately plunged into the job that would occupy him constantly for many weary, difficult years.

First, Washington assembled his top officers and held a council of war. It was apparent that the first order of business was to get the army organized.

Up to this time the men were basically a militia, or rather a group of militias, hailing from various towns and colonies. They were independent men, mostly farmers who had never been another man's servant and were used to making their own decisions. They did not like having their personal liberties limited by the responsibilities of army life. The discipline so necessary for making a large group of men work effectively together would take time and hard work to achieve. Some of the men were simply unruly. There was profanity, stealing, and drunkenness in the camp at times. Of course not all the soldiers were guilty, but these vices were too common to satisfy the upright commander of the army.

So, the very day after assuming command, Washington issued this general order:

Wisdom involves skillfully dealing with people to accomplish godly goals. Psalm 90:12 says, "So teach us to number our days, that we may apply our hearts unto wisdom."

The Continental Congress having now taken all the troops of the several colonies, which have been raised, or may be raised hereafter for the support and defense of the liberties of America, into their pay and service, they are now the troops of the UNITED PROVINCES OF NORTH AMERICA; and it is hoped that all distinctions of colonies will be laid aside, so that one and the same spirit may animate the whole, and the only contest be, who shall render, on this great and trying occasion, the most essential service to the great and common cause in which we are all engaged. It is required and expected that exact discipline be observed, and due subordination prevail through the whole army, as a failure in these most essential points must necessarily produce extreme hazard, disorder, and confusion, and end in shameful disappointment and disgrace. The general most earnestly requires and expects a due observance of these articles of war, established for the government of the army, which forbid profane cursing, swearing, and drunkenness; and in like manner, he requires and expects of all officers and soldiers not engaged on actual duty, a punctual attendance on divine service, to implore the blessing of Heaven upon the means used for our safety and defence. . . .[29] (George Washington, July 4, 1775, General Orders)

Rev. William Emerson (US-PD).

It seems a shame that such an order was necessary, but how wonderful that the commander-in-chief of the army understood the bad nature of profanity and the importance of attending "divine service" — in other words, church attendance. Washington was wise enough to know that the success of an army is dependent on the blessing of God.

LIFE IN THE CAMPS

Washington arranged for his men to be organized by colonies so that men might live and fight beside their friends and neighbors. He also hoped in this way that jealously between colonies might not be a problem. All together, the American army now numbered around 16,000 men.

We get a glimpse of the everyday life of the Continental soldier from letters written from camp to family and friends. William Emerson, a chaplain in the army at Cambridge, wrote such a letter shortly after Washington assumed command. It gives an interesting view of camp life:

New lords, new laws. The generals, Washington and Lee, are upon the lines every day. New orders from his excellency are read to the respective regiments every morning after prayers. The strictest government is taking place and great distinction is made between officers and soldiers. Every one is made to know his place and keep in it, or be tied up and receive thirty or forty lashes according to his crime. Thousands

Continental Army Color Guard

General Thomas Gage by John Singleton Copley, 1788 (CC0 1.0).

are at work every day from four till eleven o'clock in the morning. It is surprising how much work has been done. . . . It is very diverting to walk among the camps. They are as different in their form as the owners are in their dress, and every tent is a portraiture of the temper and taste of the persons who encamp in it. Some are made of boards and some of sail-cloth; some are partly of one and partly of the other. Again, some are made of stone or turf, brick or brush. Some are thrown up in a hurry; others are curiously wrought with doors and windows, done with wreaths and withes, in the manner of a basket. Some are your proper tents and marquees, looking like the regular camp of the enemy. In these are the Rhode Islanders, who are furnished with tent equipage and everything in the most exact English style. However, I think this great variety rather a beauty than a blemish in the army.[30]

Of course most of the men in the army at Cambridge were from the New England colonies, with the majority of them from Massachusetts, but others were continually coming from the other colonies to join them.

In some colonies, Pennsylvania in particular, enthusiasm was so great that something had to be done to keep the number of volunteers to manageable levels. One colonial newspaper carried an interesting story about how one militia leader enabled himself to select the best men without offending others who were not chosen. He drew a picture on a board of a man's nose. The picture was the size of a real nose. He then placed the board 150 yards from the firing line and had the men shoot at it. Those who could hit closest to the nose would be the ones selected to join the company and go to Cambridge. When the firing was done, over sixty of the men had hit the nose. The newspaper article concluded by saying, "General Gage, take care of *your* nose."[31]

AFTER THE TEA PARTY

On the night of December 16, 1773, a group of Boston men dressed as Indians boarded tea ships in Boston Harbor and dumped many thousands of dollars' worth of tea into the water. This incident went down in history as the Boston Tea Party. The British government punished Boston by closing the harbor in the Boston Port Bill. Because the town of Boston got most of its supplies by ship, this meant a desperate time for the people of the town.

The other towns and colonies up and down the Atlantic coast were not long in responding. Towns near and far sent wagonloads of food and other goods into Boston to relieve the distress of their fellow patriots. A man from nearby Pepperell wrote: "Providence has placed you where you must stand the first shock. . . . If we submit to these regulations, all is gone." This man was William Prescott, a colonel in the Massachusetts militia. He continued: "Our forefathers passed the vast Atlantic, spent their blood and treasure, that they might enjoy their liberties, both civil and religious, and transmit them to their posterity. . . . Now if we should give them up, can our children rise up and call us blessed?" This same William Prescott would soon command the American forces at the battle of Bunker Hill.[32]

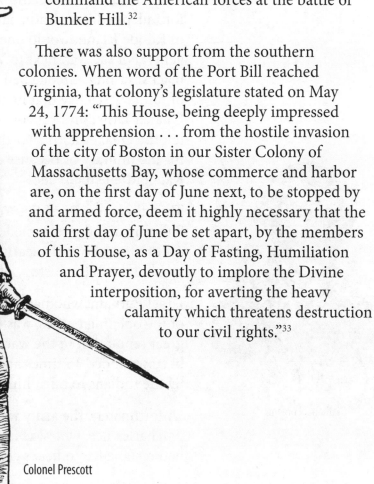

There was also support from the southern colonies. When word of the Port Bill reached Virginia, that colony's legislature stated on May 24, 1774: "This House, being deeply impressed with apprehension . . . from the hostile invasion of the city of Boston in our Sister Colony of Massachusetts Bay, whose commerce and harbor are, on the first day of June next, to be stopped by and armed force, deem it highly necessary that the said first day of June be set apart, by the members of this House, as a Day of Fasting, Humiliation and Prayer, devoutly to implore the Divine interposition, for averting the heavy calamity which threatens destruction to our civil rights."[33]

Colonel Prescott

Daniel Morgan

Washington's Leaders

"Daniel Morgan's riflemen," composed mostly of Virginia pioneers, were among the best of the recruits. Some of the New England men were not as warm in their welcome to the Virginians as they might have been, because of their prejudice against the Irish. Most of the Virginians were descended from Irishmen. But they soon earned the respect of the New Englanders with their legendary marksmanship. It was said that they could load their guns while running through the woods and that any man among them could hit a running squirrel at 300 yards.

The clothing of Morgan's men was unique also. Every man wore a long hunting shirt on which were written the well-known words of Patrick Henry, "Liberty or Death." Their leader was certainly a standout. He was a huge man of almost unbelievable strength. He had survived a savage flogging for hitting a British officer during the French and Indian War, and had lived after having been shot through the back of the neck, the bullet coming out his cheek after having knocked out his teeth on the left side.

Other leaders in the camp would also win fame while fighting for independence. Nathanael Greene, the "Fighting Quaker" of Rhode Island, would one day be regarded as the most able general of the war, next to Washington. Trained in the trade of blacksmithing, Greene had become so fascinated with the study of military science that he received a sound whipping from his Quaker father and yet continued his studies. Young Greene had left the Quaker faith after this, perhaps because of his fondness for the military or because of the influence of his devout wife, Kate Littlefield Greene.

Then there was Benedict Arnold and John Hart and John Sullivan, and the esteemed Artemas Ward, Heath, Knox, and other men who at this early time dreamed of the part they would take in the history of a nation being born.

Israel Putnam, who had left his plow in the field when he heard of the opening battles, was there also. "Old Put" had earned a great reputation in the war with the French and Indians. He had been wounded 15 times and miraculously survived an attempt by the Indians to burn him to death.

Unfortunately, the army was also burdened with the likes of Charles Lee, who was next to Washington in rank. Lee had resigned an officer's commission in the British army

Nathanael Greene

and volunteered to fight on the American side. He was a seasoned officer with experience in several European conflicts. But his personal ambition to replace Washington as commander–in–chief made him unpopular in the army and seems to have influenced him in some poor battle performances. Washington and the struggling young nation would have been saved a number of setbacks had this unreliable and treacherous officer stayed on the other side of the Atlantic.

This flag was designed by and is named for American general Christopher Gadsden during in the 1770s. The Gadsden Flag with its "Don't Tread On Me" message is a symbol used by the Tea Party movement.

So camp life went on with its odd mix of officers and men. They had different levels of experience and training. They were enlisted for various periods of time. There were united by a passion for freedom and divided by loyalties to their own colonies. They had a common cause, but not a common country. They had many different flags floating over their camps. The most common one was the Gadsden flag, a yellow field showing a rattlesnake poised to strike and the words, "Don't tread on me."

All in all, it was a motley group that Washington was striving to bring into some form of discipline and order, while at the same time working to keep the British bottled up in Boston. There was frequent firing between British and Colonial lines, and occasional minor skirmishes, but no major engagements. A letter in the *New York Gazette* painted an accurate picture of life in the American camp:

> During a severe cannonade at Roxbury last week, a bomb thirteen inches in diameter fell within the American lines and burnt furiously, when four of the artillerymen ran up and one kicked out the fuse, saved the bomb and probably some lives — a stroke of heroism worthy of record. The regulars have so hardened the provincials by their repeated firing that a cannonading is just as much minded as a common thunder shower. All things look well. The provincials are now as strongly posted as are the regulars. Neither side is willing to attack the other in their lines…[34]

John Sullivan

No doubt, camp life was monotonous much of the time. But the monotony would soon be broken. America was just about to go on the offensive and carry the war deep into enemy territory. Soon, Benedict Arnold would lead an expedition against Quebec.

Soldiers standing at attention

CHAPTER 8

DEFEAT AND VICTORY IN BATTLE

SOME EARLY SUCCESS IN CANADA

While Washington was holding the British and organizing his army at Boston, other important events were transpiring in other places. General Schuyler was now in command of the division along Lake Champlain, where Benedict Arnold had gone to capture Fort Ticonderoga, only to find that Ethan Allen was a step ahead of him. Arnold had been successful in seizing the British boats on the lake, even though he had only a few followers. But he did not like being in a position lower than that of Ethan Allen. He finally wrote an angry letter to the Massachusetts Provincial Congress, resigning the position he had been awarded by them. He returned to the camp at Cambridge with many and bitter complaints about how he had been treated.

Benedict Arnold was anything but a coward. He never asked his men to do anything he would not do himself. When the time came for bold action, his example was magnetic to the men who answered to his commands. He did, however, have a jealous nature and was not slow to take up a grudge when he felt he had been treated with less respect than he deserved. Washington had a generous appreciation for Arnold's talents, and was quick to make use of them. If Washington's

Benedict Arnold

Benedict Arnold felt he had been wronged by not getting the credit he deserved. He was not willing to forgive those he felt had wronged him. Forgiveness is picturing how Jesus died on the Cross for my sins so that God's love can flow through me to others who have wronged me.

Arnold's column is shattered in fierce street fighting during the Battle of Quebec, by Charles William Jefferys, 1916 (PD-Art).

wishes had been followed, Arnold might have stayed loyal to the American cause and rendered outstanding service throughout the duration of the war. But that was not to be.

Arnold, along with a number of other men in the colonies, was strongly in favor of an invasion of Canada. In fact, Arnold had written to Congress to submit a plan by which he was confident that 2,000 men could easily take the entire country. He stated that Carleton, the Canadian governor, had only 550 men under him who were prepared to give battle and that it was very likely that the gates of Montreal would be willingly opened to the first strong force of Continentals that arrived at the town. He badly wanted to be the leader of that force and was willing to assume all responsibility for the expedition.

Congress was not so eager. They had no clearly stated power, and many of the members were not willing to take action more than that which was absolutely necessary to protect themselves. Many still cherished the hope that the king and Parliament would eventually listen to their pleas for peace.

Fort Chambly, Chambly, Qc, Canada. Photo by Denis-Carl Robidoux, 2013 (CC BY-SA 3.0).

Ethan Allen had also written to Congress about an invasion of Canada, and in fact had visited Philadelphia himself to try to get pay for the men who had served with him at Ticonderoga and to get permission to raise a new regiment. It was reported that Allen and some of his leaders appeared before Congress and stated their needs. The assembly was very impressed by the rough frontiersmen who stood before them and willingly gave their approval for the new regiment. Allen and his men happily hurried back to join Schuyler and Montgomery, who were in command of the captured posts of Crown Point and Ticonderoga.

The expedition into Canada was finally authorized, partly out of fear that the British might try to retake Ticonderoga. In September of 1775, the forces of Montgomery and Schuyler appeared at Fort St. Johns, south of Montreal. The fort had more men defending it than the Americans had thought. Instead of wasting lives in a doomed assault, Schuyler hurried back to Ticonderoga for reinforcements. The extra men were quickly sent, but they arrived without Schuyler. He had been taken ill and could not return.

Major-General James Wolfe by Joseph Highmore, c.1760 (PD-Art).

Full command then fell to Montgomery. He proved himself equal to the task. After a 50-day siege he captured Fort Chambly and Fort St. John's. Then, pushing on, he triumphantly entered Montreal on November 12, 1775.

THE QUEBEC CAMPAIGN

Without wasting time the young officer proceeded to Quebec. Montgomery had served under General James Wolfe in the capture of this fort during the French and Indian War in 1759. Perhaps he had learned some lessons in that experience that encouraged him to believe that the fort would fall to him as it had to Wolfe.

Meanwhile, Benedict Arnold was getting his wish. Washington had granted him command of a force with which to assist Montgomery at Quebec. The detachment included two companies of the Pennsylvania troops, a thousand New England infantrymen, and Dan Morgan's riflemen. Winter was on its way, and it would not be an easy expedition. The route lay along the Kennebec and Chaudiere Rivers, through a vast wilderness.

But this was the sort of challenge that Arnold seemed to enjoy. His bold example cheered his followers and encouraged them to go on, pushing through thick brush, wading through frosty swamps or rowing across swift rivers. Many of the men grew sick, and some died along the way. Their shoes wore out, their clothing was in tatters, and their supplies ran out.

Endurance is the inward struggle to endure tribulation with determination.

"Behold, we count them happy which endure. Ye have heard of the patience of Job, and have seen the end of the Lord; that the Lord is very pitiful, and of tender mercy." —James 5:11

Even the game of the forest was scarce. Before the 33-day march was over, two hundred men had perished. Another 200 had turned back for Cambridge, carrying with them others who were too sick or injured to continue. It is said that some of the men brought their wives along on this desperate journey and that some of them bore the hardships even better than the men. There would be other times in this war when heroic American women would share the hardships of the forts and camps. Their presence was a constant encouragement to the hard-pressed colonial warriors.

The Death of General Wolfe by Benjamin West, date unknown (PD-US).

At long last, the fort at Quebec stood before them. Arnold, with his 700 remaining men, crossed the St. Lawrence, climbed the Heights of Abraham, and boldly challenged the garrison to surrender the fort or come out and fight. The garrison of the fort saw no reason to do either. They were protected and comfortable inside their fort walls. There was everything to lose and nothing to gain by going out to battle. On the contrary, their wisest course of action was to take no action while Arnold and his force withstood the rigors of the cold Canadian winter. Winter alone might be a strong enough enemy to defeat Arnold.

There was little for the plucky American to do but wait. But Benedict Arnold had never been good at waiting. He chafed at the delay while he awaited the arrival of Montgomery. Finally, on December 3, Montgomery and his men arrived, bringing the total number of Americans to 1,200.

Again they demanded of General Carleton, the fort's commander, that he come out and fight. But the Briton was far too wise to accept such a foolish challenge. At last the two American commanders decided to storm the fort. It was a long chance, but there was little else they could do but march away through the winter storms with nothing to show for their great trouble.

David Wooster, Esq'r., (PD-Art).

They devised a plan to attack the fort from both sides at once. In order to have the best chance of surprise, they launched their assault at 2 o'clock a.m. on December 31 in a blinding snowstorm. It was bitterly cold, and the snow blowing so thick that a man could hardly see three feet in front of him. On one side of the town Montgomery approached, while Arnold came from the other. Then bullets began to fly and the fight was on.

Smallpox is a very contagious disease that causes fluid-filled bumps on the skin and can kill the person infected. In the late 1700s, smallpox killed an estimated 400,000 people in Europe each year. One-third of all blindness was blamed on the disease as well.

Helped by the storm and the surprise, Montgomery doggedly and steadily moved forward. It looked as if he was indeed about to breach the fortifications, when suddenly he was struck by three balls and fell dead in the snow.

His soldiers were stunned by the loss of their brave commander. They slowed, hesitated, and then stopped. Just at that moment,

Portrait of George Washington at Dorchester Heights., by Gilbert Stuart, 1806 (PD-Art).

reinforcements arrived to support the defenders. Without a leader, Montgomery's men fell back. Had they just held the ground they had gained, Quebec might have fallen, for Arnold was fighting like a giant on the other side of the stronghold. His flashing sword seemed to be everywhere at once while his shouts of encouragement kept his men fighting, stubbornly and recklessly. Then a bullet struck his leg and suddenly he was down.

Arnold was carried from the field, seriously wounded. Mighty Dan Morgan and his riflemen rushed forward to shore up the line. Then they stormed the battery and were soon inside the town. But Montgomery was not there to meet them. They were on their own, surrounded by enemies and without support. There was no choice but to surrender. The attack had failed, Morgan and his men were prisoners, and Quebec was still in the hands of the British.

Benedict Arnold did not know how to give up. He had lost the assistance of Montgomery and now had less than a thousand men in his force. Moving back to a point three miles from Quebec, he dug entrenchments and built a camp. He hoped he could still win the fort by starving the garrison out. If he could keep supplies from being brought into Quebec, he had a chance.

General Carleton knew that once spring came and the ice melted in the St. Lawrence River, he would be reinforced. Believing that he could survive the rest of the winter on the supplies he had in store, the British commander simply waited.

The cold, harsh winter brought great hardship in the American camp. Hunger and cold were fearsome enemies to be faced. Worse yet, smallpox broke out in the camp. Patriot reinforcements arrived, bringing the entire force up to 3,000 men, but 800 of them became ill with smallpox. Carleton still knew he had little to fear from an attack.

On the first day of April, General Wooster arrived from Montreal. Because he was of a higher rank than Benedict Arnold, he assumed command. It was warmer now and as the ground thawed the men were able to work again. Cannons were placed in batteries where they could fire upon the town, but Quebec's fortifications were strong. Little damage was done. About this time, Arnold's horse slipped and fell on the officer's wounded leg. Finally, Arnold gave up.

Totally unfit for service at the present, he requested permission to retire to Montreal. Arnold did not like Wooster any more than he liked Ethan Allen, so Wooster granted permission and Arnold departed without any great sorrow on the part of either man.

In May, General Thomas came with reinforcements for the Americans, but Carleton had also received additional troops. The patriots had to beat such a hasty retreat that they left some of their sick men behind, along with some of their supplies. The British treated the sick Americans with mercy, and when they were well they were allowed to return to their homes. Soon the entire invading American army had been driven south, and the invasion of Canada was at an end.

Henry Knox, by Gilbert Stuart, 1806 (PD-US).

TAKING BACK BOSTON

But there was better news from Boston. Washington had driven the British out of the city.

Colonel Henry Knox had raised the idea of transporting cannons from Fort Ticonderoga to Boston soon after Washington arrived at Cambridge. Knox was eventually given orders to do that very thing and he started for Ticonderoga in November of 1775. Over three cold winter months, he and his men performed the nearly miraculous task of moving 60 tons of cannons, ammunition, and other equipment 300 miles along rutted roads, across frozen rivers, and through woods and swamps. Teams of oxen pulled the armaments on sleds through the snow. Historian Noah Brooks called this feat of Knox "one of the most stupendous feats of logistics" in the entire War of Independence.

Both armies understood the importance of Dorchester Heights. Along with some other hilltops around Boston, the Heights commanded a view of Boston and the harbor that could be swept with cannon fire. The harbor was as important as the city itself, for Boston was surrounded by patriot forces on the land sides and only by way of the harbor could supplies and reinforcements be brought to the British. Washington had considered trying to take Dorchester Heights when he first took command at Cambridge, but wisely observed that the army was

Defending Quebec from an American attack, December 1775, by F.H. Wellington, 1860 (PD-US).

not ready to deal with a British attack on the position. The subject came up again in February of 1776, but it was agreed that the British strength was too great and the supply of gunpowder too low to make the attempt. But when, at the end of February, Knox arrived at the end of the grueling expedition to get the cannon, he had with him extra supplies of gunpowder and shells. Washington decided it was time to act.

He first placed some of the cannons on other heights around the town as a diversion. These guns opened fire on Boston on the night of March 2, and the British replied in kind. The action was repeated on the night of March 3. While these diversionary duels were going on, Washington was preparing to fortify Dorchester Heights.

The Death of General Montgomery at Quebec. 1775. Copy of engraving by W. Ketterlinus after John Trumbull, 1808 (PD-US).

HAND OF PROVIDENCE AT DORCHESTER HEIGHTS

On the night of March 4, the batteries opened up again. While they distracted the enemy, 2,000 American troops marched up Dorchester Heights hauling cannons and equipment. They placed hay bales beside their path on the side toward the British to muffle the sound of their movements. All night long, patriots hauled cannon and built fortifications. General Washington was there, encouraging his men and reminding them that March 5 was the sixth anniversary of the Boston Massacre. It was foggy down at the foot of the hill, but clear as a bell on the top of the hill. By 4 a.m. they had built solid fortifications, including rock-filled barrels that could be rolled down the hill on attackers.

When the sky grew light on March 5, General Howe looked in amazement at the fortifications on the heights and exclaimed, "The rebels have done more in one night than my whole army would have done in a month."[36]

Washington knew that the British had to either take the heights or leave Boston. Admiral Shuldham, commander of the British fleet, told Howe that he would have to withdraw his ships from Boston Harbor unless the American works were taken, so General Howe determined to attack Dorchester Heights. He put together a plan to move 2,400 men under cover of darkness to set up the assault. But Washington got word of his intentions and moved more of his troops to the hilltop until he had a force of 6,000 in place.

Howe's plans for an attack were foiled by a sudden severe storm. That night a "natural disaster" occurred in favor of the American troops. A terrible storm blew up such as no one had seen. It blew the British ships into disarray and broke their masts. In the morning the general saw his ships wrecked and knew by the time he got things repaired, the Americans would have a real advantage.

Rev. William Gordon, a local preacher, later said, "When I heard in the night how amazingly strong the wind blew I pleased myself with the reflection that the Lord might be working delivery for us and thus prevent the diffusion of human blood. It proved to be so."[37]

Morning dawned on the following day and showed that the Americans had not let the storm delay them. They had built their fortifications higher and stronger during the storm. Now the redoubt was too strong to be taken. There was nothing for the British to do but abandon Boston. Without the shedding of a single drop of blood, the British quickly withdrew their 10,000 soldiers from the city of Boston on March 17, 1776. The victory at Dorchester Heights gave great confidence to the Americans!

The British threatened to burn the town if they were fired upon as they departed. Washington's men were not all pleased at letting the redcoats go without some punishment, but the general was not willing to cause the destruction of so much private property as would go up in flames. Boat after boat splashed its way from the wharf to the waiting ships and the redcoat soldiers took their last looks at the city they had dominated for so long. The people of Boston breathed a heartfelt sigh of relief at the departure of the British soldiers. They had their town back once again.

Storytime with Uncle Rick

America's Struggle

Writing the Declaration of Independence, 1776

CHAPTER 9

A DESIRE FOR INDEPENDENCE!

THREE STRIKES AGAINST KING GEORGE

While armies were marching, planning, and fighting, three other important events took place that were not violent in nature. Yet these events hastened the separation between England and her colonies on the eastern coast of North America.

The first of these events happened in England, not the colonies. Congress had sent a delegate to meet with the king and Parliament to deliver a last appeal for peace and justice. As we already know, most Americans, including most delegates in Congress, did not yet want to be independent of England. They said unhesitatingly that they still loved England. They were Englishmen. Some of them had lived in England. Many of them were the children and grandchildren of people who lived in England. Some of them still felt loyal to England because of love. Others owned property that they feared would

Triumph of Patriotism, Washington entering New York.

On July 5, 1775, the Second Continental Congress approved the *Olive Branch Petition* as a last-ditch effort to avoid war with Great Britain. Thomas Jefferson wrote the first draft, but his language was considered too offensive by some members of Congress and so John Dickinson rewrote most of it. The petition suggested some compromises that could be made between the king and the colonies. It assured the king that his subjects in America were loyal and did not want independence, but only asked for their rights as Englishmen. Dickinson hoped that his humble language in the petition and the recent bloodshed at Lexington and Concord would persuade the king to compromise and mend his relationship with the colonies. Unfortunately for the king, he was young and proud and responded negatively. The war was just beginning.

be lost or destroyed should war come. Still others were just the kind of people who are uncomfortable with great and sudden changes. For one reason or another, most residents of the colonies were not eager to join with the other colonies and launch out into the strange new world of independence.

Many people today think that the Revolutionary War was an unbiblical rebellion against authority. That is not true. The truth is that it was the king and Parliament who were in rebellion. This is because England was governed by a constitution that guaranteed all English subjects certain rights. When England failed to protect those rights in her American colonies, it was an illegal and unconstitutional act. More illegal acts followed as the British government fought to keep her colonies under control.

But nearly all Americans still felt that they were being treated unjustly by the British government. And when the Continental Congress sent a man to London to appeal one final time for peace and the rights of Englishmen in the colonies, it was hoped that his mission would be a success and it would begin to right the wrongs of the past many years.

They were disappointed. The king and Parliament not only declined to grant the request, they would not even read it. They refused to meet with the delegate from the colonies. Instead, they published the Proclamation of Rebellion, declaring the colonies in rebellion and stating that violent measures would be used to stop the rebellion. This was the first event. Now men such as Benjamin Franklin, John Adams, Thomas Paine, Sam Adams, and others began to speak out more boldly. They had all believed for some time that the only hope for justice and safety lay in independence. But they had kept their thoughts to themselves much of the time for fear of causing more confusion and dissension than already existed.

Hessian Soldier

The second decisive event was the wanton destruction of the town of Falmouth, Maine. That town, now known as Portland, was burned on October 16, 1775. Four British ships under the command of Captain Mowat had sailed into the harbor and set fire to several buildings in Falmouth. The blaze soon spread, and homes, churches, public buildings, and places of business were all treated alike. When the sun set that evening, less than a fourth of the town remained standing.

Over a thousand people were suddenly without shelter in the advance of a harsh Maine winter. There was no excuse for the attack except as revenge. When news of the attack spread through the colonies, many people who had been undecided about independence suddenly made up their minds.

The third event nearly overshadowed the news of the second. On October 31, Congress heard the terrible news of the burning of Falmouth. But about the same time, word came that King George had taken the radical step of hiring mercenaries to fight alongside his redcoats in subduing the colonies. What were loyal Englishmen to think of a king who would hire foreigners to come and kill them?

The rumor had floated around before, that the king was about to hire mercenaries to help him bring his American colonies to heel. But even the most loyal Tories had denied that their gracious king would ever stoop so low as to use hired killers to attack his own subjects. Why, a king's job was to lead and protect his people. How could one ever make war on them? And use hired foreigners to do so? Impossible.

Yet it had happened. The rage and astonishment was not limited to England and America. The Empress Catherine of Russia angrily refused King George's request when he first approached her about "borrowing" some of her soldiers. Then she used some of the same language to describe his character as some in the colonies were using.

Empress Catherine of Russia by Dmitry Grigorievich Levitzky, 1777 (PD-Art).

But the king had finally found his mercenaries. He hired them from the German state of Hesse. They were called Hessians. So it was that some of the most successful officers and 20,000 of the best-drilled soldiers in Europe embarked upon ships and were sent off by their corrupt prince as hirelings for a corrupt king to kill people with whom they had no quarrel.

The Hessians were sincerely hated in America. When people know that their lives, families, and property are threatened with destruction, it is hard to look at the situation objectively. So most Americans did not stop to think that the Hessians themselves had little choice in the matter. In true European fashion, they were little more than serfs; pawns of their royal masters. They were paid but a small portion of the amount given by King George for their services. The bulk of the gold went to their German prince.

But the angry Americans called them "Dutch butchers," and the contempt the colonists felt for them is hard to fully appreciate today. In addition, it was hard for the colonists and the Hessians to understand each other. The Hessian dialect sounded gruff and harsh to the English speakers of the colonies. They were professional soldiers who clung to the official uniform, which gave them a strange and foreign appearance. They had high fur hats, long jack-boots up to the thigh, and thick moustaches (which some people claimed they darkened daily with boot-black), which looked strange to the normally clean-shaven men of the colonies.

The hiring of the Hessians was the third of the three major events, apart from the battlefield, that rather suddenly compelled the separation of the colonies from their mother country.

Why did the name of Richard Henry Lee not appear on the list of committee members? After all, it was his resolution that they were refining and putting on paper. But his wife had become seriously ill and he had to leave Congress for a time to go home and take care of her.

THE DECLARATION OF INDEPENDENCE

North Carolina became the first colony to cease to be a colony. She instructed her delegates to the Second Continental Congress to vote for independence. One by one, the other colonies declared themselves in favor of independence, until only New York remained to take an official stand. Yet the general feeling of the people was well-known, so the other delegates to the Congress proceeded as if confident that New York would undoubtedly join the resistance soon.

On June 7, 1776, Richard Henry Lee of Virginia had stood in Congress to read a resolution. Lee was one of the great orators of the colonies, and in his clear, ringing tones he read:

> That these united colonies are, and of right ought to be, free and independent states; and that all political connection between us and the State of Great Britain is, and ought to be, totally dissolved.
>
> — The Declaration of Independence

John Adams was quick to second the resolution. For the safety of the two men, Congress directed the secretary to leave their names out of the records of the discussion for the day. Soon, the entire English-speaking world would know who

The Announcement of the Declaration of Independence

they were, but not until the rest of the delegates had taken a public stand along with them.

The discussion on the resolution was delayed until the first of July. The delegates hoped that, by then, every colony would have made a united commitment and instructed its delegate how to vote. A committee of five men was appointed to prepare a formal declaration reflecting the intent of the resolution: Thomas Jefferson (Virginia), John Adams (Massachusetts), Benjamin Franklin (Pennsylvania), Roger Sherman (Connecticut), and Robert Livingston (New York).

On the first day of July, 1776, the resolution was brought up for action. Thomas Jefferson, the young chairman of the declaration committee was not a great speaker but a superb writer. Nevertheless, Jefferson had requested that venerable John Adams would write the document. But Adams, wise and far-sighted as he had been in suggesting Washington as commander-in-chief, deferred to Jefferson. In his autobiography, Adams listed four reasons for his insistence on Jefferson as the penman:[38]

Thomas Jefferson

☆ First, "That he was a Virginian and I a Massachusettsensian."

☆ Second, "That he was a Southern man and I a northern one."

☆ Third, "That I had been so obnoxious for my early and constant zeal in promoting the measure, that every draft of mine would undergo a more severe scrutiny and criticism in Congress than one of his composition."

☆ Fourth, "And lastly, and that would be reason enough if there were no other, I had a great opinion of the elegance of his pen and none at all of my own. I therefore insisted that no hesitation should be made on his part. He accordingly took the minutes, and in a day or two produced me his draft."

Because Richard Henry Lee was absent, Adams was called upon to defend the resolution he had seconded. He did not have quite the gift of poetic speech that Lee possessed, but he was a brilliant and passionate man. The speech that he presented that day was so powerful that it was used as the subject of historical declamations in school rooms for generations afterward.

John Adams

The resolution was voted on July 3, 1776. The delegates had agreed it had to be a unanimous decision. Delaware was split. John Dickinson was against. Thomas McKean for it. Caesar Rodney was away squelching a Loyalist uprising. McKean sent a messenger (Caesar Rodney) to tell him he was needed at the statehouse in the morning to break the tie vote.

The resolution did have some opposition. It would have been very surprising for it to have none. Good John Dickinson, who

Richard Henry Lee

had contributed some brilliant writings to the American cause in his "Letters From a Farmer in Pennsylvania," still felt that the time was not right to declare independence. He protested:

> "The country would not be any stronger, proposed alliances with France, Spain, or other foreign nations were all uncertain. There would be no hope of future favours from Great Britain. The colonies themselves had no settled government, and first all these details should be arranged, then America might take her place among the nations of the world. . . ." — all of which was logical and worthy to be considered. But in the end, such arguments were viewed as similar to insisting on learning to swim before risking going into the water.[39]

Some delegates probably heard Mr. Dickinson's reasoning and were reminded of the ancient words of Solomon: "He that observeth the wind shall not sow; and he that regardeth the clouds shall not reap" (Ecclesiastes 11:4).

The resolution declaring the colonies to be free and independent states was unanimously adopted on July 2, 1776. Jefferson's Declaration was slightly modified and adopted on July 4. It was signed that same day by John Hancock, the president of Congress and Charles Thompson, the secretary. Most of the other members of Congress would sign it on August 2.

Signing the Declaration of Independence.

THE LIBERTY BELL

At two o'clock in the afternoon of July 4, a great crowd was assembled in the street outside the Pennsylvania State House where Congress was meeting. Rumors had spread like wildfire in the past two days, and all Philadelphia was aware of what was about to happen.

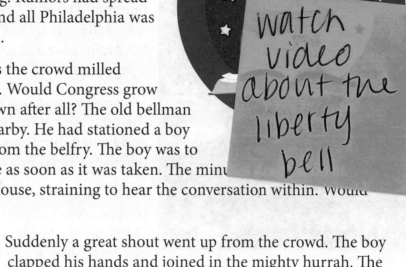

But how the minutes dragged on as the crowd milled around, muttering and speculating. Would Congress grow afraid and vote the Declaration down after all? The old bellman was up in the belfry of a church nearby. He had stationed a boy where he could easily see the lad from the belfry. The boy was to inform him of the result of the vote as soon as it was taken. The min... people crowded near to the State House, straining to hear the conversation within. Would the announcement never come?

Suddenly a great shout went up from the crowd. The boy clapped his hands and joined in the mighty hurrah. The old man knew the time had come. With all his strength he pulled on the bell rope and the sweet, clear notes of the Liberty Bell rang out across the city. Independence!

Cannons began to boom, people shouted, sang, shook hands, slapped each other on the back, laughed, and cried. In the evening, bonfires lit up the countryside for miles around. Horsemen breathlessly mounted their saddles and spurred in all directions to take the glad news to every city and settlement. Soon enough the exultant people would be reminded that there is a cost in blood and treasure that must be paid for freedom. But for today and tonight, the business at hand was thankful celebration.

THE NEW NATION CELEBRATES

The news reached George Washington and his army at New York. They had traveled there when the British abandoned Boston, guessing correctly that New York was the logical place for a fleet to land and disembark an army of conquest. A local newspaper reported:

> This afternoon, (July 10, 1776) the Declaration of Independence was read at the head of each brigade of the Continental army posted at, and in the vicinity of, New York.

Oliver Wolcott

It was received everywhere with loud huzzas and the utmost demonstrations of joy; and tonight the equestrian statue of George III, which Tory pride and folly raised in the year 1770, has by the Sons of Freedom been laid prostrate in the dirt — the just desert of an ungrateful tyrant! The lead wherewith the monument was made is to be run into bullets, to assimilate with the brains of our infatuated adversaries, who, to gain a peppercorn, have lost an empire.[40]

Indeed, the king made of lead did much better service than the king of flesh, for the statue was melted down and turned into thousands of bullets to be used in defense of freedom.

Oliver Wolcott was a signer of the Declaration of Independence. At the time of the reading of the Declaration of Independence to the troops in New York on July 9, he was there serving in the Connecticut militia. When Washington had the document read to the troops they became very excited and pulled down the lead statue of King George. Wolcott loaded up the broken pieces of the headless statue on a wagon and took it home. His wife, daughter, a son, and neighbor ladies melted it down, making over 42,000 bullets. His 11-year-old daughter Mary Ann made 10,140 herself! Wolcott then returned to Congress to add his name to the Declaration of Independence and was made a general. He later used those very bullets to fight against the British at the Battle of Saratoga.

Soldiers pulling down the statue of King George.

In Boston, July 17 was the day of the great celebration as Colonel Crats read the entire Declaration of Independence. The huge crowd was quiet during the reading, and even the excited small boys realized that something extraordinary was going on. But when the final paragraph was pronounced and the eloquence of Jefferson's pen had sunk deep into the hearts of the assembled patriots, such a shout went forth that shook the whole city.

It was not only in the cities that the Declaration was read and celebrated. In towns and hamlets all throughout the colonies there were banquets and bonfires, fireworks and cannon fire, charges of powder blown up beneath anvils. Differing dates were chosen in various places for the celebrations, but none of them were lacking in noise and enthusiasm. There was yet much to be done and much to be suffered in the fight for independence, but the colonies had made up their minds. America was free.

Reading the entire Declaration of Independence.

GUESS WHAT JOHN ADAMS SAID ABOUT HOW HE THOUGHT WE WOULD CELEBRATE INDEPENDENCE DAY?

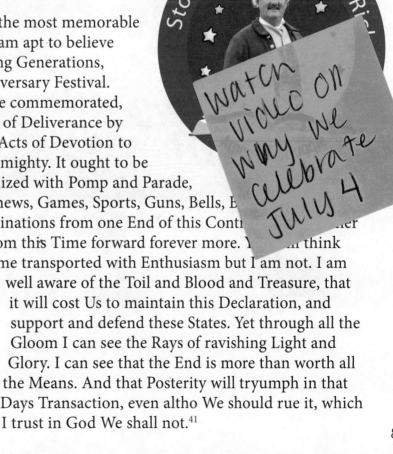

The Second Day of July 1776, will be the most memorable Epocha, in the History of America. I am apt to believe that it will be celebrated, by succeeding Generations, as the great anniversary Festival. It ought to be commemorated, as the Day of Deliverance by solemn Acts of Devotion to God Almighty. It ought to be solemnized with Pomp and Parade, with Shews, Games, Sports, Guns, Bells, B Illuminations from one End of this Cont er from this Time forward forever more. think me transported with Enthusiasm but I am not. I am well aware of the Toil and Blood and Treasure, that it will cost Us to maintain this Declaration, and support and defend these States. Yet through all the Gloom I can see the Rays of ravishing Light and Glory. I can see that the End is more than worth all the Means. And that Posterity will tryumph in that Days Transaction, even altho We should rue it, which I trust in God We shall not.[41]

87

1775

LEXINGTON

The Battle of Lexington

CHAPTER 10

BATTLES NORTH AND SOUTH

ENCOURAGEMENT FROM THE SOUTH

The colonies had now declared themselves independent of Great Britain. They thought of themselves as independent "states." A state is a group of people organized under a government. So the colony of Virginia now became the independent state of Virginia. She would no longer have a colonial governor appointed by the king. She would elect her own governor. She would no longer have laws made by a colonial assembly that answered to the king's governor. Her laws would be made by a state assembly elected by the people of Virginia. She would no longer be protected by the British army, but by her own militia and the Continental Army. Her taxes would not be set by Parliament (as Parliament had tried to do with the Stamp Act and the Tea Tax), but by her elected representatives in the state government. The people of Virginia would make the decisions for Virginia. It was the same in the other colonies.

There was still no United States of America. No one knew how that would all work out in the future. But Virginia, like Massachusetts and New York and South Carolina and Pennsylvania and all the rest of the 13 former colonies, was independent of England. The people of each state ruled their state through elected representatives and governors. For each state, it was like being a small country, working together to fight against England through their representatives in the Continental Congress.

The states were independent of Britain, but not yet united into an American nation. There was much work ahead. Many hard years would pass before the states would unite and form the

An American Rifle Man

Commitment is devoting myself to act upon my promises. Psalm 37:5 says, "Commit thy way unto the Lord; trust also in him; and he shall bring it to pass." The patriots had a high level of commitment to the cause of liberty. They knew nothing good comes without struggle and work and they committed their lives to doing whatever it took to establish a country where men would be free to serve God.

Sir Henry Clinton

United States of America. The states were not nearly as "united" as they needed to be in order to defeat Great Britain and make the king recognize that he did not own the American colonies any more.

At the time of the Declaration, however, there had been some encouragement that if the new states would unite they could remain free. In the north, there had been the battles at Lexington and Concord in April of 1775. Then there was Bunker Hill on June 17 in which the patriots had lost, but only after inflicting great damage to the redcoat army. And finally the British had been forced to evacuate Boston on March 17, 1776. The patriots knew that the king would send more ships and more soldiers to America to try to keep his colonies, but they had seen that they had a chance for independence if they joined together to fight.

In the south, two battles had occurred that also offered encouragement. One was in North Carolina, which had been the first colony to declare herself independent. The battle that took place there was a great encouragement to the people of all the colonies. It was called the Battle of Moore's Creek Bridge.

There were many Scotsman who had crossed the Atlantic and made their homes in North Carolina, South Carolina, and Georgia. Most of these people were loyal to the king. Believing that the Scotch Tories would band together to help him, the British general Sir Henry Clinton had sailed to the Cape Fear River to invade North Carolina. The colonial governor had promised that 1,600 Scotch loyalists would join him after he arrived. Clinton also expected reinforcements to arrive in ships coming from Ireland.

But the patriots of North Carolina soon figured out the threat and were not caught napping. They hastily put together some militia forces and on February 27, 1776, met the loyalists at Moore's Creek Bridge, hoping to stop them from marching to the coast to join Clinton's army. They had not been in place long when the Tories approached. The battle began, but did not continue long. The Tory leaders were killed in the first charge and their force scattered. The patriots captured 900 of them, which was most of their company. They also captured a large amount of gold money and, more importantly, many weapons.

The Battle of Concord, April 19, 1775.

The patriots had been outnumbered two to one, yet they had triumphed. The encouragement to the colonies was the same as that from the victories at Lexington, Ticonderoga, and Boston in the north. Soon, the one thousand patriots who had stopped the Scotch increased to 10,000 as enlistments exploded.

THE REGULATOR MOVEMENT — FIRST BLOOD

Historians normally point to the battle of Lexington and Concord as the first bloodshed in the War of Independence and in fact this is correct. But there was armed conflict between citizens and the British government in North Carolina four years before that had an effect on the sentiment of resistance in the colonies that later developed into the struggle for independence.

Like most of the colonists in the northern states, the people of North Carolina did not want to sever the ties between their colony and the mother country. But there was corruption in the government that offended some of the citizens and led to increasing conflict until it finally erupted in armed confrontation.

Residents of the inland, or back country, of North Carolina believed that royal officials were charging them excessive fees, falsifying records, and otherwise taking money dishonestly. These people eventually banded together to resist these outrages and regulate their own affairs. From this idea they got the name Regulators.

The Regulators believed that they were being unfairly taxed because their land — less productive mountain land in the western part of the colony — was being taxed at the same rate as the land in the eastern part of the state, where the land was more level, easier to cultivate, and more fertile.

Even more offensive was the abuse of power by government officials. Sheriffs appointed to collect taxes would destroy records of money they had collected so that they could later go back to taxpayers and demand more taxes from them. Registrars, court clerks, and judges were also charged with taking more money than authorized.

The royal governor of the colony, William Tryon, was widely seen as corrupt because he had built a huge mansion for himself at public expense in New Bern. He justified the expenditure by using the building as a center of colonial government business.

The Battle of Lexington

Edmund Fanning

Taxes were raised to pay for the palace, and much opposition was created in the citizenry of the colony.

Between the extravagance of the governor's mansion, the corruption of government officials, and the perceived unfairness of taxing western land as if it were as valuable as eastern land, the stage was set for widespread civil unrest.

As early as 1764, people in some large western counties began to protest publicly. Appointed officials who were thought to be corrupt were the targets of threats and violence. The previous governor, Arthur Dobbs, had issued a proclamation against taking illegal fees, but it had been largely ignored. Unrest and dissatisfaction continued to spread among the people.

Trouble intensified in 1770 when a mob attacked Edmund Fanning, a dishonest public official who held multiple offices in the colony. He was dragged down a flight of stairs, striking his head on each step. Another official's home was entered and his personal belongings thrown out the window.

The Regulators asked for a public meeting with colonial officials to air their grievances. The officials did not respond, which created more uniting among the Regulators and even more determination to claim their rights. The governor, Tryon, was also a former army officer, and he determined that the proper way to deal with this resistance was military force. He got the colonial assembly to approve the use of force, then called out the militia and led them from New Bern to the western frontier to settle the question of authority in North Carolina.

As Tryon's force approached the Regulator camp west of Hillsborough, the Regulators tried one more time to negotiate with him. The governor responded that he would only discuss their complaints if they would first lay down their arms and disperse within the hour. This infuriated the Regulators and the battle began.

Even though the Regulators outnumbered the militia, they were at a disadvantage because they had no training as a fighting force. They also had no clear chain of command or adequate supplies. The fight, called the Battle of Alamance, ended after only two hours with the dispersal and retreat of the Regulators.

The militia took a few prisoners, six of whom were hanged for treason. Several more were convicted of treason but were pardoned by King George on Tryon's recommendation. Tryon then issued an offer of pardon for the Regulators who would swear

Attack on Fort Moultrie.

an oath of allegiance to the royal government. Over 6,000 of them took advantage of the offer. But as we know from history, it was only a few years before North Carolina's militia and the former Regulators forgot their differences and united to oppose the British army in the fight for independence.

The Regulators had never advocated the end of British government in 1771, but rather the end of corruption by certain officials. But many of them joined the patriots when independence became the issue of the day in 1775.

Sir Peter Parker's Attack Against Fort Moultrie, by James Peale, date unknown (PD-Art).

The Battle of Sullivan's Island

Sir Henry Clinton decided that South Carolina must be an easier target than North Carolina, so he backed off and waited for reinforcements which arrived on Sir Peter Parker's ships in May. Clinton and Parker wanted to take Charleston, South Carolina. But to do so, they would have to first take the little fort on nearby Sullivan's Island, which was guarding the harbor.

They were sure this would not be difficult, so their discussions were not about whether they could conquer the fort, but how to do so with the least loss to their own force. Clinton figured that as soon as he took the fort, he would easily take Charleston, and the rest of South Carolina would be at his mercy.

The fort had been built under the command of Colonel William Moultrie and he was in charge still. It was constructed of double log walls, filled in between with sand. There were about 1,200 men under his command, while in the city of Charleston was General Charles Lee with 5,000 Continental soldiers and militiamen.

Proverbs 11:2 says, "When pride cometh, then cometh shame: but with the lowly is wisdom." General Lee's pride made him think he was wiser than Colonel Moultrie; that is why he scoffed at the log walls of the fort. But Moultrie ended up putting Lee to shame with his successful defense of the fort.

Lee thought of himself as quite a military expert. He never forgot that he had served in Europe and he was not likely to allow others to forget it either. That was quite a distinction in the minds of many people, certainly in the mind of General Lee. He made fun of Moultrie and the rough fort he had built. He was generous in giving Moultrie advice as to just how things ought to be done. But Moultrie had a mind of his own in military matters. He was not nearly as impressed with General Lee as General Lee was with himself, even if the man had fought

93

Colonel William Moultrie

in Europe. John Rutledge, who was then president of the South Carolina Congress felt the same way. He had more confidence in Moultrie than in the blustering General Lee.

GOD USES WINGED ENEMIES TO DEFEAT THE BRITISH

It was June 28, 1776. Clinton's plan was to land 3,000 of his soldiers on a sand bar in the harbor and have them wade across the shallow channel to attack the fort. If the colonials gave them any trouble, Parker's ships would take care of that with his cannons. He was planning on a bayonet charge and was sure that the poorly equipped patriots would never stand against his trained regulars. News traveled slowly before the invention of the telegraph, or perhaps he had forgotten the persistence of the homespun-clad militiamen on Bunker Hill.

The redcoats landed on the sandbar, but bad news awaited them. They discovered that the water between them and Sullivan's Island was deeper than expected. Instead of being up to their waists, it was over the head of the tallest soldier. As they stood confused, thousands of bloodthirsty enemies appeared: a swarm of mosquitoes. The winged bloodsuckers fell upon the British soldiers in clouds. Between the effort of managing to stand and keep their weapons dry in the midst of the shoals, the redcoats could do little to help in the attack on the fort. Most of the fighting was between the fort and the ships. The fight against the mosquitoes was a losing battle.

The Americans did not seem intimidated by the cannon shot from the ships, and General Lee's prediction that the walls would fall in less than 30 minutes proved to be far from true. The fort was low on gunpowder and could not return a shot for every shot from the ships, but still the gunners inside the palmetto log walls made every shot count. After ten hours of fighting, only one of the ten British ships was fit to sail, the admiral's flagship was almost a wreck, and the loss in British killed and wounded was 205. The Americans had lost only 37, and the palmetto walls were practically unharmed. Only one of the fort's guns had been silenced in ten hours of brisk fighting.

The soft palmetto logs absorbed the bombardment rather than cracking as the cannonballs struck. Some of the balls reportedly even bounced off the log and sand walls. Colonel Moultire and his 400 men fought the British all day long in the hot Carolina sun. The battle ended with most of the British ships badly damaged. Finally, they all sailed away. This victory was a huge encouragement to the patriots in the cause of independence. The fort was renamed Fort Moultrie in honor of its brave commander. "Carolina Day" is still celebrated in Charleston to honor the bravery of the fort's defenders.

Renaming the fort Fort Moultrie in honor of its commander seemed appropriate because the brave commander, though he had never "fought in Europe," certainly understood the value of sand and palmetto logs. He and his sturdy men had saved Charleston and South Carolina from the British for the time being. Clinton and Parker took three weeks for repairs to their ships and then sailed away for New York.

The battle at Sullivan's Island, like the fight at Moore's Creek Bridge, came just in time to help provide the colonies with the confidence they needed to sign the glorious Declaration of July 4.

Sergeant Jasper at Fort Moultrie.

Washington
Praying

CHAPTER II

LONG ISLAND—
A MIRACULOUS ESCAPE

ATTEMPTS TO END THE WAR —
COMPROMISE AND POISON

A man had come to America with Peter Parker, who was to play an important role in the struggle between the king and the colonies. This was Lord Cornwallis. When Clinton returned to New York from the Carolinas, Cornwallis immediately got busy helping General Howe. The British had been soundly beaten at Boston and had sailed away to Halifax. But after they had time to rest and get re-equipped, they were ready to return to the lower colonies and get revenge for their humiliation in Massachusetts.

They had sailed for New York, and Washington was expecting them. Although he did not know for sure, Washington did know that New York would be the logical place for the redcoats to land and renew the struggle. For that reason, he had left Boston and marched his men south to New York. He expected the conflict to now be transferred to the middle colonies, and indeed he was right.

New England did not suffer as much in the later years of the war as she had in the beginning. The British had found out how rough the coast was there, and how tough the men were. New York offered more support because of its large Tory population and the fact that much of the wealth of the colonies was located there, which made for easy capture. Also, because of good harbors and inland waterways, the British ships

Lord Cornwallis

Let us not forget to give credit to General Howe for his persistent efforts to avoid bloodshed. He was a loyal British officer, but he considered the patriots to be his countrymen and would much rather have reconciled with him than conquer them. If King George had listened to more Englishmen like General Howe, history might have been very different.

General Howe

could move about with considerable freedom to support the redcoat soldiers.

The southern colonies had also not been seriously troubled since the defense of Fort Moultrie. There was no great wealth there for easy taking and the patriots were very stubborn in their resistance. Howe figured that if the British could secure New York and the Hudson River region, their troops in Canada could march up through Lake Champlain and join their comrades in Albany. Then they would have the colonies split into two parts. That should make the "rebellion" as he called it, easy to stop.

As we have learned, General Howe had some sympathy for the colonies. He had not wanted to come across the ocean to fight them, but he had his orders and must obey. Still, he hoped to offer an "olive branch" and bring about peace with as little additional bloodshed as possible. Meanwhile, Washington was preparing for renewed hostilities. He arrived in New York before Howe and did his best to build defenses. Because of his small force he could not accomplish nearly as much as he desired, and in fact could not afford to place any troops at all on Staten Island to oppose the British landing there. So it was that the redcoats easily came ashore on that island on June 28, 1776.

When Washington had come to New York, Governor Tryon had fled for safety to a British ship off the coast. He was not a merciful man like General Howe and wanted to end the war as quickly as possible by any means necessary. Along with David Matthews, the mayor of New York, he formed a plot that was both clever and cruel. The goal was to blow up the powder magazines of the Americans and capture General Washington to be either murdered or tried and hanged for treason. When the plot was discovered, there were reports that Washington's cook had even been bribed to put poison in a dish of peas, a favorite food of the general.

Below is a newspaper report on the plot, taken from the *Pennsylvania Journal*:

> Since Friday last, a most barbarous and infernal plot had been discovered among the Tories in New York. Two of General Washington's guards are concerned; a third whom they tempted to join them made the first discovery. The general report of their design is as follows: upon the arrival of the British troops, they were to murder all the staff-officers, blow up the magazines, and secure all the passes of the town. Gilbert Forbes, a gunsmith in the Broadway, was taken between two and three o'clock on Saturday morning and carried before our Congress who

were then sitting. He refused to make any discovery, upon which he was sent to jail. The Reverend Mr. Livingston went to see him early in the morning, and told him he was very sorry to find that he had been concerned, that his time was very short, not having above three days to live, and advised him to prepare himself. This had the desired effect; and he requested to be carried before Congress again, promising to discover all he knew. Several have since been taken, between twenty and thirty, among them the mayor. They are all now in confinement. Their party, it is said, consisted of about five hundred.[42]

Colonel Patterson

We can be sure that General Howe had no sympathy for the evil plot hatched by Tryon and his cronies. When he arrived, he first tried to make peace. He sent a letter to Washington promising forgiveness to all who would stop fighting the British government and "aid in restoring tranquility." He addressed the letter to "George Washington, Esquire," because he did not have permission from the king to recognize any such body as the Continental Congress or any man whom they had appointed commander of an army.

With his usual dignity, Washington refused to receive the letter. He said that Lord Howe was a commander, and therefore should recognize Washington as another. When Howe's messenger returned, the general was still so hopeful of preventing further bloodshed that he sent another letter a few days later. The letter was carried by an influential officer of high rank, Colonel Patterson. Howe hoped that Washington would listen to him. Washington did agree to meet with the colonel, but as the letter was again addressed to George Washington, Esquire, he declined to open it. Colonel Patterson was disappointed in the failure of his mission, but the gracious way in which Washington received him made Patterson a great admirer of the American general.

THE BATTLE TAKES SHAPE

Now General Howe saw that Washington was not going to yield on the point. But still hoping to obtain peace without more fighting, he sent the offer of pardon to the British colonial governors and asked them to publish it abroad. Unfortunately, those gentlemen were not in a position to do much with it. Tryon was on shipboard, and was not anxious to return to land until a safe landing place could be arranged. Other governors had been thrown in jail by the Whigs. However, Congress came to the aid of Lord Howe. They arranged for the proclamation to be printed and distributed. But the people paid no attention except to treat it as a great joke.

But General Howe had been losing time while attempting to settle things peacefully. While Howe had been extending the olive branch, Washington had been busily strengthening his position. Brooklyn Heights had seemed the best place to fortify and defend, so he had placed trusty Nathanael Greene there with a force of 9,000. For the past several days they had been working feverishly to build fortifications.

General Nathanael Greene

When Howe finally realized that the Americans were determined to oppose him, he quickly decided to throw most of his force against Greene's position. He realized that if he could dislodge Greene and take his position, he would have control of New York. Unfortunately for Washington, his favorite general was taken ill suddenly. It was a critical time. Washington would have moved over and taken command himself if he could have. But he could not leave the main part of the city unguarded in case Howe changed his plan suddenly and left Greene's position alone to attack the other.

Howe did not move quickly or carelessly. He knew all about the battle of Bunker Hill and took very seriously the idea of attacking patriots in fortified positions. He spent several days in planning. Then he sent a force up the Hudson River in ships to indicate that he was about to attack the main part of the city. Washington had to stay there in case the attack came. The Americans had sunk some wrecked old ships in the Hudson to make it hard for the British ships to advance, but the redcoats easily avoided them.

In the days leading up to when the redcoats left Staten Island to attack Long Island, there were a number of interesting smaller skirmishes between them and the patriot households now stuck behind enemy lines. Occasionally, some of the boys would get in a canoe and float along the Staten Island shore at night to take shots at the camp of the Hessians, then paddle away at top speed. One British sloop got stuck in shallow water off Elizabethtown Point and was set on fire by a crowd of men and boys who had been hastily alerted by neighbors. From time to time, the opposing sides exchanged long-range potshots across the water.

The redcoats, especially the Hessians, launched a number of hostile raids on the livestock and poultry of the Whig housewives. These thrifty ladies, not content to give up without a fight, contended jealously for their pigs and poultry in any manner they could manage. Many a Hessian forager tried for supper and received a scalding or a broomstick assault instead.

The coming of the Hessians.

On August 22, 1776, General Howe moved against Greene's Long Island works with 25,000 men. In Greene's absence, the lines were commanded by Sullivan and Putnam. When he began his move, his intentions were communicated to General Washington by an unexpected source. Again, the *Pennsylvania Journal* tells the story:

> This night [August 22] we have reason to expect the grand attack from our barbarian enemies; the reasons why follow: the night before last a lad went over to Staten Island, supped there with a friend, and got safe back again without being discovered. Soon after he went to General Washington, and upon good authority reported that the English army, amounting to fifteen or twenty thousand, had embarked, and were ready for an engagement; that some ships of the line and a number of other vessels of war were to surround the city and cover their landing; that the Hessians, being fifteen thousand, were to remain on the island and attack Perth Amboy, Elizabethtown Point, and Bergen, while the main body were doing their best at New York; that the Highlanders expected America was already conquered, and that they were only to come over and settle on our lands, for which reason they had brought their churns, ploughs, etc.; being deceived they had refused fighting, upon which account General Howe had shot one, hung five or six, and flogged many. . . . There is an abundance of smoke today on Long Island, our folks having set fire to stacks of hay, etc., to prevent the enemy's being benefited in case they got any advantage against us. All the troops in New York are in high spirits, and have been under arms most of the day, as the fleet have been in motion, and are now, as is generally thought, only waiting for a change of tide. Forty-eight hours or less will determine it as to New York, one way or the other.[43]

General George Washington

General Washington had about 18,000 men at his command. Half of them were inside New York with him. The other 9,000 were in the works on Long Island, which Nathanael Greene had been busy fortifying all summer. It was a shame, from Washington's point of view, that Greene was away because of his illness. Greene was thoroughly familiar with the roads and byways on Long Island, where Putnam was not. Greene probably would have been able to place his forces more effectively than Putnam did, though it is still unlikely that he could have held his ground against such vastly superior forces.

Defeat and Retreat

After landing on Long Island, Howe took still more time to look around and finalize his plans. Then he had his brother take his ships and pretend to attack New York so that Washington would have to stay there when Putnam was attacked.

Howe himself led the largest body of troops, taking with him Clinton and Cornwallis. They marched all night long over the Jamaica road to get in the rear or on the flank of the patriots. He sent the Hessians over the Bedford road to attack Sullivan who was stationed there. Because most of the Whigs had fled the area, there were mostly only Tories left on the island. These loyalists were happy to keep the movement of the redcoats secret, so the patriots had little early warning of the British advances.

Sullivan suddenly found himself and his little force in a trap between the Hessians and the British. Unable to fight effectively, Sullivan's men were quickly confused and overpowered. Most of those who were not killed were taken prisoner, as was Sullivan himself.

Meanwhile, Brigadier General William Stirling and his Maryland patriots held their position through four hours of desperate fighting against the Highlanders. Finally, he saw that he must retreat. He was nearly surrounded, and the only path of escape was across Gowanus Creek. With the tide coming in to swell the depth of the water, he had to fight fiercely to get his men in a position to cross.

Here, young men of Smallwood's Marylanders and Haslet's Delawares, sons of wealthy families, distinguished themselves in valiant fighting. Putting up a desperate rear-guard struggle to allow their comrades to escape across the

General John Sullivan and General George Washington

102

creek, they finally fought their way to the bank of the creek and strove to follow their comrades who had already crossed. Many of them were killed. Some became stuck in the mud and were sitting ducks for British bullets. Stirling himself was captured. Only about a dozen of the Maryland men escaped after their heroic effort.

Either in terms of territory gained or lives lost, Long Island was clearly a great defeat for the patriot army. But two good things came out of it. First, the country saw for the first time just how important it was for all the colonies to strive together. The British were able to mass great numbers of men in battle and they would have to be opposed by numbers greater than any one or two colonies could muster.

The second blessing in disguise was the retreat from the island. The several thousand Americans who had not been killed or captured retreated to the defenses at Brooklyn Heights. Howe, apparently remembering his lessons from Bunker Hill, did not choose to launch another bloody frontal assault. Instead, he set his men to digging entrenchments ever closer to the American

Battle of Long Island by Alonzo Chappel 1874 (PD-US).

American Army retreating from the Battle of Long Island.

defenses on the Heights. At the same time, he ordered ships to sail up the East River to get behind the patriots and block their escape by water.

But the ships were slowed down by a contrary wind that sprang up unexpectedly, and they arrived too late. Acting under cover of night, Washington collected every available boat and had his men rowed across the river to Manhattan Island. Because he had left many campfires burning in the camp and the entire operation was conducted in strict silence, the British sentinels did not suspect their departure. But there were many men still remaining on Long Island when morning approached, and Washington watched uneasily as the sky grew slowly lighter. Then, a thick fog seemingly came out of nowhere and settled over the American position, hiding the activity of the fleeing patriots from the British camp. Through these providential occurrences in the weather, George Washington's Long Island veterans would live to fight again.

God's hand was often evident in the War of Independence. Humanly speaking, a tiny young nation with no navy, no treasury, and no organized army had no chance against the strongest military in the world. But time after time God raised up exactly the man, the idea, or even the weather that was needed to save the day — just as at the evacuation of Long Island.

THE RIDE OF SYBIL LUDDINGTON

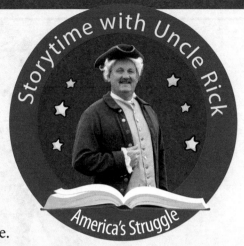

Storytime with Uncle Rick

America's Struggle

It was April 26, 1777. The sun was going down behind the clouds and the gathering darkness turned the distant trees into shapeless forms of shadow. The Ludington family was preparing to settle down for the night. Suddenly, their domestic peace was interrupted by the sound of a horse's hooves beating a rapid drumming on the road. The drumming ceased as the rider slid his mount to a stop in front of the farmhouse. Colonel Henry Ludington stepped to the front door just as a voice from outside called his name. Opening the door, Ludington admitted a tired man in mud-spattered clothes.

Exhausted and breathless, the messenger hurriedly poured out his story. The British were attacking Danbury, he said. They were destroying the supplies that had recently been moved there and stored for the American army. Even worse, they were abusing the people and burning the town. The militia must be assembled to march right away.

Colonel Ludington stared at the man. Of course he would call the militia together. He was their leader. But at that moment, all his 400 men were dismissed to their homes. Whom could he send to call them? This messenger and his horse were worn out. Besides, he was not from this area. He did not know the patriots from the Tories round about.

Then, 16-year-old Sybil stepped forward and offered to go. Yes, it was a four-mile ride on a rainy night. No, she was not a strong man to defend herself from drifting Tories and robbers. But she was a good rider and she knew where all the militiamen lived. Very soon she was on her horse and galloping away.

All through the night Sybil rode. She carried with her a stout stick to beat on doors and perhaps on the head of a robber if she should need to. Some of the men she alerted mounted their own horses and took off in various directions to call their comrades. When day broke over the Connecticut hills, a tired Sybil was reining in her horse before her father's cottage and nearly 400 militia members had assembled. Sleepy-eyed and shuffling, they were all nonetheless ready to take revenge on the redcoat raiders who were retreating from Danbury. Before the day was over, some of the redcoats had paid with their lives for their depredations.

In Carmel, New York, there stands today a larger-than-life stature of Sybil Ludington atop her horse, Star. In her hand is a stick.

Washington:
Man of Action

CHAPTER 12

BATTLES AROUND NEW YORK

THE RETREAT FROM LONG ISLAND

Washington was exhausted. For two days and two nights, he had hardly had a moment's rest or peace. Now he crossed the river to direct the actions of his battered forces on Long Island. He could not know what the next British move would be, so he and his men would not be free from anxiety for many hours to come.

Perhaps the enemy would storm Brooklyn Heights and try to overwhelm the defenders. If so, they might be taught another lesson similar to the one they had learned at Bunker Hill: it was a dangerous thing to attack Americans entrenched on a hill. On the other hand, the patriots were worn out and discouraged from the defeat of the day before. Could they make a determined stand? The question was not answered, for all that Howe did was to arrange his troops in a semi-circle and dig in. There were some skirmishes between outposts, but no frontal assault came.

Redcoats paddling to shore in a flatbottom boat.

There was soon debate in England over why Howe hesitated. London was over 3,000 miles from the fighting in New York, so of course people there thought they knew all about what should have been done. Some said Howe had eaten too much (as he was rumored to frequently do) and was more inclined to rest up than to start another battle. Others were probably closer to the truth when they said that Howe had some sympathy for his American brethren and hoped that he had wounded their army badly enough that he could end the war without too much more bloodshed. Whatever the reason, he

Proverbs 21:1 says, "The king's heart is in the hand of the LORD, as the rivers of water: he turneth it whithersoever he will." We do not know why Howe made the decision not to attack again and follow up his previous victory, but again, it seems that God spared the American cause in a most unexpected way.

Retreat from Long Island

did not attack, and several thousand American soldiers huddled unmolested behind their earthworks waiting to be told whether to fight, flee, or fortify.

Whatever the reason, his hesitation gave Washington an opportunity, and even while exhausted the commander-in-chief was not one to let a chance be wasted. He sent out scouts to see what the British fleet was doing. They reported that Admiral Howe had his ships arrayed across the Narrows and had nearly completed the circle around Washington and his men. What was his intention? Did the British intend to surround the Americans on Long Island by land and sea, and then starve them out? Or were the ships in place to carry redcoat soldiers to Manhattan Island and attack the patriot force Washington had just left there? There was no way of knowing. So what was to be done?

The American Revolution, Massachusetts, British soldiers and men working, an idealized view of Boston as a European city, by Franz Xaver Haberman, c.1770.

Storytime with Uncle Rick

America's Struggle

Washington held a council of war with his officers. It was decided that the best course of action was to evacuate Brooklyn Heights and join the troops in New York. At least then the army would not be divided, to be conquered in two pieces. General Thomas Mifflin of Pennsylvania suggested that his men take a position as rear guard while the rest of the army marched to the shore to be ferried to Manhattan. Washington agreed. To conceal his real intentions from discovery, he gave orders to the entire force to pack their equipment and prepare for a night attack. But at 11 p.m. that night, instead of an order to attack, the troops were ordered to fall in and march down to the river. Washington had ordered his men on Manhattan to collect every available boat (supposedly to ferry over to Long Island New Jersey troops who might come as reinforcements) and prepare them for a mass movement across the river. Now the sick and wounded, then the healthy troops, began to fill the boats.

It had been raining that day and evening, but Washington had ordered his cannon to bombard the British trenches actively to cover his retreat. At the same time, General Mifflin's men fanned out across the Brooklyn Heights defenses, building up the campfires to give the illusion that the camps were full of men. Hour after hour, soldiers stepped aboard the boats and were rowed across the river by sturdy fishermen of Marblehead and Gloucester in Massachusetts. These same fishermen would prove invaluable later in getting Washington's army across the Delaware River moving to and from Washington's great triumph at the Battle of Trenton.

The night passed and morning dawned. As the sky grew light, Washington chafed as he saw that his army would soon be visible to the British and many hundreds of his men were still not safely away. But then, one of the acts of Providence that seemed to attend the American army again and again in times of darkest danger, intervened. Seemingly from out of nowhere, a cloud of fog descended across the American lines. Even as day broke upon the British trenches, their view of the patriot lines was totally obscured. The evacuation continued well into the morning as Mifflin and his men silenced their cannons, marched to the shore, and boarded boats and barges.

Benjamin Talmadge by Ezra Ames, c.1800 (PD-US).

Major Benjamin Talmage was still on the island and he recorded what happened in his memoirs: "After dawn of the next day approached, those of us who remained in the trenches became very anxious for our own safety and when the dawn appeared there were several regiments here on duty.

"At this time, a very dense fog began to rise out of the ground and off the river. It seemed to settle in a peculiar manner over both encampments. I recollect this peculiar Providential occurrence perfectly well. And so very dense was the atmosphere that I could scarcely discern a man six yards distance. We tarried until the sun had risen but the fog remained as dense as ever."

The fog remained until the last boats left Long Island. Washington was the last man to leave. Later in the morning, the British noticed that the Americans did not seem to have pickets on the outskirts of their lines. When patrols cautiously advanced upon the Brooklyn Heights defenses, they found them empty. Washington had escaped with every man, horse, and cannon. Once again, a Providential occurrence spared the American army from destruction.

Another miraculous event occurring during this retreat was recorded by Washington Irving in his *Life of Washington*. A Tory lady near the shore saw what was going on and ordered her servant to quickly run and tell the redcoats. But the first scarlet coat the man encountered was worn by a Hessian, who did not understand English well enough to grasp the message. Defeated, the servant was detained in camp for a few hours and then returned home. Had the servant ran into anybody else, the British would have been able to surprise the American Forces in the midst of their retreat.

British troops were hurriedly dispatched to the river. When they arrived, the fog had lifted enough for them to see four boats upon the East River. The only boat close enough to be captured contained three vagabonds who stayed behind to plunder. Otherwise, thousands of men, with nearly all of their supplies had miraculously retreated to New York.

Here we see the American General Greene say: "The best effective retreat I ever read or heard of!" This event was so astonishing that surely the explanation given by many of the Colonists was true: That God was defending the cause of liberty.[44]

Howe would soon be knighted for his complete victory in the capture of Long Island. Meanwhile, he hoped that the battered American army would now give up the fight for independence.

In that hope, he sent patriot General John Sullivan, who had been captured in the battle, to Congress, with an offer of peace and pardon. The response from Congress was the opposite of what Howe had hoped. Still, they appointed a committee of three men to meet with Howe. The men were the prominent John Adams, Franklin, and Rutledge. But the meeting only served to convince Howe that the Americans would never agree to peace unless the British were willing to grant the right of independence to the colonies. The war would continue.

Unusual Heroics

On Manhattan Island, Washington held another council of war with his officers and it was decided that Manhattan could not be successfully defended. The sick and wounded were sent off the island and into New Jersey. Washington led most of his army to the banks of the Harlem River. While the rest of the army withdrew, Israel Putnam and 4,000 men provided a rear guard.

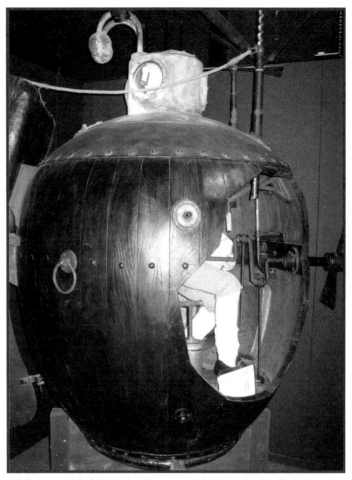

A full-size model of the Turtle submarine on display at the Royal Navy submarine museum. Photo by Geni, 2008 (GFDL CC-BY-SA).

There is a story told of an event said to have happened at this time that proved to be an advance look into warfare in centuries to come. A young mechanic named Bushnell, from Connecticut, had invented an early form of submarine which he called the "marine turtle." It was about ten feet long and six feet wide. Propelled through the water by hand-cranked paddles, it could take on water and expel it by means of a hand pump to dive or surface. The purpose of the turtle was to attach explosive devices to the hulls of British ships after approaching underwater.

Washington had his doubts about this strange boat, but he permitted a brave young man named Ezra Lee to attempt an attack on Admiral Howe's flagship, the *Eagle*. Lee was to paddle the turtle to where the *Eagle* was moored off Governor's Island, screw the "torpedo" to the hull of the *Eagle*, set the timing device on the bomb, and then paddle for shore. The turtle contained only about 30 minutes' worth of air, so Lee would have to approach on the surface in the dark, submerge, attach his torpedo, and paddle away in that short period of time.

111

The U.S. Sloop *Saratoga* (left center) and the U.S. Brig *Eagle* (right) engaging the British flagship *Confiance* (center), by Edward Tufnell, 2012 (PD-US).

At midnight on September 6, Lee entered the machine at the dock near Whitehall and started away on the first adventure if its kind. Washington and several officers who were in on the secret waited all night on the dock to see the outcome, though none of them really thought Ezra had a chance. As the dark night faded into gray dawn, even the hope of his survival seemed very dim indeed.

But just at that moment, a column of water shot into the air near the faint outline of the *Eagle*. They could see signs of frantic activity on board and on the shore nearby. It appeared that no serious harm had been done to the ship. But what had become of brave Ezra Lee? The officers waited until they felt that they must give Lee up as drowned, when suddenly he was discovered in the water near the wharf. Friendly hands helped him up and he was surrounded with congratulations on his brave attempt. He had been unable to attach his bomb to the hull of the *Eagle* because he had struck metal plating. Still, it was a noble attempt and some of those present realized that they had observed the beginning of a new type of warfare.

Historians disagree on whether this attack on the *Eagle* really took place, or whether it was just a story concocted to build American morale. But it rings true in face of the fact that both Ezra Lee and inventor Bushnell existed and did, in fact, experiment with submerged and floating explosives. Lee later blew up a British barge with a floating bomb, killing four redcoats. Bushnell famously sent kegs of explosives floating down the Delaware River to blow up British boats on contact. No serious damage was done to the ships, but the nerves of His Majesty's sailors were so put on edge that not only the barrels but every log and floating piece of wreckage that came down the Delaware became a target for their guns, producing a great waste of powder and shot. All in all, the experiment must at least have been great fun for Bushnell and his patriot henchmen.

Another significant event of these days was the capture and execution of American spy Nathan Hale. Washington had despaired of holding the New York area against overwhelming odds, making an orderly retreat while seeking to know something about the plans of the British now in possession of Long Island. What would Howe do next? He needed a spy on the island to tell him what the redcoats were doing. If he could find out what could be observed of British preparations, it might help to guess where Howe would go next and when.

I only regret that I have but one life to lose for my country.

Nathan Hale

Captain Nathan Hale of Connecticut volunteered and was provided with passes and letters from Washington that would give him the services of the American boats in the area. With this assistance he crossed to Long Island and made many sketches and notes. But when he attempted to recross the water, he was captured. He was taken before General Howe.

The General was no bloodthirsty warrior. He was sorry to send a young man to his death, especially one who bravely confessed that he was a spy for his country. But the rules of war called for death to spies. Hale was sentenced to be hanged.

Unfortunately for Hale, he was turned over to the brutal provost marshal (head of military police), William Cunningham. Cunningham refused Hale's request for a Bible to read. Nor would he allow a minister to come and comfort the young man. Howe had given Hale permission to write letters, including one to his mother. Cunningham destroyed the letters. Still, Hale maintained his courage to the last and died with the heroic words,

> "I only regret that I have but one life to lose for my country."

Loyalty is being committed to the welfare of those I serve, even to the detriment of my own comfort. "Most men will proclaim every one his own goodness: but a faithful man who can find?" (Proverbs 20:6). Nathan Hale was willing to give up his own reputation, as being found a spy was a disgrace, but he wanted to be useful to the cause of liberty. He knew General Washington needed information to make a wise decision and the lives of many depended on it. He willingly gave his life to help purchase freedom for an entire country of people.

The unnecessarily cruel execution of Hale created an intense feeling among the Continentals. The brutality of it increased the determination of those brave men who knew him or heard the story. A song was written telling the story of Hale's mission and death, and was often sung around patriot campfires for the remainder of the war.

THE BALLAD OF NATHAN HALE
Revolutionary Songs and Ballads

THE BREEZES went steadily through the tall pines,
A-saying "oh! hu-ush!" a-saying "oh! hu-ush!"
As stilly stole by a bold legion of horse,
For Hale in the bush, for Hale in the bush.

"Keep still!" said the thrush as she nestled her young,
In a nest by the road; in a nest by the road.
"For the tyrants are near, and with them appear
What bodes us no good, what bodes us no good."

The brave captain heard it, and thought of his home
In a cot by the brook; in a cot by the brook.
With mother and sister and memories dear,
He so gayly forsook; he so gayly forsook.

Cooling shades of the night were coming apace,
The tattoo had beat; the tattoo had beat.
The noble one sprang from his dark lurking-place,
To make his retreat; to make his retreat.

He warily trod on the dry rustling leaves,
As he passed through the wood; as he passed through the wood;
And silently gained his rude launch on the shore,
As she played with the flood; as she played with the flood.

Nat Goodwin had the title role in the 1898
play "Nathan Hale."

The guards of the camp, on that dark, dreary night,
Had a murderous will; had a murderous will.
They took him and bore him afar from the shore,
To a hut on the hill; to a hut on the hill.

No mother was there, nor a friend who could cheer,
In that little stone cell; in that little stone cell.
But he trusted in love, from his Father above.
In his heart, all was well; in his heart, all was well.

An ominous owl, with his solemn bass voice,
Sat moaning hard by; sat moaning hard by:
"The tyrant's proud minions most gladly rejoice,
For he must soon die; for he must soon die."

The brave fellow told them, no thing he restrained —
The cruel general! the cruel general! —
His errand from camp, of the ends to be gained,
And said that was all; and said that was all.

They took him and bound him and bore him away,
Down the hill's grassy side; down the hill's grassy side.
'Twas there the base hirelings, in royal array,
His cause did deride; his cause did deride.

Five minutes were given, short moments, no more,
For him to repent; for him to repent.
He prayed for his mother, he asked not another,
To Heaven he went; to Heaven he went.

The faith of a martyr the tragedy showed,
As he trod the last stage; as he trod the last stage.
And Britons will shudder at gallant Hale's blood,
As his words do presage, as his words do presage.

"Thou pale king of terrors, thou life's gloomy foe,
Go frighten the slave, go frighten the slave;
Tell tyrants, to you their allegiance they owe.
No fears for the brave; no fears for the brave."

1776.[45]

Fanny Murray by Henry Robert Morland, date unknown (PD-Art).

Remembrance and Retreat

The Americans had been busy strengthening their fortifications around New York. New trenches were dug and earthworks increased. But it served only to delay the loss of the city, because of the greater numbers of the British forces. Many of the patriot soldiers were still in fear of the British redcoats. It seemed that many had forgotten the Battle of Bunker Hill. The splendid British army with their abundant equipage seemed very intimidating to the under-supplied Americans. Washington had a force, but it was not reliable.

Howe sent ten ships up the Hudson to where their fire could rake across the city. While they were pouring their fire into the American lines, Sir Henry Clinton landed 4,000 men at one point while a division made up mostly of Hessians landed at another. Brigades of New England men were sent to oppose them, but the demoralized Americans forgot Lexington and Bunker Hill and remembered only the very recent battle on Long Island. Their officers threatened and begged, but could not rally their men. Even when Washington himself rode up and tried to rally them, they would not listen.

When these forces landed, Howe might easily have cut off the retreat of Putnam, who was withdrawing in the face of such overwhelming odds. But now providence put forth an unlikely deliverer who preyed on Howe's well-known weakness for food.

There are a number of character qualities to be learned from the quick thinking of Mistress Murray. She showed alertness and creativity by having the idea of delaying the British officers with an invitation to lunch. She displayed generosity by investing her own food supply in the patriot cause. She showed endurance and determination in making the effort to detain the officers with additional courses, desserts, and drinks. Her cleverness and dedication probably saved many lives, both British and American, by preventing a bloody battle. Undoubtedly, she helped the American cause.

Mistress Murray, a quick-witted lady of deep patriot sentiments, had heard of Putnam's plight. Cleverly using her resources to best advantage, she invited Howe and his officers to a delicious luncheon. Howe, along with Clinton and others, stopped at her home to dine, intending to make their visit brief and then hurry along to catch up with Putnam. But the charming hostess kept insisting on another course, another dessert, and another drink. By the time they left their feast, Israel Putnam and his men were safe with their comrades on the bank of the Harlem.

On September 16, 1776, there was a brief battle in which the patriots lost about sixty men and the redcoats many more. Now

Howe was in possession of New York itself and the Americans were entrenched on Harlem Heights. Neither was in good position to attack the other, so it was expected that the British would settle down in New York for the winter. But a fire started on the morning of September 21, and a southwest wind quickly spread it from building to building. When it was over, nearly 500 buildings had been destroyed including homes, churches,

The Battle of Harlem Heights

and businesses. A month later, Howe attempted to land men from boats in an effort to position troops behind those of Washington. Washington continued to move back from New York, leaving units to fight rear guard actions at various strong points. At length, Washington settled behind earthworks that stretched 13 miles from White Plains to Fordham in front of the entire British army. Here he would rest and reorganize for a month, until Howe gave up and decided to attack him head-on.

During this time, various outrages were committed by the British and Hessians against the patriot homes in the vicinity. One Highland soldier, stealing vegetables at night from a patriot woman's garden, was surprised and captured at gunpoint by the woman's 12-year-old son and taken prisoner to the American camp. Local men who slipped out of camp to visit their families in the area were mercilessly hunted down by the British and Tories. If caught, they were killed, sometimes in front of their own children. But often they escaped, including one man whose wife came to his rescue. Chased to his home by Tories, this patriot soldier was quickly buried in a large pile of ashes. Breathing through a long goose quill, he was completely covered by ashes and survived the search of his home when the Tories came and demanded his surrender. The loyalists went away shaking their heads in confusion.

Washington's Retreat

CHAPTER 13

RETREAT AND VICTORY

THE MIGHTY REDCOATS ROLL ON

After Washington retreated following the Battle of White Plains, the only patriot stronghold remaining on Manhattan Island was Fort Washington. Washington ordered the fort to be evacuated if it seemed necessary. But Colonel Magaw, in command of the fort and nearly 3,000 men, chose to try to defend it. When Howe sent a demand for the surrender of the fort, Magaw replied that if Howe wanted the fort, he should come and take it. Howe had warned that no quarter would be given, which he really did not mean. But the threat hardened the resolve of the men inside to defend their fort to the death against the overwhelming numbers Howe could send against them.

The attack on Fort Washington was bloody and terrible. The Americans fought with the courage of desperation, but the British had five times as many men. In the end, though they had lost only 150 men and the British had lost 500, Colonel Wagaw surrendered. Some of his men were bayoneted by the Hessians after they surrendered.

Washington decided, after another council of war, to retreat from New York and enter New Jersey. He left General Heath in the Highlands to oppose any invasion that might come from Canada, and another force with General Charles Lee at North Castle to come to Washington's aid at any time he was needed.

George Washington

Lee's failure to come quickly when summoned by Washington would cause great problems. This is why it is so important that we learn obedience while we are young.

Lee had not obeyed orders. He caused much trouble for many men and the danger they endured because of one man's decision to disobey! He personally paid a price for his disobedience.

Forcing a passage of the Hudson River, between Forts Washington and Lee, by Dominic Serres, c.1776 (PD-US).

Lee was now in place of General Artemas Ward as Washington's second-in-command. Lee enjoyed a great amount of respect in the colonies, even though we now know that he was as much a traitor as Benedict Arnold. He had fought in Europe, and in the minds of the common people that was a high distinction. He had a persuasive tongue, and he enjoyed using it. He had just come from the south and was known as the "Hero of Charleston," though he had had very little to do with the defense of Sullivan's Island.

But it was more surprise than attack. When pickets reported the approach of a huge British force, Major General Nathanael Greene led a hurried evacuation of the 2,000-man garrison. There was very little time to escape, so Greene elected to leave many of his cannons and supplies in order to have the best chance of saving his men. He marched them toward Hackensack, where Washington was expecting them. Greene managed to get his men across the one bridge over the Hackensack River before the British could get ahead of him. About two hours after the main body of the force left, Greene returned to the fort, rounded up several hundred stragglers, and started them down the road after their comrades.

When the British reached Fort Lee, they found much useful material of war. It included stores of ammunition, 1,000 barrels of flour, 50 cannons, and 12 drunken soldiers. They captured about 150 other Americans in the vicinity. Now Cornwallis saw the opportunity to strike a killing blow at the American army. He determined to pursue Washington into New Jersey.

General Washington organized the fragments of his collected army and began retreating across New Jersey with a heavy heart. He now had fewer men with him than Howe held prisoner at New York. He had been beaten and beaten and beaten again. Every battle on the islands of New York, except Harlem Heights, had been a defeat. His army was shrinking. Everything looked dark.

Worse, the confident British were close behind. The people of the region were discouraged with American prospects, and many of them who had been friendly to the cause of independence now came out on the side of Britain. Some patriot families picked up and moved with the small portion of their belongings that they could carry with them. They were terrified by rumors of what the conquering redcoats and "Dutch butchers" might do, and indeed the report of what had happened at Fort Washington made such things easy to believe.

General Howe and his brother, the Admiral, had certain powers from the king to offer pardons to patriots who repented and swore allegiance to King George. They sent out a notice offering forgiveness to all who would appear before the governor or another officer in His Majesty's service within sixty days. Many of the more timid souls of New Jersey accepted the offer.

But not all the local folk were intimidated. Some hardy patriot wrote a scornful reply:

Washington organized the fragments of his collected army.

> In this rarity we see slaves offering liberty to free Americans; thieves and robbers offer to secure our rights and property; murderers offer us pardon; a perjured tyrant by the mouths of two of his hireling butchers 'commands' all the civil and military powers, in these independent states to resign all pretensions to authority, and to acknowledge subjection to a foreign despot, even his mock majesty, now reeking with blood and murder. This is truly a curiosity, and is a compound of the most consummate arrogance and folly of the cloven-footed spawn of despairing wretches, who are laboring to complete the works of tyranny and death. . . . Messieurs Howe and W. Howe, pray read your proclamation once more, and consider how modest you appear; and reflect on the infinite contempt with which you are viewed by the Americans, and remember the meanest freeman scorns the highest slave.[46]

Endurance is the inward struggle to endure tribulation with determination. Washington was discouraged, but he would not give in to it and quit. He continued to endure. Read on to find the outcome!

Tory writers spread their propaganda as well, each side evidently hoping to bruise the confidence of the other. But while the penmen fought their battles of words, Washington led his army in an orderly retreat across New Jersey. Philadelphia had heard that Washington was retreating and Cornwallis was advancing. Panic spread through the city and the surrounding region. Every day, men deserted the American army and ran away.

Maj. Gen. Sullivan

But still the iron man, Washington and his shrinking band of faithful followers kept on. They were hungry, wretched, forlorn, fearful, homesick, and discouraged. How small seem the problems Americans face today when we remember what the patriots of Washington's little army endured.

THE PURSUED FOX TURNS

Washington delayed briefly at New Brunswick while burning the bridge across the Raritan, then continued toward the Delaware. Still, Lee had not joined Washington. The commander's army numbered only about 3,000 men and Lee was still only as far as Morristown. At last, the Delaware was reached and every boat in the vicinity taken to move soldiers across the river. This gave the little army a short time to rest and recover, as a British crossing would be delayed until more boats could be obtained, which would take some time.

> Losing Lee proved to be a blessing in disguise. Remember that in your own life, little buddies. Often when it appears that bad things are happening to us, God is using those very circumstances to bring about our good.
>
> " 'For I know the plans that I have for you,' declares the LORD, 'plans for welfare and not for calamity to give you a future and a hope." —Jeremiah 29:11; NASB

Meanwhile, the irresponsible General Lee had fallen upon hard times. Preferring to stay in better accommodations than he could get in camp, Lee had stopped at White's Tavern in Basking Ridge, New Jersey. Settled comfortably about three miles from his army, he was surprised and captured by a patrol of two dozen redcoats. It was early morning and Lee was writing some letters before breakfast. He was taken away wearing only his nightshirt and dressing gown.

Lee begged piteously for his life, while his captors amused themselves by reminding him that he could be hanged for deserting the British army. They had no intention of actually hanging Lee, but could not resist the pleasure of tormenting such a cowardly, whimpering prisoner.

Of course, many in the patriot camp thought they had lost a hero and were very discouraged by the news. But Lee was replaced by the brave Sullivan, who had been retrieved in a prisoner exchange. He immediately took command and set forth to join Washington, as Lee had long ago been ordered to do. A general had been lost, but it proved to be a blessing in disguise.

Gathering the straggling elements of his army on the other side of the Delaware, Washington knew something had to be done soon, or the cause would be lost forever. The British were confident that he was already beaten, though they had failed to catch him on the right side of the Delaware to deliver a fatal blow. Many of the redcoat soldiers had been sent to Newport and other places since it was thought that Washington did not have enough of an army left to cause much trouble.

The Hessians would be left to take care of any unfinished business. Cornwallis himself had plans to sail for home in a few days. Even with the addition of troops arriving with Sullivan and Gates, Washington had only around 6,000 men. Those seemed as nothing against the hordes of redcoats and Hessians that the king could put in the field at any time.

But Washington had bold plans. He intended to launch three separate counter-attacks at once. General Gates was to strike Count Dunop with his 2,000 men at Burlington. The Hessian force at Trenton was to be hit by General Ewing, crossing the Delaware opposite the town. Washington, with Knox, Sullivan, and Greene would cross the river a few miles above Trenton and advance on the town from the north.

But more discouraging news now piled on Washington. Gates pleaded illness and headed for Baltimore, where Congress had retreated ahead of the approaching redcoats. Cadwalader, who took his place, failed to get his army across the river, which was full of floating ice. Ewing also failed to perform.

Perhaps any man besides Washington would have given up now. But not he. At sunset on Christmas Day, he and his 2,400 men assembled on the bank of the Delaware where he planned to cross. It was stormy and the icy wind whipped up the waves. Chunks of floating ice bobbed on the current. But General John Glover and his Marblehead fishermen were used to navigating on the ocean. They had been up to the task of ferrying the American army off Long Island after the defeat there, and this river would not stop them.

Unboarding after crossing the Delaware.

Storytime with Uncle Rick

America's Struggle

For ten long, freezing hours the boats paddled back and forth across the Delaware. Washington stood all the time, watching the crossing from the riverbank. He seemed not to notice the storm and cold. At last, he and the last of his men boarded boats and were rowed across.

Now there were nine miles of rough, half-frozen road to cover between them and Trenton. In the teeth of a blinding storm of sleet and snow the ragged army marched. It was miserable. The men were wet and so were their weapons. Their thin, ragged clothing was sparkling with ice. Some of them were without shoes and had their feet wrapped in rags or burlap. Some left blood-red footprints in the snow. Yet they marched on, apparently drawing unlikely strength from the iron resolve of their general.

Washington had expected the Hessians to be less than vigilant after having celebrated Christmas in the hearty manner common to the German people. He was not disappointed. The few British light cavalry troops posted at Trenton were away on foraging expeditions, leaving the Hessians to eat and drink and carouse. Their commander, Colonel Rall, had been invited to a Christmas supper at the home of Abraham Hunt, who was loyal to neither side but did business with both. Far into the wee hours of the morning Rall and his officers sat playing cards with Hunt and imbibing drinks that did nothing to make them more alert or intelligent.

Suddenly the colonel's servant dashed into the room — against strict orders — and handed Rall a note. He said it had been given to him by a man who said the colonel must read it immediately, being of greatest importance. But Rall was in a celebratory mood and delayed reading the message. He tucked it into his pocket to read later.

Had Rall known that the note came from a loyalist who had seen the American army approaching Trenton, the history of the War of Independence might have been far different. He learned of Washington's approach in a much noisier way than reading a note.

The Americans were approaching in two divisions. The first, led by Sullivan, came along the lower road. The other, led by Greene, traveled the upper road. Much of their gunpowder was wet, but they used their bayonets to drive the outer pickets back into the town. Then their cannon boomed and quickly cleared the streets of Trenton from Hessians. Colonel Rall rushed from Hunt's house and tried to rally his men. Along with 16 others, he went down in a hail of bullets. The battle was over quickly and nearly a thousand hired Hessians were prisoners. The Americans had lost only four men and two of those had frozen to death on the march.

ACROSS THE DELAWARE
by Will M. Carleton

The winter night is cold and drear,
Along the river's sullen flow;
The cruel frost is camping here—
The air has living blades of snow.
Look! pushing from the icy strand,
With ensigns freezing in the air,
There sails a small but mighty band,
Across the dang'rous Delaware.

Oh, wherefore, soldiers, would you fight
The bayonets of a winter storm?
In truth it were a better night
For blazing fire and blankets warm!
We seek to trap a foreign foe,
Who fill themselves with stolen fare;
We carry freedom as we go
Across the storm-swept Delaware!

The night is full of lusty cheer
Within the Hessians' merry camp;
And faint and fainter on the ear
Doth fall the heedless sentry's tramp.
O hirelings, this new nation's rage
Is something 't is not well to dare;
You are not fitted to engage
These men from o'er the Delaware!

A rush—a shout—a clarion call,
Salute the early morning's gray:
Now, roused invaders, yield or fall:
The refuge-land has won the day!
Soon shall the glorious news be hurled
Wherever men have wrongs to bear;
For freedom's torch illumes the world,
And God helped us cross the Delaware![47]

A SURPRISE FOR CORNWALLIS

Washington crossed back over the Delaware, but still the
remaining Hessians in the region fled to more distant towns.
They had heard of what happened in Trenton and did not care
for a taste of the same medicine. Four days later, Washington
re-crossed the river and again occupied Trenton. The town was in

Cornwallis

his hands along with 6 brass cannon, 1,200 stand of arms, nearly a thousand prisoners, 12 drums, and 4 unit colors.

It did not take long for the news to travel to New York, where much of the British army was camped. Cornwallis canceled his travel plans and headed immediately for Princeton, near Trenton. He feared that Washington would attack there next, or at New Brunswick where many British supplies were stored.

Washington had sent General Greene with a small force of 600 men to harass Cornwallis as he marched, but he could not do nearly so much to slow the British down as did the horrible condition of the roads in winter. It was January 2 when Cornwallis left Princeton with almost 8,000 men and headed for Trenton. He marched for several hours over the rough roadways and arrived near sundown at the Assanpink. Washington was encamped across this little stream.

Cornwallis did not hesitate long. He sent his columns marching across the bridges to attack "the old fox" as he called Washington. But a heavy fire from the patriots drove the redcoats back. He recalled his men and decided he was content to wait until morning. But he felt triumphant. Washington was just over that little stream, and outnumbered several times over by the British. Tomorrow the old fox would be bagged.

Washington gathered his officers and asked their advice. It appeared a retreat was in order. Even if they could hold the bridges over the Assanpink, there were several fords where the redcoats could cross to attack them. His men were badly outnumbered and still tired from days of fighting and marching. His staff was united in their opinion: the only thing to do was make their getaway in the darkness and put as many miles between them and the British as possible. They could fight again after the men had gotten some rest and more supplies collected.

Washington was a man of amazing leadership ability. He often wisely asked for advice from his officers, but when a hard decision had to be made, Washington took the responsibility and acted firmly.

But Washington offered a suggestion that made them stare. They would indeed leave their camp, with just enough men remaining behind to keep the fires burning and give the impression of digging trenches. The rest of the army would start for Princeton and attack the remaining redcoats there. His officers gave many objections. The roads were too muddy to travel anywhere fast. The enemy was too strong for an attack to succeed. Other problems were cited.

But even as they talked, the wind died away and an intense cold settled in. Before long the mud began to freeze and the roads became passable. Washington gave his orders and his men obeyed. The army collected itself and marched away in the dark. Enough men were left behind to ply the picks and shovels within hearing distance of the British pickets and keep dragging fence rails to the fires.

It was sunrise and they were nearing Princeton when they ran into the advancing force of redcoat Colonel Smallwood, who was on his way to join Cornwallis. Smallwood's men, thinking that the Continentals were fleeing from Cornwallis, immediately fell upon them in battle. But rather than a ragged batch of refugees, they met an organized army prepared for an attack on the town Smallwood had just left. The opposing lines swayed back and forth in the struggle.

But it only lasted about half an hour, when the British lines were cut in two pieces and one went rushing back toward Princeton while the other fled down the road toward Brunswick. They left 200 of their comrades lying dead or wounded and another 300 prisoners.

Back on the stream bank near Trenton, Cornwallis opened his eyes to the morning light and stared in astonishment. Across the stream was an empty camp. At the same time, he heard a sound like thunder far off toward Princeton. It was not hard to discern that it was not thunder. Washington, the old fox, had slipped out of the trap and was attacking Princeton.

Without delay, Cornwallis started up the road to Princeton in support of his comrades. But the sun was beginning to melt the frozen roads and soon mud slowed his progress to a crawl. When he did arrive, the battle was over and he saw no Americans but some men tearing down the bridge he needed to cross Stony Brook and enter Princeton. His cannons scattered the demolition crew, but not before they had removed the bridge planks and escaped. The redcoats splashed through the icy waters of the creek and rushed toward Princeton. But at the west end of the village they were halted by a shot from a huge cannon and Cornwallis stopped, thinking Washington was making a stand there. He sent out scouts to reconnoiter, then marched on. When he entered Princeton there was not a Continental in sight. Washington had slipped away again and was chasing two British regiments in the direction of New Brunswick. So first Trenton, and now, on January 3, 1777, Princeton was added to the ragged American army's list of amazing successes. The crisis of the Revolutionary War had passed.

Attack on Princeton

Battle of Princeton

CHAPTER 14

THE BATTLE OF VALCOUR ISLAND

A TINY NAVY

The year 1776 had been of mixed success for the American patriots. Lexington and Concord, Bunker Hill, and the evacuation of Boston had cheered the colonists and shown both them and the British that Americans could stand against the mighty redcoat army. The battles in and around New York had discouraged the patriots and taken a heavy toll in lost men and equipment.

Washington had succeeded in ending the year with an unexpected triumph in New Jersey by taking Trenton and Princeton just before the close of December.

There had been another battle up north as well, which was a source of encouragement to the struggling patriots. The battle had ended in defeat for the Americans, yet again they had made a brave showing against their enemies. They had left the British bloodied enough to make them show more respect to their homespun adversaries. This battle was between the brave men under Benedict Arnold and those following Sir Guy Carleton of the British army.

The British had long been planning to split the colonies apart by invading southward from Canada. The plan was to capture the forts along Lake Champlain and Lake George, then hold the Hudson River. This would open an undisputed waterway between Montreal and New York. It would also create a water barrier to keep either part of the separated colonies from breaking through to each other.

Sir Guy Carleton

The Americans experienced some wins and some losses, but they pled to God, believing that their cause was a just one and that they would ultimately win. Steadfastness is unwavering or determined in purpose. I Corinthians 15: 58 says, "Therefore, my beloved brethren, be ye stedfast, unmoveable, always abounding in the work of the Lord, forasmuch as ye know that your labour is not in vain in the Lord."

Soldiers were quick at loading their muskets.

After withstanding the American assault on Quebec, the British believed that General Carleton could take back the forts of Crown Point and Ticonderoga and then move on to New York or Albany. He had already put together a large force, including reinforcements of men and ships from England.

General Horatio Gates had now replaced Philip Schuyler as the officer in charge of the northern army, though Washington was sure that Schuyler had been a far better man for the job. Now a council of officers was held and the decision was made that Benedict Arnold was the best man to lead a force in driving back, or at least harassing, the British force that would soon come from Canada.

Always a man of boldness and energy, Arnold threw himself into the preparations. He was joined by reinforcements from the coast of Connecticut and Massachusetts, many of them men experienced in building and sailing ships. In only a few weeks they had cut trees from the nearby forest, made beams, and built small ships. By the middle of August 1776 a small squadron had been built and rudely equipped.

The little fleet consisted of a sloop with 12 guns, two schooners with 8 guns each, a schooner with 12 guns, and five "gondolas" with 5 guns each. This tiny "navy" would soon face the might of Carleton with his 20 gunboats, over 200 transports, and many thousands of men.

Arnold had planned to go down the lake to near Rouse's point. But he learned that Tories and Indians were assembling nearby and made the decision instead to fall back. His fleet had received some modest reinforcement, but rumors that Carleton had 12,000 men in addition to his many vessels made caution seem the wisest course for the Americans. So Arnold found a narrow channel between Valcour Island and the New York shore where he felt somewhat protected and there awaited the attack of the British.

The redcoat ships appeared early on the morning of Friday, October 11, 1776. The sight of the huge fleet must have sent shivers down the spine of many a brave American. They were vastly outnumbered by a fleet manned by experienced sailors.

Another officer might have turned tail and fled. But Arnold was determined to fight. He moved among his men, talking personally to them. He shared words of courage and resolve, showing by his own example that a stand would be taken and defended. He appeared wherever his presence could lend a mite of strength.

Slowly, the white sails of the British ships grew closer. The Union Jack floated boldly from tall masts. Then suddenly a puff of smoke appeared from the side of one ship and a cannonball came skipping across the water toward the new Yankee boats. The battle was on.

Battery and Bowling Green in 1776

Within an hour, all the British ships had come up, and every vessel on both sides was fully engaged. For nearly five hours the surface of the great lake was covered with a layer of smoke. Sixty Americans had been killed or wounded, the ships' sails were tattered by cannonballs, and some of the masts had been splintered by enemy fire. Yet there was no thought of giving up in the mind of the intrepid Arnold. He employed his own hands in aiming some of the guns, all the while shouting encouragement to his men.

Finally, a very dark night ended the battle without a clear victor. Yet the odds were so much against the patriots that Arnold knew he could not fight long when morning again lit up the skies. He consulted his officers and it was decided to take advantage of the strong north wind to try to sail away without the retreat being discovered by the British. About 10 o'clock that night the battered little fleet weighed anchor and crept slowly and quietly away from the enemy. Arnold's own ship brought up the rear. They were nine miles away before Carleton discovered that he had been tricked.

The British ships immediately set out in pursuit, but the wind had changed and the sailing was slow. It was not until the early morning of the 13th that the British were close enough to fire upon the retreating patriots. Arnold's ship was still in the position of rear guard. Soon they were taking a terrible fire from three of Carleton's gunboats.

Finally an American ship, the *Washington*, struck her colors and surrendered. The crew was taken prisoner, including the treacherous Joe Bettys, who would soon commit treason and murder. He would eventually be pardoned by the mercy of George Washington, but even then would return to villainy and finally be captured and hanged.

Another "Benedict Arnold"

Storytime with Uncle Rick
America's Struggle

One of the heroes of the battle on Lake Champlain was Joe Bettys of Ballston, Virginia. Like Arnold, he had proven himself brave and skillful in the fight against Carleton. Also like Arnold, he would later turn against his country and fight just as savagely against America as he previously had fought against Britain.

Bettys was described as "bold, athletic and of untiring activity; revengeful and cruel in his dispositions; inflexible in his purposes; his bosom cold as the marble to the impulses of humanity; he ranged the border settlements like a chafed tiger snuffing every tainted breeze for blood."[48]

At the beginning of the war, Bettys was living in Ballston. He volunteered early in the war and was soon a sergeant in the regiment of Colonel Wynkoop. But he had a proud, independent spirit which did not serve him well in the disciplined life of a soldier. Eventually he was prosecuted for rude language to an officer he claimed had mistreated him. He was demoted to the ranks.

Colonel Ball, knowing personally of Bettys' courage and resolve, arranged to have the soldier transferred to the command of Benedict Arnold on Lake Champlain and restored to the rank of sergeant in the summer of 1776. In the fight between Carleton and Arnold in October of that year, Bettys displayed great courage and outstanding service. During that four-hour battle, he fought until every officer on his ship was either killed or wounded. Then he assumed command of the ship himself and fought with such recklessness and bravery that he was noticed by General Waterbury, Arnold's second-in-command. Seeing that Bettys' ship was sinking, Waterbury ordered him and the few other surviving men to board his own ship. He placed Bettys by his side on the quarterdeck and gave orders to his own crew through him. On they fought, until the ship was also crippled. Only two crew members besides Bettys were still able to fight. General Waterbury was wounded. Finally, he ordered the colors struck and the ship surrendered to the British. Waterbury later spoke highly of Bettys' courage and competence in the battle.

The captured Americans were taken to a British fort in Canada. There it was discovered that the loyalty of Bettys was primarily to Bettys himself. The British were able to persuade him to renounce his commitment to America and become a traitor and spy. Because of his knowledge of the country and his sneaky cleverness, he was just as effective in his efforts against his former comrades as he had been while fighting beside them. Sometimes he was used as a messenger, sometimes as a spy. Sometimes he served in both roles at the same time. He returned to his home territory in northern Virginia and even in Ballston, the home of his family and former neighbors, he managed to recruit men to join the king's army.

During one of his spying missions he was captured. He was tried, condemned, and sentenced to be hung. But strangely, he was pardoned by General Washington and given another chance to repent and abandon the British. Washington had been begged for leniency by Bettys' aged parents and some other honest citizens of Ballston. Part of the reason for the pardon may have been the appeals of influential Whig citizens, some of them members of the Ball family of Ballston. Washington was, in fact, related to the Balls through his mother, Mary Ball Washington.

But if honor, gratefulness, or humility had ever been part of Bettys' character, they had long since ceased to be. Very soon he was back in the service of the British and up to his old tricks. Instead of repaying the unexpected kindness he had been shown upon his promise to reform, he became a relentless scourge of his former friends and neighbors.

He returned home and recruited more soldiers for the king. He kidnapped and carried off some of the most influential patriot leaders. Those he especially hated lost their lives to murder or their homes to fire.

Soon no patriot on the borders felt safe. Sometimes he fell on his victims in the dark of night. At other times, he was seen walking around in broad daylight, undisguised and seeming as careless of his own life as he was of others' lives. He declared that he would never be captured alive, and that anyone attempting to take him must do so at the risk of theirs. His threats were taken seriously, as it was known that he always had at his beck and call a group of cutthroats as desperate and evil as himself.

Many and risky were his adventures during this time. And it was not only the borders that were in danger of his assaults. One time he entered Albany and attempted to capture the honorable General Schuyler but failed.

But not everybody lived in fear of Bettys. The men of the borders were strong and brave. Several times, attempts were made to capture the outlaw. But none succeeded until the winter of the years 1781 and 1782.

A suspicious man had been seen in the area of Ballston on snowshoes. Three alert patriots there named Perkins, Cory, and Fulmer thought there was little doubt that the stranger was Bettys, so they armed themselves and began stalking him. By a circuitous trail, they traced him to the home of a well-known Tory. They approached very cautiously and were able to get close to the house undiscovered. Then suddenly they rushed up to the front of the house and broke down the door.

Inside, they found Bettys sitting at a table eating a meal. They were upon him so suddenly that he was caught off guard. He tried to fire his musket, but had forgotten to take off the deerskin cover from the lock and the weapon was useless. Before he could grab his pistols which lay on the table in front of him, the three men had him in their grasp. Soon he was sitting, a prisoner under guard.

The traitor now seemed to be resigned to his fate. He asked for permission to smoke, which was granted. As he fumbled with his tobacco box, Cory noticed that he appeared to throw something very small into the fire. The object was only about an eighth of an inch long, but it was grabbed hastily and flung across the floor along with a handful of burning coals. The burned hand was worth the cost, for the object proved to be a tiny lead box containing a rolled up scrap of paper. On the paper was writing that the patriots could not understand. It was a spy message, written in code and intended for the British commander in New York. There was also an order for 30 guineas to be paid to Bettys when the message was received.

Now the famed courage of Bettys deserted him. He begged to be allowed to burn the message. He offered a hundred gold guineas for permission. But his captors steadfastly refused. Again he was tried for his crimes, and this time the hangman gave him no chance to commit any more evil.

Battle of Plattsburgh, artist and date unknown (PD-US).

Soon Arnold's flagship, the *Congress,* was under attack by seven British vessels. Full of holes and barely able to move at the pilot's command, still the *Congress* floated and her cannons kept firing. Arnold did not seem to know how to give up. But finally, the battle became so hopeless that he sent some of the other ships to sail toward the shore and ground themselves. Then, under Arnold's orders, their crews set them afire so they could not be taken and used by the British.

When the other men had safely reached shore and their vessels were all burning, Arnold and his crew gave up the fight and followed them. He organized his men and marched rapidly for Crown Point. So fast did the patriots move that the Indians sent by the British to form an ambush were too late to get ahead of them. Arnold safely made it to the fort at Crown Point and found that what remained of his fleet had arrived there ahead of him. All that remained were one schooner, one sloop, and one gondola.

British ship-of-war

The British had lost about 40 men in the battle and the Americans had lost around 80. But the patriots had done so much damage to the British fleet that Carleton was not sure if he should attempt to follow up his costly triumph. Hastily, the Americans abandoned Crown Point and retreated to Ticonderoga, a much more important fort to hold.

The men in Ticonderoga spent a few days in fear of a British attack. They were vastly outnumbered and not at all eager for a fight. Carleton's superiors later accused him of failing to take advantage of his costly victory on the lake. Surely he would have taken Ticonderoga easily, they said. But Carleton replied that the cold season was upon him and that he was risking getting stuck in the ice if he tarried. So it was that after just a brief pause, Carleton sailed away for Canada. It had been another battle in which the British had won the day, but been badly damaged by the destruction of some of their ships and the loss of some of their men. Carleton had suffered serious losses and really accomplished nothing but the destruction of a few crude ships made of green lumber during the previous summer.

Though Benedict Arnold would finally go down in history in shame as a traitor, there is no doubt that this battle had been well-fought, thanks to his courage, determination, and skill. He had many enemies, for he seemed to make enemies easily. Yet even they acknowledged that the battle on Lake Champlain had been a success due to him.

But when Congress again undertook the task of appointing new generals, Arnold was passed over. He was certainly qualified for the honor, as his courage and ability in battle had proved. Washington was solidly in favor of his promotion. But again the petty jealousies between colonies prevailed, and Congress said that Connecticut had plenty of officers in the army. She would have to wait until some men from other places had received their deserved recognition.

> Humility means acknowledging that any good I have achieved is a gift from God, and my life is to be used as an instrument in His hand.
>
> "Humble yourselves in the sight of the Lord, and he shall lift you up."
> —James 4:10

Arnold was furious. He threatened to resign from the army as soon as he heard the news. Only the personal pleading of General Washington himself persuaded him to hang on a while longer in hopes that his merits would finally be recognized and rewarded. Though there is no excuse for the treachery committed by Arnold later in 1780, one can understand how disappointed and insulted he might be. He had fought bravely and suffered much in the battles before Quebec and on Lake Champlain. He had proven to be a man of brilliance as much as a man of courage.

It is too bad that Arnold was not the truly great man that Washington was. Washington was repeatedly treated with disrespect and suspicion by Congress and other leaders. Yet he remained loyal to his country and plowed ahead with his task even when many people thought he was failing and should be replaced. But there are very few men in whom the qualities of leadership and humility are found in such great supply as in George Washington. Washington would have suffered the neglect of Congress and gone on faithfully doing his duty. Arnold failed to humble himself and eventually allowed his pride and bitterness to make him a traitor.

But that was in a later season of the war. Arnold had certainly shown himself to be a mighty man of valor on Lake Champlain, and America still owes a debt to his tarnished memory for the wonderfully brave leadership of his men.

General John Burgoyne

CHAPTER 15

BURGOYNE'S CAMPAIGN BEGINS

HIGH HOPES IN CANADA, A REVERSE IN CONNECTICUT

The year 1777 opened with high hopes on the part of the British. It was true that they had failed to "bag the old fox," Washington. He had even closed the year of 1776 with a couple of victories that could primarily be credited to his determination and brilliance. But still, he was up against the military might of Great Britain, supplemented with the trained and equipped Hessian troops.

It was still the fond hope of the British army to open a waterway along Lake Champlain from Montreal to New York and Albany. This year, the attempt was to be made under the leadership of a man who claimed not to know the meaning of failure. His name was General John Burgoyne.

"Britons never retreat" was a favorite saying of Burgoyne. He had been a soldier almost from a boy, and he was used to winning. He had won distinction when his nation assisted Portugal in her war with Spain. He had a pleasant disposition and made friends easily. He was proud of his work as an author, having written some plays and poems that were admired by King George and his court. Burgoyne was welcome at the palace in London.[49]

Burgoyne had considerable ability as a general, too. He was quite confident in his own ability, and quite contemptuous of the "country bumpkins" who opposed him. It was this very over-confidence that would be his downfall.

John Burgoyne

Boasting is when one praises oneself or is haughty in spirit. Proverbs 27:1-2 says, "Boast not thyself of tomorrow; for thou knowest not what a day may bring forth. Let another man praise thee, and not thine own mouth; a stranger, and not thine own lips." Remember that, little buddies, and it will save you much trouble in your life.

A friend who had considerable influence with the king arranged for Burgoyne to have command of the force that would try once again to invade the American colonies from Canada. No man in England was happier than Burgoyne at this news. And no man had more confidence in his success. Many were the boasts heard from Burgoyne over what he would do to the "country bumpkins." It was just as well that he got some boasting done before the campaign, as he would have little chance for it afterward.

Pride is the opposite of humility. The Bible says, "A man's pride shall bring him low: but honour shall uphold the humble in spirit" (Proverbs 29:23). We shall see how Burgoyne's pride helped to bring him low.

Carleton had retreated into Canada. New York and Newport were in the hands of the British. Burgoyne intended to approach Albany by way of Lake Champlain. At the same time, Colonel Barry St. Leger had a large force of regulars and Indians and was to lead them up through the St. Lawrence from Montreal and to march through the Mohawk Valley to join Burgoyne at Albany.

While these two armies were in motion, a third force under General Clinton was to come up the Hudson from New York and join the other two men. This would split the eastern colonies off from the middle and southern colonies. Then the colonies on one side of the waterway could be attacked and conquered while the colonies on the other side were held back from joining to help them. It was a good plan, but there is a difference between planning and doing. General Burgoyne was to learn this to his sorrow.

John Burgoyne, after Allan Ramsay, 1758 (CC BY-SA 4.0).

THE DANBURY FARMERS TEACH BURGOYNE A LESSON

Before we go further into the story of Burgoyne's invasion, however, it is important to know about an event that happened down in Connecticut and would have an important effect later. Throughout the winter of 1776–1777, the patriots had been gathering war materials and storing them at Danbury, Connecticut. Word of this was carried by spies to the British command in New York. The redcoat generals decided to pay a visit to Danbury to capture these stores and teach the "farmers" a lesson that would quickly restore their loyalty to King George.

So it was that William Tryon, who had failed in dominating both North Carolina and upstate New York, was given a force of 2,000 men to do the job. He sailed away with his men to Fairfield, Connecticut, landed there, and marched across country to Danbury. He managed to seize the stores and then, to make the lesson even more colorful, set fire to the town. Then he started his army marching back to Fairfield. By this time riders had spread the news of his attack throughout the area and the patriots were responding in a manner that must have reminded the redcoats of Lexington and Concord in 1775. Old men, boys, and militia members came streaming across the rocky Connecticut hills and followed the retreating invaders. From behind rocks, trees, and stone walls they fired Indian fashion then ran on to reload and fire again. It was a galling fire they laid down, and the redcoats could do little about it.

Benedict Arnold was in New Haven, Connecticut, at this time, and he soon got word. For the moment, he chose to forget his resentment at being denied promotion and gathered 600 men to attack Tryon. At Ridgefield, he joined the militia commanded by Wooster. There a battle took place on April 27, 1777. Arnold was at his best, fighting like a demon while shouting encouragement to his men. He had two horses shot from under him, yet never slowed down. Finally, the British were soundly defeated and almost captured. Those who did get away left behind 200 men who had been killed or taken prisoner.

Arnold had distinguished himself, and no one could deny it. Congress promoted him to major general at last and presented him with the gift of a fine horse. But Arnold was still not satisfied. He continued to feel resentful, and when Washington offered him the command of the Americans at Peekskill, he declined. But despite this, he was still to have an active part in the exciting events of the coming summer.

General Horatio Gates

A Confident General Marches to Conquest

Early in the summer, General Burgoyne, or John Burgoyne Esquire, as he wrote his name, or Gentleman Johnny, as he was sometimes called because of his love of fancy clothing and high living, was ready to advance from Montreal. By the first day of June he was at Fort St. John at the foot of Lake Champlain with 7,000 men.

Because of the quarrels among the colonies, the enemies of General Philip Schuyler had succeeded in having him replaced by General Gates at the head of the army opposing Burgoyne. This would last only a few weeks until Schuyler was again given command and Gates was assigned to a lower position. This would be a great offense to Gates, who was petty and vain. He refused to serve under Schuyler and left the region for a time.

Burgoyne set sail in the middle of June. His force had grown to near ten 10,000 men with the addition of Indians, Tories, and Canadians. Three thousand of the soldiers were Hessians, commanded by the stouthearted General Riedesel. The fleet must have made an impressive sight as it set sail on that beautiful June morning across the blue waters of Lake Champlain. Its colorful appearance reflected the cheerful confidence the men under Gentleman Johnny felt in their prospects of success. In the lead were many birch-bark canoes full of war-painted Indians. Along with them were barges full of soldiers under the experienced General Frazer, a couple of armed frigates, and a number of other armed vessels.

American scouts patrolling the shore of the lake soon spied and reported the fleet to General St. Clair, in command at Fort Ticonderoga. "Fort Ti," as it was usually called, was once again to fall without a battle.

For a week in late June, Burgoyne's fleet halted at the falls of the Bouquet River while more of his Indian allies joined him. There was feasting and jollity, and Gentleman Johnny made a speech in which he reminded his Indian friends to remember the requirements of civilized warfare. Yet he sent out a proclamation through the region that the inhabitants should not aid the rebels in any way, lest he let loose his hordes upon them.

He left a small garrison to hold the fort at Crown Point and then pushed on for Fort Ti. He expected that the patriots would make a stand there and he looked forward to the contest.

In Ticonderoga, St. Clair had about 3,000 men. He was fairly well equipped and the fort had been strengthened since it had been controlled by the Americans. But less than a mile away, a high rocky hill known as Sugar-loaf Hill or Mount Defiance stood 600 feet above the waters of the lake and was plenty high enough that cannon mounted on its summit could easily fire into the fort below. Many times the American officers had been urged to secure it, but it was very steep and apparently it was assumed that no attacking army would go to the trouble of dragging guns up to the top. It was a sad oversight.

All through the night of July 4, the British general Phillips and his men dragged a few cannons up the narrow, rocky passageways they built in the hillsides. The next morning, the astonished Americans saw their enemies looking down at them from the height they had thought could not be fortified. They were in trouble.

General St. Clair

Fortunately, the redcoats were not quite ready to attack. St. Clair had a meeting with his officers and made the decision to evacuate the fort. They would move out that very night under cover of darkness. His abandonment of Ticonderoga was much criticized by the patriots later, but it may have been the only way to keep his army from being destroyed or captured.

The plan called for dividing the force. St. Clair would lead most of the men in a retreat through the Green Mountains. The officers' wives, the supplies, and most of the guns and ammunition would be carried by water to Skenesborough and then on to Fort Edward where General Schuyler held his force. St. Clair hoped to meet them there, arriving from another direction.

The Americans had hastily thrown together some obstructions in the lake, hoping to slow down the approach of the British fleet and give their own vessels more time to escape.

It was about 3 a.m. on July 6. Part of the garrison had already left the fort, and the rest was getting ready to march away. Suddenly, one of the houses in the fort caught on fire. This was later said to have been an accident, but many people suspected the work of a treacherous officer. Whatever the cause really was, the light of the burning building lit up the inside of the fort and British sentinels saw that the fort was being evacuated. Less than an hour later, their own flag was flying above the walls of the fort and Ticonderoga had once again fallen without firing a shot.

General Frazer and 900 men went in pursuit of the fleeing patriots. The Hessians under Riedesel were ordered to follow behind Frazer and give him support. Burgoyne himself took all the remainder of his army except for 1,000 men left behind to hold the fort, and started up the lake in pursuit of the force that had fled with the stores and ammunition.

Prudence is exercising caution in all situations; forseeing the consequences of my actions. The Bible says, "A prudent man forseeth the evil, and hideth himself: but the simple pass on, and are punished" (Proverbs 22:3.) It was prudent to think about what might happen and prepare as best as they could for the situation they might encounter.

The men with St. Clair, fleeing through the hills in the dark, were frightened and disorganized. They were fleeing in disorder, hoping that somehow they might soon join forces with Schuyler, or at least find a good spot to make a defense against Burgoyne and hold him back until Schuyler could come to their aid.

St. Clair had no way of knowing whether or not he was being pursued. When he reached Hubbardton, he pushed on, but left Colonel Warner and Colonel Francis behind to form a rear guard.

This was a mistake, but not a foolish decision. The day was hot, his men were exhausted, and they did not know that Frazer and the Hessians were coming. Warner decided to give his men a night's rest, but wisely decided to chop down a number of trees and much of the brush in order to entangle the British soldiers if they did catch up.

A SURPRISE ATTACK

The next morning, July 7, the patriots were cooking an early breakfast at 5 a.m. Suddenly, they were shocked by a sudden attack by Frazer's men. One regiment panicked and fled, but most of the men held their ground bravely. The British were hampered in their approach by the brush and trees, and so could not mount an effective and organized attack. Each man fought from such cover as he could find, and the zeal of the triumphant redcoats was matched by the desperate determination of the Americans. Both sides were fighting bravely and well. It was something of a standoff for a while. Finally, the British began to give way.

Then the sound of an approaching host was heard. The Hessians had followed far behind the redcoats, but were now catching up to help their British allies. The patriots, not knowing whether Burgoyne's entire force might be upon them, broke and ran.

General Riedesel

142

Meanwhile, John Burgoyne Esquire was in pursuit of the Americans who had fled up the lake on boats. They arrived at Skenesborough barely ahead of the British and were not yet prepared to defend themselves when the redcoats arrived and opened fire. The Americans abandoned their boats after setting them on fire, along with most of their supplies, and fled for Fort Anne. Somehow, they made it.

General Arthur St. Clair

St. Clair heard at almost the same time about the defeat of Colonel Warner at Hubbardtown and the loss at Skenesborough. His own followers were demoralized and they were down to about half the number he had led away from Fort Ti. He was running low on supplies. The country behind him was under the control of Riedesel and Frazer. But he was determined to do all he could, so he led his troops in haste to Rutland and Bennington, and eventually joined Schuyler at Fort Edward. Warner and his exhausted, fleeing men finally rested at Bennington.

Burgoyne was delighted with his success thus far. All this he had accomplished in less than a week, and he seemed to be driving his opponents before him. He was quick to send a glowing report to England, which pleased the king nearly as much as it pleased Gentleman Johnny himself.

View of Mount Defiance from Fort Ticonderoga, photo by Mwanner, 2009 (CC BY-SA 3.0).

General Philip Schuyler

The Americans had not made a very impressive showing against the gentleman general. Yet, besides the failure to deny the British access to Mount Defiance, it may be said that the patriots were doing the best they could under difficult circumstances. Congress, without the power to tax, could not give them much aid. The troops were undisciplined through lack of training, and their equipment was poor in comparison to the well-supplied British. While they had some excellent officers, they were also burdened with some who owed their jobs to friends in Congress rather than to their own proven competence. In fact, John Adams was heard to declare that the Americans would not be able to hold a post until they first shot some of the generals.

Washington himself could not come to the aid of his friend, Schuyler. Howe was in New York with a large army, and Washington did not know where he might strike next. It might be in New England, or perhaps in Philadelphia. Either way, Washington could not afford to deplete his army by sending troops to help Schuyler oppose Burgoyne. Burgoyne had left a large detachment of Hessians in Vermont, indicating a possible attack on Boston. This increased Washington's uncertainty.

Meanwhile, Burgoyne had settled for the moment at Skenesborough and was preparing for a march on Albany. His ranks were swelling as more Indians and Tories joined his ranks, encouraged by his successes. But his delay gave the patriots something they had not had before — time to do some work that would slow Burgoyne's advance. They made diligent use of that time to destroy bridges and build obstructions in the road Burgoyne must use.

But Schuyler had less than 4,000 men at Fort Edward, so he dared not give battle. He fell back to Moses Creek, then to Saratoga, then to Stillwater. Fortunately, Burgoyne's delay at Skenesborough gave the patriots time to make sure he did not advance too quickly once he started again. When he left Skenesborough, the redcoat general only progressed about one mile per day. It was July 30 before he reached Fort Edward.

Now, Burgoyne at last began to falter. He was starting to run low on supplies, having traveled so far from his home base. In addition to that, there were enemies beginning to assemble behind his troops. The Americans of the region had begun to recover from the fear Burgoyne's rapid advance had caused. The Indian allies of the British had been allowed to commit outrages that were far beyond the limits of civilized warfare, and the patriots were growing furious. They became determined to resist to the utmost the advance of an enemy who would use such allies.

But Gentleman Johnny was blissfully unaware of the hatred he was causing. He fondly hoped that there were many Tories in the area who would flock to him and help him secure the supplies he needed. To that end, he sent Colonel Baum and nearly a thousand men to attack Bennington, Vermont, where the patriots had stored supplies and horses. He would score a double blow by striking again at New England and seizing the badly needed supplies. Baum's force was made up mostly of Hessians, with some Canadians, Indians, and Tories. Local Tories served him as guides. Behind him were reinforcements under Breyman, and he was counting on more Tories to join him as he moved forward. Baum was confident that the American "peasants" would never stand up to his trained soldiers and his cannons. It looked as if he would soon impress his British master with the prisoners and supplies he presented to him.

Surrender of the British General John Burgoyne at Saratoga (American General Horatio Gates with his arms spread), by John Trumbull, 1822 (PD-US).

The Battle of Bennington

CHAPTER 16

BENNINGTON AND FORT SCHUYLER

JOHN STARK OF NEW HAMPSHIRE

Colonel John Stark was a son of New Hampshire. An experienced fighting man, he had served with distinction in the French and Indian War before the colonies dreamed of independence. Hard and rugged as the hills among which he grew up, he had again proven his mettle at Bunker Hill, Trenton, and other battles. After Trenton, General Washington asked him to go home to New Hampshire and recruit more soldiers for the patriot army.

Stark agreed, but when he returned to his home state he learned that another soldier had received the promotion he himself had hoped for. While he had been fighting in New Jersey, Enoch Poor had been made a brigadier general. Stark believed that Poor had refused to march his militia regiment to Bunker Hill to fight, choosing instead to keep them in New Hampshire. Stark felt that he had been passed over for promotion unfairly. He was an experienced fighting commander and woodsman. Now a man with no combat experience and apparently little will to fight had been promoted over him. On March 23, 1777, he resigned his colonial commission in disgust, but promised his services to New Hampshire if they were needed.

Colonel John Stark

New Hampshire quickly responded by offering him a commission as a brigadier general. Stark accepted on the condition that he would fight as a militiaman, not under the orders of the Continental Army. Quickly, he assembled a force of militia numbering almost 1,500. The men supplied their own

"Yonder are the Hessians. They were bought for seven pounds and tenpence a man. Are you worth more? Prove it. Tonight the American flag floats from yonder hill or Molly Stark sleeps a widow!"

—John Stark

General Benjamin Lincoln

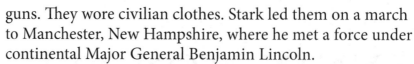

guns. They wore civilian clothes. Stark led them on a march to Manchester, New Hampshire, where he met a force under continental Major General Benjamin Lincoln.

Lincoln directed him to reinforce Schuyler on the Hudson River. But Stark was not taking orders from anyone in the Continental Army. He believed Lincoln, like Poor, had been unfairly promoted over him. Lincoln was wise enough, however, not to have a confrontation with Stark. He did not dispute the colonel's desire to operate independently against Burgoyne. Stark made plans to reinforce Schuyler, but first to defend Bennington against Baum's approaching force.

As he marched toward Bennington, he was informed that many Indians had been seen in the woods nearby. He sent 200 men to drive the Indians away, but they soon reported to him that behind the Indians was a large force of Hessians. Baum was approaching Bennington.

Stark immediately sent word to Lincoln at Manchester to send help, and moved out to confront the approaching Hessians. When the advance units of the two armies met, there was a skirmish. Realizing that he had encountered major resistance, Baum halted his army and ordered defenses to be built on high ground near the Walloomsac River. He sent a message to Breyman to quickly bring up the Hessians with him.

The next day was rainy. Stark waited, rather than attacking Hessians in a rainstorm when it would be impossible to keep his powder dry. The Germans made good use of the delay by plying their picks and shovels to strengthen their fortifications on the hill. Stark received reinforcements in the form of bodies of militia from western Massachusetts. The Massachusetts men were eager to fight. In fact, they complained that they had been called out before but had not yet been used in a battle.

One preacher, who had responded at the head of a company made up of men from his congregation, voiced this complaint to Stark. The Yankee officer replied,

> "If the Lord should give us sunshine once more, and I do not give you fighting enough, I will never ask you to turn out again."[50]

He intended to keep his promise.

The next day, the Lord sent the desired sunshine. The Massachusetts militia would indeed get all the fighting they desired. At noon on August 16, 1777, Stark formed up his men. They were about to advance up the hill the Hessians had

Enoch Poor

148

fortified. He had already been sending small groups of his men around the sides of the hill to take positions on the sides and in the rear of the enemy. Dressed in civilian clothes, they attracted little notice by the Hessians. They were thought to be some of the Tories whose support had been promised to them.

All things considered, Stark's men faced a monumental task. They were untrained and poorly armed and faced experienced troops that were considered among the best soldiers in Europe. The Hessians had cannons to use and had been given valuable time to fortify their position. But John Stark pointed with his sword to the entrenchments on the hill and shouted to his men,

> Boys, there are the Hessians. They were bought for seven pounds and tenpence a man. Are you worth more? Prove it. Tonight the American flag floats from yonder hill or Molly Stark sleeps a widow![51]

Soon the sound of guns came from the rear of the hill. Stark ordered his men forward, and from front, rear, and sides, the hill was assaulted by clambering, shouting men. Closer and closer they came to their enemies. Hotter and hotter grew the firing. Baum and his Germans were fighting bravely, but the enraged Americans could not be held back. The Hessians wondered why Breyman had not yet come to their aid. They longed for the desperate day to end and darkness to put an end to the frantic fighting.

Then there was a slight lull in the firing from the hilltop and the Americans swept forward and over the breastworks. But the Hessians were not beaten yet. With no time to reload their weapons, they reached for the short broadswords they all carried and fought hand to hand. Stubbornly, they resisted, but little by little Stark's men drove them back. Then, suddenly the Hessians broke and fled. The Americans owned the hill!

The battle had been won. The victorious Americans began to tend the wounded and plunder the camp. But very soon they were scrambling to pick up their rifles again, because the other Hessian force under Breyman arrived and pitched into them.

Volunteer Heroes of the Revolution

1. Green 2. Wayne 3. Putnam 4. Washington
5. Stark 6. Knox 7. Hamilton

THE SIEGE OF FORT SCHUYLER

For a moment it appeared that the great victory was about to turn into a defeat. The tired Yankees were at first driven back by the onslaught of Breyman's men. But just at that moment the men from Manchester arrived under Colonel Warner and threw themselves into the fight with all their energy. Stark's men turned the cannons they had taken from Baum and turned them against Breyman. Sharpshooters poured deadly accurate fire into the Hessian flanks. The Germans were driven back, foot by grudging foot. The air was filled with the shouts of battle, the cries of the wounded, and the unceasing pop and boom of muskets and cannons.

Darkness was approaching when the Hessians fell back before the American onslaught. Finally, their lines broke and they fled back the way they had come.

The victorious Yankees pursued their retreating enemies for only a short distance. They had fought a double battle in the summer's heat, and they were exhausted. Stumbling back to the hilltop defenses, they took time to collect their spoils and celebrate their hard-won victory. They counted 4 cannons, 700 prisoners, 1,000 sets of weapons, and 1,000 swords. Over 200 Hessians had been killed or wounded. The Americans had protected their stores at Bennington with the cost of only 14 killed and 42 wounded.

Burgoyne had now had another reminder of the foolishness of boasting.

"Boast not thyself of to morrow; for thou knowest not what a day may bring forth." —Proverbs 27:1

But the numerical tally did not come close to the real value of the victory. The effect on the Americans was electric. Their bravery and enthusiasm seemed to instantly return. At the same time, Burgoyne felt his first blast of discouragement. Where were all his Tory allies? Where would he get supplies for his army? His Indians were leaving him, further depleting his force. Perhaps the peasants were not quite so conquered as he had boasted. Perhaps he had spoken a bit too confidently when he had boasted that Britons never retreat.

Also in August of 1777, another battle took place that demonstrates how the fear of the invading British was fading in the hearts of the patriots. This battle was won as much by cleverness as by courage.

The British colonel Barry St. Leger had loaded his men on a fleet of skiffs, bateaux, and canoes to carry them south from Montreal into the Mohawk Valley of what is now the state of New York. With his redcoats was a large force of Indians under the famous chief Joseph Brant, or Thayendanegea, as the Mohawks called him. He was also assisted by "Johnson's Loyal

Greens," a troop of Tories who had left the Mohawk Valley and moved to Canada.

Early in August, St. Leger crossed Oneida Lake and advanced toward Fort Schuyler, which was located where the city of Rome, New York, now stands. This force of 1,700 was prepared to assault the old fort, commanded by young Colonel Peter Vansevoort. Vansevoort was among the standouts of the American army, but he had only a few hundred men to hold out against the much larger force of St. Leger.

Courage is standing alone for righteousness and yielding my fears to God. Joshua 1: 9 says, "Have I not commanded thee? Be strong and of a good courage; be not afraid, neither be thou dismayed: for the LORD thy God is with thee whithersoever thou goest." If God calls you to do something, little buddies, he'll be with you and give you strength to accomplish it. Give him your fears and he'll give you the courage you need.

Notified that St. Leger was coming, Vansevoort did his best to strengthen the defenses of the feeble old fort. But when he learned from a captured spy and some friendly Oneida Indians that his enemy was growing near, the young soldier knew he was in a very poor condition to defend his post.

Soon, St. Leger and his army were before the walls of the fort. The Britisher sent a demand for its surrender and at the same

General Burgoyne addressing the Indians.

Colonel Marinus Willett

time he distributed a printed proclamation through the region. The paper promised protection to all who would accept his terms of peace, but threatened severe punishment to all who would resist. The patriots of the valley knew what he meant: he was willing to loose the Indians among his troops to make unrestrained war against men, women, and children. But he, like Burgoyne, was beginning to learn that the hardy Americans were in no mood to receive either promises or threats from their enemies.

Colonel Vansevoort had no thought of giving up. He sent a brief reply that left no doubt of his intention of holding the fort. But he was in poor condition to hold his ground. His men were few, his provisions were low, and powder was scarce. He had received a few reinforcements with the arrival of Colonel Willett, but still he was outnumbered two-to-one by St. Leger.

A militia force under old General Herkimer gathered in the valley and now marched toward Fort Schuyler. But they met a force of Indians under Brant and had a desperate battle. Herkimer took a musket ball in his thigh, but the brave old man just sat with his back against a tree and continued to direct the battle. At last, the Indians were driven off, but the patriots had not been able to get to the fort and reinforce their comrades.

Hearing of this battle, St. Leger again sent a messenger to Vansevoort demanding the surrender of the fort. He falsely said that his Indians had beaten the militia under Herkimer and that, furthermore, Burgoyne had captured Albany. Vansevoort had no way of knowing how much of the message was true, but he had no intention of giving up his fort. His subordinate, Colonel Willett, gave the British officer carrying the demand a thorough rebuke, calling the British "hordes of women and children killers." The fort did not surrender.

The siege was renewed. Food remained scarce, and ammunition was nearly gone. Messengers had been sent to General Schuyler, desperately pleading for help, even though he himself was fighting to defend a fort with too few men and too little by way of supplies. But the siege continued for several days.

A SURPRISING VICTORY

Then, to the amazement of every man in the fort, the British fled. So suddenly did they leave that their tents remained standing and their guns were left in the trenches. What could have happened?

The Bennington Flag is a popular revolutionary flag that invokes the "Spirit of 76".

It was the heroism of General Schuyler that had saved them. Even though some of his own officers had accused him of treason in weakening his already weak force, he had sent Benedict Arnold rushing with a company of men to help Colonel Vansevoort. On the way, Arnold met with Colonel Willett and another officer who had slipped out of the fort to bring one last desperate plea for help to General Schuyler.

The force, along with Willett and his companion, stopped at Fort Dayton. There they learned of a gathering of Tories in a house nearby, and Arnold sent Willett with a force to capture them. They were successful, and 20 prisoners fell into their hands. Among them was a man who would be the key to saving Fort Schuyler, even though he was one of the most treacherous of the Tories.

This man was Hanyost Schuyler. He was known as one of the lowest and coarsest specimens of humanity in the valley. He had been a notorious spy and ruffian, so when a court martial was held the next day at Fort Dayton, it took very little time for him to be found guilty and sentenced to be hanged. The man's mother and brother lived nearby, and quickly approached Arnold with a plea to spare his life. But Arnold was unmoved. Their Hanyost must die.

Then an idea occurred to a Major Brooks in Arnold's command. He said that Hanyost might be worth much more alive than dead. He proposed a scheme to Arnold.

The plan was to allow Hanyost to escape from the guardhouse and flee to St. Leger's camp. There he would convince the Tories and Indians that Arnold was on his way with a huge force to relieve the fort and destroy the British attackers. He must make his story so convincing that the redcoats would immediately break off their attack and run. His brother would be held at Fort Dayton as a hostage until word came that he had succeeded. If he wanted his brother's life to be spared, he must make his mission a success.

Storytime with Uncle Rick

America's Struggle

Herkimer Mortally Wounded

Arnold immediately liked the idea. He had heard of the bloody battle in which General Herkimer had fallen. He was not sure he had enough men to break through St. Leger's troops and relieve Vansevoort, so the ruse was worth a try. If successful, it would save patriot lives.

Arnold and Brooks worked out the details of the plan, then went to share it with Hanyost and the guard watching him. After dark that night, the double traitor "escaped" from the guardhouse and the guard did not fire his gun in alarm until Hanyost was too far ahead of pursuit to be caught. Several soldiers were sent to pursue him, but the traitor had disappeared into the darkness. Everyone in the fort who did not know the plan was deeply disappointed that such a villain had escaped the noose.

For once, Hanyost Schuyler was true to his word and country. The promise of his brother adorning the noose he had escaped made Hanyost a most willing deceiver. He reached St. Leger's camp, where he knew many of the Indians. He told a pitiful story of having been captured by the rebels and his daring escape. He showed them holes in his hat, which he said had been made by patriot bullets as he fled. When the Indians asked him how many men were with Arnold, he pointed to the leaves on the trees and claimed that the men with Arnold were more in number than the leaves. As this report spread through the camps, the Indians began to grow very uneasy.

A friendly Oneida had also been let in on the secret and had cheerfully agreed to go to the St. Leger camps to back up Hanyost's story. He did this very convincingly, arriving some time after Hanyost. Then, into the camp strode two other Oneidas, whom he had met on the trail and who were happy to join in the deception. All telling essentially the same story, the three Indians acted amazed and awed by the number of soldiers coming to attack the British, Indians, and Tories.

It was all too much for the superstitious Mohawks. They decided on immediate retreat. St. Leger tried to hold them, even offering the rum the Indians loved so much. But they flatly turned him down. Drink had lost its charm in the face of an enemy many times their number. Despairing, St. Leger begged them to at least form a rear guard and protect his troops while they withdrew. They again refused. They accused him of sacrificing them to save his own men. It was every man for himself.

There was nothing for St. Leger to do but order the siege raised and get his men to safety. Gathering his entire force of redcoats, Tories, and Indians, he withdrew so suddenly that, according to some reports, his tents were left where they stood, the artillery was abandoned, and dinners were left cooking over campfires.

It seems the Oneida Indian who added so much to the trick had about him quite a spirit of mischief. As the army hastily withdrew he followed in the rear, occasionally shouting, "They are coming! They are coming!" just for the pleasure of watching the redcoats race each other to the boats on the lake. None of the Britishers felt safe until there was a goodly stretch of Lake Oneida between them and the patriots of the Mohawk Valley.

General Horatio Gates

CHAPTER 17

THE DOWNFALL OF BURGOYNE AND THE BATTLE OF SARATOGA

THE BRITON RETREATS

Six days after the flight of St. Leger, Burgoyne heard the news. Again he was informed that sometimes Britons did indeed retreat, and in this case it was in fear of a rumor. He was growing a bit less pompous as he gained more experience with the American "peasants."

The situation of Burgoyne's own army was no longer excellent. The dashing and daring Arnold had been sent to the aid of the patriots and his enthusiasm and confidence gave courage to the men around him. Lincoln's men were following those of Burgoyne, and now New England men were daily joining up with his band. It looked as if they could block Burgoyne's retreat, or at least harass his men from behind. Dan Morgan's riflemen and other regiments had come north, and their long rifles were to play a significant part in the events following the fight at Bennington.

At this time, most of the soldiers had confidence in General Gates, though he would later prove to be far less of a general than Schuyler, the man whom he had replaced. A great danger to the American army in the north was the jealousy between Gates and Arnold. Gates did not like the fact that Arnold had openly sided with Schuyler against him. Arnold did not like the fact that he had to take orders from a man whose military abilities he did not particularly respect.

But all this was unknown to the common soldier, and when Gates ordered the army to move to within 10 or 12 miles of the enemy lines, the men were ready to follow. Four days after Gates moved his army to Stillwater, Burgoyne made a bridge of boats and crossed the broad Hudson River.

General Burgoyne

Jealousy is very destructive. The American army was weakened by the jealousy between Arnold (left) and Gates. As Christians, we are sometimes tempted to be jealous of others, especially if we feel that they are getting credit for something we have accomplished. But part of growing up spiritually is learning to think of the greater mission of the gospel rather than thinking about who gets the credit for what gets done. James 3:14–15 says, "But if you have bitter jealousy and selfish ambition in your hearts, do not boast and be false to the truth. This is not the wisdom that comes down from above, but is earthly, unspiritual, demonic" (ESV).

THE BATTLE OF FREEMAN'S FARM

On the other side was Bemis Heights, fortified by the American soldiers under the direction of a Polish officer named Kosciuszko, who had crossed the ocean to join the American army when he heard of their struggle for freedom. Kosciuszko was an extraordinarily gifted engineer, and he had built strong fortifications.

Burgoyne was growing desperate. His path of retreat was blocked, though he had never intended to use it, and no help had come to him up the Hudson from the British army in New York. He was determined to make an attack as soon as he could get situated to do so. But meantime, his ranks were being badly harassed by Dan Morgan's eagle-eyed riflemen. When Morgan and the others figured out that Burgoyne meant to attack Bemis Heights, they decided not to wait to receive him in those strong fortifications. Instead, they took the initiative and attacked Burgoyne at Freeman's Farm.

Gates was not interested in attacking Burgoyne. His plan was to wait in the security of Bemis Heights and fight a defensive battle. But when he learned that a battle had already begun, he sent men to reinforce those already involved in the struggle. However, he did not send enough men for fear of weakening his own position. Meanwhile, Arnold raged like a trapped tiger, frantic to join the fight but unable to get Gates to give the order. Had Gates committed his entire force, it is likely he would have conquered Burgoyne handily. Instead, he huddled in his defenses.

At first, the Americans seemed to be winning the battle. Their sharpshooters, firing from their hiding places had caused havoc among the enemy. Arnold, chafing at the delay, finally persuaded Gates to order him forward, but Gates would only allow him to lead his own division of New Hampshire men. The rest of his army he held with him on the heights.

Now the British received help with the arrival of Fraser and Riedesel. Arnold sent a message to Gates, begging for 2,000 more men. With them, he said, he could drive the British before him. But Gates refused out of caution and the opportunity was lost. After several hours of bloody combat, sundown ended the battle. Both sides claimed victory, the sharpshooters having caused great losses in both armies. The British losses were probably higher than those of the Americans, though the redcoats held the field after the battle.

The battle has become known as the Battle of Freeman's Farm rather than the Battle of Bemis Heights. Freeman's Farm is one of the decisive battles of the Revolutionary War, leading directly to Burgoyne's surrender.[52]

John Neilson House, Bemis Heights, served as the headquarters for the Generals Enoch Poor and Benedict Arnold during the Saratoga campaign, by Benson Lossing, 1851 (PD-US).

Indeed, the former name is more appropriate, since Gates would not leave the Heights and did no fighting at all. Yet his report to Congress gave all the credit to himself and did not even mention Arnold's heroic part in it. It almost seemed that America was conspiring against Arnold. Time after time he had proven himself both fearless and skillful as a soldier, yet time after time he was denied the credit he deserved, and saw others promoted over him. The soldiers knew the truth, but the continuing quarrel between Arnold and Gates threatened the success of the army almost more than the British did.

View from Mount Defiance, Ticonderoga, New York. Photo by Mwanner, 2009 (CC BY-SA 3.0).

A Humiliating End to a Proud Campaign

Arnold was eager to have Gates follow up the battle by hitting Burgoyne again and harder. But Gates delayed. Burgoyne was growing more vulnerable as time went by. Lincoln's men were tearing his army from the rear, seizing supplies and cutting off men as prisoners. They even attacked Ticonderoga, but failed to take the fort even though they did what the British had done only two weeks before: move cannons atop Mount Defiance. But the British would not give up as St. Clair had done.

Burgoyne's supplies were getting dangerously low. If this continued, starvation might force him to surrender. Still, he hoped that Clinton would send help from New York. He resolved to fight his way through the "peasants," though they were constantly receiving reinforcements and now numbered 16,000. He had sent men out to forage for supplies, but the Americans controlled much of the country around them. Burgoyne sent out a force of his best fighters under Fraser to see whether the growing patriot force could be driven back. At least, he hoped, they could help the foragers collect supplies.

The Americans quickly showed that they were in no mood to be driven. There was a short but furious engagement, and then Fraser fell back to the location of the previous fight on Freeman's Farm. There he rallied and again faced the Americans. Benedict Arnold, unable to restrain himself any longer, now entered the fray. Leaping into his saddle and with no permission from Gates, he galloped like the wind to the battlefield. His men roared with cheers when they saw that he had joined them. At about the same time, Morgan pointed out Fraser to some of his

159

General William Fraser

best marksmen and told them to fire at only him. Soon Fraser was carried out of the battle with a mortal wound.

Fraser's fall seemed to take the courage out of his men. They were pushed back until they reached their own entrenchments. But Arnold led such desperate attacks on them that soon they retreated farther.

A wounded Hessian raised his gun, even as he lay on the ground, and fired it at Arnold. The bullet killed Arnold's horse and passed through the same leg that had been so seriously wounded at Quebec. One of Arnold's soldiers saw his general fall and rushed to kill the Hessian with his bayonet, but Arnold called to him and asked him to spare the man's life. The soldier did so, and Arnold's kindness in this incident stands in his favor against the dark and treasonous deeds that later ruined his reputation forever.

Burgoyne's men had been driven from the field. The next day he collected his army as best he could and marched back toward Saratoga. Hearing of his coming, the patriots in his path packed up as much of their property as they could carry and set fire to the rest in order to deny it to the redcoats.

General Schuyler's wife was one of those who destroyed their own property. Her husband had been a wealthy man before the war, and in addition to his mansion in Albany, he owned a lavish country estate and farms near Ticonderoga. Mrs. Schuyler, hearing that Burgoyne was retreating to Saratoga and stealing or destroying everything of value in his path, had gone to her country home to supervise the removal of her furniture. While there, she received a message from her husband. The general instructed her to burn their fields of ripening wheat so that the British could not use it. He asked her to direct their tenants to do the same. What a sadness Mrs. Schuyler must have felt as she put the torch to the lush fields and watched their smoke rise to the sky. Shortly after she left on the return trip to Albany, Burgoyne arrived and added her splendid estate house and barns to the ashes.

Compassion is being willing to expend effort to help alleviate the suffering of those in need. Proverbs 3:27–28 says, "Withhold not good to them to whom it is due, when it is in the power of thine hand to do it. Say not to thy neighbor, Go, and come again, and tomorrow I will give; when thou hast it by thee." Little buddies, when you see others in need or hurting, remember to show compassion to them.

But the British army was now surrounded. Supplies were running out, and each man's rations were reduced. Still Burgoyne heard nothing from Clinton. In fact, Clinton was doing his share of fighting. He had started up the Hudson to meet Burgoyne and had taken several American forts on the way, his superior numbers forcing General Putnam to abandon some without a fight. Now the British could travel by boat from New York as far as Albany.

On October 8, Clinton wrote a note to Burgoyne saying,

> I sincerely hope this success of ours will facilitate your operations.[53]

This message was hidden in a small silver bullet and given to a messenger to slip through the American army to Burgoyne's army. The next day, Clinton's force landed at Kingston, New York, and set fire to the town.

Another Clinton arrived too late to stop him. This was the patriot General George Clinton, who would serve New York as the state's longest-serving governor and America as vice president under two different presidents. He had been a member of the second Continental Congress. Somehow, the messenger of the British Clinton fell into his hands. The man was seen swallowing something as he was taken prisoner. The American Clinton forced him to swallow an emetic, which is a medicine used to make a person vomit. Up came the bullet and the message was found. The spy was quickly hanged, and the message never reached Burgoyne.

Gates was wise in allowing Burgoyne to state some conditions to his surrender. Had he insisted on an unconditional surrender, Burgoyne would have held out longer and Sir Henry Clinton might have reinforced him and changed the outcome of the battle. Unconditional surrender would have added to the glory of the victory for Gates, but it was not worth the risk to the greater cause.

GRACE TO AN ENEMY

Constant skirmishes and sharpshooter firing continued between the two armies, but finally the British had no option but to surrender. Retreat was cut off and there was no word of help arriving from New York. On October 17, 1777, they gave up the fight. Gates demanded an unconditional surrender at first, but Burgoyne refused. Such a surrender meant great shame to a general, and John Burgoyne, Esquire, was too proud a man for that. Gates was aware that Clinton was quickly approaching, so he wisely decided to allow Burgoyne a more honorable surrender. He agreed that the British could march out of the camp with the honors of war. They would then be marched to Boston, where they would board ships to take them home after having given their paroles that they would fight no more against the Americans. Gates even allowed the officers to keep their side arms as a gesture of respect.

The Camp Fire at Saratoga

It did not take long for the newspapers of the colonies to inform the people of the great victory over Burgoyne. There were many celebrations at the news, but since Gates had sent the first report of the surrender to Congress portraying himself as the hero, little credit was given to those who had really earned it, especially Arnold and Schuyler. Arnold was predictably incensed by this intentional oversight, but the great Schuyler held his peace. As time went on, even the British prisoners would comment on the humility and generosity of General Schuyler.

Indeed, so great was the praise heaped on the undeserving Gates that a plot was hatched to remove Washington from the head of the army and replace him with Gates. The group of men who formulated the plan was known as the Conway Cabal. It is fortunate for America that this plan never succeeded.

Kindness is treating others as you would like to be treated by them. Ephesians 4:32 says, "And be ye kind one to another, tenderhearted, forgiving one another, even as God for Christ's sake hath forgiven you." General Schuyler gives us a great example of kindness to those who had destroyed his home and crops just a few days before.

After the surrender, as Burgoyne and some of his company were traveling toward Boston as prisoners, they were invited to stop for a time at the mansion of General Schuyler near Albany. Here there occurred a most beautiful example of humility and kindness. Though it was only a few days since Burgoyne had destroyed the home and crops of Schuyler near Ticonderoga, he and his officers found a warm welcome at Schuyler's Albany home. They were treated with such kindness and courtesy that they were amazed.

General Schuyler had been detained at Saratoga, where he saw the sad ruins of his beautiful country estate. But he wrote to his wife urging her to make every preparation to give the best possible reception to the Burgoyne party. Evidently she followed his instructions, because the Madame de Riedesel wrote that their reception was not like that of enemies, but of intimate friends. She said,

The messenger cried, General Burgoyne and his whole army are prisoners of war!

All their actions proved, that at the sight of the misfortunes of others, they quickly forgot their own.[54]

The British commander was indeed warmly welcomed by the Schuylers and lodged in the best suite in the house. In the evening, he and his party were served an excellent supper. The honors were done with such grace and kindness that Burgoyne was moved to tears. He said with a sigh,

Indeed, this is doing too much for the man who has ravaged their lands and burned their dwellings.[55]

To Schuyler he said, "You are too kind to me, who have done so much injury to you." Schuyler generously replied, "Such are the fortunes of war. Let us not dwell on the subject." What a great, humble man!

The Murder of Jane McRae

Storytime with Uncle Rick
America's Struggle

One incident that rallied the patriots in the Hudson Valley against Burgoyne was the death of a young woman named Jane (or Jennie) McRea. Jane was engaged to be married to Mr. David Jones, a lieutenant in Burgoyne's army. She had received a letter from him saying that he hoped to see her soon at Fort Edward as the redcoat army advanced southward along the Hudson. Though most of the patriot settlers had fled the region after Forts Ticonderoga and Edward fell to the British, Jane stayed behind to meet her beloved. She went to visit a neighbor, Mrs. Sara McNeil, who was preparing to leave for Fort Edward for safety. But Burgoyne's advance party of Indians captured the two women and started north, pursued by American militia. Along the way, Jane was killed and scalped. The Indians claimed that she was killed by a stray shot from their pursuers, but the general belief of the time was that she had been murdered by one of the Indian scouts and her scalp taken to Burgoyne for a bounty. Mrs. McNeil claimed later to have seen Jane's scalp at Fort Edward. The incident was reported in several newspapers, and the details were often exaggerated to make the story more sensational. In later years, it found its way into various books of fiction with the details adjusted to fit the narrative, but the immediate effect of the story was to infuriate the patriot settlers of the Hudson Valley region and swell the ranks of volunteers to the militia. Jane could rightly be considered a martyr to the cause of liberty, because her death certainly contributed to Burgoyne's defeat.

American soldiers at
Valley Forge, Pennsylvania

CHAPTER 18

HOWE TAKES PHILADELPHIA

TRYING TO FOOL A FOX

Like most of the high American generals, Washington and Greene expected that General Howe would take his army, or at least a part of it, up the Hudson to join forces with Burgoyne. But this never happened, perhaps for two reasons. The first possible reason is the presence in New York of the faithless American general, Charles Lee. He was giving the British advice on how the rebellion could be ended. His counsel may have affected British decisions.

The second reason is the early success of Burgoyne. It may be that Howe felt that Burgoyne was succeeding on his own. When the Americans were driven out of Fort Ticonderoga without a shot being fired, and when the American army fled from Burgoyne, Howe probably figured that Burgoyne, with the help of St. Leger, was getting along fine for the moment. That left Howe free to attempt something near to his heart, the capture of the "rebel capitol," Philadelphia. There was the seat of the Continental Congress, there was the place where the Declaration of Independence had been signed, and there was the home of that incorrigible old rebel, Ben Franklin, who even now was in France seeking help from that government for the rebellion. Philadelphia would be a most

Alertness is being keenly aware of what is taking place around me so I can be prepared with a right response. Proverbs 3: 6 says, "In all thy ways acknowledge him, and he shall direct thy paths." Washington was very alert and prayerful, which made him such a great leader.

satisfying prize. Besides, occupying Philadelphia would place his army between the northern and southern colonies. When Burgoyne succeeded in his march south, that would strengthen the wall between the two regions, and each could then be conquered in turn.

In June 1777, Clinton was left in New York while Howe took an army of 18,000 men and started to march across New Jersey. Washington now had only about 10,000 men to oppose him. He left his station in the highlands and moved his army to New Brunswick. This place was too strong to be attacked, and Howe hesitated. A frontal assault was unwise, yet he was afraid to just go around the position and head for Philadelphia. That would have left the "old fox" behind him with a considerable force of men. So, after some skirmishing, Howe changed his plans and returned to Staten Island.

Once more, Washington expected Howe to move up the Hudson. But Howe made no such move. He kept a fleet of boats moving on the waters around New York to confuse Washington about his intentions. At one time, it looked as if Howe would go up the Hudson. At another time, it seemed he was on his way to Boston. Yet another time, it looked as if he was headed to Philadelphia.

When Howe thought he had Washington thoroughly confused, he quickly embarked 18,000 men on 228 boats bound for Philadelphia. At the same time, he wrote a letter to Burgoyne telling him that he was setting sail for Boston. The messenger was to allow himself to be captured so Washington would intercept the message and run off toward Boston while Howe marched for Philadelphia.

News traveled slowly in the days before electricity and telephones. Washington had to rely on spies, scouts, and horseback messengers. Think how different those days were from now, when we can learn news from the other side of the world in only seconds! General Washington had to be alert and flexible at all times.

But the trick was nothing new, and Washington was not fooled. He started his army across New Jersey to get between Howe and Philadelphia, with his scouts instructed to stay alert and notify him immediately if there was any sign of a change of direction and a move up the Hudson. On July 31, Washington heard that Howe's fleet had been sighted off the Delaware River. Washington moved up to Germantown to oppose him. But the next day, he got word that the British fleet had set sail again. He now expected that Howe would quickly return to New York and sail up the Hudson. But then came the news that Howe had sailed for the south. That would probably mean that he intended to attack Charleston.

The Battle of Germantown

There was not much to be done about that. Howe could easily sail his army to Charleston before Washington could move his men several hundred miles over the rough roads of the day. So Washington decided to go north instead and attack New York, protected only by the 7,000 men under Clinton.

But on August 25, news came of the victory at Bennington. And Washington also was notified that Howe had landed his troops on the Chesapeake Bay. He was marching his army toward Philadelphia.

The "old fox" decided the time had come to fight. Perhaps, if events favored him, he could do serious damage to Howe despite the redcoat army's superior numbers. At least he could stop or delay him in going north to help Burgoyne. Having heard of Bennington and Arnold's victory over St. Leger, Washington now expected Burgoyne to fail in his mission if he remained without heavy reinforcements.

At Chadd's Ford on the Brandywine River, he took his stand. The shores were rough and covered in thick woods. To the rear was high ground. The river current was swift. All in all, it seemed a barrier that even the highly drilled redcoats and

Hessians could not take. He hoped that his men were now experienced enough to stand against professional soldiers.

General Sullivan's men were in the front lines, but though they fought bravely, they were slowly pushed back. Fighting along a two-mile front, the patriots lost over a thousand men. The enemy held the ground.

THE FIGHT FOR PHILADELPHIA

Still, Washington had accomplished much. Even as the frightened Whigs of the region packed their belongings and fled to the mountains, the patriot army retreated in good order, without panic. On the day after the battle, many of Washington's soldiers wanted to form up and fight the advancing enemy again. But Washington was too wise to permit this.

Washington was prudent. Even though his men wanted to fight again, he knew the big picture. They had been beaten up the day before and needed time to rest and recover. Besides, they had lost the advantage of the good position they had found on the banks of the Brandywine. The "Old Fox" would not fight again until his army was ready and he could choose the place.

He knew he was not prepared with enough numbers to fight again so soon. But for two weeks his men harassed the enemy column, slowing its advance so much that they did not enter the city until September 26. Washington's hope had been that by harassing Howe he could keep him from sending much-needed help to Burgoyne up north. He had lost a battle, but succeeded in his higher goal.

One of the skirmishes between Washington's men and the British involved "Mad Anthony" Wayne, one of the boldest fighters in either army. Wayne had been given command of 1,500 men by Washington and ordered to try to seize part of the British baggage train while harassing them in every other way possible at the same time. Wayne selected a quiet, secluded spot as a camp for his men near Paoli. There he was reinforced by another 1,800 men, mostly from Maryland. Now he felt safe from the enemy for the moment. Unfortunately, some Tories learned of his camp and reported the information to Howe.

Howe did not wait to act upon the report. He ordered General Gray to attack and seize the camp. Gray was called the "no-flint general" because he was known to order his men to remove the flints from their guns before a battle in order to force them to use their bayonets. On a dark and stormy night, Gray advanced toward the camp. His men were ordered to use their bayonets and give no quarter. There seems to have been no excuse for this brutal order.

Their movements covered by the dark of night and the sound of their approach masked by the noise of the wind, the redcoats overcame Wayne's pickets then rushed the camp. The brave patriots tried to mount an organized defense, but the redcoats seemed to come from everywhere. The British were hard to see because of the darkness behind them, while the scrambling Americans were exposed by the light of their campfires. Over 150 were killed or wounded and another 75 taken captive, some of them bayoneted after they had surrendered. But the courage and skill of Mad Anthony saved most of his force. He organized a masterly withdrawal and managed to lead his remaining men to rejoin Washington at Chester. He would remember the brutal attack later at Stony Point.

General Wayne

The British now occupied Philadelphia. But not far away were Forts Mercer and Mifflin, both strong enough to cause problems for Howe. So Howe decided the forts must be captured. In October, the imposing fleet of the general's brother, Admiral Howe, arrived to join him, and the two men put together a plan to take the forts. General Howe sent part of his army overland to assist the fleet of his brother as he cannonaded them from the water.

This was the opportunity for which Washington had been waiting. With many of Howe's men leaving Philadelphia for the attack on the forts, the force left in Philadelphia was much smaller. Washington would attack while the enemy was at his weakest. Hopefully, the body of troops left behind would fall to him in the same way it had the year before at Trenton.

On October 3, Washington marched his men out of camp at sunset. They would march through the dark hours to the village of Germantown at the edge of Philadelphia where most of the British troops were encamped. Soon after dawn, they attacked. It was a desperate fight, with lines of men thrashing and weaving back and forth across the field. Washington's men had attacked in four columns, but one of the columns got confused in a dense cloud of smoke and fog. Its leader, General Stephen, was later charged with being drunk at the time. The column mistook Mad Anthony Wayne's men for the British and fired a number of shots into their ranks before they could be stopped. Stephen was later court-martialed and dismissed from the army. This incident caused so much confusion in the American ranks that they were soon retreating. They left nearly 700 of their men on the field, fewer than were lost by the British.

Some historians believe that the genius of Washington and the courage of his men at Germantown, even though they were defeated, did as much to bring France into the war on the side of the Americans as did the defeat of Burgoyne. At least it was plain that the Americans were learning to fight. The redcoats still controlled Philadelphia, but the patriots seemed as far from giving up as they had ever been.

The Howe brothers took the two forts with little difficulty. This left Philadelphia and the Delaware River in their hands. But now winter was approaching and fighting must cease, or at least die down.

ONE WINTER, TWO ARMIES

In Philadelphia, the redcoats had every comfort they could ask for. Much of the population was Tory in sentiment and they welcomed the British as conquering heroes. Many were the parties, balls, and dinners enjoyed by the king's officers and their Tory friends. Supplies were plentiful. In the spring there would be fighting and dying to do, but for now comfort was the order of the day.

Not so for the little patriot army. They were camped out in a place called Valley Forge, near present-day Norristown, Pennsylvania, on the Schuylkill River. It was to be a terrible winter. It was not that the weather was worse than the average Pennsylvania winter, but that the little army was so ill equipped. There were not nearly enough tents, stoves, food, clothing, or even tools with which to construct huts. Most of the soldiers wore threadbare clothes, and many of them were without shoes, with only rags or burlap sacking to wrap around their bleeding feet. Their homes were huts constructed of logs, sod, stones, and any other material that could be scraped together from the surrounding wilderness. The huts were small, smoky, and without decent bedding. Sickness was a constant companion, as the bodies of the half-starved men grew weaker and less resistant to disease.

Three cheers for Mrs. Martha Washington! How the soldiers loved her in that terrible winter of 1777–1778. Rather than staying in her comfortable mansion at Mount Vernon, Martha traveled to Valley Forge with a caravan of vehicles carrying food, clothing, and cloth to the hungry army of her husband. She spent the winter visiting sick soldiers, knitting socks (along with some of the other officers' wives), and comforting the dying. Week after week she shared the lean fortunes of her husband and his men, looked upon as an angel of mercy by the suffering soldiers. Upon coming out of church one Sunday with her husband, Martha was met with the cry from hundreds of throats, "Long live Lady Washington!"

Still, the patriots were ready to fight. Baron von Steuben, the rough but kindly old veteran from Germany, pounded new self-respect and resolution into the hungry, frostbitten men as he trained and drilled them unceasingly. They learned to move better as units, performing complicated maneuvers with increasing skill. Despite the shortage of ammunition, von Steuben drilled and drilled them on reloading in a minimum of time. Once in a while the lean, shivering patriots managed to forget that they were hungry and cold and were able to feel like real, trained, battle-ready soldiers.

But the British were in Philadelphia, warm and well fed, enjoying the company of the many loyalists of the town. While the Americans at Valley Forge starved and froze only a few miles away, the redcoats passed the winter days in comfort. They could wait until more pleasant weather to renew the struggle.

American soldiers at Valley Forge, Pennsylviania

PATRIOT MARY KNIGHT

Of the many brave women who helped the army survive the hard winter of 1777–1778, one whose story has come down to us is that of Mary Knight. Mary was a devoted patriot and the sister of an American general. She often trudged through deep snow to carry baskets of food to the camp in Valley Forge. Often she made her way past the British outposts disguised as a market woman with her burden of food or medicines. Her brother, General Warrell, once came to her for a hiding place when he was separated from his company and being hunted by the British. For three long days Mary concealed him in a cider barrel in her cellar, feeding him through the bung of the barrel. Parties of redcoats searched the house four times, but none ever discovered the general in his unique hiding place.

171

Molly Pitcher
at the
Battle of Monmouth

CHAPTER 19

A Turning Point in the War

At Last — Help from France

America needed help.

She was poor, and short on experience, supplies, and manpower. Congress knew this and was looking for help across the ocean.

France was the most likely source for this help, so Congress had sent wise, shrewd old Ben Franklin to make friends there. At the beginning of the war, France was angry over the loss of her colonies in America. In addition, France had been at war with England many times, and there was much hatred between the two countries. It seemed as if France was fertile ground in which to sow the seeds of an alliance. It was not that France had a great love for the American colonies; after all, they were English in heritage and had fought with the English against the French in the French and Indian War. The leaders of France were much more interested in doing harm to England than in doing good to the colonies. Either way, their help would be welcome.

In fact, France had already been helping the patriots. Some money had been forthcoming, and France had also allowed American privateers to fit out their ships in her ports and retreat to them when pursued too closely by British ships. Openly, France still pretended to be presently at peace with England. In fact, her king was believed

At a brilliant party in Franklin's honor, he was crowned with laurel.

Bravery means to face danger in control of our fear. Isaiah 41:10 says, "Fear thou not; for I am with thee: be not dismayed; for I am thy God."

One brave patriot, along with some comrades was chopping the beams under a bridge just as the advance of the British approached. While his companions fled, this unnamed hero continued swinging his axe as the enemy opened fire upon him. The last stroke broke through the beam and the bridge collapsed just as several musket balls struck him down, dead.

to be rather on England's side than that of her colonies. But young Lafayette was not the only Frenchman who had sailed across the Atlantic to help the struggling patriots, and much sympathy had been aroused among the French people by clever old Dr. Franklin. He had won the hearts of Frenchmen high and low by his simplicity, ready wit, and humble manners. He had a quaint style of dress that was free of any pretension or vanity, and in fact "Franklin hats" and "Franklin coats" were quite in fashion for a while.

All the while, Franklin was working hard for one purpose: to get France to openly declare to the world that she was a friend of the new nation struggling to be born in America and give her solid support. The obstacle in his path was the fear of many Frenchmen that the main burden of the war would fall upon their country, and that there would be little of profit for her at the conclusion of the war. They knew that France had much to lose in blood and money by fighting England again, but just what would be the reward if the struggle was successful? Most Frenchmen had hatred enough for England, but what was really to be gained by fighting the British again as a friend of America?

But Burgoyne had surrendered and Washington had displayed brilliance in leading the attack on Germantown, even though the battle failed to gain the desired result. There was clearly a nation being built in the New World, and Franklin finally persuaded France that she had something to gain by having her as a friend. Early in 1778, a treaty of alliance was made.

A promise was made that a fleet of 16 ships would sail to America under the command of Admiral d'Estaing, along with an army of 4,000 men. Naturally, this led to an immediate declaration of war against France by England. Now the British government changed her tune rather drastically toward her colonies. She offered the colonies everything they had demanded at the beginning of the war if they would return to loyalty to the king and help him fight the French. No more quartering of soldiers, no more taxation, no more interfering with colonial governments, no more interfering with courts, etc. England was again embroiled in a war against a major European power and decided it was time to make peace in the family.

But it was too late. Had England made the same offer three years earlier, all would have been different. Most American colonists had not originally wanted independence, but just their constitutional rights as Englishmen. But now the British had burned their towns, sent the brutal Indian tribes against them, seized their property, and killed their neighbors and relatives. America had declared herself a free and independent nation,

Franklin in France

and there would be no going back. The war must continue.

Their leader, General Washington, was more trusted by the people in the spring of 1778 than he had been the previous year. There had certainly been a crisis for him; as the leader he was the logical one to blame for the failures around Philadelphia, and those were compared with the apparent success of Gates in the defeat of Burgoyne. But some understood that it had been Schuyler and Arnold far more than Gates who had determined the outcome in the north. And the wisdom and dignity of Washington had defeated the movement to replace him with Gates, so that when the trial was over there was a natural reaction in the feelings of the people, and Washington stood higher in the public regard than before.

The Army at Valley Forge

There was plenty of alarm in the redcoat army when news came of France's involvement in the war. Now there was to be war not on one side of the Atlantic but on both. In fact, because the ruling families in France were related by blood to the ruling families of Spain, that country also took sides against Britain. Not long after, little Holland decided it was in her best interest to befriend America as well, so another enemy was added to those who opposed England. So it was that England's forces must be seriously divided, greatly weakening her ability to recover her lost colonies. Though France would not contribute huge amounts in materials and men to combat in America, the effect of the alliance with her was to have a very large impact.

THE RACE FOR NEW YORK

Howe had sailed from Philadelphia for England, leaving Sir Henry Clinton in command. As soon as Clinton heard of France's decision to enter the war, he decided to abandon Philadelphia and return to New York, fearing that it would be the first place to be attacked by the French. But now he had a new problem. The Tories of Philadelphia expected him to help them escape the wrath of the patriots who would be in control of their city upon Clinton's departure. Philadelphia had contained a good number of Tories originally, and many more citizens had accepted the offer of pardon and safety from General Howe. These people were terrified at the thought of the patriot soldiers who had suffered through the terrible winter while the Tories of Philadelphia made their enemies comfortable. Those soldiers were still at nearby Valley Forge. They were better drilled and trained than ever before, and there were far more of them because many of the men who had been fighting Burgoyne had now come to join them. The Tories would stand no chance of defending themselves if attacked. They begged Clinton for help.

Clinton gave in to their appeal. In June 1778 he used the fleet of ships intended for his soldiers to carry the timid Tories to New York and prepared to march his men across country. He planned to march to Brunswick, New Jersey, and there meet Admiral Howe's fleet on their return from ferrying the Tories to New York. Once aboard ship, his army could make their way to New York also.

> "Many a man proclaims his own loyalty, but who can find a trustworthy man?" —Proverbs 20:6 (NASB).
>
> No doubt General Charles Lee told everyone he was loyal to America and to General Washington. Yet Lee was a constant thorn in Washington's side, causing discord among the officers and instigating distrust toward the commander-in-chief. The truth was that Lee was mostly loyal to himself.

Meanwhile in Valley Forge, Washington was making his own plans. In doing so he had to contend with General Charles Lee, who had been retrieved in a prisoner exchange. Lee was such an unfaithful man that America would have been better off had he remained a prisoner of the British. He constantly opposed Washington's plans. He was against following the redcoats as they retired from Philadelphia; he did not think the Americans were yet ready to stand before the king's disciplined regulars. He was a persuasive speaker, and more of a threat to Washington and the army than anyone knew. They were unaware of the treasonous work he had been doing as a prisoner in New York.

In spite of everything, Washington took his army, which now numbered 15,000, and moved toward Philadelphia. On the morning of June 18, 1778, Clinton marched out of the town, and by nightfall Washington marched in. He had made his advance so quietly and discreetly that some of Clinton's men who straggled behind the others were captured.

It would not have been surprising if the American army had visited punishments on the Tories who had failed to escape the city. But Washington was in a hurry and was not disposed to waste time taking revenge on helpless people. Benedict Arnold, whose left leg had been again wounded in the fighting against Burgoyne, was left in charge of a small American force to maintain control of Philadelphia.

The members of Congress now returned to the city and resumed their business. Two of the Tories were tried and hanged for their crimes, but the rest were eventually pardoned. The two who were executed were among those who had guided the redcoats in a night attack on an American force.

Washington, informed of Clinton's plans, decided to march quickly across New Jersey in a line north of the enemy and get ahead of him. Then he would pick out a place most advantageous to him and give battle to the redcoats. Clinton, though his army was a little larger and much better equipped than Washington's, did not yet want to fight. His goal was to reach New York and join the force there in defending the city against an expected attack from the French.

The temporary camp at Monmouth

THE BATTLE OF MONMOUTH

Now the American army was ahead of Clinton. Washington halted his men at Hopewell for a rest. The men were so worn out that it seemed necessary, and it gave Washington a brief respite to hold a council of war with his officers. He proposed sending a detachment to attack the British immediately, while he himself followed with the main army. Again Charles Lee opposed him, and he spoke so eloquently that a majority of the officers voted against Washington's idea. But Nathanael Greene, Mad Anthony Wayne, and others urged Washington to go ahead, and as his own judgment agreed, he decided to do so.

Clinton had received word that Washington was now ahead of him, so a change of plans was necessary. He redirected his course and headed for the Navesink Highlands, there to board Howe's ships and be conveyed to New York.

On June 28, the Americans overtook Clinton at Monmouth Courthouse, and there occurred the famous battle of Monmouth on one of the most brutally hot days ever recorded in New Jersey. It was reported that the temperature reached 96 degrees before the sun was fully up. It was in this battle that General Charles Lee finally was discovered to be a treacherous and disloyal officer.

In Camp at Valley Forge

Lee was in command of the advance of the army, ordered to attack the enemy while Washington brought up the rest of his force. But after his men had fired only one volley, he ordered a retreat. The men did not understand this, as it had seemed that they were well positioned and, in fact, holding their own quite well against the enemy. Mad Anthony, when he heard of the order, was beside himself with grief and rage.

177

Washington rebuking Lee at Monmouth.

As Washington rode forward, he began to meet soldiers moving away from the battle. Stopping a fifer and asking him the meaning of this development, he was told that the patriots were retreating. Washington sternly ordered the man to repeat those words to nobody on pain of severe punishment. Riding onward, the general encountered so many retreating men that he realized the division was indeed leaving the field of battle. Now the fighting blood of Washington was truly up. He sent forth his aides with orders to regroup and stop the retreat. Soon he faced General Lee and demanded to know the meaning of his order to retreat.

Lee, terrified, tried to stammer out an explanation that his order had been misunderstood. The commander was too upset to listen to excuses. It seemed that all his hopes and plans, possibly along with the prospects of the entire nation, might be blasted by the treachery of one false patriot. Leaving the stuttering officer, Washington galloped off in a rage to repair the damage. At last, though, he understood what kind of man Charles Lee really was.

Once Washington had his army under control, the battle became a masterful series of moves by both Washington and General Cornwallis, who was leading the rear guard of Clinton's army. When darkness put a merciful end to the fighting, both armies were still on the field. But in the middle of the night Clinton formed up his exhausted men and slipped away toward New York. Washington then took up a position outside the city but did not attack. He made plans instead to keep the British bottled up there so that they could not do more damage to the surrounding area or move out to join another British force.

After the battle, Lee wrote an insulting letter to Washington, defending himself and attacking the "tinsel dignity" of his commander. Washington quickly had Lee arrested and ordered a court martial. Due to Washington's humble forbearance, Lee was only sentenced to a year's dismissal. There is no doubt that he deserved a heavier punishment, but such was the greatness of Washington's character that he bore insults and insubordination, suffering wrong rather than to risk doing wrong even to an enemy. But Lee had not learned his lesson. He began writing disparaging letters about Washington to various newspapers. Soon he was expelled from the army for good.

MOLLY PITCHER

In 1777, William Hayes enlisted in Proctor's 4th Pennsylvania Artillery. As he endured the winter of 1777–1778 in Valley Forge, he was joined by his wife, Mary. Mary, like the other women known as "camp followers," tended to sick soldiers, washed laundry, and cooked meals for the men. During the battle of Monmouth in the summer of 1778, she spent many sweltering hours carrying water to the patriot soldiers amidst flying bullets and cannonballs. The common practice was for gunners, when they needed water to cool their cannons to shout "Pitcher!" to let a water carrier know of the need. The same was done by any soldier who was thirsty. Mary, whose nickname was Molly, often heard the cry of "Molly! Pitcher!" During the awful heat of the Battle of Monmounth, according to reports from various soldiers, there came a time during that day's fighting that William Hayes fell on the battlefield, either from a wound or from heat exhaustion. When he did, his wife picked up his ramrod and began helping to serve the cannon in his place. She continued in this work for several hours. After the battle, General Washington heard about her heroic service and issued her an honorary commission as a sergeant. She went by the nickname "Sergeant Molly" for the rest of her life.

Storytime with Uncle Rick

America's Struggle

MOLLY PITCHER

by Kate Brownlee Sherwood

'T was hurry and scurry at Monmouth town,
For Lee was beating a wild retreat;
The British were riding the Yankees down,
And panic was pressing on flying feet.

Galloping down like a hurricane
Washington rode with his sword swung high,
Mighty as he of the Trojan plain
Fired by a courage from the sky.

"Halt, and stand to your guns!" he cried.
And a bombardier made swift reply.
Wheeling his cannon into the tide,
He fell 'neath the shot of a foeman nigh.

Molly Pitcher sprang to his side,
Fired as she saw her husband do.
Telling the king in his stubborn pride
Women like men to their homes are true.

Washington rode from the bloody fray
Up to the gun that a woman manned.
"Molly Pitcher, you saved the day,"
He said, as he gave her a hero's hand.

He named her sergeant with manly praise,
While her war-brown face was wet with tears —
A woman has ever a woman's ways,
And the army was wild with cheers.[56]

Washington near the village of White Plains.

CHAPTER 20

BATTLES IN VARIOUS PLACES

FIGHTING EAST AND WEST

After the Battle of Monmouth, Washington moved his army to the Hudson River, camping at White Plains. Clinton, fortified inside New York City, feared that he would now be attacked from the land by Washington and from the sea by the French. But Washington, despite several successful battles, had by now concluded that the way to win the war was not by pitched battles, which could cost American dearly in blood and treasure, but rather by simply making the British so weary of the war that they would finally abandon it. He would hold the enemy in New York if possible, so they could do little more damage to the countryside. Then he would wait to see what the new alliance with the French would accomplish.

D'Estaing's fleet of six frigates and 12 ships-of-the-line arrived at the mouth of the Delaware River on July 8, 1778. Learning there that the British had gone to New York, they then set sail for that port. There an attack was planned, but it was feared that the large ships in the fleet could not get through some of the shallow channels around the city. So the plan was changed and it was decided to attack Newport, Rhode Island, the only other port city then occupied by the British.

Nathanael Greene

"America must raise an empire of permanent duration, supported upon the grand pillars of Truth, Freedom, and Religion, encouraged by the smiles of Justice and defended by her own patriotic sons."

—Nathanael Greene

Lt. Col. Robert Pigot, by Francis Cotes, c.1765 (PD-Art).

Prospects for the attack looked good. General Sullivan, in command at Providence, was reinforced by a company of picked men under Nathanael Greene. Greene was a native of Rhode Island and knew both the land and the people well. When some New England militia arrived, the patriot force grew to 9,000 patriots and 4,000 Frenchmen. They faced a total of only 6,000 redcoats under Sir Robert Pigot. With the help of d'Estaing's fleet, it was confidently expected that Newport would fall easily.

But there was tension between the French and American leaders. Still, the attack might have gone over very well, had not a British fleet arrived just as final preparations were being made. The French fleet immediately withdrew and sailed out to fight the British ships. But before they could engage the enemy, a fierce storm arose and forced both fleets to look to their own survival.

Once the storm was past, the French admiral insisted on taking his soldiers and sailors to Boston for ship repairs. The American officers argued that the work could easily be performed in Providence, but the Frenchman was insistent.

Of course this was discouraging to the Americans. They thought of the French as very fickle allies. A third of the patriot soldiers abandoned Newport and went home to take care of their crops. Seeing this, Pigot, the British commander, attacked the American fortifications on Butt's Hill near Newport but failed to drive the Americans away.

In November 1778, the French fleet sailed away to the West Indies, forcing Clinton to send 5,000 of his troops off to reinforce the British army there. Fearing an attack from Washington now that the New York defenders were fewer in number, he recalled Pigot and his 6,000 men from Newport, and that port city was relieved without bloodshed. So the French had indeed aided the Americans, although it was more indirectly than directly. The patriots were still disgusted by the fickleness they had seen, but at least the British army in America had been weakened.

It was in 1778 that General Sullivan led an expedition against the Tories and Indians involved in border warfare on the fringe of the colonies. Having succeeded in arousing the Indians to violence with promises of land and gold in exchange for patriot scalps, the British found that they were unable to control their allies and prevent their conducting warfare in their own way, apart from any European reservations against wholesale slaughter. The result was that the settlers of the border

Comte Charles Henri d'Estaing

regions lived in constant terror, and their brethren in the more settled regions to the east were incited to intense anger and a greater determination to fight the British to the end.

In July, the horrible Wyoming Valley massacre took place in which Tories who had previously lived in the valley joined their Indian allies in butchering their former neighbors. Then in November there was another massacre, this time in Cherry Valley. Fifty men, women, and children were killed, and the valley was left a smoking ruin.

The Wyoming Massacre, Alonzo Chappel, 1858 (PD-Art).

On February 27, 1779, Congress passed a resolution authorizing Washington to take whatever measures he deemed necessary to stop these outrages by the Tories and Indians on the frontier. Washington pondered which of his generals should be sent. It would be no easy job. It would mean hundreds of miles of travel through pathless forests and a day-and-night watch against attacks by the most deadly and stealthy enemies to be faced anywhere. At last, he settled on the choice of General Sullivan.

Sullivan divided his force, sending part of it up the Mohawk River and leading the other himself up the Susquehanna. In late August the two companies met, joined forces, and attacked the Tories and Indians at Newtown, where the city of Elmira now stands. The patriots drove the enemy before them and finally their lines broke and they fled.

Sullivan then advanced farther, determined to teach a lesson that the enemy could not fail to understand, and which would show the Indians that their own welfare depended on staying out of alliances with the brutal Tories. Indian towns were burned, crops were destroyed, and many braves were killed. Sullivan hoped to proceed and capture Fort Niagara, but sickness among his men and lack of supplies forced him to return east without accomplishing that. Nevertheless, he had accomplished his goal: though there would continue to be depredations against lonely homesteads, the mass slaughters of Wyoming Valley and Cherry Valley were not repeated.

Visiting the French Fleet

On the Hudson — The Storming of Stony Point

In the year 1779, there was only one major open attack between the British and American armies. This was the taking of Stony Point on the Hudson River. Stony Point had been captured by Sir Henry Clinton on his tardy advance to help John Burgoyne in 1777. In July 1779, Washington resolved that the fort should be taken back. Mad Anthony Wayne was the officer chosen to lead the attack.

Wayne led his men on a stealthy advance through the swamps, and they gathered at a point about a mile and a half from the fort. Then, Wayne and his officers sneaked closer to the fort to look it over and make their plans. The fort would not be easy fruit to pick. The waters of the Hudson protected three sides of it, while there was a swamp in its rear, and it reposed on a high bluff. It was equipped with cannons and garrisoned by experienced soldiers. But all that just meant that the choice of Mad Anthony Wayne had been a wise one.

Wayne was assisted by a man named Pompey, a slave of a Whig who lived near the river. Pompey had numerous times gone to the fort with strawberries to sell to the officers. Now Pompey told the officers that it was hard for him to leave his master's work in the daytime and he needed permission to come after dark. The redcoats agreed, and he was given the password: "The fort's our own."

Kindness — George Washington was a Bible-believing man. No doubt he was familiar with Matthew 5:44–45, "But I say unto you, Love your enemies, bless them that curse you, do good to them that hate you, and pray for them which despitefully use you, and persecute you; that ye may be the children of your Father which is in heaven: for he maketh his sun to rise on the evil and on the good, and sendeth rain on the just and on the unjust."

Washington gave orders to punish severely any American soldier who abused prisoners. He wanted to shame the British, who did abuse prisoners. He issued an order saying, "Treat them with humanity, and let them have no reason to complain of our copying the brutal example of the British Army in their treatment of our unfortunate brethren who have fallen into their hands."[58]

On the night of July 15, 1779, Pompey and two soldiers approached the first sentinel at the fort. Pompey gave the password, and then he and his companions seized the sentinel, and tied and gagged him. Other sentinels were captured, and a little after midnight the attack began. Wayne had ordered his men to use their bayonets only, except for a few who attacked from one side with loaded weapons. Using this ruse to draw the defenders to one side of the defenses, Wayne then sent the remainder of his men forward. There was a fierce response of musket fire from the defenders, but the patriots kept forcing their way forward with their bayonets. Each man had pinned a piece of white paper to his hat so that his comrades could tell him from a redcoat in the dark.

Mad Anthony himself was struck in the head with a musket ball. It was only a shallow wound, but Anthony thought he was probably dying. He ordered his men,

March on! Carry me into the fort, for I will die at the head of my column![57]

However, he soon recovered and in a short time he was commander of the fort.

Unlike the British at Fort Washington and elsewhere, Mad Anthony's men did not abuse the British once they were made prisoners. Wayne had lost 15 men who were killed and 83 were wounded. The British had lost over 60 who were killed and had over 500 captured.

Anthony Wayne

Mad Anthony was so excited about his victory that he immediately sent a letter to Washington advising him of the happy news. There was great rejoicing among the Continentals, but Washington thought the fort would be too hard to hold, so plans were made to abandon it. First, of course, the Americans stripped the fort of everything that could be useful to a fighting army. When the British returned to the fort, it was indeed not much more than a stony point.

The country, greatly encouraged by this clear victory, soon rang with the praises of Mad Anthony. Congress voted him a medal in honor of it, and even Charles Lee, who had no more love for Anthony than he had for Washington, wrote him a very flattering letter complimenting him on his triumph. But perhaps the most gratifying result of the battle for Wayne was the knowledge that the bayonets of his men had avenged the losses he had suffered in 1777 when General Gray, the "no-flint general," had surprised his camp and slaughtered so many of his brave men.

The Jersey Shore

Among the little known but very interesting chapters in the War of Independence is the role of the small privateers along the Jersey Shore during these days. Beginning the war with no navy at all, America had to scramble to find ways to do damage to the king's ships. While John Paul Jones (sometimes called the Father of the American Navy) was just beginning to earn his reputation on the first American naval vessel to sail, many daring adventurers called "privateers" took to ships and even rowboats to attack British shipping. Privateers were not in the American navy, nor were they pirates. They were adventurers who sailed privately owned vessels to attack British shipping. A privateer was issued a Letter of Marque by the American government that authorized him to capture British ships and turn them into an admiralty court to be sold. The privateer made a profit on each

Delaware River at Gloucester

ship he captured, with its cargo. These boats, owned by individuals rather than the American government, took great risks for the sake of hindering His Majesty's navy and of obtaining plunder for their owners and crews. Some of these vessels were quick little sloops that could strike suddenly and quickly outrun the heavy British vessels sent in pursuit. Some of them were whaleboats, powered by several pairs of oars. Small cannons would sometimes be mounted on these little vessels.

The *New Jersey State Gazette* published a story on June 23, 1779, that accurately describes the nature of this small-scale but very daring style of naval warfare:

> An open boat called the *Skunk*, mounting two guns and twelve men, belonging to Egg Harbor, sent in there, on Wednesday last, a vessel with a valuable cargo, which makes her nineteenth prize since she was fitted out. Upon one occasion this boat had quite an adventure when commanded by Captain Snell and John Goldin. They thought they had discovered a fine prize off Egg Harbor in a large ship wearing the appearance of a merchantman. The boat approached cautiously, and after getting quite near, the little *Skunk* was put in a retreating position, stern to the enemy, and then gave him a gun. A momentary panic ensued. All at once the merchantman was transformed into a British 74, and in another moment she gave the *Skunk* such a broadside that, as Goldin expressed it, 'the water flew around them like ten thousand waterspouts.' She was cut some in her sails and rigging, but by hard rowing made good her escape, with Goldin to give the word, "Lay low, boys! Lay low, for your lives!"[59]

This was a sample of the action taking place from Cape May to Sandy Hook. The patriots had no vessels that could compete with the mighty British frigates, but their whaleboats, manned sometimes by 20 or more oarsmen, and their little sloops could sometimes do great damage. Sometimes they sustained serious damage and patriot lives were lost, but the hardy sailors were always ready with boat or musket or both, and for the remainder of the war gave the British a lively time all along the coast.

ALL IS WELL

One particularly successful privateer was Captain Adam Hyler. Hyler had been a sailor in the British navy, but at the outbreak of the war had thrown in his lot with the patriots. Despite the threat of being hung from a yard-arm as a traitor if captured, he chose to stand for independence. He lived in New Brunswick, New Jersey, where he built whaleboats and collected a dedicated and bold band of followers. His men practiced rowing the long, quick whaleboats until they could move them across the water silently and swiftly as the wind.

Storytime with Uncle Rick

America's Struggle

The boats were hidden along the shores of Amboy Bay and the Raritan River. The vessel that dared to despise these humble craft or relax its vigilance, was in for trouble. Many times the crew of an unsuspecting vessel would suddenly find themselves prisoners and their ship seized by a handful of daring men who drove their long rowboat silently over the waves, then just as silently climbed aboard their victim. Of course, a tiny crew with tiny boats could not take part in any great naval engagements, but still they were a perpetual threat and an unending source of fear and distraction to British boats in and around New York.

On one occasion, Hyler took one gunboat and two whaleboats and attacked five British vessels, within a quarter mile of a large British guard ship. After 15 minutes of sharp fighting, the crews of the British boats abandoned them and took refuge in a small fort onshore. From there they fired 12 swivel guns at their captured ships, but Hyler defied the danger and boarded all five boats without losing a single man. He captured 50 bushels of wheat, some cheese, some dry goods, a cask of gunpowder, and a number of muskets. Then he set the boats on fire so that the enemy could not reclaim them. The exception was one boat on which he found a woman and four small children. That vessel was left unharmed as Hyler and his crew rowed quickly and quietly away.

One British sailor, captured by Hyler, gave this account of the episode:

> I was on deck on a very pleasant evening with our sentinel fixed. Our vessel was at anchor near Sandy hook and the Lion man-of-war about a quarter of a mile distant. It was calm and clear, and we were all admiring the beautiful and splendid appearance of the full moon. While we were thus attentively contemplating the serene luminary, we suddenly heard several pistols discharged into the cabin, and turning around perceived at our elbows a number of armed people, fallen as it were from the clouds, who ordered us to surrender in a moment or we were dead men. Upon this, we were turned into the hold and the hatches barred over us. The firing, however, had alarmed the man-of-war, who hailed us and desired to know what was the matter. As we were not in a situation to answer, Captain Hyler was kind enough to do it for us; telling them through his speaking trumpet that all was well. After which, unfortunately for us, they made no further inquiry.[60]

Whaleboats

Antique Church Hymnal

CHAPTER 21

THE FIGHTING PREACHER AND TREASON

MINOR ENGAGEMENTS, ARNOLD AND ANDRE

In the later years of the war, both sides were getting tired of the struggle. Each hoped the other would wear out and give up first. No great battles occurred in the north, though there were a number of small engagements. Let us look at a few of these to get a general understanding of what the War of Independence was like in the north during these days.

Near the end of summer in 1779, after General Anthony Wayne had seized and then abandoned Stony Point, a force of 300 men under Major "Light-Horse Harry" Lee (father of General Robert E. Lee) advanced upon Paulus Hook in New Jersey. At that city, which is now known as Jersey City, Clinton's redcoats had built a fort.

In addition to Lee's 300, a reserve force of Stirling's men came behind him. The people of the region did not pay much attention as the force marched along because large foraging parties were often abroad in the country trying to find food for men and horses. But at three in the morning on August 19, Major Lee carefully arranged his men and advanced quietly on the fort. The sentinels were in their places, but had dozed off in a sense of false security that arose from having lived some time without fighting.

Before anyone in the fort knew what was happening, Lee had seized 150 redcoats, and the rest had hastily run into the middle of the fort. Rather than attacking the well-fortified position with

Image from the book, *Son of Light-Horse Harry*.

Discretion shall preserve thee, understanding shall keep thee: Lee used discretion by knowing when to attack and when to withdraw. He received honor for making the wise decision.

— Proverbs 2:11

Major "Light Horse Harry" Lee

his small company, Lee wisely withdrew with his prisoners. Congress awarded him a gold medal for this gallant deed.

The following year, Lee accompanied Mad Anthony Wayne and his troops in an attack on the blockhouse at Bergen Neck in an attempt to drive off some cattle the British held there and take them back to the hungry American army. They did not have with them heavy guns to break through the walls of the blockhouse, but they did succeed in capturing a large number of cattle.

In the summer of that year a large British force crossed from Staten Island in New York to Elizabethtown in New Jersey and started out to drive Washington's army from their camp at Morristown. But they were of course seen by local patriots and the alarm was carried out by several riders. A cannon called "the old sow," placed on a hilltop for just such an emergency, was fired. Quickly a crowd of men and boys appeared to harass the British with gunfire from behind trees and stone walls. Soon the redcoats had had enough and returned to where they had started.

A few days later, Clinton led another British force out with the same goal in mind. But the patriot farmers and militia stopped them at Springfield, where they occupied high ground and fought so savagely that again the redcoats turned back. Washington's camp at Morristown was left alone for the time.

Give 'em Watts, Boys!

Now we turn to one of the very sad stories of the War of Independence. The Reverend James Caldwell, pastor of the Presbyterian Church in Elizabethtown, served as a chaplain in the American army. Before the war, he had been an energetic advocate for independence. Perhaps his family's history of suffering religious persecution, both in Europe and more recently in the British colonies in America, had bred in him a powerful love of freedom. During the war, he was known as "the Fighting Chaplain," and the British had issued an offer of a reward for his capture. While serving in his home pulpit, he was sometimes known to place pistols on either side of his Bible and have a row of muskets leaning against the wall in case of attack by redcoats or Tories. Thanks to his fervent preaching before and during the war, his church supplied 31 officers and 52 enlisted soldiers to the American army. Caldwell himself was elected chaplain of the third New Jersey brigade and served under Colonel Elias Dayton, a member of his church.

Storytime with Uncle Rick

America's Struggle

As popular as he was among the patriots, Caldwell was just as hated among the British. They called him "the rebel high priest."

As chaplain, Caldwell went wherever the army went. This gave him opportunity to minister not only to the soldiers, but also to civilians in nearby towns. He preached, ministered at funerals, and performed baptisms. As in his hometown, he quickly gained a reputation for his powerful, heartfelt preaching.

A night raid on Elizabethtown by the British left the courthouse and the Presbyterian church in ashes. Caldwell lost many personal papers and church records. When the fighting came close to home, Caldwell sent his large family to a house in a safer area. But in 1780, the British army was coming closer to this place as well. Caldwell asked his wife to quickly find another place for her and her children while he must stay with the army.

But Hannah Caldwell did not want to move again. Perhaps she felt safer in her house in a village than out on the open road. Whatever her reasons may have been, she sent her older children to stay with friends and stayed at home with her youngest children. "They will respect a mother," she repeatedly said.

But one day a company of Hessians came marching by the house. Mrs. Caldwell retreated to a back room with her baby. One soldier jumped the fence and strode up to the window. Seeing Hannah inside, he fired his musket through the window, shattering glass and sending a ball through the young mother's chest. As her baby screamed in terror, she died on the floor. Other soldiers rushed into the house, stealing valuables and smashing furniture. Mrs. Caldwell's body was carried outside and later the house was torched. She lay outdoors for several hours before the Hessians left and sympathetic neighbors carried her away for burial.

The murder of this minister's wife incensed both the army and the people of the community. Parson Caldwell threw himself harder than ever into the cause of freedom. During the battle at Springfield, the soldiers ran low on wadding for their muskets. Wadding was a small patch of rag or paper in which the bullet was rammed down the barrel of the musket. The gun would not fire properly without it. So Caldwell rushed to a nearby church and returned amid the fighting, his arms loaded down with Watts' hymnals. He quickly passed out the books, shouting, "Give 'em Watts, boys! Put Watts into 'em!"

"GIVE THEM WATTS, BOYS!"

Give 'em Watts, boys!

James Caldwell did not survive the war. On November 24, 1781, he was coming off a ship on which he had business. Because he was carrying a bag, he was stopped by an American sentry named James Morgan. Sentries had been ordered to be watchful for British goods being smuggled on ships. Caldwell stopped at Morgan's order, but Morgan shot him anyway.

Morgan was tried for murder. There were rumors that Morgan had some connection with the British and had been influenced by them to kill Caldwell. Though the British connection was not proven, Morgan was still found guilty and hanged.

CALDWELL OF NEW JERSEY
By Bret Harte

HERE 's the spot. Look around you. Above on the height.
Lay the Hessians encamped. By that church on the right
Stood the gaunt Jersey farmers. And here ran a wall —
You may dig anywhere and you'll turn up a ball.
Nothing more. Grasses spring, waters run, flowers blow,
Pretty much as they did ninety-three years ago.

Nothing more, did I say? Stay one moment; you've heard
Of Caldwell, the parson, who once preached the Word
Down at Springfield? What, no? Come — that 's bad, why he had
All the Jerseys aflame! And they gave him the name
Of the "rebel high-priest." He stuck in their gorge,
For he loved the Lord God — and he hated King George!

He had cause, you might say! When the Hessians that day
Marched up with Knyphausen they stopped on their way
At the "Farms," where his wife, with a child in her arms,
Sat alone in the house. How it happened none knew
But God — and that one of the hireling crew
Who fired the shot! Enough! — there she lay,
And Caldwell, the chaplain, her husband, away!

Did he bear it — what way? Think of him as you stand
By the old church to-day — think of him and that band
Of militant ploughboys! See the smoke and the heat
Of that reckless advance — of that straggling retreat!
Keep the ghost of that wife, foully slain, in your view —
And what could you, what should you, what would you do?

Why, just what he did! They were left in the lurch
For the want of more wadding. He ran to the church,
Broke the door, stripped the pews, and dashed out in the road
With his arms full of hymn-books, and threw down his load
At their feet! then above all the shouting and shots,
Rang his voice — "Put Watts into 'em — Boys, give 'em Watts!"

And they did. That is all. Grasses spring, flowers blow
Pretty much as they did ninety-three years ago.
You may dig anywhere and you'll turn up a ball —
But not always a hero like this — and that's all.

Wilhelm von Knyphausen

THE TREASON OF BENEDICT ARNOLD

The year 1780 was a melancholy year. The army and the populace were discouraged by the lack of progress toward independence. In May, the 5,000-man force in Charleston, South Carolina, had fallen to the British in a huge blow to American morale. Meanwhile, small skirmishes in the north and the frequent raiding by foraging soldiers and outlaws who thrived on the confusion of wartime kept the country around the army encampments in a constant state of tension. The deaths and suffering of innocent civilians such as Hannah Caldwell added to the general air of discouragement.

In addition to all this, economic problems were rampant. Congress had voted to print paper money, but the currency was losing its value. The British had printed loads of counterfeit bills that looked exactly like continental money. Then they spread this fake money liberally throughout the colonies. Soon, Continental money was worth only a fraction of its original worth. Few people

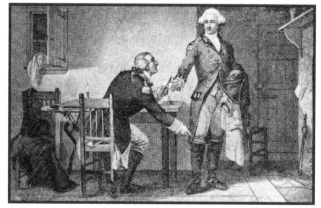

The Treason of Benedict Arnold

Peggy Shippen (wife of Benedict Arnold) with one of her children, possibly her daughter Sophia

dared to accept it as payment for fear it was fake. Everyone who owned it grew poorer.

Just when it seemed that the young nation and its hard-pressed leaders had all they could possibly bear, another blow fell. Benedict Arnold, an American general and hero of several hard-fought battles, turned traitor.

You will remember that it was Arnold at Saratoga who, without permission from Gates, galloped into the battle, rallied his comrades, and gloriously won the day. You also remember that when Gates wrote his letter to Congress reporting on the battle, he gave himself all the credit for the victory, though he had done nearly nothing to win it. It was this, and similar instances of watching others get the credit and rewards when he was more deserving, that tipped Arnold toward becoming a turncoat.

In 1778, Arnold was given command of Philadelphia. The British General Clinton had withdrawn from the city, and a small American force was left to hold it. Arnold, still recovering from a serious wound in his leg and therefore unfit for combat duty, was placed in charge.

Congress returned to the city, and this brought opportunities for Arnold to dispute with its members over the government's failure to reward his service. Indeed, he had a valid argument. But his natural energy and hot temper increased the tension between the two parties.

So it was that handsome, popular Arnold spent months in Philadelphia making friends among the citizens and enemies in Congress. He was also incurring debts, for he loved high living and circulating among the "best" families of the city. It was from one of these families, who were Tory sympathizers, that he took a wife, beautiful young Peggy Shippen.

Benedict Arnold's craving for glory was part of the reason for his disloyalty. He resented the fact that he had not received enough praise for the great things he had done on the battlefield. Rather than trying to get praise for himself, he should have left it to God. God's way is not for us to seek praise or praise ourselves.

"Let another man praise thee, and not thine own mouth; a stranger, and not thine own lips." —Proverbs 27:2

It is not known exactly what part Peggy may have taken in the plot that Arnold hatched. What is known is that he managed to get himself appointed by Washington to the command of the fort at West Point on the Hudson River, and to make an agreement with the redcoat General Clinton to turn that fort over to the British. This would have been a terrible blow to the patriots, as West Point was critical in preventing British ships from using the great river as a waterway.

Had Arnold been a man of Washington's high character, he would have borne the abuse he had suffered with patience and humility. Time would have proven to the nation that he was indeed worthy of promotion and no doubt great honors would have come to him eventually. But bitter, proud, and under pressure to pay heavy debts, he chose instead to negotiate a deal with General Clinton that would reward him with a large sum of money and the rank of brigadier general in the British army.

Why was West Point so important? Located on a sharp bend on the Hudson River, the fort had big guns commanding the river all the way across. Had the British captured it, they would have had control of the entire river and a waterway from Canada to New York, which would have split the colonies in two. It was something for which the British were willing to pay generously.

Arnold's messenger between himself and Clinton was a British officer, Major John Andre. After months of negotiation, Arnold and Clinton had finally arranged the details of their agreement. Then, in September of 1780, Andre sailed at night up the river on the *Vulture*. On the shore he was met by Benedict Arnold. Arnold gave him papers to take to Clinton. These papers included maps of West Point's defenses, which Arnold had allowed to fall into disrepair. He had also scattered his forces so that the British could attack the fort and take it without trouble. After an hours-long conference, Andre placed the papers inside his shoes, and the two men parted.

The *Vulture*, however, was not where she had been. Patriot marksmen had been firing at her from the shore and causing alarm even though it was dark, so she had drifted a distance farther down the river to get out of their range. Now Andre could not return to New York on the boat, but he was supplied with a pass signed by Arnold and began to make his way toward White Plains on horseback.

Andre expected to encounter British outposts, but it was his misfortune to be stopped by three American sentries. Believing them to be Tories, he identified himself as a British soldier. The men captured him and searched him, finding the papers in his shoes. Even though he had a pass signed by Arnold and identifying him as "John Anderson . . . being on public business by my direction" they refused to let him go. He offered them a bribe of 400 guineas, but still they refused and took him to Colonel Jameson. Jameson, never dreaming that his brave commander had any part in the espionage, forwarded the papers with a letter to General Arnold.

Capture of Andre

Arnold's Escape

The package found Arnold in his quarters. His young wife and their baby had just joined him two days earlier, and they sat at breakfast along with some of the other young American officers. General Washington himself was expected to join them soon. Opening the letter, Arnold quickly saw that his plot was about to be discovered. He excused himself from the table and went to his room, frantically planning his escape. He called young Peggy to join him, and quickly told her of his danger. She screamed and fainted in his arms. Quickly he laid her on the bed and kissed their baby. There was no time to do more for her. He rushed from the house and mounted his horse. Galloping down a little-used path toward the river, he was taken aboard a barge and rowed 18 miles down the river to the *Vulture*. Once aboard, he was safe.

Now he must care for his wife. He wrote a letter to General Washington, confessing his crime and declaring that his young wife had no knowledge or part in the plot. He begged Washington to allow Peggy to return to her family in Philadelphia or to join him on the *Vulture* if she desired.

This letter and the captured papers made the treachery clear to Washington. He talked to the hysterical young wife personally, but she was beside herself with grief, shock, and terror. All he could get from her were tears and sobs, but after he received the letter from Arnold, the great, kind-hearted general assured Peggy that her husband was safe among the British.

Andre, on the other hand was not safe. Though he tried to portray himself simply as a British officer attempting to corrupt an American general, he was wearing civilian clothing and carrying secret

Escape of Benedict Arnold

messages. He was convicted of spying and sentenced to be hung. He begged General Washington to be shot by a firing squad as a soldier instead of suffering the shameful noose, but was sadly refused. With such a plot discovered, the entire American nation was fearful and suspicious. Only the most serious measures could be accepted.

Last Moments of Major Andre

When the noose was around his neck, the brave young Britisher was asked if he had anything to say. Like Nathan Hale, he faced death with courage. He replied,

> I pray you to bear me witness that I meet my fate like a brave man.[61]

Andre's execution had been delayed until October 2. In the days between his capture and his death, his courage and manners had made him a favorite of the American officers who dealt with him. He had walked to the noose arm-in-arm with two of them. In the moments both before and after his execution, many in the crowd were in tears.

Mrs. Arnold went first to Philadelphia, but people there believed that she had been a part of her husband's plot. After all, her family members were known to be loyal to the king. Ordered to leave the city, she traveled by coach to meet her husband, who was now in New York. All along the way she had the unpleasant experience of seeing her husband hanged and burned in effigy. In one town, the "celebration" was just being prepared as she entered the town in her coach. Out of sympathy for her, the observance was delayed until she had traveled on. After the war, she lived with her husband in New Brunswick, Canada, and later in England. Sadly, neither she nor her children would ever outlive the shame of bearing the name of a traitor.

After the war, Arnold and his family lived in both England and Canada, but Arnold's lack of character and reputation for treachery followed the family for the rest of his life and beyond. He was involved in a number of questionable business deals, and suffered in other ways from not being known as a trustworthy man. It is well to learn from examples like Arnold. It takes years to build a reputation of virtue and only a few acts to tear it down.

Washington visiting the ill.

CHAPTER 22

SUFFERING SOLDIERS

SUFFERING IN THE CAMPS

The soldier's life in the northern camps of the American army during the year of 1781 was always difficult and sometimes agonizing. War has been described as "long periods of boredom punctuated by short periods of abject terror."[62] For the Continental army in those days there was little of terror but much of other agonies.

There were few active engagements with the enemy because each side seemed determined only to hold the last position it had taken. The British sat in New York, the Americans in the Hudson highlands and the hills of New Jersey. The long inactivity ground on the soldiers' nerves, and many must have wondered why they were there.

Washington at Valley Forge

In addition to this, they had received little of the pay that was due them. And when they were paid, it was in Continental currency that lost much of its value because of the large quantities of counterfeit money the redcoats in New York printed and distributed through the countryside. Camp life was a life of hunger, exposure, homesickness, boredom, and despair. As the years crawled by, the end of the war seemed as far away as it had in the very early days of the struggle. Men huddled in threadbare tents or huts of logs or stone, all poor protection from the elements.

Washington wrote to a friend describing the trials of the army's life. He said that the men were sometimes five or six days without bread, and many days without meat. A time or two, they had been without either for two or three days. He told

Washington loved his soldiers! How it hurt him to see them suffer. Worse yet, he had to punish them for foraging when he knew how hungry they were. It is a terrible thing to be at war. Sometimes it requires a leader to use harsh discipline even though he sympathizes with his men. George Washington was a giant among men, able to do very hard things in view of the "big picture." He never forgot that his army had to succeed in order to fulfill the dream of freedom.

General Henry Knox

how he had thought it impossible to continue holding the army together, how in fact it would have fallen apart had not the community leaders of various counties appealed to the citizens for such provisions as they could spare. For a time, the soldiers ate bread made of horse feed — Indian corn, buckwheat, rye, and wheat. Washington went on to express his wonder that, though there had been a few desertions, there had been no general mutiny.

Starving, freezing, sleeping five or six men together with one blanket each and a mattress of crumbling straw, the men suffered through the winter months together. Sometimes provisions were available, but held back from delivery to the army by several feet of snow on the roads. Under these circumstances it is not hard to understand why men slipped out of camp to go on unauthorized foraging trips. Washington began to get complaints from neighboring farmers that their chickens, ducks, pigs, and even cattle were being stolen by starving soldiers. Of course, the commander could not allow this to go on, for if the farmers were ruined there would be no one to supply the army, and then everybody would be hungry. The army would have to disband.

So the strictest actions were taken to compel the starving men to stop foraging. In a few cases, repeat offenders were executed. Usually, the punishment was a public whipping. The number of stripes given depended upon the seriousness of the offense. There was always a fair trial, but the punishment was harsh. Up to a hundred lashes might be given on a man's bare back, each stroke of the knotted cords cutting through flesh. For some reason, the fifers and drummers were assigned the unpleasant task of administering the punishment. Sometimes a man under punishment would bite down on a bullet between his teeth to keep from crying out from the awful pain. It was noticed that sometimes the bullet would end up flattened and jagged when the whipping was over.

Cheerfulness is choosing to have a good attitude even when circumstances are tough to bear and uplifting others. "Rejoice in the Lord always: and again I say, Rejoice" (Phillipians 4:4). These patriots' wives didn't have to go to camp. They did it of their own will to make hard circumstances more tolerable for the soldiers.

The harshness of camp life was relieved from time to time by celebrations and festivals of sorts. Many of these were planned by the sympathetic wives of the officers, many of whom suffered without along with their husbands for as much time as they could possibly be away from home.

The wife of General Henry Knox is kindly remembered for the "parties" and "functions" she organized for the men. And the cheerful, courageous, and patient way Mrs. Nathanael Greene bore the hardships of army life was much noticed and admired by the soldiers. It was said that that kind lady had nearly as much influence on the men of the army as she had on her husband.

They celebrated special days, such as the Fourth of July and the anniversary of the alliance with France. Parades took place, featuring the effigies of prominent Tories or Britishers. One might see the image of King George or Lord North, the British prime minister, carried along in the procession with glee, to be burned in bonfires after dark. Sometimes these celebrations lasted well into the night hours.

But hunger, deprivation, despair, and the failure to receive their pay finally boiled over into outright rebellion. It happened first among the Pennsylvania troops. These men, about 2,000 in number, were suffering through the winter near Morristown. Desperate in their hunger and suffering, they at last decided that they must revolt against their officers.

The Mutiny

These soldiers had suffered all the same hardships as the rest of the army, but they had an additional complaint. When these men had first enlisted in the army, they had signed on rolls that specified a term of enlistment of either three years or the duration of the war. Since the enlisting officers had not dreamed that the war would continue more than three years, they had not been strictly careful about explaining the terms of enlistment or directing the recruit to the proper column on which to sign his name. The result was that many men who had signed up for a three-year enlistment were not allowed to go home at the end of the three years. They were told instead that their enlistment had been for the remainder of the war.

Even the officers among the Pennsylvania troops were feeling mistreated, and some of them allowed their complaints to be heard by the men. Because they felt the same way as the enlisted men felt, they were less strict in their discipline than they should have been. The mutterings of revolt grew louder.

On the first day of 1781, the mutiny began. The men had selected a sergeant major for their commander and called him a major general. On a prearranged signal, all the men except a part of three regiments, formed up with their weapons. Without their officers, they marched to the magazines and took a supply

201

of provisions and ammunitions. They took six cannons and horses from General Wayne's stable to pull them.

Mad Anthony Wayne

The officers collected all the men who had not mutinied, and tried to use this force to restore order. But the mutineers fired a volley that killed Captain Billing and several other officers. Several of the mutinous soldiers were killed as well. The mutineers then ordered the soldiers who had not rebelled with them to come over to their side or be bayoneted. The outnumbered men did so.

Mad Anthony Wayne, commander of the Pennsylvania troops, tried to reason with the men, using his authority and influence to get them to return to duty until their grievances could be addressed through the proper channels. They would not listen, so he cocked his pistol as if to threaten the ringleaders. Instantly several bayonets were presented against him. The men said,

> We respect and love you; often have you led us into the field of battle, but we are no longer under your command; we warn you to be on your guard; if you fire your pistols or attempt to enforce your command, we shall put you instantly to death.[63]

Wayne protested that they were about to sacrifice the cause of their country; that the enemy would soon find out about this rebellion and move to take advantage of it by attacking the Americans. The men replied that they were still loyal to the cause of independence and that if attacked they would take the field under the command of Wayne and his officers to fight heroically. But they repeated their complaints that they had received no pay for over a year, that their clothing was worn out, that they were starving, and that they had been taken advantage of in respect to their terms of enlistment. They told him they intended to march on Philadelphia and take their grievances to Congress.

So off they marched, in regular military order. When they camped at night, they were careful to station pickets. To prevent them from stealing private property in order to eat, General Wayne supplied them with such rations as he could. He and two other officers accompanied the men on their march. These two men were Colonels Stewart and Butler, officers loved and respected by the men. The three officers carefully mixed among the men, observing their behavior and listening to their views. They were treated with civility and respect by the men.

On the third day of their march, they reached Princeton. Here, General Wayne requested that they bring their claims to him in writing. They did so, sending three sergeants as a delegation. They made three demands:

☆ First, a discharge for all those who had enlisted for three years and had not reenlisted and received the bonus for doing so

☆ Second, an immediate payment of all their back pay and clothing

☆ The rest of the bonus they had been promised for enlisting and appropriate future pay for those who remained in the army.

General Wayne, of course, did not have the authority or the means to agree to these demands, so he referred the men to the civil authorities in their home state.

Meanwhile, at his headquarters on the Hudson, General Washington received news of the mutiny and called a council of war to figure out a solution. He and his officers had a great fear that other troops, having much the same reason to complain as the Pennsylvanians, would mutiny as well.

There is no doubt that the patriot soldiers of Pennsylvania were suffering. General Washington, General Wayne, and their other officers understood that, and were suffering with them. Often people have rebelled under much less difficult circumstances than those faced by the Continental army. Let's be very careful of our words so that we aren't part of the problem in tough times, instead of part of the solution.

These developments did not go unnoticed in the British camp. When Sir Henry Clinton heard of it, he immediately began searching for a way to use the rebellion to turn the swords of the patriots against each other. He quickly sent two messengers to the dissatisfied Pennsylvanians with a message that if they would lay down their arms and march to New York they would be received as friends and brothers. He promised that they would be given all their back pay in hard cash. They would be well clothed, pardoned for all past offenses, and protected by the British government. No military service would be required of them, although they were welcome in the British army if they chose to volunteer.

How hard it must have been for the poor, starving soldiers to turn down Clinton's offer! Yet they loved their country and their neighbors more than themselves.

The offer must have sounded attractive to hungry, poor, exhausted men. But still, it was scornfully rejected by the Americans. Desperate they were, but they were still patriots. The mutineers delivered the written messages to General Wayne but refused to give up the messengers, preferring to hold them until their grievances could be settled.

A committee of Congress was appointed to look into the matter, and they conferred with the executive council of the state of Pennsylvania. That council worked out an agreement that was accepted by the rebellious troops. Some of them were discharged after swearing that they had indeed enlisted only for three years.

Washington had been right in worrying that the actions of the Pennsylvania men would soon be copied by other troops, who had the same problems as the Pennsylvanians did. On January 20, some New Jersey troops declared that they too, were about to leave the army. Washington knew that he had to act fast and decisively. These men also had reasonable complaints, but if they were not brought back into line immediately, he knew he would lose his entire army. Desperate measures must be taken.

In Numbers 11, the people of Israel are complaining against God. They seem to have forgotten that He had delivered them form a cruel bondage. All they seem to remember about Egypt is that they had more to eat there. Now they are complaining against God even though He is supplying them miraculously with food. They're tired of manna and they want meat. So God gives them what they want — millions of quail, blown in by the wind cover the ground. Soon everybody is eating meat. But they are also getting sick. Perhaps they ate too much, or perhaps the quail had a virus of some sort that affected humans. In any case, God gave them what they asked for and they found that they were worse off than before. It is not wise to ignore problems, but it is never wise to accuse God of not treating us fairly. He always knows things that we don't.

The commander ordered a Massachusetts brigade to march from West Point to Pompton, where the rebellion was rising. The soldiers responded quickly and appeared at Pompton so suddenly that the mutiny was quickly over. Two of the leaders were sentenced to be shot. That resolved the issue and though Washington was greatly pained to have to use such harsh measures, there was no other way to keep his army from falling to pieces.

In the Prisons

As bad as the suffering was in the patriot camps, there were other soldiers whose plight was even more miserable. These were the Americans who had been captured in battle and were now languishing in British prisons.

Prisoner custody was a problem for both countries during the war. Other than holding prisoners indefinitely, the options were few. Sometimes, especially on the American side, large numbers of prisoners were allowed to go free on parole, which simply means they gave a solemn promise that they would not take up arms again as long as the war lasted.

The Old Bridewell prison.

Sometimes prisoner exchanges could be arranged. When officers were involved, normally one army would exchange a prisoner of a certain rank to get back one of their own officers of the same rank. Occasionally, a large group of enlisted men would be exchanged for an equal number of enlisted men. Without question, the British army was much harder on prisoners than the Americans were. Washington even issued orders for his army to treat prisoners with as much consideration as its own soldiers were treated. On the other hand, King George had issued orders declaring all "rebels" to be traitors, and therefore not eligible for treatment as prisoners of war according to the laws of war. This led to severe neglect and routine abuse of prisoners. Normally, traitors were hung. But the British did not usually resort to hanging, for fear it would result in the same treatment for their men who were being held prisoner by the Americans.

Another prison in New York was the New Bridewell, used to house privates from the Continental and militia units. Oliver Woodruff spent the winter in the New Bridewell prison, where he "never saw any fire except what was in the lamps of the city. There was not a pane of glass in the windows and nothing to keep out the cold but the Iron Gate." Three sugarhouses along the waterfront area of New York, which were used to store rum, sugar, and molasses were converted into prisons for the British. Van Courtland's, Rhinelander's, and Liberty Street sugarhouses were commandeered and refitted into prisons. The largest and most infamous of the three was the five-story Liberty Street building. The Liberty Street prison was spacious and Spartan, but lacked adequate sanitary facilities. These sugarhouses tended to be dirty, too hot in summer, and too cold in winter.[64]

In New York City, churches, warehouses, and sugar houses had been turned into houses of confinement and were packed with suffering men, yet these prisoners were far more fortunate than the men who ended up in the holds of British prison ships.

The old Sugar House & Middle Dutch Church, by George Hayward, 1858 (PD-US).

These floating jails were ships that had become unfit for battle and so had been anchored near New York City, where they were overcrowded with the unfortunate men who had fallen into the hands of the redcoats. Some of these ships were the *Hunter, Good Hope, Prince of Wales, Whitby, Scorpion*, and the *Falmouth*. But the worst one, the one most detested by every decent human being who knew what she was like was the *Jersey*.

Every night, the guards would cry, "Down, rebels, down!" and the men would be driven down into the hold where the filth, foul air, and crowding were unbearable. In the morning the call came, "Rebels, bring up your dead!" and the dead would be brought up. They would be wrapped in a blanket, if a blanket was available, then buried in shallow graves on the Long Island shore.

The food was horrible, and there was little of it. The guards were brutal. It was said that over 11,000 prisoners died on board that awful ship. Most attempts at escape were not successful, but conditions were so terrible on the *Jersey* that men kept trying.

One young prisoner was taken to the shore to get water. While the guard watched, the half-starved young man dipped the heavy wooden bucket into the spring and started back to the skiff. Suddenly, he swung the bucket and knocked down the guard, then sprinted toward the nearby woods. The guard stumbled to his feet and fired his gun at the fleeing prisoner. He missed his target, but the noise alerted other guards.

The chase began, and soon the desperate young patriot was running frantically through the woods with the redcoat guards crashing through the brush behind him. Reaching a road, he had to hide himself for hours at a time behind stone walls, in barns, among the woods, and any place that offered a brief shelter. Knocking at a farmhouse to beg for help, he was nearly captured. He moved on in desperation until finally, nearly exhausted, he was taken in by a kindly Quaker woman who put him in bed and then baked his filthy prison clothes in her oven. The next day, her husband took the young fugitive down to the bay and found a boat in which he rowed him over to the Connecticut shore and safety at last.

The *Jersey* prison ship

A group of four men successfully escaped by seizing a skiff that had brought some visitors out to the ship. They were fired upon as they hastily rowed away, but none of them was killed. A larger group of prisoners tried to escape one bitter winter day by running across the ice. A few of them got away, but several froze to death, too weak from starvation to get to shore.

Escape was rare, and the guards on shore were so numerous that it was very hard to get away. There were frequent visits from British recruiters who offered the men a chance to escape their chains by joining the redcoat army. They told the prisoners that their comrades were steadily being defeated anyway, so there was no purpose in remaining in prison. Very few of the Americans ever accepted the offer, preferring to suffer and die in the black hold of a rotten ship rather than betray their country.

Launching of the *Prince of Wales*, Man of War at Portmouth.

Storytime with Uncle Rick

America's Struggle

There were several women in the Setauket spy chain that operated during the revolution and kept General Washington supplied with information regarding the movements of the British troops in New York and on Long Island.

One of the most interesting stories concerns Ann Smith Strong (she was called Nancy in the spy records), wife of Judge Selah Strong, who lived in Setauket. The British army was having a great deal of trouble with American saboteurs and anyone who rode about very much out of uniform was suspected of unfriendly intentions. The Setauket Spy Ring began in 1778 and operated for six years. The spies were never found out by the British. Actually, their identities were kept secret for over 150 years until historian Morton Pennypacker broke their code. He wrote a book called *George Washington's Spies on Long Island and in New York*. The majority of the letters in the spy ring were written by Abraham Woodhull and much of their work helped to reveal the treason of Benedict Arnold and led to the capture of Major Andre.

Nancy Strong played a large part in informing Abraham Woodhull. Robert Townsend was a patriot disguised as a redcoat. He would talk to British generals in a tearoom in New York City and then write a letter sharing information to be delivered to George Washington. A Setauket innkeeper, Austin Roe, would ride to New York to pick up supplies, collect the letters, and when back in Setauket, hide them in a hollow tree near Abraham Woodhull's farm. A whaleboat manned by Caleb Brewster was to take the secret messages across the sound to General Washington. Nancy signaled the location of the whaleboat to Abraham Woodhull, who was a neighbor and could see her clothesline from his house. He would collect the letter and deliver it to Caleb Strong, who would then row it across Long Island Sound to Fairfield, Connecticut.

Since Caleb Brewster was a well-known figure in Setauket, it was not safe for him to always land his boat in the same spot, so he had six landing places. Abraham Woodhull could not always know whether Brewster was in the village or

at which landing place his boat was hid, so Nancy made it her business to keep track of him and passed this information on to Woodhull through her clothesline. Most of the petticoats worn by the women in those days were red, so if Mr. Woodhull saw a black petticoat waving on Nancy's clothesline he knew Brewster was in town. Each of the landing places had a number, and by counting the handkerchiefs hanging on Nancy's clothesline he knew at which landing place Mr. Brewster's boat was hidden. The great-great granddaughter of Nancy's son Thomas told the story to her children and said it was Nancy's son Thomas who she sent daily to look for the whereabouts of the whaleboat. She didn't let him know why she wanted to know for his own protection as he was often stopped by the British occupying the area. When he'd return with the information she would hang her petticoats and handkerchiefs on the clothesline to alert Abraham Woodhull.

Nancy was not discovered by the British, but her husband, Judge Strong, was arrested for "surreptitious correspondence with the enemy,"[65] and thrown into prison on one of the worst British prison ships. Nancy got permission to visit him and took a boat load of food, which probably saved his life and the lives of other prisoners. Later on she secured his release, probably by supplying the British with food from her farm in exchange for her husband. Judge Strong then had to flee to Connecticut for safety and remain there until the end of the war. Nancy's place in the spy ring was an important one, and she occupies a front place in the line of Colonial America's great women.[66]

Colonel Cleveland's
War Prize

CHAPTER 23

THE WAR IN THE SOUTH

MILITIA BATTLES

In the later years of the struggle for independence, although the sufferings of the people in the northern colonies was great, the majority of the active battles took place in the south. King George had failed in conquering the people of New England. Next, he tried to regain control over the middle states but found them just as hard to manage. The British had won many victories in both regions, but some of them had been costly in terms of men and material expended. In addition, the spirits of the Americans had not been crushed by their defeats. Rather, they seemed more determined than ever to fight and rid themselves of the redcoat invaders.

British Map of Southern Colonies

But the British were also very determined. Failing to bring the north and middle regions to their knees, they now moved the bulk of their operations to the south. There were but few cities in the south, where the people were more scattered in lonely homesteads and small settlements. There were large numbers of Tories who could be recruited to fight against their neighbors, and the slave population was quite large. If the redcoats could persuade the slaves to revolt against their masters, there would be a considerable force to ally with the king's regulars to conquer the southern territory. Then, even if he ended up losing the war, His Majesty would have a good chance of holding on to his colonies in the south at least.

Kings Mountain was a unique Revolutionary War battle because it was one of the only battles during the war fought entirely between Americans. There were no British troops serving there. Many of those living in the South at the time were divided, so some fought for independence and others for loyalty to England. When Major Patrick Ferguson came to crush the rebels in the area of Kings Mountain, Colonel Benjamin Cleveland rallied his militiamen into fight. Cleveland's horse was shot out from under him, and so he later took Major Ferguson's white horse as his "war prize," for Ferguson had died in the battle (www.nps.gov/kimo/moreintroinfo.htm).

The Maternal Homestead

There was strong feeling in the south on both sides of the independence question. Most men, whether Whigs or Tories, held firmly to their convictions. This made the fighting very bitter between the two sides. Then, as the British tallied up more victories and their Tory allies committed more outrages on the civilian population, the patriots grew all the more determined. Nor was all the abuse on the Tory side. Sometimes Tories, falling into the hands of the independence party, suffered rough treatment as well. Still, in areas where the British were in control, Tory depredations usually far exceeded those committed by patriots in American-controlled territory. The result of all of this was that the record of the war in the south tells of instances of robbery, murder, and cruelty as well as honorable combat in open battle.

In the fall of 1778, two groups of Tories moved quickly and unexpectedly into Georgia from eastern Florida. One party marched overland to attack the little garrison at Midway, while the other traveled by boat toward Sunbury. Arriving at Sunbury, they sent a demand for surrender to the commander, Colonel McIntosh. He sent back their messenger with the curt reply that

> "if the redcoats wanted the place, they must come and take it."

The loyalists may not have been expecting such firm resistance, or perhaps they felt that their numbers were not sufficient for the task of taking Sunbury. At any rate, they turned around and marched back to Florida.

The other group kept on going, though they were badgered along the way by small groups of patriot militia that fired at them from cover. But when they finally found themselves at the Ogeechee River they were faced by a force of 200 Continentals prepared to deny them a crossing. In addition to that threat, they received a message that a force of angry patriots was on its way from South Carolina. They gave up the expedition and turned back.

On the homeward march, they stopped at the village of Midway and took out their frustration on that patriot community. They destroyed the crops in the fields, burned every dwelling, led away the slaves, and stole all the horses and valuables they could find.

The leader of the patriots in the region was General Robert Howe. Howe determined to strike back at the Tory forces, so he collected and led a force of 2,000 men to St. Augustine, carrying the war into the enemy's country. But a wave of terrible sickness broke out among his men just as he prepared to attack, so he had to retreat in order to save his army from a danger greater than they would have encountered in battle.

General Clinton now decided to attack the south in force. He set his sights on Savannah, Georgia, as his first major conquest. He ordered General Prevost from eastern Florida to advance on Savannah with his men, while Colonel Campbell was bringing a force of 2,500 men from New York on the fleet of Sir Hyde Parker. The fleet arrived on December 23, 1778, and in a few days the redcoats were safely landed.

General Robert Howe was now given the task of defending Georgia, but there he had only a force of about 600 Continentals and perhaps 250 militiamen. He took the best position he could find near Savannah, surrounded by the river on one side and dense swamps on the other. The only approach to his position was a frontal assault against solid fortifications.

Colonel Archibald Campbell, by George Romney, c.1790 (PD-Art).

Howe thought that even outnumbered as he was, he could hold his position. This was because of the work of a local slave. This man knew a path through the swamps that led to the rear of the patriot position. He reported this to the British, then leading the way himself, he guided one redcoat force to the American rear while another company attacked the frontal exposure. Caught between two attacking forces, the Americans were nearly wiped out. Around 100 of their men were killed and 450 taken prisoner. All the guns, ammunition, and stores fell into the hands of the redcoats. A few Continentals escaped, and these made their way into South Carolina. Georgia was in the hands of the British. What made the rout even more bitter to the American memory was the fact that when Savannah fell, 2,000 patriots were marching from North Carolina to help them.

Now the redcoats made their headquarters at Augusta and Ebenezer. From these centers they sent out recruiters to incite the Tories of the region to rise up and fight for the king. Their efforts were successful, but it was not only honorable loyalists who turned out. There are many opportunities for troublemaking during the lawless seasons of war, and a number of criminals and desperate men joined with the British, eager for a chance to rob and pillage. Soon crowds of ruffians were committing crimes and depredations of all sorts under the pretense of loyally serving their king and country.

These outrages, of course, served to rouse the patriots even more. Soon brave Colonel Pickens, with a band of picked

General William Moultrie

fighters from the Ninety-six district fell upon a band of these marauders and drove them from the field in a rout. Their leader and 40 men were killed.

The origin of the name of this district is a mystery. Some believe it was named because of its distance of 96 miles from the nearest Cherokee village. Others say it has to do with early units of geographic measurement. We cannot say for sure, but the British built an earthen fort at this western South Carolina location in 1780, and Nathanael Greene led an unsuccessful siege against it in 1781.

DEFENDING SAVANNAH

As the plans of the British for a southern campaign became clear to the American leaders, they placed General Benjamin Lincoln in command of the troops there. To his regular force was added the little remnant of Howe's company and some reinforcements from North Carolina, so that his total force numbered around 2,500 men.

The redcoats had also been strengthened by the arrival of more regulars from St. Augustine. Now, encouraged by their easy capture of Savannah, they planned an attack on Port Royal Island. They landed there on February 3, 1779, but they were met by the men of William Moultrie who put up such a savage resistance that the redcoats were routed, losing nearly all their officers and a large number of men.

The depredations of the Tories in the south had so aroused the patriots that 70 of the loyalists were sentenced to die for their crimes. However, second thoughts came, and in the end only five of them were executed. The patriots realized that brutality on their part would only increase the brutality of the Tories.

> Never give up if you're doing what you know God wants you to do. Exert all your energies to the task and leave the outcome to the Lord!

The British had been extending their reach by building outposts up the river from Savannah into the inner parts of Georgia. Now, Lincoln ordered General Ashe to take his 1,500 North Carolina militiamen, along with the remnant of the Georgia Continentals, and move into that part of the country as well.

General Prevost, learning that Ashe was camped at Brier Creek, decided to attack him. First, he pretended that he was about to attack Charleston. This was to make sure Lincoln would not come to the aid of Ashe. Then Prevost moved as if to attack Ashe from the front, but quickly crossed Brier Creek with a large force and struck Ashe's company from the rear. The redcoats attacked so suddenly and furiously that the American militia fled without firing a shot. The battle-hardened Continentals held out for a little while, but they were vastly outnumbered. Soon 300 of them were shot or taken prisoner. Only about 450 made their way back to join Lincoln. The panicked militia dispersed and the men returned to their homes.

Lincoln had lost about a quarter of his army, but he was not inclined to give up. He was a veteran fighter who had been a part of the army that defeated the mighty John Burgoyne. He had been strengthened by some reinforcements, so leaving 1,000 men to garrison the forts, he led his remaining 4,000 men off to try to regain lost territory.

British General Augustine Prevost by Mather Brown, date unknown(PD-Art).

Prevost intended now to take Charleston, a very important seaport and population center. With 2,400 redcoats and many Indian allies, he marched toward the city with only the small force of Moultrie to oppose him. Moultrie, lacking the numbers to stop Prevost, instead retired toward Charleston. As he went, he burned or destroyed every bridge over the many rivers in the region in order to slow the redcoat advance.

So it was that when Prevost arrived to demand the surrender of Charleston, the city had made some preparations for defense. They were aware that Lincoln was on his way to assist them, so they held out grimly until he drew near with his army. Now, Prevost was forced to withdraw to avoid being trapped between two enemy forces. There were some small battles between patriot and British companies, but Prevost hurried back toward Savannah and little had been accomplished by either side.

There was little change in the situation until September, when French Count d'Estaing arrived with his fleet. This event gave the struggling patriots a fresh charge of hope, and with the promise of French assistance, Lincoln prepared to march on Savannah. Many of the militia now rallied to the call from Lincoln and a significant force was growing. But the British in Savannah had not been idle either, and they had been busily adding to their fortifications. When the Americans arrived and surrender was demanded, Prevost replied that he intended to defend the place to the utmost.

On October 4, the American and French guns opened on Savannah. For several days the cannonade continued, but without any sign of a willingness to surrender by the British. The militia, always confident and eager until events went against them, now shouted for an attack to be made. Finally it was, and the attacking force looked impressive. There were 3,500

Count Casimir Pulaski

French troops, about 350 militia, and some 600 Continentals. For a while they fought bravely, but at last they were beaten back. Their losses amounted to around 600 French and 240 Americans.

In the battle the brave Count Pulaski fell — the Polish officer who had come to America to help the colonies fight for freedom. This, along with their numerous losses, greatly discouraged the Americans. The militia scattered to their homes. The fleet of d'Estaing set sail back to France. The outlook was gloomy indeed.

The patriots would soon learn that their only hope of success in the south was not in opposing the trained forces of King George in the open field, but rather using small companies of raiders to attack and then fade away into the swamps. Cleverness must take the place of numbers, for numbers were not available, at least not such large numbers as it would take to defeat the British.

One such raider who had some early success in guerilla warfare was a man named Colonel John White. Even as Savannah was under siege, White captured five armed British ships with only six men who were as bold as he was himself. On the night of September 30, he set up a false camp on the banks of the Ogeechee River where the ships lay at anchor. He and his men built many campfires to convince the British sailors that a huge patriot force was nearby. Then he demanded the surrender of the ships on the threat that American cannons would quickly blow them to pieces if they resisted. The ships gave up, and White's tiny band took 140 prisoners. It was just such daring that would keep American hopes alive in the south in spite of numerical inferiority and many reverses on the field of battle.

When the news reached Clinton in New York that the French fleet had departed for home, he decided to go south himself to assist in completing the conquest that had begun with the taking of Savannah. He left the Hessian General Knyphausen in command in New York and sailed for the Carolinas. He had a rocky trip, for storms took some of his ships and he lost men and horses. But still he arrived in Charleston in February, eager to fight and conquer.

The Fall of Charleston, Defeat of Gates and the Battle of Kings Mountain

General Lincoln had returned to Charleston with the remnant of his army and had been laboring hard to improve the defenses of the town. Hundreds of slaves from the area were put to work as well as the soldiers. Receiving word that reinforcements would soon be coming from the north, Lincoln began to take heart. The few little American ships could not hope to stand against the mighty fleet of Clinton, so Lincoln had them divested of their guns, and the cannons were brought into the city to assist in its defense.

In April 1779, Clinton sent word to Lincoln that the city was being approached by land and sea and that there was no hope but to surrender. Lincoln bravely refused, and the battle began. The British lines were pulled tighter and tighter. Patriot bands who tried to come to the aid of the city were cut off. Meanwhile, 3,000 more redcoats had come from New York to swell Clinton's ranks. At last, on the 12th of May, Lincoln had no choice but to surrender. Help had not arrived, and the British guns were causing great destruction and death in the town. To resist further could only result in more misery and eventual defeat.

The "Old Fox," George Washington

Clinton was delighted over his success. The little army he had captured in Charleston was the only force of significant size that the Americans had in the south. Now he eagerly embarked on his plans to mop up. The many Tories in the state came forward to help. Clinton, ever fond of a proclamation, made one now. He offered pardon and protection to all Whigs who would return to loyalty, and rewards for the Tories who would organize to help keep order in the state.

The infamous Colonel Tarleton was sent out with cavalry and infantry to assist the Tories and stop the patriots who were reported to be marching down from North Carolina. On May 29, 1780, he met and defeated the patriot force of Colonel Buford in the battle of Waxhaws. The actions of his men on that bloody day were brutal. Most of the surrendering men were murdered with bayonets and swords. "Tarleton's quarter" became the bitter rallying cry that enraged and united the patriot resistance in the Carolinas for the remainder of the war.

After the fall of Charleston and the battle at Waxhaws, South Carolina was for the most part quiet. Clinton was deceived into believing that he had accomplished his mission and the patriot resistance would never be rebuilt. Also, there was the prospect of a French-American attack on New York. So he left Cornwallis and 4,000 men in the state and sailed back to New York to keep an eye on the "old fox," Washington.

FRANCIS MARION

Francis Marion was an American officer who was not captured at the fall of Charleston. He had been sent out of the city along with the other sick and wounded officers because he had a broken ankle from a fall. After Charleston was surrendered, Marion left his farm and hid in the swamps to keep from being captured by raiding British or Tory bands. Collecting a small company of patriot neighbors, he began guerilla warfare. His band would capture British stragglers, attack redcoat camps unexpectedly, capture horses and material, and then disappear back into the depths of the swamps.

British Colonel Banastre Tarleton chased Marion's men 26 miles one day before they dispersed and seemingly melted into the swamps. Giving up the chase in disgust and frustration, Tarleton said, "As for this old swamp fox, the devil himself could not catch him." The nickname "Swamp Fox" stuck to Marion for the remainder of the war. You can learn more about this great, brave patriot in my audiobook, *Uncle Rick Reads Marion's Men*.

Storytime with Uncle Rick

America's Struggle

People used to write poetry about historical events. You can learn much from reading historical poetry. You'll love this one about Francis Marion. Notice the reference to Marion praying.

But the quiet was only the calm before the storm. Small bands of determined patriots gathered under the leadership of another "fox," Francis Marion, and other brave guerilla leaders such as Pickens and Sumter. These bands made it their business to cut off small parties of redcoats and keep the British army so busy chasing them through the swamps that Cornwallis would not dare to weaken his force by sending large numbers of his men north to help oppose Washington.

THE SWAMP FOX

By William Gilmore Simms

We follow where the Swamp Fox guides,
His friends and merry men are we;
And when the troop of Tarleton rides,
We burrow in the cypress tree.
The turfy hammock is our bed,
Our home is in the red deer's den,
Our roof, the tree-top overhead,
For we are wild and hunted men.

We fly by day and shun its light,
But prompt to strike the sudden blow,
We mount and start with early night,
And through the forest track our foe,
And soon he hears our chargers leap,
The flashing saber blinds his eyes,
And ere he drives away his sleep,
And rushes from his camp, he dies.

Free bridle-bit, good gallant steed,
That will not ask a kind caress
To swim the Santee at our need,
When on his heels the foemen press —
The true heart and the ready hand,
The spirit stubborn to be free,
The twisted bore, the smiting brand —
And we are Marion's men, you see.

Now light the fire and cook the meal,
The last, perhaps, that we shall taste;
I hear the Swamp Fox round us steal,
And that's a sign we move in haste.
He whistles to the scouts, and hark!
You hear his order calm and low.
Come, wave your torch across the dark,
And let us see the boys that go.

We may not see their forms again,
God help 'em, should they find the strife!
For they are strong and fearless men,
And make no coward terms for life;
They'll fight as long as Marion bids,

And when he speaks the word to shy,
Then, not till then, they turn their steeds,
Through thickening shade and swamp to fly.

Now stir the fire and lie at ease -
The scouts are gone, and on the brush
I see the Colonel bend his knees,
To take his slumbers too. But hush!
He's praying, comrades; 't is not strange;
The man that's fighting day by day
May well, when night comes, take a change,
And down upon his knees to pray.

Now pile the brush and roll the log;
Hard pillow, but a soldier's head
That's half the time in brake and bog
Must never think of softer bed.
The owl is hooting to the night,
The cooter crawling o'er the bank,
And in that pond the flashing light
Tells where the alligator sank.

What! 't is the signal! start so soon,
And through the Santee swamp so deep,
Without the aid of friendly moon,
And we, Heaven help us! half asleep!

But courage, comrades! Marion leads;
The Swamp Fox takes us out to-night;
So clear your swords and spur your steeds,
There's goodly chance, I think, of fight.

We follow where the Swamp Fox guides,
We leave the swamp and cypress tree,
Our spurs are in our coursers' sides,
And ready for the strife are we.
The Tory camp is now in sight,
And there he cowers within his den;
He hears our shouts, he dreads the fight,
He fears, and flies from Marion's men.[67]

219

Ferguson showed himself to be very courageous.

Meanwhile, Congress was deciding how to help the southern colonies, and soon Delaware and Maryland troops were on their way south. They were first under the leadership of Baron de Kalb, but since he was a foreigner who did not know the men or the country well, it was decided to replace him with Horatio Gates. Gates would prove, despite his glowing reports of his own prowess against Burgoyne, that he was not up to the job.

Gates assumed command on July 27, after the army reached South Carolina. Determined to make an immediate attack, he moved his army in the direction of the British at Camden. Some militia joined him along the way, raising the number of his force slightly and creating an added burden on his supplies. Gates halted on August 13, about 13 miles from Camden. His force numbered around 3,600 men. Cornwallis was at Camden with about 2,000 men, and since many of them were sick, he did not want to risk a battle. Still, a retreat under such conditions seemed even worse, so he made plans to fight.

On the night of the 15th, Cornwallis led his men out of Camden in the hope of surprising Gates in the dark. At the same time, Gates, having sent away his sick and wounded, was moving forward, intending to find a better position. The two armies met as if by accident, and both found it an unpleasant surprise.

Gates had portrayed himself as the hero who conquered Burgoyne, but he was so badly whipped at Camden that he rode 170 miles in retreat after the battle. It took his army days to catch up with him. He was soon replaced by an excellent officer, General Nathanael Greene.

During the night, both sides held their ground, but as daylight came, the redcoats surged forward with a shout, and the green Virginia militia ran for their lives. The tough Continentals held their ground for a while, but after the militia fled they became surrounded. The retreating Continentals were chased by Tarleton for 20 miles. The Americans lost several hundred prisoners, all their cannons, and Baron de Kalb, who was one of those killed.

Fortunately for Gates, so many of Cornwallis's soldiers were sick that he decided not to follow up on his victory immediately. Gates rallied the tattered remnants of his army at Hillsboro while Cornwallis issued more proclamations threatening death to any man who had borne arms with the British and later gone over to the Americans. The order only served to harden the resolve of the patriots.

Cornwallis had dispatched Major Ferguson to cut off an American force under Colonel Clarke, which had threatened the fort at Ninety-six. As Ferguson was moving to obey this order, patriots in Virginia, North Carolina, and Tennessee were gathering to march against him. Soon there were 3,000 of them, including 1,600 on horseback, and nearly all of them expert marksmen. Finding himself unable to get away, Ferguson took a strong position on Kings Mountain, sent a message to Cornwallis asking for reinforcements, and prepared to defend himself.

The death of British Major Patrick Ferguson at the Battle of Kings Mountain by Chappel, Alonzo, 1863 (PD-US).

The frontiersmen attacked Ferguson in three columns, each ascending a different side of the mountain. Each column was driven back with bayonets, but their unerring marksmanship took its toll, and the redcoat ranks grew thinner. Finally, Ferguson himself was killed and his men surrendered. The Americans took several hundred prisoners, practically the entire force of redcoats. They also captured hundreds of weapons. Their own losses were very light.

Col. Patrick Ferguson's grave site.

General Nathanael Greene

F Peale

CHAPTER 24

GENERAL GREENE IN THE SOUTH

GREENE VS. CORNWALLIS

The times were dark for the patriots in the southern states. Lincoln had been forced to surrender the entire American army at Charleston, Gates had blunderingly lost an important battle, and there was terrible guerilla warfare going on between the Whigs and Tories. News from the north was not very encouraging, as the two armies were not active so it seemed there was little progress toward ending the war from that direction. And all the time, money was scarce. Such conditions would certainly have discouraged all but the strongest men.

America did not yet have many wealthy men, but some of those few helped out with loans to the army. The most notable of these is Robert Morris, a personal and loyal friend of Washington. He gave so much of his own money to the cause that he had little of his fortune left at the end of the war. Some other loans came from France, and some other countries agreed to help America with loans, with France promising to pay them should the Americans fail. Even with all this help, war is so expensive that it was not enough.

Early in 1779, young Lafayette had gone home to France for a while. There, he pleaded with the government to give America more help. He was an eloquent and passionate

General Nathniel Greene

Robert Morris was a living illustration of the quality of generosity. Generosity means giving unselfishly to the needs of others. Proverbs 3:27 says, "Withhold not good from them to whom it is due, when it is in the power of thine hand to do it." Robert Morris certainly demonstrated generosity to the cause of liberty. He personally gave $2 million to the cause of liberty. The country was never able to repay him and he later spent time in debtor's prison but he never regretted giving his fortune to help obtain freedom.

Washington and Rochambeau in the trenches at Yorktown.

speaker, and finally France agreed to send ten ships and a force of 6,000 men to America's aid. Count Rochambeau was to be in command of those troops while Admiral de Ternay was in command of the fleet. It was understood that George Washington would be in command of all forces, so it was hoped that there would be less friction between French and American commanders than there had been the previous time.

Washington would find that Rochambeau was a friend in need and a friend indeed. In fact, it was to meet with Rochambeau that Washington had been away at Hartford when Arnold's plan to betray West Point was supposed to have taken place. Returning sooner than expected, Washington had spoiled Arnold's plan and forced him to flee for his life.

There was much joy in July 1780 when the French fleet and soldiers arrived at Newport. Not only were they a substantial force, but they also brought with them the promise of yet more men and ships to come. But the plan was delayed for a while, for the British navy kept the additional troops from departing France for a time and also kept the French fleet at Newport bottled up in the harbor. So the Americans were forced again to rely on their own efforts, but the time would soon come when the help from France would make a critical difference.

The bitter struggle in South Carolina continued, but things were changing for the better with the coming of General Nathanael Greene. Like some of his brother officers, Greene had been criticized by some men in Congress and finally gotten so tired of it that he had resigned from his post. But Washington was his friend, and the commander-in-chief well knew the value of Greene's leadership. So, appealing to Greene on the basis of honor and friendship, Washington persuaded him to take over command of the army in the south from Gates. On December 2, 1780, Greene arrived in Charlotte and took over.

Lafayette was America's friend and became a dear friend of Gen. Washington. When he was an old man he came back to America to visit, and crowds came out to honor him all around the country.

However, the reliable Baron von Steuben, who had so skillfully trained the starving troops at Valley Forge, did not come with Greene. Steuben had been left in Virginia to face Benedict Arnold. Arnold, who had turned traitor and joined the enemy, was very bitter at his former countrymen and with 1,600 angry

New York Tories had been sent out to do all the damage to the country that he could.

But Greene did have some very able help. With him, Washington had sent Henry "Light Horse Harry" Lee, the dashing cavalry commander. In addition, Kosciuskio, the brilliant Polish engineer, came along and would soon prove to be of great value to Greene.

The British force was considerable. Arnold had taken the place of General Leslie when that officer had left Virginia to help Cornwallis. Leslie commanded 3,000 top British troops and, along with other reinforcements, he now swelled the ranks of Cornwallis to 11,300 well-equipped and well-trained men.

Notice these passages in Scripture where God worked on behalf of His people, even when they were outnumbered by the enemy, or His promise to do so. The founders of our country saw many instances where God worked on their behalf. They often would call a day of fasting and prayer to thank and acknowledge God's intervention on their behalf.

> There is no king saved by the multitude of an host: a mighty man is not delivered by much strength. An horse is a vain thing for safety: neither shall he deliver any by his great strength. Behold, the eye of the LORD is upon them that fear him, upon them that hope in his mercy; to deliver their soul from death, and to keep them alive in famine. Our soul waiteth for the LORD: he is our help and our shield. For our heart shall rejoice in him, because we have trusted in his holy name. Let thy mercy, O LORD, be upon us, according as we hope in thee (Psalm 33:16–22).

> And when the servant of the man of God was risen early, and gone forth, behold, an host compassed the city both with horses and chariots. And his servant said unto him, Alas, my master! how shall we do? And he answered, Fear not: for they that be with us are more than they that be with them. And Elisha prayed, and said, LORD, I pray thee, open his eyes, that he may see. And the LORD opened the eyes of the young man; and he saw: and, behold, the mountain was full of horses and chariots of fire round about Elisha (2 Kings 6:15–17).

> And he said, Hearken ye, all Judah, and ye inhabitants of Jerusalem, and thou king Jehoshaphat, thus saith the LORD unto you, Be not afraid nor dismayed by reason of this great multitude; for the battle is not yours, but God's (2 Chronicles 20:15).

Baron Steuben at Valley Forge

Greene had only around 2,300 men to face this intimidating force, and more than half of them were green, inexperienced militia. Whatever success Greene would have must come from the skill of the generals and the unconquerable spirit of the men whom they commanded. Surprisingly, the first thing Greene did was to divide his already small force.

But Greene was not foolish. He knew just what he was doing, and soon the country would as well. He sent Dan Morgan with 500 men to watch the movements of the British at Camden and to collect all the provisions he could find for the army. Francis Marion was told to make his presence felt in lower South Carolina, then General Greene led his troops south toward the Pee Dee River. The war was on.

VICTORY AT COWPENS AND THE RETREAT TO VIRGINIA

Late in December, Morgan sent Colonel William Washington, a cousin of General Washington and a dashing cavalry commander, with his horsemen and 200 militia toward Ninety-six, where they encountered an advancing party of Tories. They whipped the Tories in a surprise attack, carrying away 40 prisoners and many horses; 150 of the enemy fell, killed or wounded.

After the arrival of Leslie and his men, Cornwallis had decided to move into North Carolina and "pacify" that state too. But now to do so would leave the daring Morgan and his men behind him, and that did not seem a safe thing to do. No, Morgan must be defeated. That would send a message to the rest of the conquered state as well. Tarleton was just the man for the job. That brutal and bold leader was sent out with 1,100 men to bag Morgan.

Tarleton approached Morgan's force rapidly. Hearing of this development, Morgan realized that he was outnumbered two to one and in no condition to meet his enemy. He began to retreat. But Tarleton was very quick. He allowed his men almost no sleep in his eagerness to catch and beat Morgan. Soon, Morgan found that he was losing his lead. Very well, if he could not escape, he certainly could fight. He drew up his men at a place called Cowpens, near the North Carolina border. The day was January 17, 1781.

He arranged his army very carefully. In the rear he placed Colonel Washington and his cavalry. In front he placed the untried militia troops. Between them, he arrayed his experienced Continentals. He ordered the militia to fire a volley and then retreat to take up positions behind the regulars. He hoped that they would then make a stand with their comrades.

General Dan Morgan

When Tarleton saw the homespun garb of the militia in front of him he attacked immediately, confident that he would soon have the Americans flying in fear. The militia did not fire until the redcoats were within 50 yards. When they did fire, many of the enemy went down. Then they fell back behind the line of Continentals as planned. The British, thinking that they already had the Americans on the run, plunged ahead. But then the militia joined the Continentals in a countercharge and hit the redcoats head on. At the same time, Colonel Washington's cavalry swung around from the rear of the Americans and slammed into the redcoats from the side.

The Battle of the Cowpens

The effect on the redcoats was instant panic. Confused by being struck from two sides at once, "Tarleton's Legion," exhausted from sleepless marching, quickly decided that wisdom lay in the course of retreat. Many of the infantry became prisoners, and Washington pursued the cavalry of Tarleton so rapidly that he was able to engage that officer in a horseback sword battle and leave him with a serious cut on one hand.

Most of the "Legion" escaped and hurriedly made their way to the army of Cornwallis to tell him the surprising story of their defeat in the battle of Cowpens. The statistics were ugly from the British side: 110 killed, 500 taken prisoner, 229 wounded, along with 100 cavalry horses, 800 sets of arms, and 35 baggage wagons. Meanwhile, one special delight to the Americans was the capture of two cannons that had been taken from Burgoyne at Saratoga and retaken by Cornwallis at Camden. The American losses were only 12 killed and 60 wounded.

Morgan was proud of his men and elated with their victory. He quickly sent his militia to Virginia with their prisoners. He followed with the rest of his men as a rear guard. But Cornwallis, furious and determined, was soon on his trail. It was the beginning of one of the most memorable pursuits in American history.

Eleven days after the battle at Cowpens, Morgan's men found themselves across the Catawba River just ahead of Cornwallis. A hard rain was falling, keeping the redcoat leader from following through the swollen stream. Two days later, he managed to cross, but found that his captured troops were too far ahead of him to be recovered.

Morgan had sent riders to summon all the patriots of the region to join him, expecting to have to fight Cornwallis as he tried to cross the river. But on the last day of January, General Greene himself

Morgan's Riflemen

rode into camp after having made a 150-mile ride to lead Morgan and his men to join the rest of the army himself.

Greene arranged his force to oppose Cornwallis in crossing the river, but the militia failed, as they often did. The redcoats were soon across the river and in pursuit of the much smaller force ahead of them. At times, the armies were so close to each other that the leading British soldiers could see the rear guard of the Americans. Again there was a river to be crossed, and again the Americans got across the Yadkin just ahead of the British, taking all available boats with them. The wily Greene, also something of a "fox," similar to Washington, moved out with an additional lead on the redcoats just as an unexpected rainstorm swelled the river to uncrossable depths. The British had to march far up the river to find a ford. The patriots of the region rejoiced, praising God and declaring that Providence had again held back the redcoats.

At Guilford Courthouse, Greene rejoined his army. Cornwallis was now frustrated and desperate. He had failed to catch up with Morgan and force a battle, and he now wanted to cut Greene off in his retreat to Virginia. He also had heard that reinforcements were coming to Greene, and he wanted to cut them off before they reached him. The American general, in turn, did not want a battle with his smaller force; but he did want to keep Cornwallis at a distance if he could, so he sent 700 men with Light Horse Harry and Colonel Washington to "bother" the enemy. In fact, they bothered Cornwallis so much that Greene crossed the Dan River, taking all the boats, just as the vanguard of the British appeared. The river was too deep to be crossed, so a frustrated Cornwallis marched on to Hillsboro. The remarkable retreat of the patriot army had covered 200 miles, covering 40 miles on the last day. The suffering on both sides had been indescribable as the two armies strove to outrun each other at a pace that taxed all the powers of the human body and mind.

At Hillsboro, Cornwallis paused to forage for supplies and call for Tories to join his force. But the Tories were demoralized by recent British failures and were not quick to respond. Finally, several companies were formed and began to march toward the main body of Cornwallis's army. Tarleton was to meet them on their way, but a mile short of the meeting point Pickens and Light Horse Harry Lee attacked and scattered them. Some of those who escaped ran into Tarleton's Legion and were mistaken for patriot militia. They were fired on by their own comrades. This unfortunate Tory band is sometimes known as the "lost regiment."

Greene's Successful Failures

Late in February, Greene once again crossed the Dan River, leaving Virginia for North Carolina. He wanted to cut off supplies to Cornwallis, while also avoiding an open battle with the British. Three weeks after returning, Greene was reinforced by militia until he had around 4,200 men. Now he was superior in numbers to Cornwallis's army of 2,400. But most of his men were militia, not nearly as effective in battle as the British regulars. Greene took a position near the backwoods settlement of Guilford Courthouse, and finally, Cornwallis got the battle he had long been seeking.

It was a fierce battle, this 15th of March in 1781. For a while, the untrained American militia performed well, but eventually Greene saw that the British were moving to cut off any route of retreat and ordered his men off the field. They left behind them 400 of their comrades struck down on the field. The British had lost 600 in killed, wounded, and missing. Of course, Cornwallis claimed a complete victory in the battle and promptly made another proclamation. He offered to pardon all rebels who returned to loyalty to the king and called upon all Tories to assist in restoring royal government in the area. Indeed, it was a British victory in that they held the field after the Americans retreated, but it was an expensive one. Cornwallis seemed to be in control of Georgia and both Carolinas, but he knew his grip was doubtful at best. Within a few weeks he gave up his hard-won prize and headed for Virginia.

Now the positions of the two armies were reversed. Greene had thought that the scrappy Cornwallis would fight again, but evidently the redcoat general had had enough of winning battles that seriously weakened his army with losses. As soon as Greene saw that Cornwallis was departing, he decided to be the pursuer instead of the pursued for a change. He began following the redcoats, but when he came to Deep River he changed his mind and stopped his army. Cornwallis kept marching until he reached Petersburg, Virginia. Greene turned his attention back to the Carolinas.

Greene rested his army, released most of the militia

Battle of Guilford Courthouse, 1781, artist and date unknown (PD-Art).

Total Rout of the Loyal Recruits

to go home, and in early April started back toward Camden, South Carolina, where Gates had been so badly defeated and where now Colonel Rawdon was in charge of the British forces. He sent Francis Marion, Pickens, Lee, and other cavalry leaders with their fast-moving bands of men into different parts of the state to cut off supplies on their way to the redcoats. They were also ordered to attack the many small outposts the British had established, generally working to keep the enemy scattered and confused, doing all the damage possible to him all the while.

Greene knew he was too weak in numbers to attack Rawdon's fortified position, so he chose a situation he thought he could defend and waited for the British commander to attack him. Rawdon did so on April 25. For a while, the battle favored the Americans, but in the end Greene withdrew, leaving the British once more with territory held and large numbers of men lost. On the 10th of May, Rawdon set fire to Camden and marched away.

Meanwhile, the scattered bands of American raiders were fulfilling their mission. Outpost after outpost fell into their hands. Little garrisons were taken at Orangeburg, Fort Motte, Nelson's Ferry, Fort Granby, and Silver Springs. Lee and Pickens joined forces to capture Fort Cornwallis, and the Swamp Fox forced the redcoats out of Georgetown. These were not huge victories in terms of numbers, but they served to encourage the patriots to keep fighting and kept the British and their Tory friends in constant anxiety wondering where these mysterious raiders would next appear.

At the fort of Ninety-six, Colonel Cruger was in command of 500 British soldiers. With his small army, Nathanael Greene laid siege to the place. Directed by Kosciusko, the Americans erected batteries and dug tunnels to within six feet of the fort. The patriots were confident that the British would soon be in their hands, but then Greene received a report that Rawdon was on his way with strong reinforcements to relieve them. Facing Rawdon with his few men was out of the question, so Greene quickly made plans to take the fort by assault.

The patriots fought desperately, but in the end failed to take the position. Greene began another of his strategic retreats that always seemed to hurt the British more than their victories could help them.

In September, there was another large battle at Eutaw Springs, about 30 miles from Charleston. Greene had increased his force to around 2,000 men and decided it was time to stop retreating. He still did not have a sufficient force to attack Rawdon, especially since Rawdon had recently been reinforced by Cruger's men coming from Ninety-six. But when Francis Marion appeared with a sizable force of men, Greene made the decision to fight. The two armies met on September 8, 1781.

Battle of Eutaw Springs

The Americans, skillfully placed by their leaders for maximum effectiveness, drove the British before them. Then the redcoats took a stand near a large, three-story brick house, and the patriots could not move them from their position. Hand-to-hand, with bayonets and clubbed muskets, the soldiers shouted and fought. One side seemed just as determined as the other. Finally, the Americans withdrew and the British declared victory. And it was true that they had not been driven from the field. But they had lost more than 1,100 men killed, wounded, and captured. The Americans had lost only around half that number. It was another very expensive triumph for the redcoats. The next day, the British hurried back to Charleston. They would remain bottled up there for the remainder of the war.

COL. ISAAC HAYNE

Col. Isaac Hayne was a captain in the American army in Charleston when the city fell. Like the other American officers, he was paroled upon his promise that he would not take up arms against the British again as long as they held the city. Later, the British broke the agreement and summoned all the paroled officers to join the redcoat army or go to prison. Haynes would have chosen to go to prison, but his wife and several of his children were suffering from smallpox and near death. He went to the British commander in Charleston and was assured that if he would take the oath of loyalty to King George, he would not be required to take up arms against his former comrades. But later, when the successes of Greene had left little but Charleston in British hands, Hayne was summoned to join the British army. Considering his oath voided because of this action by the British, Hayne went to the American camp and rejoined the army. He was later captured and hanged by the British because they considered him a traitor for having violated his oath of allegiance — even though they had broken the agreement first.

Storytime with Uncle Rick

America's Struggle

231

Marquis Cornwallis

CHAPTER 25

CORNWALLIS IS TRAPPED

HUNTING A TRAITOR

We have already learned some things about Benedict Arnold's treasonous work for the British. Now we must return to him again and watch his movements later in the war. Arnold knew very well that he was hated and despised by his former comrades, the Americans. It was not long before he found out that he was not going to be popular among the British either. Before Arnold had sailed from New York with his army he had been living in a house in the Broadway area of the city, next door to Sir Henry Clinton. He met many British officers and quickly learned that a turncoat is not respected in any army.

Benedict Arnold

General Washington had an extra reason for wanting to see Arnold suffer the consequences of his crime. The general had invested much thought and energy into trying to create a plan by which Arnold could be captured and punished. It was necessary to make an example of such people in order to serve a warning to others who might be tempted to sell out their country for gold. There was no way of knowing how many American soldiers might have been involved in the plot between Arnold and Andre, or who might be thinking that since Arnold had gotten the gold and not been captured, the danger of being caught might not be as great as the chance of reward. It would not be good to let potential traitors be encouraged by Arnold's success in escaping capture. It was even possible that some high-ranking officers had been involved with Arnold and, if so, they must be found out.

In 1780, while the army was at Tappan, several plans had been suggested for this purpose. One of them received Washington's

Loyalty is being committed to the welfare of those I serve, even to the detriment of my own comfort. Benedict Arnold would have done well to remember this. John 15:13 says, "Greater love hath no man than this, that a man lay down his life for his friends." Little buddies, remember to be committed to those you are responsible to serve.

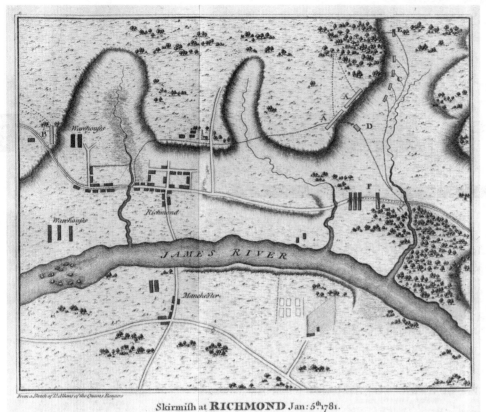

Skirmifh at **RICHMOND** Jan: 5ᵗʰ 1781.

A. *Rebel Infantry*. B. *Rebel Cavalry*. C. *Queen's Rangers*. D. *Queen's Rangers Cavalry*. E. *Yagers*. F. *British Army*.

A map showing the attack on Richmond, Virginia under forces of Benedict Arnold in 1781 (PD-US).

approval, and he sent for Major Lee to consult with him. Lee was totally trusted by Washington and could be counted on to remain silent about any arrangements made. The two men got together and decided that Lee would select from his command some trustworthy man who would pretend to desert to the British in New York. He would be given letters to two friends of Washington in the city and with them would come up with a plan to capture Arnold. The "traitor" was to be taken prisoner and returned to the American army, but he was not to be killed.

The young man chosen by Lee for this daring job was Sergeant Major John Champe. At first, Champe was unwilling. His patriotic heart rebelled at the idea of even seeming to desert his country. But after much discussion he yielded to the appeals of Washington and his beloved commander, Lee. At 11 p.m. on October 20, 1780, Champe quietly rode out of camp on horseback. In his pocket he carried three guineas, a gift of Lee, and a few personal belongings. Only a few minutes passed before someone discovered he had left, and it was assumed that he had deserted the army. Major Lee had a hard time delaying his indignant soldiers in pursuing Champe. In fact, the pursuit was so vigorous that Champe barely had time to reach the shore and be received aboard a British ship. The captain of the ship listened to his story and gave him a letter to Sir Henry Clinton. Clinton received Champe cordially and very soon the young spy found himself assigned to the "American" legion that Arnold was just then raising among deserters and Tories. The assignment was exactly what Champe had hoped for.

THE ESCAPE OF SERGEANT CHAMPE

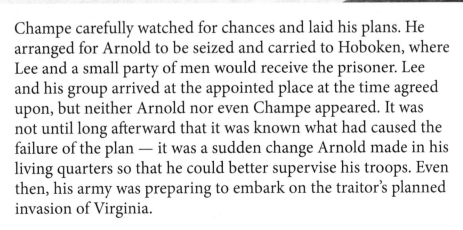

Benedict Arnold's defection to the British had prompted a number of other American officers to do likewise. This set the stage for John Champe of Aldie, Virginia, to convince the British that he was just another deserter, seeking a home in the British army. Washington and Lee were confident that if Champe could win Arnold's confidence it would not be hard to kidnap the traitor. He was weak and crippled from two serious wounds in his left leg. Champe and a conspirator or two could tie and gag Arnold and hustle him to a boat in the river. If observed, they would reply that they were taking a drunken sailor back to his ship.

Indeed, Champe was successful in winning the confidence of Arnold. The turncoat gave him the job of recruiting Tories in New York for the British army. Champe watched Arnold's habits and noticed that he walked alone in his garden each evening. That would be the perfect time to snatch him.

But good plans do not always go as expected. The very day before Champe planned to kidnap Arnold, orders came to sail to Virginia, and Champe found himself sailing south to help make war on his home state. He marched with the British army for months before he was able to escape, make his way into the mountains, and finally travel north to rejoin Washington. After his discharge, he was honored with the position of doorkeeper and Sergeant-at-arms for the Continental Congress.

Champe carefully watched for chances and laid his plans. He arranged for Arnold to be seized and carried to Hoboken, where Lee and a small party of men would receive the prisoner. Lee and his group arrived at the appointed place at the time agreed upon, but neither Arnold nor even Champe appeared. It was not until long afterward that it was known what had caused the failure of the plan — it was a sudden change Arnold made in his living quarters so that he could better supervise his troops. Even then, his army was preparing to embark on the traitor's planned invasion of Virginia.

The unexpected result of Champe's plan was that not only was Arnold not taken, but Champe was forced to go along on the Virginia raid. He found himself a part of the army that was to invade his own country. Several weeks went by before Champe saw an opportunity to escape from the British army. When he returned to his friends, they were amazed by the boldness of what he had done and covered him with honors and praise. But everyone knew that if he was ever captured by the British, he would be hanged as a deserter. For that reason, he was discharged from the army with the thanks of his great commander and a rich reward.

Meanwhile, Arnold was marching through Virginia with 1,600 men. Arriving at Richmond, he destroyed large quantities of stores, including salt and tobacco among other valuable items. From Richmond, he marched to Portsmouth on the coast where he made his headquarters. From there he sent small units out in several directions, destroying public and private property everywhere they went.

So great were the ravages committed by Arnold's men that Washington sent Lafayette with 1,200 men to oppose him.

Washington and Layfayette at Valley Forge by John Ward Dunsmore, 1907 (PD-US).

Lafayette had been marching south already to join the southern army, but Washington felt it necessary to delay that movement because of the damage being done where Arnold had no large American forces to oppose him.

The Fight Moves to Virginia

Now Washington renewed his hope that the traitor might be captured, so he wrote to Rochambeau and Destouches at Newport, asking them to send 1,000 men and the entire French fleet to help Lafayette. But Destouches only sent three ships, and when they arrived at Portsmouth they did not dare to attack Arnold's fleet, so they turned tail and sailed back to Newport. The only thing they had to show for the excursion was the capture of a 50-gun British ship, the *Romulus*.

The failure of the French to follow Washington's orders was a serious breach of the agreement between France and America. Not only did Washington not get the help he needed, but also he did not have accurate information on which to make plans. Great trouble follows when people fail to show the character quality of dependability.

But Washington was still intent on capturing Arnold. On March 6, he and some of his officers held a council with Rochambeau to discuss plans. The result was that they decided to have the French fleet — all of it this time — carry Rochambeau's entire force of 1,100 men down to Virginia. But the French admiral was not in a hurry, and when he finally arrived off the coast of Virginia he found he was opposed by the British Admiral Arbuthnot, who was there and ready for battle. The French engaged the English ships, but after only an hour of fighting they withdrew. The very next day they sailed back to Newport. Washington had once again seen that he could not depend on the navy of France.

A few days later, General Phillips of the redcoat army brought 2,000 troops to join Arnold. Together they marched their powerful force to Petersburg, causing great suffering to the patriot homes and towns along the way. Baron Steuben was in Virginia, but he had too few men to risk an engagement with the main force of the British. Now Cornwallis, withdrawing after his costly victories in the Carolinas, arrived at Petersburg. He found that General Phillips had died of a fever, so he took over command of the troops. Another 1,500 men had just come from New York, so the redcoat commander found himself in charge of a considerable army.

Lafayette had been sent to oppose this horde, but he was facing problems in the ranks. His army was far too small to begin with.

In addition, his men were mostly New England soldiers who suffered greatly in the Virginia heat. Their clothes were wearing out, and there was no money to replace them. They deserted in such numbers that young Lafayette (Cornwallis scornfully referred to him as "the boy") was struggling against despair. Finally, he assembled his men and appealed to them. He reached out to their patriotic sentiments and told them how dangerous was the job he had been sent out to do. He urged them to stay and fight alongside him. Further, he raised some money on his own promise to repay in Baltimore and bought some clothing for them. His men responded, and there were few desertions after that time.

> Lafayette was an example of many fine character qualities. In battle, he was brave. To his men, he was kind, humble, and generous. To Washington, he was loyal and respectful. He was a role model for others to follow, one who showed such depth of character in his life.

Cornwallis soon crossed the Pamunkey River and divided his forces. The hated Tarleton was sent on a mission to capture the Virginia Assembly, which was meeting in session at that time in Charlottesville. Tarleton was not a good man, but he was certainly an energetic one, and he almost succeeded in his mission.

He managed to catch seven Assembly members and destroy a large store of supplies the patriots had been collecting at Charlottesville. The other part of Cornwallis's army had been sent to capture American stores at point of Fork, but the patriots came out in force and managed to save part of them.

Fight of the Romulus, by Vincent Courdouan, date unknown (CC BY-SA 2.0 FR).

Lafayette now received the exciting news that Mad Anthony Wayne was on the way to join him with 800 men of the Pennsylvania line. How the young general rejoiced at this news! Soon, he and his ally would have an army large enough to make an impression on the legions of Cornwallis. Meanwhile, Lafayette had moved his war supplies from Richmond to Albemarle Old Courthouse and, since this could hardly be kept secret with Tories in the country, the British soon knew of it. Cornwallis moved to a position between "the boy" and his base of supplies, hoping to capture the material the patriots so desperately needed to continue the fight.

But Lafayette was not easily bested, and he followed along after the redcoats until they were only a few miles away from his supply depot. Cornwallis considered himself to be in an excellent position, for he held one of the two roads to the place and he was confident Lafayette would not try to use the other road.

But as we have seen, Lafayette was not easily beaten. While Cornwallis was gleefully congratulating himself on a clever move, "the boy" made a nighttime march over a road the British had thought impassable. Cornwallis was unpleasantly surprised soon after to find that Lafayette was now between the British and the supplies. Giving up on capturing them, Cornwallis marched his red legion back to Richmond.

Cornwallis did not know exactly the size of Lafayette's force. Some of the patriot farmers had come out to join him, and Baron Steuben's men had also arrived to swell his ranks. Cornwallis thought the patriot army even bigger than it was, so he was hoping to avoid a fight for the present. He had more disturbing issues also, as he had received a letter from Henry Clinton in New York demanding that Cornwallis send some of his force back to that city. Clinton said he had just learned that the Americans were planning a combined French and American attack on him and he wanted help.

Washington and Lafayette at Mount Vernon, by Thomas Prichard Rossiter and Louis Rémy Mignot, 1859 (PD-US).

Cornwallis

Clinton indeed had learned of an impending attack, but it was a myth. He had learned of it in the manner by which he learned a number of things. This was Washington's favored ruse of sending letters by messengers, intending to have the riders captured by the British. He had used this method for some time to keep Clinton in a constant state of agitation so that he would not dare to leave New York for fear Washington would attack the city while it was lightly defended. Yet the "old fox" was indeed considering an attack at some time, having "cried wolf" enough times that Clinton never knew whether to believe rumors of an attack or not.

CORNWALLIS IN A CORNER

On July 4, Cornwallis marched his army to a ford on the James River and sent part of his force to the other side. Over a period of three days, most of the supplies and baggage were carried across. Nine miles away, Lafayette waited until he thought most of the army had crossed, leaving only a small rear guard. Then he launched an attack.

This was exactly what Cornwallis had hoped for. In reality, he had left most of his army in the position of a rear guard to dupe Lafayette into attacking a much larger force than he expected. The little American army nearly fell into a deadly trap.

Boldness is facing confrontation with the assurance that God will bless the outcome if I'm standing firm for truth. Samuel Adams explains how the colonists viewed this.

> There is One above us Who will take exemplary vengeance for every insult upon His majesty. You know that the cause of America is just. You know that she contends for that freedom to which all men are entitled — that she contends against oppression, rapine, and more than savage barbarity. The blood of the innocent is upon your hands, and all the waters of the ocean will not wash it away. We again make our solemn appeal to the God of heaven to decide between you and us. And we pray that, in the doubtful scale of battle, we may be successful as we have justice on our side, and that the merciful Savior of the world may forgive our oppressors.[68]

The British outposts fell back as Mad Anthony Wayne struck. This was what they had been

The Battle of the Saints, by Thomas Whitcombe, 1783 (PD-Art).

told to do. Very suddenly, Wayne found himself facing the main body of the British, now emerging from the woods. It did not seem safe to turn his back and retreat, so he did what came naturally to him: he charged. Sheer boldness had done much for him at Stony Point and other places, and it did not fail him now. Despite the fact that he only had 800 men against several thousand British, Wayne held his own through the hottest kind of fighting. He was relieved when Lafayette saw what was happening and came to his aid. Together they managed to get their entire force withdrawn to the shelter of a deep swamp.

Mad Anthony Wayne

Cornwallis might have followed up their retreat with a successful charge, but he did not like the position of the patriots. They might be leading him into just the sort of trap that he had laid for them. Besides, in the swamp it is hard to maneuver large groups of men, so his numerical advantage might have been overcome by the nature of the battleground. Instead of advancing, he formed up his men, marched them across the river by night, and continued on to Portsmouth. There the contingent of men who were to be sent to Clinton boarded ships, but just before they set sail another messenger came from Clinton. Now Cornwallis was ordered to hold all his men. A fleet of ships was coming to aid him, so he should select a safe post and wait for them to arrive.

Cornwallis selected Yorktown on the York River, and soon his men were occupying and fortifying that place. The plan was for a British fleet to come from the West Indies to join him. All he had to do was hold off the little American army under Lafayette and Wayne until the reinforcements could arrive. Then, with a huge force, he would march out and serve Virginia with a taste of what South Carolina had suffered. So Cornwallis settled comfortably into Yorktown, with nothing to do but wait. Soon the entire South would be in the palm of his hand.

With this frame of mind, it must have been a very unpleasant surprise when the first sails Cornwallis saw belonged to 28 French ships under Count de Grasse. Even as they sailed into the Chesapeake, word came to the redcoat general that the combined armies of the Americans and the French were marching upon him from the north. Cornwallis was trapped.

Surrender of Cornwallis

Second Battle
of the
Virginia Capes

CHAPTER 26

WASHINGTON MARCHES SOUTH

A TRICKY "OLD FOX"

Now we must turn our attention to the northern states again to understand what Washington was doing. Being a man of action, he had been irritated for a long time because circumstances forced him to wait. Many people, both in the army and in Congress, thought he should have been moving his army and attacking the enemy. But Washington, though eager to fight, was also very wise. He knew it was better to bear the criticism of those who thought him overcautious than to act unwisely for the sake of quieting his critics.

In early 1781, Washington had already decided that his best chance of defeating the enemy was to wear him out rather than facing him in open battle where his large numbers and superior equipment could be used to advantage. No, he would bide his time unless another opportunity like the ones he had been given at Trenton and Princeton should come his way. Those battles had been wonderful successes, just when his army and the nation had needed encouragement most. But his troops had been defeated in almost every other battle they had fought since.

Rochambeau

Caution is knowing how important right timing is in accomplishing a task. Proverbs 3:6 says," In all thy ways acknowledge him, and he shall direct thy paths." Washington used caution in making his plans. He knew many lives were dependent on proper timing.

Count de Grasse

Still, no patriot could have been as frustrated with the inaction as the great commander-in-chief. All the while he was being criticized for not moving, no one in the country wanted to move more than he did. The criticism of his fellow Americans must have been very hard for him to stand.

Finally, in the spring of 1781 it began to look as if some decisive action might be possible soon. He and the French army commander Rochambeau had met in Wethersfield, Connecticut, to discuss the matter. They had decided the time might be right to make an attack on New York. If they accomplished nothing else, it might cause Clinton to send for part of Cornwallis' force for reinforcement, thus weakening the British army in the south where Greene and his allies were struggling with a lack of men and supplies.

You will remember that the French and English were at war against each other at this time. There had been much fighting between them in the West Indies, where de Grasse was in command of the French. The plan now was for de Grasse to suddenly break off operations against the British and sail quickly to the aid of the American and French forces in America.

It's incredibly hard to stand firm and do what you think is best when under criticism. However, we are responsible to God for our decisions, not man. We need to stand firm in doing what we believe is right even if others criticize us for it.

De Grasse sent a message in mid-August that he would have to return to the West Indies soon, so if the armies wanted his help they must move southward to meet him. In that way, he could fight and then sail back to the Indies as soon as possible. By this time Washington also knew that Cornwallis had bottled himself up in Yorktown, Virginia, so the "old fox" changed his plans and decided to take his combined armies south and fight Cornwallis before help could be sent to him. If de Grasse could get to Yorktown before the British fleet from New York, a fatal blow might be struck. It appeared that the success at Trenton and Princeton might be repeated.

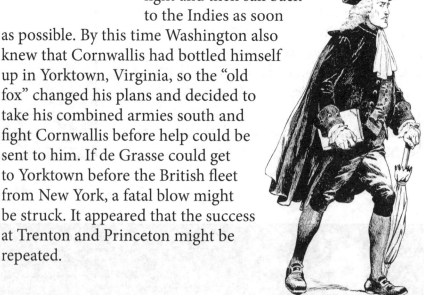

Rochambeau

SERVING IN AN UNEXPECTED WAY

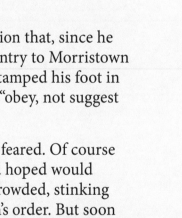

First, steps had to be taken to hold Clinton in New York. Several stealthy moves were made, among them the trick used by Washington and others of having falsified letters fall into the hands of the enemy. One messenger who carried such a letter was a young man named Montagnie. Montagnie was a Baptist preacher and a soldier in Washington's army on the Hudson. This young soldier was a faithful and dependable man, as Washington learned after making careful inquiries. The general summoned young Montagnie to his office and told him he was needed to carry some messages. The dispatches would be sewed inside his coat lining. He would ride through the Ramapo Pass and carry them to Morristown.

Montagnie was surprised at being summoned to the commander's office, and honored at being selected for an important mission. But he protested when informed of the route he would be taking. He knew the surrounding country and was aware that Ramapo Pass was a long, narrow defile between the wooded hills of New Jersey. It had a wide, swift creek on one side and steep cliffs on the other. It was known to be a place where the "cowboys," a loyalist guerrilla band, often used to pass through on their raids.

Montagnie was not one to argue with his general, but he dared to mention that, since he knew the entire area well, it might be wiser for him to travel across country to Morristown and avoid the danger of capture at Ramapo Pass. At this, Washington stamped his foot in pretended anger and declared that it was the duty of the young man to "obey, not suggest plans to his superiors." So off went Montagnie.

He was indeed captured by the "cowboys" just as he had feared. Of course he had no idea that this was just what Washington had hoped would happen. Now, crammed with other prisoners into a crowded, stinking sugarhouse he was naturally resentful of Washington's order. But soon after his capture he saw a newspaper in which a long account of his capture was given, along with an account of how papers found on his person had revealed to General Clinton that Washington and Rochambeau planned to attack New York very soon. Clinton was now hard at work to prepare his men and the city for the onslaught. Hopefully, Montagnie quickly figured out that Washington had sent him on a fake errand in order to help win the war in a short time.

Count de Rochambeau

Thomas McKean

THE ARMY MOVES AT LAST

Now Washington's army moved fast. By different routes, various units advanced toward a rendezvous with the French. At Perth Amboy they made a big show of preparing to attack New York. All of this so deceived Sir Henry Clinton that he had no inkling of what Washington was doing until the entire combined army was across the Delaware and marching rapidly southward. It was not until then that the soldiers themselves learned what was going on, because the plan had been kept absolutely secret. When they found out their true destination, most of the soldiers were delighted.

Soon, word of the march was spreading through the countryside and the people turned out to welcome the army as it marched. Shouts of "Long live Washington!" rang from crowds of joyful people as the long line of lean, determined men passed through their towns and settlements.

There was no joy in Sir Henry Clinton's headquarters, however. Clinton was beside himself when he finally learned what the "old fox" was doing. The Americans were too far ahead for him to catch up with them, and the fleet that could carry his soldiers to help Cornwallis had not yet come from the West Indies. There was nothing he could do.

Once the army crossed the Delaware, they found the roads to be in better condition. More importantly, the land was much flatter than the hilly terrain through which they had been marching. Whereas they had been marching 12 to 15 miles each day, now they could increase their speed to 24 miles per day.

When they arrived in Philadelphia, the regimental bands began to play lively marching music. The army was led by the French cavalry, their resplendent uniforms making a brave and noble appearance.

One French officer wrote in his diary:

> The streets and the line of march were crowded with people who were absolutely amazed to see such a fine army. . . . They could not conceive how, after a long and tiring march over frightful roads, we could be in such good condition, or how we could have brought so much artillery in our train.[69]

The combined army (French and American) passed in review before Congress. Washington and Rochambeau stood on either side of the president of Congress, Thomas McKean.

Near the town of Chester, a message came bearing good news. The French fleet had broken through the British blockade and had landed 3,000 French soldiers. Yorktown was under siege, and Cornwallis was trapped. A wave of happiness swept through the ranks. There was hard work ahead, but the general feeling was that the long war was nearing an end.

When the Americans reached Head of Elk in Maryland, Washington, Knox, Rochambeau, and a few others crossed the Chesapeake Bay to Virginia.

Marquis de Lafayette

Washington slipped away from his army for a few days to visit his beloved Mount Vernon, which he had not seen in six years. He and his entourage, including Count Rochambeau, rode 60 miles in one day to reach the plantation. On the third day of their visit, Washington got word that the French Admiral de Grasse had left Chesapeake Bay with his entire fleet. Had the French navy failed him again?

It had not. Clinton had sent additional ships to Cornwallis in an effort to break the French naval blockade. The effort had failed and the battered English fleet had been forced to withdraw. Soon, Washington and his company, encouraged by news of the defeat of the English navy, rode to Williamsburg to join Lafayette and his besieging army.

They arrived at Williamsburg on September 14, and immediately began to develop their plans. How great their anxiety must have been! So many things can happen in wartime to upset the best-laid plans of the most brilliant strategists.

Most of Washington's men were still on the way. Some had sailed from Head of Elk and were now headed down Chesapeake Bay. The rest were marching an extra 200 miles to go around the bay by land.

Cornwallis made a feeble attempt to break up the naval blockade by sending fire ships floating down the James River toward the moored French fleet. The burning ships created a dramatic sight, but did little damage.

Three months after marching south, the troops finally stood before Yorktown. They unloaded the heavy siege guns that had come by ship and dug long trenches that would extend the entire length of the British defenses. Batteries of cannon were placed in the American trenches to deter the redcoat works from close range. For the first time in the entire war, Washington had more men and more guns than his opponent.

Now he hoped to batter Cornwallis into submission with his big guns and avoid the bloodshed of an infantry assault on fortifications.

Letters, diaries, and journals written by American soldiers at Yorktown show that there was an anticipation that this might be the final battle of the war. Sergeant Joseph Martin wrote,

> We prepared to move down and pay our old acquaintance, the British, at Yorktown, a visit. I doubt not but their wish was not to have so many of us come at once as their accommodations were rather scanty. They thought "the fewer the better cheer." We thought, "the more the merrier." We had come a long way to see them and were unwilling to be put off with excuses.[70]

In New York, General Clinton was desperate. He could not send direct help to Cornwallis. He wracked his brain for some sort of maneuver he could perform to make Washington think his presence could not be done without in the north so that he would turn around and return. When he finally came up with a plan, it was such a cruel one that it would do as much to cause the Americans to hate the British army as any other single event in the war.

Benedict Arnold was no longer in Virginia. He had been sent north after Cornwallis had arrived to replace General Phillips. Now Clinton planned for Arnold to lead a force against New London, Connecticut. This was the very region in which Arnold had grown up, having been born in nearby Norwich. When

A south view of Oswego, on Lake Ontario.

news of his treachery against his country had become known, there was no place in the country where his name was more despised than in Connecticut. He well knew this, and his bitterness caused him to jump at the chance to visit his revenge on the region.

The American army had stored a large stash of military supplies at New London, but had left only a skeleton force to protect it. Arnold's soldiers had the help of local Tories in quickly overwhelming patriot resistance. The redcoats would loot the town and then set fire to everything in sight, causing the equivalent of half a million dollars in damages. This destruction would seal Arnold's reputation as one of the lowest specimens of humanity. All the bravery and brilliance he had ever shown in battle would now be overshadowed by the villainy of this act.

Governor and Mrs. Jonathan Trumbull, Sr., by John Trumbull, 1783 (PD-Art).

Villainy at New London

Onlookers were startled and frightened to see 24 British ships come sailing into their harbor. The soldiers landed in two divisions, Colonel Eyre commanding the force on the Groton side and Arnold himself leading the men on the New London side. There were about 800 men in each division. Most of them were Tories and Hessians, the two groups in the entire British army most likely to be eager to murder and destroy.

Fort Trumbull was named after a great patriot. It takes its title from Jonathan Trumbull, Connecticut's wartime governor. After the battles at Lexington and Concord, General Gage sent a request to Trumbull (who had been appointed by the king as governor) for assistance. He got a cold reception, and Trumbull made it clear that he was on the side of the patriots. He told Gage that his troops had done things that would "disgrace even barbarians" in the "most unprovoked attack upon the lives and property of his Majesty's subjects." Trumbull was a personal friend of Washington during the war and was always willing to lend advice or assistance. Trumbull also served as paymaster general to the Northern Department of the patriot army. When his mother's untimely death forced him to resign his post, he requested that his remaining back pay be distributed among the men of the army. Trumbull was the only colonial governor to take sides with the patriots in the war.

There were only a few Continental soldiers at New London, but they bravely tried to make a stand and defend Fort Trumbull. They soon saw that they had no chance of accomplishing anything against such a huge force, so they abandoned their fort and crossed over to the Groton side. There they joined Colonel Ledyard in attempting to hold Fort Griswold. With not even militia to oppose him, Arnold was left free on the New London side to vent his bitterness on his former friends and neighbors. Houses, churches, stores, and ships at the wharves were soon in flames. The whole town was burning. The redcoats plundered and destroyed everywhere, not even allowing the people to try to save their furniture from the flames. One report later stated that the fires had consumed 31 stores, 18 shops, 65 houses, the courthouse, the jail, and many other buildings.

Across the water, Colonel Eyre was following Arnold's order to take Fort Griswold. When he called for the surrender of the fort, Colonel Ledyard refused. Then began a desperate and bloody battle. The little garrison fought with guns, clubs, and spears against the hundreds of enemies besieging them. Nearly 200 of the redcoats had fallen when at last Colonel Ledyard realized that he had no choice but to surrender to avoid the slaughter of all his men. Colonel Eyre had been killed in the attack, so it was Major Bromfield, a Tory from Connecticut, who accepted Ledyard's sword. As soon as his hand closed on the weapon,

Fort Trumbull, by Seth Eastman, date unknown (PD-US).

he thrust it through Ledyard's body, killing him. Then his men followed his evil example and fell upon the surrendered patriots, killing 70 and wounding 35 of them. It was nothing short of a massacre.

Not satisfied with their orgy of brutality, the Tories took some of the wounded prisoners and piled them on a cart at the edge of the hill. Giving the cart a push, the Tories sent the wounded men rolling down the steep slope toward the river to drown. The fort was set on fire, the roaring flames competing with the cries of the remaining wounded. Not even a drink of water was given to the suffering men. It was a day of villainy seldom exceeded anywhere.

But alarm guns and horseback messengers were being heard from, and soon angry citizens were swarming from the surrounding countryside. At last they were so numerous that Arnold realized it was time to return to his ships. He called his men back from their depredations and marched them down to the wharf, but a number of them fell to patriot bullets before reaching the safety of their ships.

The traitor Arnold sailed back toward New York that night with his army and 40 prisoners. He had succeeded in wreaking vengeance on a helpless town, but he had failed in distracting Washington. Time would show that the great commander would not turn aside from the purpose that was driving him with deadly determination — the cutting off and defeat of Cornwallis's army at Yorktown in Virginia. Clinton was still a threat; he could take his army up the Hudson and attack West Point or he could invade New Jersey and lay waste to the countryside. Either way, he would do damage to the cause of freedom. But either way, he would not pull Washington away from his purpose.

> Determination is purposing to exert all your energies in accomplishing a task regardless of the opposition. Washington knew his best chance was to cut off Cornwallis's army at Yorktown and he knew he had to throw all his might into making that happen. He even resisted the distraction of Arnold's atrocities in Connecticut, understanding that the attack on New London was just a ploy to pull him away from his golden chance to conquer Cornwallis.

Cornwallis Surrenders
to Washington

CHAPTER 27

CORNWALLIS SURRENDERS

LAYFAYETTE IS LOYAL AND AWAITS ORDERS

Part of the French fleet had blockaded the York River even before Washington arrived in Virginia. Another part of the fleet was anchored at Lynn Haven Bay. The ships had landed 3,200 French troops to join Lafayette's army. Count de Grasse, the French admiral, was eager to attack Cornwallis from the sea and had urged Lafayette to collaborate with him in making one. But Lafayette was both prudent and loyal. He said he would wait until General Washington arrived to take command.

French warship *Ville de Paris*, artist unknown, 1764 (PD-US).

When the sun came up on September 5, 1781, the sails of a large fleet appeared above the horizon at Cape Charles. At first, de Grasse thought it was more of his French ships arriving from Newport. But it soon became apparent that they were the British ships of Admiral Graves, so the French admiral sailed out to meet them, prepared for battle. But though there were some minor engagements between them, no major battles took place as the two fleets faced each other for five days.

It may be that de Grasse was just holding his opponent, waiting for the expected French ships from Newport to arrive. In any case, it worked, and soon de Grasse was able to sail back to his former position, able to prevent help from coming to Cornwallis by sea.

Soon after Washington arrived, he went with Knox, Rochambeau, and others to visit de Grasse on board the flagship of the French fleet, the *Ville de Paris*. News had come to the

Loyalty is being committed to the welfare of those I serve, even to the detriment of my own comfort. Layfayette left his home and comfort in France to join in America's struggle for freedom. America appreciated his service and honored him for years to come. Every schoolboy and girl knew of the sacrifice Layfayette made to help attain our freedom.

admiral that more ships had also come to reinforce the British fleet, under command of Admiral Digby. De Grasse was now spoiling for a fight and was eager to sail out and engage the British vessels. But to do so would leave the possibility open of Cornwallis escaping by sea, as the blockading French ships would be drawn far away in maneuvering for battle. Washington immediately saw that such a decision could mean disaster for his fondly held plan of capturing Cornwallis at Yorktown. No doubt he employed all his eloquence and passion in pleading for cooperation from de Grasse. In light of how fickle the French assistance had proven to be thus far, he must have been intensely anxious as he waited for the admiral's decision.

Finally, de Grasse agreed to cooperate with Washington. When the army being transported from Head of Elk arrived, plans were at once developed for an attack on the British entrenchments.

Gloucester Point stood opposite Yorktown, and this point was held by Colonel Tarleton with a force of some 700 men. In order to keep him from interfering with Washington's attack on the main body of the British, the French General de Choisy was assigned, with the help of Virginia militia, to engage Tarleton and hold him there.

Surrender of Cornwallis to George Washington

MAKE YOUR LIFE COUNT

George Washington once said, "Make sure you are doing what God wants you to do — then do it with all your strength."[71] You might be surprised how many people you know are drifting through life, just doing enough to get by. Many people go to work, come home, eat supper, and spend the rest of the evening watching television. They don't serve others through volunteer work, improve their minds by reading a good book, or make an effort to share the gospel. They just try to have fun and avoid trying very hard at anything.

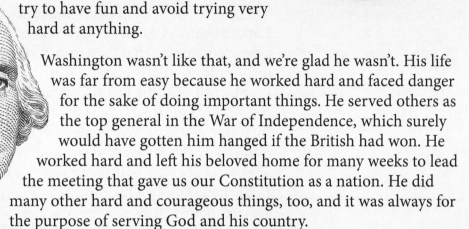

Storytime with Uncle Rick
America's Struggle

Washington wasn't like that, and we're glad he wasn't. His life was far from easy because he worked hard and faced danger for the sake of doing important things. He served others as the top general in the War of Independence, which surely would have gotten him hanged if the British had won. He worked hard and left his beloved home for many weeks to lead the meeting that gave us our Constitution as a nation. He did many other hard and courageous things, too, and it was always for the purpose of serving God and his country.

I hope you don't want to play your life away. Your country, your family, and God's kingdom need people who want to accomplish something with their lives. Ask God to show you some great works you can do and then attack them will all the strength you have. Nothing else is worth living for.

WASHINGTON

Day and night the cannons boomed. By the sixth of October, the patriots had moved to within 600 yards of the redcoat defenses. Then, working at night in fevered haste, they dug a trench parallel to that of the British. When the redcoats looked out over their fortifications in the morning, they were alarmed to find that the Americans had erected earthworks strong enough to shelter them from British fire.

A couple of days later, American and French guns opened up on the British ships that dared to come within range. Three of the British transports and one of their gunboats went down with the loss of many crewmen. Under the cover of this firing and the dark of night, the diligent Americans had extended their works, creating a second parallel of trenches and embankments. Now they were within 300 yards of Cornwallis's defenses.

Getting ready to leave Abercrombie.

Neither had the British soldiers been idle. They had advanced redoubts out beyond their main defenses in order to fire at the Americans while they worked. This proved to be very dangerous and distracting to the toiling patriots. The only solution was to take these works from the redcoats, so an attack was made on the evening of October 14. Lafayette led an American detachment toward these redoubts on the left side, while Baron de Viomenil led a troop of French soldiers to the right.

In the vanguard of Lafayette's force was Captain Aaron Ogden of New Jersey. His men were carrying unloaded guns so that they were forced to approach the enemy fortifications quietly and use their bayonets. On his command, they leaped over the fortified structure, scaled the wooden stakes, and launched a desperate bayonet charge against the surprised redcoats. So savage was their attack that in only two minutes all the British had surrendered. Viomenil and his men were were also successful, but lost 100 men in the effort while Lafayette lost only a handful. Now the redoubts would be used against their British builders. Cannon were now placed in the captured positions and turned upon the redcoats.

CORNWALLIS IS EMBARRASSED

Cornwallis was now in a very difficult position, yet he was an old British soldier and would rather die than surrender. He ordered Colonel Abercrombie to assault two batteries that were protected by French soldiers and cut through their line. The attack began at 4 a.m. on the morning of October 16. It was made with the ferocity of desperation and at first seemed to be succeeding as the French were driven back. But the fire that then came from the American trenches was so intense that the British were driven back to their own lines. Their attempt to cut their way through the enemy lines and open a path of escape had failed.

Now Cornwallis tried a different trick. He would leave his sick and wounded in camp and transport his men by boats over to Gloucester Point. Time was running out for him; a hundred guns were now pounding his position. The British navy had not come to his aid, so his situation was desperate in the extreme. He was successful in sending a few boatloads of his men across, but a sudden storm had come up and scattered the boats. Now he gave up on his second escape attempt.

On the following day, still more American and French guns had been brought up and put into action against the redcoat camp. Cornwallis was growing more desperate by the hour. At 10 a.m. on October 17, he sent a message to Washington asking for hostilities to cease for 24 hours. Washington was afraid that Clinton already had men and ships on the way to help the beleaguered British and he had no intention of allowing Cornwallis to stall for a full day lest reinforcements should come to him. So he replied that he too, was eager "to spare the further effusion of blood," but that he would only agree to a two-hour ceasefire.[72]

Cornwallis knew he was beaten. Painful as it was, he sent to Washington propositions for surrendering his army. Washington wrote a rough draft of the terms he would require and found that he and Cornwallis were fairly close to an agreement. In view of this, he now ordered a suspension of hostilities for a day and a night. It was arranged that commissioners from both armies would meet to further discuss terms.

Viscount de Noailles, by Gilbert Stuart, 1798 (PD-Art).

The American army sent Viscount de Noailles and Colonel Laurens to represent their side, and the British appointed Colonel Dundas and Major Ross for theirs. They met on October 18 at the home of a Mrs. Moore, near the right of the American lines. They were unable to come to an agreement and Washington feared that once again the British were fighting for time. He felt that the time had come for decisive action. On the next day he sent a copy of the rough draft of his terms to Cornwallis, along with a letter stating that he "expected" that the British general would have signed the terms by eleven o'clock that morning. The terms were signed.

Soon a spectacle took place that had the country folk from miles around hurrying toward Yorktown to watch. The British troops marched out of the town and presented the surrender document to General Lincoln. It contained exactly the same terms as he himself had received when forced to surrender Charleston to Cornwallis the previous year.

A double line of soldiers a mile long formed along the road by which the British army was to march in surrendering. On the right side of the road the American army was drawn up. On the left side was the French army. The surrendered army would march between them.

George Washington sat on a white horse at the head of his army. At the head of the French army, General Rochambeau sat on a bay horse. No doubt, both officers were eager to see General Cornwallis, who had been the instrument of so much suffering and death in America, ride out to offer his sword to Washington. But the redcoat general pleaded "indisposition" and sent the message that he was too ill to appear.

Instead, General O'Hara came, bringing the sword of Cornwallis. Instead of receiving it himself, Washington directed O'Hara to present it to General Lincoln. Lincoln, not wanting to add to the humiliation of Cornwallis, despite having been forced to surrender to him at Charleston, took the sword and then presented it back to O'Hara.

Next, 28 British captains came forward, each carrying a British flag in a case, and 28 American sergeants advanced to receive the colors. But there was a hesitation among the British captains when they were ordered to give up the flags. Forward rode Colonel Hamilton, the officer of the day, to find out the meaning of the delay. He was told that the redcoat officers did not like the idea of surrendering their colors to men of a rank lower than commissioned officers. Hamilton, not wanting to add to their embarrassment, courteously ordered a young American officer to receive the flags and then hand them to the waiting sergeants.

Then all the British soldiers laid aside their equipment and grounded their arms. Disarmed, they were marched back to their own lines. The following description of the surrender was given in the *New Jersey Gazette* in its November 7, 1781, edition:

> The British officers in general behaved like boys who have been whipped at school; some bit their lips, some pouted, others cried; their round, broad-brimmed hats were well adapted to the occasion, hiding those faces they were ashamed to show. The foreign regiments made a much more military appearance, and the conduct of their officers was far more becoming men of fortitude.

It is possible that the editor of that publication was indulging in a bit of fun at the expense of the army that had caused so much damage in his state.

Cornwallis's boats and sailors were assigned to the French as their prisoners and spoils. The 7,000 redcoat soldiers were claimed as prisoners by the American army. In the battle, the French and Americans had lost around 300 men. Around 552 of the British had fallen. The siege had lasted 13 days. The British army yielded to Washington a rich prize in artillery, small guns, ammunition, supplies, and equipment. Yet, the greater reward was in the glory and moral effect of the victory.

Tearing down the King's arm.

Gracious Washington permitted Cornwallis to send the *Bonetta* to New York with news of the surrender for Clinton. Many of the Tories who had been with the British at Yorktown departed with the ship, not wanting to fall into the hands of the patriots. Most of the surrendering redcoats were led away as prisoners into the interior of the country for the present.

Cornwallis and some of his officers were allowed to go to New York after having signed paroles.

REJOICING IN VICTORY

Just as Washington had suspected, help had indeed been on the way to Cornwallis as he surrendered. Clinton had sailed from New York to the aid of his friend with 7,000 of his best soldiers. Reaching the Virginia coast five days later, he received the news that he was too late. Sir Henry Clinton and Admiral Graves delayed a few days, then turned around and sailed for New York. No doubt, it was a time of great disappointment for the British officers.

But in the American camps, all was joy and relief as the word spread of the Yorktown surrender. It was hoped that this would prove to be the last major battle of the war and soon the soldiers could go home to rebuild their homes, their farms, their communities, and their country. Both officially and informally, great praise was heaped upon the American and French officers who had led the battle at Yorktown. Celebrations spread throughout the camps. Any soldiers being held under arrest were released. It was a great time of thanksgiving.

The news had to be carried to Philadelphia as quickly as possible. Washington sent his aide, Colonel Tilghman, galloping off with the happy announcement. The colonel made such superb time that in only four days he had traveled from southern Virginia to Philadelphia. He arrived at midnight, but that did not stop him from publishing his news. He found where Thomas McKean, then president of the Continental Congress, was staying and rapped loudly on

Surrender of Cornwallis

Siege of Yorktown, 1781, by Auguste Couder, 1836 (PD-Art).

the door. He made such a disturbance that the night watchman almost arrested him. Instead, every watchman in Philadelphia was soon calling out "Cornwallis is taken!"

Of course, Congress assembled quite early the next morning, and it was said that these distinguished gentlemen acted more like a troop of wild boys about to be released from school. The building rang with hurrahs when Washington's letter was read.

Congress made votes of thanks to Washington, Rochambeau, de Grasse, and other important leaders. To Rochambeau and de Grasse, they presented two of the captured cannon. They gave a gift of two captured flags to Washington and even made a gift to Colonel Tilghman, for bringing the glad news, of a fine sword and a beautiful saddle horse. A national day of thanksgiving and rejoicing was set for December 13, and it was celebrated in pulpits, communities, and homes across the happy land.

Nathanael Greene still had his hands full in South Carolina, so Washington appealed to de Grasse to use his ships to help. But de Grasse was in a hurry to return to the West Indies (where he would later be soundly defeated by the British navy) so he declined, offering instead to carry troops from the northern region to the Head of Elk in Maryland, where they could more quickly be marched south to assist Greene and others. After doing so, he quickly set sail for the Indies.

Rochambeau remained with his men for a while in Virginia. The next year, they sailed back to France. He was remembered gratefully by thousands who knew him or knew of the great help he had been to Washington.

General Washington settled his affairs at Yorktown and then hurried to Eltham, Virginia, where his wife's son, John Parke Custis lay dying. Custis had contracted camp fever during the Yorktown campaign. After his death, George and Martha Washington adopted two of his children and raised them as their own.

Traveling back to his army, Washington was hailed with great rejoicing at every hamlet through which he passed. Staying a few days in Philadelphia, he was honored by people of all classes. Attending the Congress at the State House, the general heard a congratulatory speech from the president of Congress. The genuine appreciation and admiration of the members of that body must have been very gratifying as Washington remembered times during the war when he had been doubted and even attacked by some of its members.

Count de Grasse

General St. Clair led troops by way of Wilmington, North Carolina, to assist Greene. The redcoats were driven out of Wilmington and both Virginia and North Carolina were at last free of any sizable force of the enemy.

In Georgia, Mad Anthony Wayne fought Tories, Indians, and redcoats in several battles. The patriots had the advantage in morale after the defeat of Cornwallis, and soon the enemy lost heart. In July 1782, the British evacuated Savannah; Wayne marched in and the war in Georgia was over.

South Carolina was the last southern state to expel the British. There were a number of smaller engagements, and though the numbers involved were comparatively small, the bitterness was as great as ever between patriot and Tory forces. In December 1782, the British evacuated Charleston. This left only small groups of bitter Tories to be dealt with.

NEWS FROM YORKTOWN
by Lewis Worthington Smith

"Past two o'clock and Cornwallis is taken."
How the voice rolled down the street
Till the silence rang and echoed
With the stir of hurrying feet!
In the hush of the Quaker city,
As the night drew on to morn,
How it startled the troubled sleepers,
Like the cry for a man-child born!

"Past two o'clock and Cornwallis is taken."
How they gathered, man and maid,
Here the child with a heart for the flint-lock,
There the trembling grandsire staid!
From the stateliest homes of the city,
From hovels that love might scorn,
How they followed that ringing summons,
Like the cry for a king's heir born!

"Past two o'clock and Cornwallis is taken."
I can see the quick lights flare,
See the glad, wild face at the window,
Half dumb in a breathless stare.
In the pause of an hour portentous,
In the gloom of a hope forlorn,
How it throbbed to the star-deep heavens,
Like the cry for a nation born!

"Past two o'clock and Cornwallis is taken."
How the message is sped and gone
To the farm and the town and the forest
Till the world was one vast dawn!
To distant and slave-sunk races,
Bowed down in their chains that morn.
How it swept on the winds of heaven,
Like a cry for God's justice born!

Battle between
Captain John Paul Jones'
ship *Bon Homme Richard*
and the British frigate *Serapis*

CHAPTER 28

A STRANGE WAR ON THE SEA

THE STRUGGLE FOR A NAVY

The War of Independence was a struggle between an old nation with the strongest navy in the world and a new nation with no navy at all. Still, there was plenty of fighting on the ocean during the years of the war.

The Americans, having been colonists before the war, had depended on the protection of the British navy from foreign enemies. For that reason, they had never built warships and created a navy of their own. When the war began, the need for ships of war was quickly recognized and even as early as 1775, Congress gave orders for a fleet of 14 vessels to be constructed.

In December of that year, a Rhode Islander named Ezekiel Hopkins was given command of the "fleet." Fewer than half of the ships ordered ever put out to sea, and when they did, things did not go well for them. In April of 1776, Hopkins attacked the *Glasgow*, a British sloop of war. Though Hopkins had in his command two sloops and three small brigs, he lost the battle. The news was received with anger among his countrymen, and Congress passed a "vote of censure" upon him. Before 1776 was over, Hopkins had been dismissed from the service.

An English caricature of John Paul Jones

One of the captains who served under Hopkins, however, had better success. His ship battled with the *Edward*, a British tender off the coast of Virginia, and won the day. This captain, John Barry, had the honor of taking the first enemy vessel in the war.

"Surrender? I have not yet begun to fight!"
—John Paul Jones, Memoirs of Rear-Admiral Paul Jones: Compiled from His Original Journals and Correspondence.

Persistence means tenacity or the strength to finish a task despite adversity. Second Chronicles 15:7 says, "Be ye strong therefore, and let not your hands be weak: for your work shall be rewarded."

John Paul Jones

But it was not ships owned by the infant American navy that made serious trouble for England on the water, but privateers. These ships were owned by private individuals or companies and fitted out for war, commissioned by either the Continental Congress or the Congress of an individual state to capture British vessels. Most of them had been merchant vessels before the conflict began. It was not that the Americans did not still see the need for their own navy, but Congress had little money to spend on ships. The few ships that ended up being built were usually captured by the fast, strong British ships.

But with the privateers it was another story. Just how many "prizes" were taken cannot be known, but it is estimated that the number was about 700. Considering that the mighty Royal Navy captured only 200 more than that number, it was a very good showing for a poverty-stricken infant country struggling against one of the powers of the world.

Sailing among the British Isles early in the war were two of the most successful American privateers, the *Revenge* and the *Reprisal*. These two ships had done so much damage to British shipping that English merchants feared to send their goods out of port.

But the most daring and probably the most skillful of the privateer captains was John Paul Jones. Though he claimed Scotland as the land of his birth, Jones had been to America many times on voyages and considered himself quite at home there. He had lived for two years in Virginia just before the war began.

Like most of the American leaders, Jones was a young man. But also like many of those leaders, he used daring to make up what he lacked in life experience. In 1778, he captured or sank many British merchant ships and even a sloop of war, the *Drake*. He was called a "pirate" by the English, and promised a noose suspended from a yardarm when he was caught. But catching John Paul Jones proved to be more easily said than done.

The year 1779 proved to be the zenith of Jones' career. Franklin had managed to get French assistance in fitting up five ships for Jones to command. Rather than sailing his fleet home to America to defend the coast against British ships, Jones was to concentrate on the coast of Great Britain.

It was hoped that he could do so much damage there that the British would call some of their ships back to protect the home island, rather than leaving them free to attack towns on the coast of America. Of these five ships, only the *Duras* was of significant size, and she was so old and rotten that it almost seemed foolish to take her out to sea. But the French purchased the ship and fitted her out, changing her name to *Bon Homme Richard* in honor of Benjamin Franklin (who had published *Poor Richard's Almanac*), who was very popular in France at that time.

It seemed perhaps a poor bargain, but the energetic Jones accepted her and eagerly prepared his fleet to make life even more miserable for British shipping. Just like his ships, Captain Jones' crew was also a mixed lot. He had around 380 men altogether, and only about 100 of them were Americans. The rest were gathered from ports all over the world. The other four ships in the fleet were the *Alliance*, the *Cerf*, the *Vengeance*, and the *Pallas*. The *Alliance* had actually been built in America and was under command of Captain Landais, a Frenchman who had gone to America in hopes of becoming a naval Lafayette. Landais was to be one of the worst problems Jones would encounter. He would give his commander more trouble than many a British ship.

John Paul Jones during battle, by Guttenberg, Carl, after C. J. Notté, c.1779 (PD-Art).

Time would show that Landais could not even manage his own ship well, yet he often expressed disdain for the sailing skills of Jones. In fact, each ship's captain had a degree of independence in commanding his crew and vessel, but the rude disrespect Landais showed to the squadron commander was far above and beyond what was appropriate or even common courtesy. Thus it was with a patched-together fleet, a truly motley crew, and an insubordinate captain that John Paul Jones set sail from France for the British coast in September 1779.

Jones Terrorizes the British Coast

For some weeks, Jones and his ships terrorized the eastern coast of Scotland and England. Prizes were captured, towns threatened, and the people of the islands kept in a state of nervous distraction. Then, on September 23, Jones encountered two British frigates off Flamborough Head, on the Yorkshire coast of England. They were the *Serapis*, a 44-gun ship, and the *Countess of Scarborough*, carrying 22 guns. One of the most desperate and bloody sea battles of the war was about to begin.

These two British ships had been detailed to guard a fleet of 40 merchant vessels that stretched out in line over a considerable expanse of water. As soon as Jones saw their sails, he signaled

Admiral John Paul Jones

to his other ships to join him in a chase. The merchant ships flew into a panic, but the two frigates boldly made ready for battle. Captain Landais promptly fled the scene in the *Alliance*, but Jones' other three ships advanced to fight the *Countess of Scarborough* while Jones directed the *Bon Homme Richard* to engage the Serapis. It was just after sundown when the battle began, and it appeared to be an unequal struggle. The *Serapis* was a well-equipped modern ship while the *Bon Homme Richard* was an old, rotten former merchant vessel. Yet John Paul Jones was at sea for the purpose of fighting, and he was not easily intimidated.

At first, the fight was one of booming cannons in which both ships suffered greatly. Then Captain Pearson of the *Serapis*, in trying to achieve a better position, caused his ship to collide with the *Richard*. Immediately, Jones gave orders for his men to lash the two vessels together, and the battle changed into a brawl. The sailors of both vessels fought with demonic fury using pikes, pistols, and cutlasses. The *Richard* was taking water quickly through jagged holes made by the 18-pound balls from the *Serapis*. Her two 12-pounders had been silenced, but her three 9-pounders were still hard at work spouting death and destruction into the enemy ship. Meanwhile, sailors with muskets, high in the ship's rigging, kept up a continuous fire on the crew of the *Serapis*. During this time, the captain of the *Serapis* called on Jones to surrender. Jones replied, "I have not yet begun to fight!" and that reply has gone down in history and is quoted even today. Two and a half hours into the battle, a sailor on the *Richard* threw a grenade onto the *Serapis*, exploding some munitions on the British ship. Instantly, several British sailors were blown to pieces. Decks on both ships were slippery with blood. Both vessels caught fire more than once during the fight. Dead bodies lay everywhere.

Finally, Captain Landais decided to return and help his comrades. The *Alliance* fired several broadsides, doing damage to the *Serapis* and at the same time killing 11 sailors and an officer aboard the *Richard*. Later, the theory was advanced that Landais had fired at both vessels hoping that the *Richard* would be so badly damaged that Jones would have to surrender to the *Serapis*. Then, with the *Serapis* already badly damaged and lashed to the sinking *Richard*, he could achieve a glorious victory by capturing both ships. Later, Landais would be charged with this crime, but would only be dismissed from the service as punishment. Because of his bizarre behavior aboard his ship, he was believed to be insane.

Captain Pearson had ordered the flag of the *Serapis* nailed to the mast in a gesture of defiance, but finally the battle appeared to be hopeless. The *Richard* was in a desperate plight also, and was being kept afloat by the efforts of a hundred British prisoners from previous fights working busily at the pumps. At last, a double cannon shot from the *Richard* shattered the mast of the enemy ship and Captain Pearson with his own hands tore the flag from the mast to surrender.

Through the rest of the night, the surviving crew of the *Bon Homme Richard*, along with sailors from the other American ships (except the *Alliance*, which Landais kept at a distance) struggled to fight the fires and keep the *Richard* afloat, but the next morning at 10 a.m. the gallant ship sank beneath the Atlantic waves. It was a glorious victory for John Paul Jones, but it was a costly one. More men had died than survived the battle.

Jones and what was left of his squadron made it safely to Holland, where the British demanded that the Dutch give him up as a pirate. But the Dutch had little more love for the British than did the Americans, so Jones made his escape to France.

The Bon Homme Richard

A Thorn in the Side

Captain Pierre Landais (below) was a thorn in the side of John Paul Jones for as long as he commanded a ship in Jones' squadron. He constantly refused to obey orders from Jones and often expressed his opinion that his

boss was not much of a sailor. Benjamin Franklin believed that Landais was mentally unstable and said, "If I had twenty ships of war in my disposition I should not give one of them to Captain Landais." During the battle off Flamborough Head, his cannons had done almost as much damage to the *Bon Homme Richard* as to the *Serapis*. Jones believed Landais had intentionally fired on both ships. Ultimately, Landais was dismissed from service.

The Nation Thanks John Paul Jones

In autumn of 1780, John Paul Jones once again sailed for America. Arriving in Philadelphia in February 1781, the young captain received a welcome that would seem a high honor to any man. The honors came not only from America; he had already received recognition from the governments of Holland, Denmark, France, and Russia. Congress voted to Jones the "thanks of the nation," and in later years presented him with a gold medal.

Naval power was also put to work in an assault on a British fort at Penobscot, Maine, in 1779. A redcoat force from Halifax, Nova Scotia, had begun building the fort under the leadership of a General McLean. In July of that year, the Americans decided to send an expedition from Boston to destroy the fort to prevent the British from establishing a foothold there. The expedition was intended to involve 1,500 men, but the response was far less than that number. A fleet of 19 armed ships and 24 transports made up the naval force under the command of Dudley Saltonstall, who was also the overall commander of the expedition. The land forces were led by Generals Lovell and Wadsworth.

The militia leaders and Saltonstall did not get along well. In addition, unfavorable headwinds thwarted the progress of the expedition. However, McLean was in no condition yet to repel a sustained attack, so if Lovell had acted quickly he probably would have succeeded in taking the fort. Instead, he demanded a surrender, which was refused, and instead of storming the defenses he erected a battery 750 yards away, only to find that his guns were ineffective at that range.

After three weeks of posturing and small skirmishes, the Americans prepared to storm the place. McLean frantically worked to strengthen his fortifications and defend the fort, but the attack had barely begun when it was suddenly broken off. The militia hurriedly left the fort and boarded the fleet. The British fleet of Sir George Collyer had arrived on a rescue mission.

John Paul Jones

Not only was the attack aborted, but the Americans managed to make the affair an even greater disaster. The fleet at first prepared to fight, but evidently courage was in short supply and soon the vessels scattered. Every single one was lost — some were captured, some blown up, and some set on fire by their own men to keep them from being taken by the British. Once on shore, the American militiamen and sailors had a terrible march of 100 miles through the wilderness before they reached their friends.

It had been a very disheartening fiasco, and it was investigated by the Massachusetts General Court. The outcome was that Generals Lovell and Wadsworth received commendation for their part in the expedition and the blame placed on the commander of the fleet. Every boat had been lost, and it was the worst naval disaster until Pearl Harbor, over 150 years later.

During the last three years of the war, America had only two frigates in the service. The French fleet had done very little to defend the American coast, but the privateers had shown themselves heroes over and over. Their history almost reads like fiction for the great and bloody battles they fought and the victories they sometimes achieved against great odds. Whaleboats and sloops, craft of every size and description, were at all times attacking larger boats of the enemy and many times were successful

The *Serapis* and the *Bon Homme Richard*

King George III

CHAPTER 29

WAR IN THE WEST

REDCOATS AND INDIANS IN THE OHIO COUNTRY

Most of the action of the Revolutionary War took place along the Atlantic coast. This makes sense, because that is where most of the people lived. Boston, New York, Philadelphia, Charleston, and Savannah were all the scenes of great battles. They were all cities on or near the ocean. That meant that America needed them to ship needed goods and war materials into the country. It also meant that England could send large armies to those places by ship, which was much easier than marching them over the rough roads of the time. It was natural that most of the fighting would take place in the part of America where most of the people lived and which could be reached by sea. The issue of American independence was settled in the great battles in the east.

The Death of Cornstalk

But the question of American's independence from England was not the only matter that was settled by the war. Another very important issue was settled in the country far to the west of Boston, New York, and Philadelphia. What was that issue? It was the question of just how large the United States would be when the war ended and America was a free nation. How much land would the Americans control?

If you look at a map of America in colonial times, you will see that most Americans lived between the Atlantic Ocean on the east and the Allegheny Mountains on the west. There just had not yet been enough time for the colonies to spread over the mountains.

Daniel Boone loved the Lord. He wrote in 1816: "The religion I have is to love and fear God, believe in Jesus Christ, do all the good to my neighbor, and myself that I can, do as little harm as I can help, and trust on God's mercy for the rest. (http://www.christianhistorysociety.com/booneadventures.html)

Pontiac

Only the hardy pioneers who wanted more land, the hunters and trappers who went seeking animal skins, and the men who sold and traded goods to the Indians (called Indian traders) were likely to be found west of the Alleghenies.

There was much land in that region that was claimed by England. Most of it had been won from the French after England defeated France in the French and Indian War. This region would later come to be called the Northwest Territory. It included land that is now in the states of Michigan, Ohio, Indiana, Illinois, and Wisconsin. Parts of other states were also included in the Northwest Territory. Before and during the War of Independence the region was often called the "Ohio country." The Ohio River was the southern boundary of this region.

On the other side of the river was Kentucky, which was called the "Dark and Bloody Ground." There were few Indians actually living in Kentucky, but several northern tribes crossed the river often on hunting trips. There had been much fighting between tribes over hunting rights in Kentucky, giving the region its sad nickname.

The land north of the Ohio River had been reserved for several Indian tribes. After the French had been driven out, England had made treaties with the Indians to avoid warfare with them. When England and her American colonies went to war against each other, most of the Indians in the Ohio country were on the side of the British.

Fort Detroit was where the city of Detroit, Michigan, now stands. It was on the Detroit River, a main waterway between some of the Great Lakes. The fort was many miles west of the main theater of action in the war. The reason it was still important is that the British used Detroit to organize and arm Indian tribes so that they could fight against American settlers to the southeast. These tribes mostly lived north of the Ohio River, but often crossed the Ohio to attack American settlements in what is now western Pennsylvania, Kentucky, and West Virginia.

Daniel Boone, Simon Kenton, and other pioneers rose to fame by fighting off these attacks and building lasting settlements in the beautiful but dangerous land of Kentucky.

View of the Allegheny Mountains West Virginia, by Aneta Kaluzna , 2006 (CC BY-SA 2.5).

The British were eager to encourage the Indians to make trouble in the western regions. They hoped that the colonies would send soldiers to protect the western American settlements, which would mean fewer soldiers to fight the British in the east. The commander of Fort Detroit, Henry Hamilton, even gave the Indians money to kill American settlers. To prove how many people they had killed, the Indians had to bring scalps to Detroit. This led to the nickname "Hair-buyer Hamilton."

Siege of Fort Detroit by Frederic Remington, date unknown (PD-Art).

From Detroit, the British sent forces to build more forts along the Ohio River. This made it easier to supply their Indian allies and launch attacks farther from Detroit. Much of the fighting in the west took place around these forts.

In Kentucky, just south of the Ohio, Indian attacks often targeted white hunters and settlers in lonely regions, convincing many white people to return to the East. There were fewer than 200 colonists remaining in Kentucky by the late spring of 1776. Most of them were located around the forts at Boonesborough, Logan's Station, and Harrodsburg. Even near the forts, settlers lived with the constant fear of waking up at night to the sound of Indian war cries.

INCREASING BLOODSHED IN THE WEST

In 1777, the violence grew. The British launched a series of attacks from the north. They were trying to draw American forces west in the hope of weakening patriot strength in the east. British officers based in Detroit began calling on Indians to attack the Americans, providing them with arms and rewards for their service. This led to bitter fighting, with an unknown number of Indians and American settlers killed in battles in present Pennsylvania, Kentucky, and West Virginia.

The fighting became even more bitter after angry Virginia militiamen killed the Shawnee chief Cornstalk in late 1777. Cornstalk's death was actually bad news for the Americans because he had tried to keep his tribe from going to war on either side. Like Cornstalk, many Ohio Indians wanted to stay out of the war, but their location between the British in Detroit and the patriots along the Ohio River made it very difficult to do so.

Early in the war, Virginia had attempted to defend her western border by occupying Forts Pitt, Randolph, and Henry along the

Ohio River. They soon found out that this would not work, however, because the Indians simply slipped between the forts on their way to and from their destinations. So in 1778 the Americans decided that the only way to protect their western border (the Ohio River) was to go on the attack against the Tories and Indians. Expeditions would have to be made into the Ohio country.

The first expedition was led by General Edward Hand. The mission was a disaster, but not because Hand was defeated in battle. He had led 500 militiamen from Pennsylvania toward Mingo towns on the Cayuhoga River in February of 1778 in what was supposed to be a surprise winter attack. At these towns the British had stored military supplies for the Indian and Tory raiders. But the winter weather was so harsh that the company gave up and started home. On the return march some of Hand's men, encountering some peaceful Delaware Indians, attacked them. They killed one man and a few women and children. Some of them were relatives of Captain Pipe, a Delaware chief. Even at this outrage, Pipe did not join the British in fighting the Americans, but later, his people would suffer other offenses from foolish Americans, and Pipe would lead them to join the redcoats.

Colonel Hand had other problems also. There was strong Tory sentiment in the western end of Pennsylvania to be contended with. In March of 1778, three important men deserted from Hand's group and went over to the British and Indian forces. The defectors were Simon Girty, Alexander McKee, and Matthew Elliot. Girty was an interpreter who would become famous as a traitor before the end of the war. Matthew Elliot was a local trader, and Alexander McKee had been an Indian agent for the British before the war. These three traitors would be very useful to the British during the war along the Ohio. Their knowledge of Indian ways would help the redcoats to keep their native allies loyal.

In 1777, the western settlers kept sending letters to Congress, asking them to send soldiers out west to protect them from the enemy raiders. Early in 1778, Congress recommended to the army that they send help and build a fort on the north side of the Ohio River. The plan was to build more forts after that one and eventually launch an attack from them that would capture Detroit and break up the British-Indian operations.

After making a treaty with the Delaware Indians, the Americans built Fort Laurens on the Tuscarawas River. But the fort did not last long. The Delaware chief who had made the agreement with the Americans was killed. Captain Pipe then became the Delaware leader. Soon he began taking gifts from the British.

He could no longer be trusted not to attack the fort. An even bigger problem was manpower. Congress could not get enough troops to send to the west because every man was needed for the intense fighting in upstate New York and eastern Pennsylvania. In 1779, Fort Laurens was abandoned. The Americans marched away.

Endurance is the inward struggle to endure tribulation with determination. George Rogers Clark is a great example to us of endurance. He has gone down in history as the Hero of Vincennes and rightly deserves that title. "Behold, we count them happy which endure. Ye have heard of the patience of Job, and have seen the end of the Lord; that the Lord is very pitiful, and of tender mercy" (James 5:11). Little buddies, we need to remember to appreciate the sacrifices that so many made obtaining our freedom.

George Rogers Clark
Illinois Campain

In late 1778, a young Virginia militia officer named George Rogers Clark set his sights on capturing the Illinois country from Britain. Clark would soon become the top American leader in the west. With a company of volunteers, he captured the fort at Kaskaskia on July 4, 1778. Next, he took the fort at Vincennes. Because he was short on men, he could only leave a small force there. The fort was soon retaken by the British officer, General Henry Hamilton.

A few months later, in an astonishing winter march, Clark led his militiamen almost 200 miles through bitterly cold weather and a flooded Wabash Valley to retake Vincennes, capturing Hamilton himself along with the fort and its garrison.

Lt Governor Henry Hamilton surrenders to Col. George Rogers Clark.

Joseph Brant by Gilbert Stuart, 1786 (PD-Art).

When Governor Thomas Jefferson heard about the capture of the "Hair-buyer," he ordered Hamilton to be brought to Williamsburg. There he intended to try the man for war crimes. But Jefferson changed his mind about the war crimes trial when the British threatened to treat captured American officers the same way. Hamilton was exchanged for an American soldier in 1781.

Over the next few years, raids were launched by both sides against various settlements. A British-Indian expedition into Kentucky cost the Americans hundreds in killed and captured in 1780. George Rogers Clark struck back a few months later with a raid on two Shawnee towns along the Mad River.

Late in the year 1780, Clark went east to meet with Governor Thomas Jefferson of Virginia. The two men developed a plan for Clark to lead a force of 2,000 men against Fort Detroit. This was a goal that was dear to Clark's fighting heart. The fort at Detroit had been the launching place for many bloody attacks on the American settlers.

However, recruiting enough volunteers proved to be a problem. Militiamen on the frontier did not like to go far from home, leaving their families and farms unprotected. Besides that, Continental Colonel Daniel Brodhead refused to send men from his force to help Clark because he was launching his own campaign against the Delawares, who had recently taken to the warpath on behalf of the British.

Brodhead was successful in marching into the Ohio country and demolishing Coshocton, the Delaware Indian capitol, but America's cause was hurt by this victory, because Brodhead's attack had taken men and supplies that Clark had needed for a much more important campaign against Detroit.

When Clark finally began his march toward Detroit from Fort Pitt in August of 1781, he had only 400 men in his company. Another 100 men were marching to meet up with him, but on the 24th of that month, Indians led by Joseph Brant, a famous Mohawk leader, ambushed and defeated that force. After this loss, Clark decided that he had to call off the attack on Detroit. That fort would not be taken during the entire war.

There were a number of other defeats in store for the Americans west of the Alleghenies, and 1782 became known as "the bloody year." By July, peace negotiations were underway because of British losses in the east. There would be a few more bloody engagements before the British finally gave up the war in the west.

THE BATTLE OF BLUE LICKS

One of these engagements was the battle of Blue Licks in August of 1782. British Captain William Caldwell led about 50 Tories and 300 Indians in a raid on Bryan Station, a small fort near what is now Lexington, Kentucky. Caldwell's advisor was Simon Girty, who had defected from the patriots and would go down in history as one of the most violent and treacherous traitors the war produced. Arriving at the fort around dawn, Caldwell's force found that their hope of a surprise attack would be disappointed. Some keen-eyed pioneer had spotted Indians lurking in the woods outside the stockade and alerted the others. After several attempts to take the fort, Caldwell's men gave up. Word had come that patriot reinforcements were on the way and it was time to leave.

With men from Bryan Station, the Kentucky militia set out in pursuit of the mostly Indian attackers. Mostly because of the foolishness of one hotheaded officer, they were drawn into a trap at a place called Blue Licks. There they suffered a bloody defeat, and the survivors gave up and headed for home.

In November, the final blow of the war in the Ohio country was delivered by George Rogers Clark, who destroyed several Shawnee towns as the braves fled before the dreaded frontiersman.

Because of the work of George Rogers Clark in seizing British forts and destroying Indian towns, the British gave up the entire Ohio country to America by the terms of the peace treaty that ended the Revolutionary War. It was several years, however, before the redcoats finally withdrew all their troops. The Indian tribes were not consulted regarding the treaty, so they were left with no claim on the region except their willingness to continue to fight without the help of the British. Their struggle would continue as the Northwest Indian War.

By the Treaty of Paris that ended the War of Independence, the British gave up all claims to land between the Atlantic Ocean on the east and the Mississippi River on the west. Had it not been for George Rogers Clark, Daniel Boone, and other frontier warriors, England probably would have held on to her territory in the west. America would only have been about half as large as she was when the war ended.

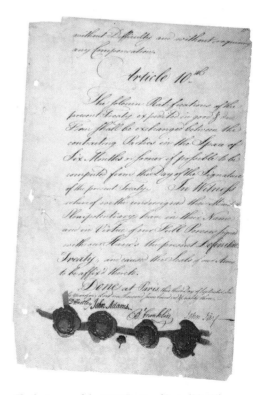

The last page of the 1783 Treaty of Paris (PD-US).

277

Washington's Farewell
to His Officers

CHAPTER 30

AN UNSETTLED PEACE

THE DUST OF WAR SETTLES

Cornwallis had surrendered. Yorktown was to be the last major battle of the War of Independence. The supporters of the king, both in America and England, were forlorn about the news. Of course, at the same time, the American patriots and their sympathetic friends in England were as happy as the loyalists were sad.

In Parliament, passions burned hot and speeches grew more eloquent as reverses in America added fuel to the arguments of those members who opposed the war in the colonies. These men kept relentlessly pushing their ideas for an end to hostilities. And though always defeated at first, it seemed that as time went on, all of Parliament was growing weary of war and the majorities against peace diminished with each vote. Finally, the party for peace won out, important supporters of the king resigned, and the end of the war was at hand. Soon, commissioners of peace would be commissioned by each of the two warring nations, and hostilities would cease entirely.

Prime Minister Lord Shelburne, by Jean-Laurent Mosnier, 1791 (PD-Art).

In America, the people waited to see what would happen next. They had lived with war for years; terrible things had been suffered, and bitterness was strong on both sides. Whigs and Tories both carried very hard feelings toward each other. Especially among the scattered homes in the countryside where no strong force of either side was in control, raids and counter-raids were still going on frequently. In the absence of an established law system, lawless men took advantage of the confusion and used the war as an excuse for robbery and murder.

"Unto Him who is the author and giver of all good, I render sincere and humble thanks for His manifold and unmerited blessings, and especially for our redemption and salvation by His beloved Son. . . . Blessed be His holy name."

—John Jay

John Jay, by Gilbert Stuart, 1794 (PD-Art).

Finally, in 1783 the war came to an official end. Benjamin Franklin, America's envoy to France, had received informal suggestions from the British government about making peace in 1782, but the plan suggested by the British did not allow for the 13 colonies to become independent and form a new country. It only allowed a greater measure of self-government while still remaining a part of the British empire. Franklin rejected the offer and insisted on a recognition of America's independence and an end to hostilities against France, America's new ally. But the old philosopher did agree to formal negotiations to end the war.

America sent John Adams and John Jay to join Franklin, and the three men met with Britain's commissioners beginning on September 27, 1782.

Franklin, shrewd old negotiator that he was, demanded that Great Britain relinquish Canada to the United States. He knew that many Englishmen, including Prime Minister Lord Shelburne, would not agree to this, but it put America in the position of making the first concession in the discussions, suggesting an obligation for England to respond with concessions in turn. The negotiations continued for two months before it appeared that a tentative agreement had been reached.

In this agreement, referred to as "preliminary articles of peace," the two powers resolved many tough issues. The British accepted American independence and boundaries. Further, it resolved the question of fishing rights on the Newfoundland banks, debts owed by Americans to British creditors before the war, and the restoration of property lost by loyalists in America during the war. It also provided for the removal of British forces still in the 13 states. The preliminary articles were signed in Paris on November 30, 1782, but they were not to go into effect until Britain and France negotiated a similar treaty. The Foreign Minister of France, Vergennes, quickly made arrangements for this to be done. France and Britain signed preliminary articles of peace on January 20, 1783. Finally, on September 3, 1783, the Treaty of Paris was signed, finalizing the end of the war.

Now the United States of America was acknowledged to be a free and independent nation, although the states were only weakly held together by the Articles of Confederation, drafted early in the War of Independence to give the colonies a form through which to cooperate in fighting Britain. Canada was the boundary on the north. Florida was the boundary on the south. The Mississippi River formed the western boundary.

It is not possible to account for the exact number of men who had fought in the war. It is estimated that about 40,000 Continentals were in the field at the same time, and about the same number of redcoats. But as many as 230,000 may have served in the Continental army for some part of the war, and there is no way of numbering the men who turned out among the Whig and Tory militias. When the war ended, the bitterness against the Tories was so great that most of the states confiscated their property. Now left in poverty and surrounded by people whom they hated and who hated them, most of the loyalists left the country. Those in the south often relocated to the West Indies, those in the north to Canada or Nova Scotia.

Likewise, there was great poverty among the patriots. Those who had spent many years in the army were usually ruined when they returned home. Whatever business they had before the war was destroyed. The struggle for survival was intense in all the colonies, and the leaders were often no better off than the working classes. But the country was new, natural resources abounded, and the former colonists were used to working hard for what they needed. The same grit and determination that had built an army and a nation were applied to building new lives and fortunes for the families of America. In a short time, a surprising amount had been accomplished toward restoration of pre-war fortunes.

Determination: purposing to exert all your energies in accomplishing a task regardless of the opposition. The patriots used determination to win the war. Now they needed to use determination to rebuild their businesses and farms.

"And whatsoever ye do, do it heartily, as to the Lord, and not unto men."
—Colossians 3:23

Some of the leaders in the war were men who had scarcely been known beyond their home regions, but now were national heroes and famed far and wide throughout several nations. Washington, Jefferson, Franklin, Hancock, and many others became justly famous for their contributions before and during the war. At the same time, many common people whose names have never been printed in history books also demonstrated great courage, determination, and wisdom during those dark days. The winning of liberty had indeed been a team effort all through America. Even the Indian tribes, fighting for one side or the other, had their share in determining the outcome.

Why did God bless America? Because it was founded upon godly principles set forth in God's Word. Alexis de Toqueville came to America from France and sought to discover why America was prosperous. This is what he concluded, "I sought for the greatness and genius of America in her commodious

Caricature of Alexis de Toqueville by Honoré Daumier, 1849 (PD-US).

harbors and her ample rivers — and it was not there . . . in her fertile fields and boundless forests and it was not there . . . in her rich mines and her vast world commerce — and it was not there . . . in her democratic Congress and her matchless Constitution — and it was not there. Not until I went into the churches of America and heard her pulpits flame with righteousness did I understand the secret of her genius and power. America is great because she is good, and *if America ever ceases to be good, she will cease to be great*" (emphasis added). You as a citizen of this country have a duty to do your part to see that America never ceases to be good and to bring her back when she strays. The United States has sent more missionaries than any other country.[73]

PROBLEMS WITH THE ARMY

Seeing the history of the world from our vantage point as modern Americans, we see that the freedom our forefathers won for us was not to benefit America alone. The ideals of self-government, hammered out and articulated in our founding documents, filtered across oceans and eventually caused sweeping changes in countries around the world.

The Founders reacted, not so much against England as against certain narrow ideas of a part of the English people. The natural desire of people to be free and determine their own destiny was already demonstrated in many Englishmen who supported the American colonies in their desire for representative government. That same desire has since been seen in many places around the globe as oppressed people in various lands have worked and fought for the freedom to live under a government that recognizes justice and liberty as the right of all mankind.

The Continental army had not yet been dissolved. George Washington was still at its head, and his troubles as General Washington were nearing an end. His difficulties as President Washington would begin in a few years. Still, there remained to be settled the problem of the poor soldiers who had suffered and risked so much to bring the war to an end. They had been paid mostly in promises, and those promises proved to be slow in being fulfilled. Their peacetime trades and businesses were gone, their farms in disrepair, and their wives and children were dependent on men who had been absent for months or years at a time. As the time of their discharge drew near, the soldiers wondered whether they would receive the pay due them or be turned out of the army to march home with ragged clothes and empty pockets.

Congress had used up all the money it had received and had contracted debts beyond that. It had made so many promises that there was doubt whether they would ever be fulfilled. A panic spreads rapidly, and before long there was talk in the camps of extreme measures to force Congress to do justice to the men who had borne the burden of war. The members of Congress certainly had no intention of doing wrong to the soldiers; in fact, many of them were also poverty-stricken after having their property destroyed by the British during the war. But it is impossible to pay money that one does not have, and that was the plight of the Congress at that time.

Congressed passed an act for the relief of the army officers in October 1780. The act granted them half pay for the remainder of their lives. But the act had to be approved by the states, and nine of them failed to do so. As the end of the war drew near, some of the officers sent an appeal to Congress asking that instead of half pay for life, they might receive their full pay for five years and whatever money was owed to them already.

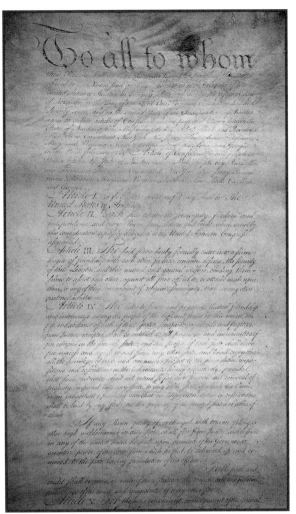

Articles of Confederation, 1777, ratified in 1781 (PD-US).

During this time, Washington was in the camp at Newburgh when he heard rumors that some of the soldiers were talking among themselves of organizing a move to force Congress to do justice in the matter of money owed to them. The general once again displayed his greatness and the loyalty he inspired when he faced his men and appealed to them not to take drastic measures. He spoke to them calmly and earnestly, showing much sympathy for their suffering and deep appreciation for their loyalty and courage through the war. In the end, the men agreed to yield to their Commander's wishes.

However, at the end of the war, trouble arose in Philadelphia. In October of 1783, Congress announced that the soldiers were to be discharged on December 3. Once again, the fear spread through the army that they were to be turned out without having received their pay. About 80 men in camp at Lancaster, Pennsylvania, went to Philadelphia where they were joined by some other soldiers, and together they marched to the State House where Congress was meeting. In an orderly troop that was estimated at 300 to 500 in number, they placed guards at the doors to hold the representatives in the building at bayonet point, if necessary. They sent a message in to Congress that they wanted something done to grant them the pay due them.

Washington giving his farewells to his men.

They demanded a response in 20 minutes and stated that if it was not forthcoming in that time, the soldiers would enter the building and unpleasant things would happen.

There was discussion back and forth between the leaders of Congress and the leading mutineers. Finally, the Congress adjourned and the members left the building, unmolested by the soldiers.

A message was sent to General Washington about the uprising. He quickly sent back a message saying that he would respond with troops immediately, and that the troops he had were dependable. The mutineers, he said, were not the faithful veterans who had borne the hardships of the entire war, but recent recruits whose selfishness was a disgrace to the army. The general started hastily for Philadelphia with a force easily large enough to disperse the mutiny, but the trouble had died down before they could arrive. Meanwhile, the Congress had moved to Princeton, where the governor of New Jersey had promised them protection.

THE GENERAL SAYS GOOD-BYE

On November 25, 1783, the British abandoned New York. It was a day of wild celebration as the last large British garrison in an American city departed. The redcoats had already pulled their soldiers from the few remaining cities they had held at the time of Cornwallis's surrender. For that reason, the celebration recognized not only the liberation of New York but the end of British occupation in America. The redcoats were gone.

As soon as they departed, the American army marched in to take possession of the city. The air was full of joyful noise as crowds of people added their cheers to the celebratory booming of cannons. At Fraunce's Tavern, Governor Clinton gave a dinner for the army officers. In the evening, the city was illuminated by bonfires and fireworks.

Fraunce's Tavern was again the meeting place of the officers on December 4, 1783, but this occasion was more somber than celebratory. The commander was going to take leave of his top comrades.

A Tearful Good-bye

The only known eyewitness account of Washington's farewell to his officers is from the memoirs of Colonel Benjamin Tallmadge. He gave a detailed description of the scene that clearly showed the deep bond of respect and affection between Washington and the officers who had served so faithfully beside him through the difficult and desperate years of the war.

It was time for General Washington to leave the army in New York and return to his beloved Mount Vernon. At noon on Tuesday, December 4, 1783, he and his officers gathered at Fraunce's Tavern on Pearl Street. It had been announced that this was the day when they must part. Just a few moments after the men entered the room, they were joined by General Washington. Despite his exceptional supply of dignity and self-control, he could not hide the deep emotion the occasion was kindling in him. Likewise, every officer in the room seemed to be bursting with feeling. A solemn quiet filled the room. The general filled his glass, lifted it to his men in salute, and said, "With a heart full of love and gratitude I now take leave of you. I most devoutly wish that your latter days may be as prosperous and happy as your former ones have been glorious and honorable." A moment later he said, "I cannot come to each of you, but shall feel obliged if each of you will come and take me by the hand."[74]

Tough, stocky General Knox was nearest the chief, turned to him and grasped his hand. Washington, his face covered with tears, embraced his friend but could not get any words out. Tallmadge wrote, "In the same affectionate manner every officer in the room marched up, kissed and parted with his general in chief. Such a scene of sorrow and weeping I had never before witnessed and fondly hope I may never be called to witness again." [75]

After this, the officers escorted Washington down to the wharf, where he would be picked up by a boat.

The men could see in each other's faces and that of their general all the joy and sadness born of the struggles, victories, disappointments, defeats, and hardships they had endured together. Those experiences were things of the past now, but their memories would go with every officer for the rest of his life. At last, the moment came when, solemn and silent, the general stepped into a boat and was rowed across to the New Jersey shore.

Thomas Mifflin

From there he proceeded to Annapolis, Maryland, where the Congress was in session. It was time to resign from the army and go home. He stayed in Philadelphia a few days before traveling on to Annapolis. He informed Congress on December 20 what the business was that had brought him there. Congress immediately voted to make the occasion public. Crowds of eager people assembled and the hall itself was filled to bursting. Mrs. Washington had come to share in the event, and she sat in the gallery with many other ladies.

Washington entered and was led to a seat. Thomas Mifflin, the president of Congress, then arose and declared to Washington that "the United States in Congress assembled are ready to receive his communications."[76] The general then arose to speak. His deep emotion was evident to everyone.

Washington's great humility is again evident in his speech to Congress. Despite the brilliance, strength, and determination he had so often displayed throughout the war, he had nothing to say in praise of himself. All the credit for the success of the struggle he gave to his men and to the kind assistance of Providence. In fact, Washington mentioned Providence, heaven, or God three times in his brief speech.

Annapolis, December 23, 1783

Mr. President: The great events on which my resignation depended having at length taken place; I have now the honor of offering my sincere Congratulations to Congress and of presenting myself before them to surrender into their hands the trust committed to me, and to claim the indulgence of retiring from the Service of my Country.

Happy in the confirmation of our Independence and Sovereignty, and pleased with the opportunity afforded the United States of becoming a respectable Nation, I resign with satisfaction the Appointment I accepted with diffidence. A diffidence in my abilities to accomplish so arduous a task, which however was superseded by a confidence in the rectitude of our Cause, the support of the supreme Power of the Union, and the patronage of Heaven.

The Successful termination of the War has verified the most sanguine expectations, and my gratitude for the interposition of Providence, and the assistance I have received from my Countrymen, encreases with every review of the momentous Contest.

While I repeat my obligations to the Army in general, I should do injustice to my own feelings not to acknowledge in this place the peculiar Services and distinguished merits of the Gentlemen who have been attached to my person during the War. It was impossible the choice of confidential Officers to compose my family should have been more fortunate. Permit me Sir, to recommend in particular those, who have continued in Service to the present moment, as worthy of the favorable notice and patronage of Congress.

I consider it an indispensable duty to close this last solemn act of my Official life, by commending the Interests of our dearest Country to the protection of Almighty God, and those who have the superintendence of them, to his holy keeping.

Having now finished the work assigned to me, I retire from the great theatre of Action; and bidding an Affectionate farewell to this August body under whose orders I have so long acted, I here offer my Commission, and take my leave of all the employments of public life.[77]

Washington then handed his commission to Mifflin. Mifflin made a brief, respectful reply, and the ceremony ended. Washington withdrew from the room in solemn dignity, and after a brief pause Congress adjourned and the many spectators dispersed. A short time later, Washington returned and bade farewell to each member of Congress personally.

Now Washington, determined to eat Christmas dinner at his own home, took his wife and headed for Mount Vernon. Wild ovations followed the happy couple on their way. Crowds gathered along the roads cheering, shouting, and making music. At last, after an almost unbroken absence of eight years George and Martha Washington reached home together.

Guess what King George said when he heard Washington would return to Mt. Vernon?

In London, King George III questioned the American-born painter Benjamin West on what Washington would do now that he had won the war. "Oh," said West, "they say he will return to his farm." "If he does that," said the king, "he will be the greatest man in the world."[78] Consider the humility of George Washington or as the founders described it, he was a great example of a disinterested patriot. By that, they meant that he wasn't interested in self-promotion, but put the best interests of his country above his own self interests.

Constitution of
United States
of America

CHAPTER 31

THE UNITED STATES CONSTITUTION

A NEW FORM OF GOVERNMENT

The peace treaty between England and her former colonies had been signed. The colonies were now free states. Each one could rule itself as the people of the state chose. And now, a watching world waited to see what these little "states" — they were, in fact, like little independent nations — would do with their hard-won freedom. Would they survive? Would they prosper? Would they continue to work together, as they had in the Revolutionary War? Would they perhaps begin to fight each other, now that England was no longer there to settle disputes between colonies?

The 13 colonies, when they declared independence, assumed the title "The United States of America." Under that name, they had won their freedom from the mother country. But what would they do now? There were plenty of elder nations in the world looking on, awaiting their chance to ridicule, sneer, or scorn. Liberty was a new idea to most European countries, with all their kings and lords. Freedom was not accepted as the birthright of all people — not by any means. The old continent had little if any confidence in the ability of the people of the upstart United States to rule themselves. Why, they weren't even a nation. They were just a collection of 13 little states. They might like each other well enough, they might get along well enough to win their independence, but what now? What would keep them from starting to fight among themselves as the nations of Europe so often did?

The Great Seal of the United States
(CC BY-SA 3.0)

The founders established our government to be a republic. Many Americans today think we are a democracy, but that is not true. The difference between a democracy and a republic rests in the source of authority. A pure democracy operates by direct majority vote of the people. When an issue is to be decided, the entire population votes on it and the majority wins. A republic, on the other hand, is rule by law. According to founder Noah Webster (left), "Our citizens should early understand that the genuine source of correct republican principles is the Bible, particularly the New Testament, or the Christian religion."[79]

The Founders understood that biblical values formed the basis of the republic and that the republic would be destroyed if the people's knowledge of those values should ever be lost.

> America's unchangeable principles of right and wrong were not based on changing feelings and emotions of people, but on the Bible. Benjamin Rush, signer of the Declaration of Independence said, "Where there is no law, there is no liberty; and nothing deserves the name of law but that which is certain and universal in its operation upon all the members of the community."[80]

A republic is the highest form of government devised by man, but it also requires the greatest amount of human care and maintenance. If neglected, it can deteriorate into a variety of lesser forms, including a democracy (a government conducted by popular feeling); anarchy (a system in which each person determines his own rules and standards); oligarchy (a government run by a small council or a group of elite individuals); or dictatorship (a government run by a single individual).

Understanding the foundation of the American republic is a vital key toward protecting it.[81]

In fact, there were plenty of people in America who wondered if a republic was even possible. They had just come through a war. There were homes and farms to be rebuilt, businesses to reestablish. The state governments were young and weak. None of the leaders had much experience in leading a republic, because the experiment had just begun. It was all not very encouraging.

Some people talked about giving up the idea of a republic and establishing a new monarchy. A monarchy is a government led by one strong leader, such as a king. After all, that was what these former Englishmen were used to, as their ancestors had been before them. Perhaps they would be all right if they just found a good man to be their king. Of course, George Washington was the first name thought of. He had led them through a terrible war that most countries of the world had thought could not be won. But when it was mentioned to Washington, he was extremely offended. He had fought the war precisely because he believed men could rule themselves and that power in the hands of a king is dangerous.

The . . . law established by the Creator . . . extends over the whole globe, is everywhere and at all times binding upon mankind. . . . [This] is the law of God by which he makes his way known to man and is paramount to all human control.

Rufus King[82]
Signer of the Constitution

While the war had lasted, the states had been held together by the Continental Congress. The Congress had drawn up an agreement called the Articles of Confederation. But this agreement was accepted only because of the necessity of working together to survive the war. It did not give Congress any real authority. They could not collect taxes, so that when the army needed money they could only suggest to the states that they raise it and send it. Sometimes, the states failed to do so, and there was great suffering among the soldiers.

So they fought through the war together, united only by the weak provisions of the Articles of Confederation. The Articles said that the 13 colonies were united and that they would be known as the "United States" of America. It further stated that they were entering into a "firm league of friendship with each other for their common defense, the security of their liberties and their mutual and general welfare." That worked well enough for a time of war, but now peace had come and many wise men in America saw that neither the Articles nor the Continental Congress were strong enough to establish a good government. Freedom had been accomplished, but union had not. Tired and weak from the difficulties of war, the young states were struggling to figure out how to live in the new world they had created.

> When Washington accepted the office of commander of the Continental Army, he said he would not accept pay for his services, only reimbursement for his expenses. "As to pay, Sir, I beg leave to assure the Congress, that, as no pecuniary consideration could have tempted me to have accepted this arduous employment, at the expence of my domestic ease and happiness, I do not wish to make any proffit from it. I will keep an exact Account of my expences. Those, I doubt not, they will discharge, and that is all I desire."[83]

In fact, now that the argument with England had been settled, the states began to quarrel with each other. They bickered about boundaries and trade. Something had to be done about taxation, but any talk of that raised bitter arguments. It was feared that there might be bloodshed, as state after state threatened to withdraw from the "confederation." Congress had little authority; in fact, the state governments had much more. Young war hero Alexander Hamilton looked sadly over the political landscape and mourned,

> A nation without a national government is an awful spectacle.[84]

Hamilton was not the only one who felt that way, but he was good at explaining his reasons to those who would listen. He wrote during the war to his friend, James Duane, who was a member of the Congress:

> We must have a vigorous confederation if we mean to succeed in the contest and be happy thereafter.[85]

He went on in the letter to list many of the provisions that would later find their place in the Constitution. What an amazing young man of only 23 years! But in those days, boys

President of this Constitutional Convention: George Washington

grew up much faster than they do now. Many young men of his day were just as bright as Hamilton.

The idea of a written constitution was a radical idea in 1783. A constitution is a set of basic principles or established practices by which a government runs a nation. The English constitution had not been written in one document, which is one reason that the king and Parliament had been able to get away with doing so many things that their constitution did not give them the right to do. There was no single document for people to look at and see whether a decision was constitutional or not.

Many American leaders wanted a written constitution. They believed it was best to spell out exactly what rights the states had and what rights the national government had. That way, there would be a way to know exactly when a government went beyond its rightful authority over the people. What was needed, they said, was a document drawn up and signed by representatives of the people in all 13 states. Then, the document should be voted on by the people of all the states.

And that is what happened. It took some time, but that should not surprise us. Anything as big as a nation should be expected to take some time to put together. In 1787, 45 delegates from 12 of the 13 states (Rhode Island did not send representatives) met in Philadelphia for a Federal Convention. This convention has been called "one of the most remarkable deliberative bodies known to history."[86]

And so it was. The president of this Constitutional Convention was none other than George Washington. Its members included Benjamin Franklin, James Madison, Alexander Hamilton, Robert Morris, Rufus King, Roger Sherman, and William Livingston. Some of the men who worked on the Constitution had also signed the Declaration of Independence. They were excellent men, the best that their states could find to send. Their love of freedom was great, their thinking was clear, and they were there not to make themselves a place in history, but to make for their fellow citizens a national government under which they could live together in unity and peace. From May to September of 1787, the Convention debated, discussed, amended, and modified their document. Then it was officially signed and sent to the states for their approval.

At first, the Convention had not intended to write a Constitution. They started out to revise the Articles of Confederation so that they were better suited to the needs of the new nation. But soon they came to see that something more was needed.

A horseman telling recent events to a group of Sunday worshippers.

The Constitutional Convention's members were thinking of the Declaration of Independence as they began their deliberations. The Declaration had stated the problems over which the colonies left the mother country. The men writing the Constitution wanted make sure that the document they wrote for America would keep those problems from happening again. For instance, England had had a national religion — Anglicanism. It was because of that religion that so many people had been persecuted. The Pilgrim Fathers had fled persecution in England because some of them had been forced to pay fines or even go to jail for worshiping as they believed the Bible taught them to worship. So, religious freedom was protected in the Constitution. In fact, it would be soon amended to make the right of religious freedom even more clear. There were also protections in the document for the freedom of speech and the press and many things that the king of England had denied the colonists.

Nobody believed the document was perfect, but most of the delegates agreed with wise old Ben Franklin that it was the best that fallible mortals could produce. It was presented to the people of the states for their approval by vote. George Washington was the first man to sign the Constitution, Ben Franklin was the oldest man to sign, and Nicholas Gilman was the youngest, being only 25 years of age.

HENRY OPPOSED THE CONSTITUTUION

Would you believe that the famous orator of the Revolutionary War was opposed to the Constitution? Asked to be a delegate from Virginia to the Constitutional Convention, Patrick Henry replied that he "smelt a rat." Henry feared that in trying to form a tighter relationship between the states, a federal government would be created that had too much power and would eventually grow into tyranny. But he attended the Convention anyway and spoke eloquently against the adoption of the Constitution. His main objection to the document was that it did not contain a Bill of Rights, specifically stating the rights and liberties of citizens. England had adopted such a document in 1689, and Henry thought it was necessary for America to do the same. The Constitution was ratified despite his objections, but enough Americans agreed with Henry that the Bill of Rights was added only three years later, in 1791.

Storytime with Uncle Rick
America's Struggle

The Constitution said that the name of the country was officially the "United States of America." It established a general government with final authority on all matters that were of national interest and union. The government was to be divided into three branches: the legislative, the executive, and the judiciary. It was the duty of the legislative branch, or Congress, to make the laws as representatives of the people. The executive branch consisted of the president of the United States and the officers he selected. Their job was to enforce the laws that were made. The judiciary branch was made up of the law courts of the United States. Its job was to decide questions and disputes about the laws. The Constitution, as the law of the land, was to be obeyed by the national government, the state governments, and the people.

A year of discussion went by as the states made up their minds. One by one, the 13 states all accepted, or "ratified," the document. On September 13, 1788, the Constitution of the United States became the supreme law of the land. At last, America was truly a nation.

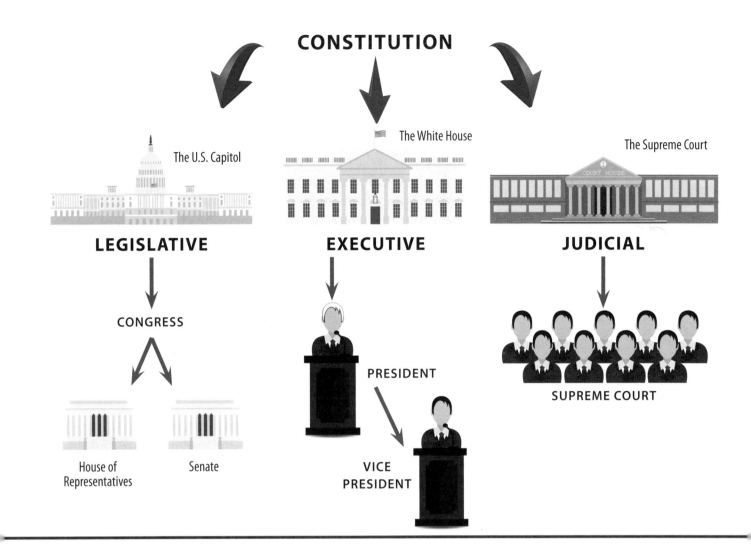

A New Constitutional Republic

The Legislative Branch made the laws. There were two levels in this branch — the Senate and the House of Representatives. Each state, whatever its size or population, had two senators, but the members of the House of Representatives were to be elected by the people of their states, according to their population. The states with larger populations would have more men in the House of Representatives than the states with fewer people living in them. The Senate and the House of Representatives together made up the United States Congress.

What was their job?

They had the power to establish taxes, coin money (America did not have paper money at that time), regulate commerce, raise armies and navies, and declare war. To pass a law required a majority of votes in both the House and the Senate. Treaties made by the president must be approved by a majority vote in the Senate.

Attorney General Edmund Randolph

The Executive Branch was to enforce the laws. It was led by the president, who was elected every four years by "electors." Electors were chosen by the people of the states. The president was the commander-in-chief of the army and navy. He also appointed public officers to carry out the details of the laws that Congress made. If the president did something very wrong, he could be accused by the House of Representatives, a process called "impeachment." He would then be tried by the Senate. If a president were removed by impeachment, or if he died while in office or resigned from the presidency, the vice president was to take his place. The only other duty the vice president had was to preside over the Senate's meetings.

The role of the Judiciary Branch was to apply the Constitution to disputes about the laws. The branch consisted of a Supreme Court and certain district courts. The judges were to be appointed by the president. They could stay in office for life, as long as they did right. If they did wrong, they could also be impeached.

Of course, not everyone liked the Constitution equally. As time went on and it was discussed more and more around the country, two different parties developed. One of these parties came to be called the Federalists. They liked the Constitution very much and thought the new federal government was just what the country needed. The other party was suspicious of the federal government and thought the individual states should have more power. They feared that Congress had too much power and that the government might develop into tyranny. This party was known as the Anti-Federalists.

During Washington's Inaugural Address, he called attention to the fact that God had providentially helped America to become a nation: "No People can be bound to acknowledge and adore the invisible hand, which conducts the Affairs of men more than the People of the United States. Every step, by which they have advanced to the character of an independent nation, seems to have been distinguished by some token of providential agency."[88]

But despite their disagreements, most people of both parties accepted the Constitution and were willing to live under it. Among the leaders of the Federalists were Washington and Franklin, both very highly respected among the people. Among the Anti-Federalists was Jefferson, also highly respected and very dedicated to limited government.

Many great men had made their mark on the nation during the trying times of the War of Independence, but when the time came to select a president, there was only one name taken seriously. George Washington was, without question, the man for the job. When the 69 electors sent in their votes, every vote was for the great general. John Adams was elected vice president. New York City was America's first capitol.

It was a glad day when George Washington took the oath of office as the first president of the United States. The ceremony took place on the balcony of Federal Hall on Wall Street.

Chancellor Livingstone administered the oath as Washington held his hand on an open Bible. When the oath was completed, Washington bent reverently and kissed the Bible. Then, Chancellor Livingstone proclaimed, "Long live George Washington, President of the United States!" Cannons boomed, the crowd roared and flags waved everywhere. Washington, the man who had led the nation through a long and terrible war and guided its leaders in the formation of its national government, now took his office as the official head of the new country.

Maj. Gen. Henry Knox

To help him conduct the affairs of the nation, Washington selected a group of men that came to be called the president's "Cabinet." These were:

☆ Thomas Jefferson, Secretary of State

☆ Alexander Hamilton, Secretary of the Treasury

☆ Henry Knox , Secretary of War

☆ Edmund Randolph, Attorney General

These trusted men would help him conduct the affairs that were his responsibility as president. Congress assembled in the Federal Building, with Vice President John Adams presiding over the Senate.

Frederick Augustus Muhlenberg was a preacher when the War of Independence began. At first, Muhlenberg was unsure of how to respond to the growing threat of war. A British bombardment of New York City in 1775 forced his wife and children to leave the city, but correspondence between Muhlenberg and his brother Peter reveals Muhlenberg's feelings about mixing his religious vocation with his political opinion: "You have become too involved in matters which, as a preacher, you have nothing whatsoever to do. . . ." The two exchanged more letters, in which Peter accused Muhlenberg of being a Tory sympathizer, and Muhlenberg responded with his convictions that man cannot serve two masters. Repeated unrest seemed to convince Muhlenberg to change his mind.[88]

He then went on to hold many important and influential offices on behalf of his country.

Frederick Augustus Muhlenberg served as Speaker of the House of Representatives. Together, a company of great men put in motion the machinery of a new government. Much of the world expected them to fail, even as they began a new experiment: government of the people by the people.

You, as citizens of our country, have a right and a duty to learn about how our government is set up, protect our freedom, and hold our elected officials accountable to do what is right when they get elected. The following information will help you to do just that.

The Early Americans had a choice — declare independence and form a "new government" or remain under English control. THEY CHOSE INDEPENDENCE!

For 170 years, the people of America had been being preparing for this new day in world history. The training had been long and demanding. They had won their freedom; now the world would see whether they were wise enough, good enough, and strong enough to be trusted with such a precious treasure. Their mission was spelled out in the first part, or Preamble, to the Constitution they had produced: "We the people of the United States, in order to form a more perfect union, establish Justice, insure domestic Tranquility, provide for the common defence, promote the general Welfare, and secure the Blessings of Liberty to ourselves and our Posterity, do ordain and establish this CONSTITUTION of the United States."

HOW THE CONSTITUTION WORKS

The Founding Fathers knew a government must provide two things in order for America to work: justice and protection. Justice means the punishment of evil and praise of those who do right (Romans 13:3–4; 1 Peter 2:14). Protection means we have a court system to punish those who hurt others, and for one citizen to appeal for fair treatment by other citizens.

This is what is required for the people to have what they all want: prosperity, peace, and freedom.

They studied all pre-existing and existing governments to find the right one. They found it did not exist. Instead, they found governments took away from the people's prosperity, peace, and freedom, because they were run by rulers who exploited the people. They made laws for themselves at the expense of the people! (Sound familiar?)

SOLUTION: Form a government of the people because the people would make laws for the good of the people.

How Do You Put the Power of the Government in the Hands of the People?

This is how they did it: Separate the power and put checks and balances in place.

How?

By doing the following:

1. Separate the main government into three heads: EXECUTIVE (President), LEGISLATIVE (Congress), JUDICIAL (Supreme Court).

2. Write down all the laws the government is to follow. (The US Constitution)

3. Have all elected officials take an oath to follow, uphold, and defend those laws. (The US Constitution)

4. Make the Congress the law-making body, because they are members elected by the people.

5. Declare all laws passed that are unconstitutional to be null and void.

6. Require a journal to be kept of all the proceedings and open to the people.

7. Have two divisions of government — the FEDERAL and the STATE. Each is to check on the other and bring the government closer to the PEOPLE.

8. Have a federal and state court system set up to check on each other.

9. Have an impeachment process.

10. Give the PEOPLE the right to vote.

11. Give the PEOPLE the right to voice their grievances.

12. Educate the PEOPLE on the laws in the United States Constitution.

Okay, let's get educated on the United States Constitution!

THE UNITED STATES CONSTITUTION is the laws our government is to rule by. Its purpose is to stop government abuse of the people.

The key is in the law! Here is the LAW:

What Are the 11 Powers of the President?

1. Is Chief of State

2. Chooses his vice president

3. Chooses governmental officials with consent of the Senate

4. Receives foreign visitors.

5. Makes treaties if 2/3 of Senate agrees

6. May require opinions and reports from government agencies.

7. Gives State of the Union Address

8. Can veto laws

9. Sees that the laws are faithfully executed

10. Can pardon for offenses against the United States

11. Is commander in chief of the military

Basically, the president is an overseer of the nation. He doesn't make laws or declare war.

WHAT ARE THE 22 POWERS OF THE CONGRESS?

(Congress consists of 2 senators from each state, and the number of representatives is according to the population.)

1. Determine if members are properly elected

2. Punish own members for disorderly behavior

3. Has complete control over federal lands and buildings

4. Has all law-making power

5. Collect taxes, duties, imposts, and excises

6. Pay the debts

7. Bring impeachment charges

8. Regulate commerce between states and with other countries

9. Establish uniform rules for naturalization

10. Establish uniform laws regarding bankruptcy

11. Can borrow on credit of the United States

12. Has power to coin and value money

13. Fix weights and measures

14. Punish counterfeiting

15. Establish post offices

16. Encourage science and useful arts, issue copyrights and patents

17. Set up federal courts

18. Define and punish piracies and felonies on high seas

19. Grant letters of marquee and reprisal

20. Call for the state militia when need to

21. Declare war

22. Keep a journal of proceedings that is open to the public

Basically, Congress is the law-making body of government; however, it is not to be involved in anything not listed.

WHAT RESTRICTIONS ARE THERE ON THE LAWS THAT CONGRESS CAN MAKE?

1. NO LAWS against religion

2. NO LAWS against the freedom of speech and press

3. NO LAWS against the right of peaceful assembly

4. NO LAWS against the right to voice grievances

5. NO LAWS against the right to bear arms

6. NO LAWS against the right to be secure in persons, houses, papers

7. NO LAWS against the right to vote

8. NO soldier shall in time of peace be quartered in any house without the consent of the owner

9. NO taking land for federal use without just compensation

WHAT ARE THE POWERS OF THE SUPREME COURT?

1. All judges appointed by the president with the advice and consent of the Senate

2. Congress can impeach judges for treason, bribery, or other crimes, not for unpopular decision

3. Judges are appointed for life on good behavior

4. Congress is authorized to restrict the jurisdiction of the Supreme Court, but this is rarely done

5. The administration of this judicial power shall extend to all cases, both in law and in equity

6. Shall have jurisdiction over any question concerning the Constitution and laws of the United States

7. Shall have jurisdiction over any question arising under the treaties or agreements made by authorities of the United States

8. Shall judge any controversies between two or more states

9. Shall judge controversies between citizens of different states

10. Shall judge an issue between a state or the citizens thereof and any foreign state or subjects thereof

11. Shall judge all cases affecting ambassadors, public ministers, and consuls

The federal Supreme Court is the guardian of the Constitution. Their job is to make sure all the laws passed are according to the United States Constitution.

The above are the powers granted to the three heads of the federal government and any time they involve themselves in any other power than what is listed, they are considered to be involved in unconstitutional activities and should be called into line by the people.

THE RESULTS

USA — In a little over a century, their formula allowed less than 6 percent of the human family to become the richest industrial nation on earth. It allowed them to originate more than half of the world's total production and enjoy the highest standard of living in the history of the world. It also produced a very generous people. No nation in all the recorded annals of the past has shared so much of its wealth with every other nation as has the United States of America.

Let's take a closer look!

PROSPERITY

What causes Prosperity?

Two things cause prosperity. The first is the free enterprise system. In this system you have the freedom to:

1. Have a job of your choice

2. Buy

3. Sell

4. Try

5. Fail

6. Make a Profit.

The second is government intervention and protection in only four areas:

1. To prevent force

2. To prevent fraud

3. To prevent monopoly

4. To prevent debauchery (these are the vices detrimental to a community, such as gambling, drugs, liquor, prostitution, pornography, etc.). Many times people try to get away with promoting such vices on the excuse of "Freedom of Speech," however, "Freedom of Speech" is restricted when it comes to harming others. You are not allowed to shout "Fire" in a crowded

building as a joke; it can cause harm and is against the law. Debauchery causes harm and can and should be restricted by a state or a community.

What Destroys Prosperity?

1. Big government

2. Too many taxes

3. Too many regulations

4. Too much interference by government

5. Too much welfare

6. Too much crime

All of the preceding does not produce any profit — they only consume the profit that produces wealth.

Government is to protect, not provide. If left alone, the people can provide for themselves and those in need, much better.

PEACE

What causes peace?

Four things provide peace:

1. A strong defense

2. A good foreign policy (Be friends with all, but stay out of their business; it will cause enemies and we can't police the whole world, without destroying our own protection.)

3. A fair and equal court system

4. Religious liberty

What destroys peace?

1. Weak defense

2. Interfering in everyone's affairs

3. Unfair and unequal court system

4. Religious restrictions

FREEDOM

What causes freedom?

1. A few good laws

2. Good protection, especially on your rights of life, liberty, and the pursuit of happiness.

What destroys freedom?

1. Laws, laws, and more laws

2. Inadequate protection

3. No justice

Let's go back . . .

The key is in the law, and the solution is in the people.

IN WHOSE HANDS DOES THE POWER OF THE US GOVERNMENT LAY?

"Every government degenerates when trusted to the rulers of the people alone. the people themselves, therefore, are its only safe depositories. And to render them safe, their minds must be improved to a certain degree" (emphasis added). "I consider the people who constitute a society or nation as the source of all authority in that nation" (emphasis added). — Thomas A. Jefferson

Each has a job to do:

The president scrutinizes the laws as to how good they are for the nation.

The Senate scrutinizes the laws as to how good they are for the state.

The House of Representatives scrutinizes the laws as to how good they are for the people.

The Supreme Court scrutinizes the laws to see that they go according to the Constitution.

The people are to make sure all government officials are doing their jobs right.

HOW?

1. Know the US Constitution

2. Vote in good and wise men

3. Voice their grievances.

If we don't like the laws our government officials are passing, then we must voice our grievances to change it. If they won't change it, then we should not vote those government officials into office again. We are responsible for what is happening in this country. We shouldn't complain if we are not doing anything to change it. How do we change things, by voicing our grievances?

How can you voice your grievances?

1. A petition (least effective)

2. A personal letter (more effective)

3. A personal visit (even more effective)

4. A paid lobbyist (very effective)

5. A peaceful demonstration (most effective)

Where are we today . . . ruler's law or people's law?

If EVERYONE is doing their job right, only "good laws" would be passed and we would be living in prosperity, peace, and freedom. The supreme law of the land, the US Constitution, is the key, and the people are the solution. Do you notice anyone not doing their job? What are you going to do about it?

How can there be a government of the people, for the people, by the people, if the people don't know the constitution and are not involved?[91]

For lots of fantastic resources about our Constitution see http://www.learntheconstitution.com/.

You must learn your duty and be involved in helping to bring our country back to where it began in following God's law, electing and holding accountable those who will rule according to the Constitution, which is based on the principles set forth in the Bible.

We the People

of the United States, in order to form a more perfect Union, establish Justice, insure domestic Tranquility, provide for the common defence, promote the general Welfare, and secure the Blessings of Liberty to ourselves and our Posterity, do ordain and establish this Constitution for the United States of America.

Article. I.

Section. 1. All legislative Powers herein granted shall be vested in a Congress of the United States, which shall consist of a Senate and House of Representatives.

Section. 2. The House of Representatives shall be composed of Members chosen every second Year by the People of the several States, and the Electors in each State shall have the Qualifications requisite for Electors of the most numerous Branch of the State Legislature.

No Person shall be a Representative who shall not have attained to the Age of twenty five Years, and been seven Years a Citizen of the United States, and who shall not, when elected, be an Inhabitant of that State in which he shall be chosen.

Representatives and direct Taxes shall be apportioned among the several States which may be included within this Union, according to their respective Numbers, which shall be determined by adding to the whole Number of free Persons, including those bound to Service for a Term of Years, and excluding Indians not taxed, three fifths of all other Persons. The actual Enumeration shall be made within three Years after the first Meeting of the Congress of the United States, and within every subsequent Term of ten Years, in such Manner as they shall by Law direct. The Number of Representatives shall not exceed one for every thirty Thousand, but each State shall have at Least one Representative; and until such enumeration shall be made, the State of New Hampshire shall be entitled to chuse three, Massachusetts eight, Rhode Island and Providence Plantations one, Connecticut five, New York six, New Jersey four, Pennsylvania eight, Delaware one, Maryland six, Virginia ten, North Carolina five, South Carolina five, and Georgia three.

When vacancies happen in the Representation from any State, the Executive Authority thereof shall issue Writs of Election to fill such Vacancies.

The House of Representatives shall chuse their Speaker and other Officers; and shall have the sole Power of Impeachment.

Section. 3. The Senate of the United States shall be composed of two Senators from each State, chosen by the Legislature thereof, for six Years; and each Senator shall have one Vote.

Immediately after they shall be assembled in Consequence of the first Election, they shall be divided as equally as may be into three Classes. The Seats of the Senators of the first Class shall be vacated at the Expiration of the second Year, of the second Class at the Expiration of the fourth Year, and of the third Class at the Expiration of the sixth Year, so that one third may be chosen every second Year; and if Vacancies happen by Resignation, or otherwise, during the Recess of the Legislature of any State, the Executive thereof may make temporary Appointments until the next Meeting of the Legislature, which shall then fill such Vacancies.

No Person shall be a Senator who shall not have attained to the Age of thirty Years, and been nine Years a Citizen of the United States, and who shall not, when elected, be an Inhabitant of that State for which he shall be chosen.

The Vice President of the United States shall be President of the Senate, but shall have no Vote, unless they be equally divided.

The Senate shall chuse their other Officers, and also a President pro tempore, in the Absence of the Vice President, or when he shall exercise the Office of President of the United States.

The Senate shall have the sole Power to try all Impeachments. When sitting for that Purpose, they shall be on Oath or Affirmation. When the President of the United States is tried, the Chief Justice shall preside: And no Person shall be convicted without the Concurrence of two thirds of the Members present.

Judgment in Cases of Impeachment shall not extend further than to removal from Office, and disqualification to hold and enjoy any Office of honor, Trust or Profit under the United States: but the Party convicted shall nevertheless be liable and subject to Indictment, Trial, Judgment and Punishment, according to Law.

Section. 4. The Times, Places and Manner of holding Elections for Senators and Representatives, shall be prescribed in each State by the Legislature thereof; but the Congress may at any time by Law make or alter such Regulations, except as to the Places of chusing Senators.

The Congress shall assemble at least once in every Year, and such Meeting shall be on the first Monday in December, unless they shall by Law appoint a different Day.

Section. 5. Each House shall be the Judge of the Elections, Returns and Qualifications of its own Members, and a Majority of each shall constitute a Quorum to do Business; but a smaller Number may adjourn from day to day, and may be authorized to compel the Attendance of absent Members, in such Manner, and under such Penalties as each House may provide.

Each House may determine the Rules of its Proceedings, punish its Members for disorderly Behaviour, and, with the Concurrence of two thirds, expel a Member.

Each House shall keep a Journal of its Proceedings, and from time to time publish the same, excepting such Parts as may in their Judgment require Secrecy; and the Yeas and Nays of the Members of either House on any question shall, at the Desire of one fifth of those Present, be entered on the Journal.

Neither House, during the Session of Congress, shall, without the Consent of the other, adjourn for more than three days, nor to any other Place than that in which the two Houses shall be sitting.

Section. 6. The Senators and Representatives shall receive a Compensation for their Services, to be ascertained by Law, and paid out of the Treasury of the United States. They shall in all Cases, except Treason, Felony and Breach of the Peace, be privileged from Arrest during their Attendance at the Session of their respective Houses, and in going to and returning from the same; and for any Speech or Debate in either House, they shall not be questioned in any other Place.

No Senator or Representative shall, during the Time for which he was elected, be appointed to any civil Office under the Authority of the United States, which shall have been created, or the Emoluments whereof shall have been encreased during such time; and no Person holding any Office under the United States, shall be a Member of either House during his Continuance in Office.

Section. 7. All Bills for raising Revenue shall originate in the House of Representatives; but the Senate may propose or

Every Bill which shall have

CHAPTER 32

THE NEW REPUBLIC

EARLY TIMES IN THE NEW NATION

Thirteen states, almost independent of each other, had joined together to win their freedom. Then they had hammered out a Constitution that bound them together as one nation. Finally, they had voted by the provisions of that constitution to select a president of the United States. In a way, it was the end of a season in history.

In another way, it was certainly a beginning. Americans had fought for their freedom, and now they must show the world whether they had the wisdom, justice, and character to make good use of it. Indeed, it was a beginning.

George Washington had been living quietly on his plantation, Mount Vernon, in Virginia. He would have loved to spend the rest of his life in peaceful retirement there, but it was not to be. Once again, his country called him to serve her. He was too good a man not to answer the call.

When Washington was inaugurated in New York City on April 30, 1789, the nation contained less than 4 million citizens. That sounds like a lot of people, until we stop to think that today many cities have a larger population than the entire nation did then. And our national population has grown to over 220 million people!

The population of America under Washington lived mostly along the Atlantic coast. Americans tended to stay near the ocean

Map of Territorial Growth 1790 (PD-US).

Wisdom is learning to see life from God's point of view or learning to exchange our natural thoughts for what God says in the Bible. Psalm 90:12 says, "So teach us to number our days, that we may apply our hearts unto wisdom." Aren't you thankful for a president who sought the Lord and got our country off to a right start?

Mount Vernon with the Washington family on the terrace, by Benjamin Henry Latrobe, 1796 (PD-Art).

because it was almost the only great highway on which they could do business. Those who happened to travel away from the coast and toward the interior of the country soon found themselves passing fewer and fewer homes, and these appeared simpler as the path wound westward. Settlements grew farther apart, and most of the houses were only cabins. By the time the traveler reached the Allegheny Mountains, he would find very few settlements of white people.

Everything to the west of the mountains was untamed wilderness, threatening the traveler with dangers from wild beasts and hostile Indians, except for small pioneer settlements in Kentucky and Tennessee. The Mississippi River was the western boundary of the United States. Few Americans would ever travel far enough to see it. To most citizens, it seemed as far away as Africa.

We must remember that the people of that day had only very slow ways of traveling from one place to another. Today, you can get in your car and easily ride for 60 miles in only one hour. Can you imagine what it would be like to pack your belongings into a wagon drawn by horses or oxen and drive that far over unpaved roads that were full of rocks and ruts? The roads of that day were dusty in dry weather and muddy when it rained. You might drive all day long and only go a few miles. There were few bridges, so if you came to a stream that was deep and swift from recent rains, you might be stuck for a while until the water went down. There were not even steamboats and railroads yet. There were stagecoach routes between the larger cities, but even in a coach it took two or three days to get from New York to Philadelphia and six days to get from New York to Boston.

The fastest and easiest way to travel in those days was on horseback. People were willing to pay a good price for a smooth-riding, long-winded horse such as a Narragansett Pacer from Rhode Island, or a Virginia "natural pacer." Often, two people would travel using only one horse, in a practice called traveling "ride and tie." This meant that one person rode the horse ahead for a distance and tied him beside the road, then walked on. The other person, who had walked from their starting point, mounted the horse when he reached it, rode past his companion for about the same distance, and tied the horse again. Then he walked on. By taking turns riding and walking, they could cover more distance without wearing out the horse by riding double.

Narragansett Pacer

When Washington became president, all the major towns were on the coast or the great inland rivers, except Lancaster, Pennsylvania. Outside of Pennsylvania, the roads were so rough that large trading towns did not develop far from a good "water highway."

Within Pennsylvania, trade was carried on by means of very large covered wagons called Conestoga wagons. Each wagon, when it was loaded with goods, required six or eight stout horses to pull it. This wagon trade made Philadelphia the chief town of North America, as more than 10,000 of these wagons ran in and out of the town. Out in the remote areas, pack horses carried goods by road, and boats called *bateaux* (plural for *bateau*) carried on trade by inland waterways, pushed along by men with poles.

It was much harder to communicate by mail then, as most letters were carried by horseback, and delivery was irregular and slow. In those days, if you received news in the mail, it had almost become history by the time you read it. There were only a few newspapers in the country, most of them published once each week.

Conestoga Wagons

Ben Franklin

Early Development, Regional Differences

Colleges began in America to train ministers of the gospel. Harvard, where eight of the signers of the Declaration of Independence received their training, had this as one of their rules: "Let every student be plainly instructed and earnestly pressed to consider well the main end of his life and studies is to know God and Jesus Christ which is eternal life (John 17:3) and therefore to lay Christ in the bottom as the only foundation of all sound knowledge and learning. And seeing only the Lord only giveth wisdom, let every one seriously set himself by prayer in secret to seek it of Him (Prov. 2:3). Every one shall so exercise himself in reading the Scriptures twice a day that he shall be ready to give such an account of his proficiency therein."[92]

Yale College, Princeton College, and The College of William and Mary had similar rules and were likewise established to train ministers of the gospel. Four of the signers of the Declaration of Independence attended Yale College, three attended Princeton College, and four attended The College of William and Mary.[93]

Books were scarce and expensive. There were schools in the major towns and cities and boys and girls could learn to read and write when they were not needed in the fields or the home for work. There were a few colleges also. Harvard, the oldest college in America, was in Cambridge, Massachusetts.

For many years after the first English colonies were settled, there was not much being done in the fields of art, literature, or science. People were too busy clearing the forests for fields and building houses and barns to have much time to paint pictures or write poetry. Most of the early books were about religion or politics, which is not really surprising. Still, the colonies were growing and developing. In the half century before the War of Independence, interest in science and literature was growing.

Benjamin Franklin became famous both in America and in Europe for his discovery that lightning is electricity. Franklin was well-known as a thinker and a writer, and his inventions included the Franklin stove, the lightning rod, and bi-focal eye glasses. He was the best-known man in the colonies.

Franklin's Electric Discovery

Ben Franklin was a scientist as well as a statesman. His most famous scientific experiment is the one in which he proved that lightning is electricity. Ben had long suspected that this was true. Because he noticed that lightning usually struck the highest parts of trees and buildings, he wished that Philadelphia had a big hill or tall building so

he could get closer to the lightning. Finally it occurred to Franklin that he could get a kite high up into the air and perhaps make contact with the lightning. So one rainy day he and his son launched a kite out in a field. The kite was not made of paper because paper would fall apart when it got soaked with rainwater. Instead, Franklin made the kite out of a silk handkerchief. Silk would catch the wind well enough, and it would not fall apart when wet. Franklin and his son moved to a shed when the rain began to fall. Franklin tied a key to the kite string. He held the string by another string made of silk that he kept dry, because he suspected that electricity would travel down a wet string and shock him. When he observed lighting in the sky near his kite, Ben moved his hand near the metal key and felt a mild electrical shock. This led to his invention of the lightning rod, which was soon saving many wooden houses from burning down after being struck by lightning. In fact, Franklin's own house is said to have been saved from burning by a lightning rod.

By the time of independence, many improvements had been made in America's towns and cities. Some of the streets had been paved with stones so that they were no longer swamps in rainy weather. More schools were being started, and Franklin and his friends had started the first public library in Philadelphia.

Still, life was simple and primitive compared to how we live today. Of course, there were no telephones, televisions, or computers. There were no electric lights. In fact, they did not even have gas lights or kerosene lamps. Most homes depended on candles for lighting. Poor people might even depend on a cloth wick burning in a cup of grease or pieces of pitch pine burning on the hearth. It is no wonder that most people went to bed early. Imagine how hard it would have been to read or sew by the weak light of a candle or burning rag.

Heating stoves were still rare. Most homes depended on a big stone fireplace built from rocks gathered in the fields. There they also cooked their simple meals. Wood was the fuel for such

Washington Irving

fireplaces, and the men and boys spent many backbreaking hours cutting and splitting firewood. Even with all that effort, the houses could scarcely ever be kept warm because they had no insulation and leaky doors and windows.

There were few factories or mines. People wore homespun clothing made from wool or flax, which was grown, spun, and woven into cloth at home. Most of the men were farmers. They and their families grew most of what they ate and what they wore. Shoes were rough and handmade. They might be ordered from a local cobbler or even made at home. The children went barefoot in the summer, and sometimes their parents did as well. Many farm implements, including plows, sleds, and wagons were made on the farm. Farming was rough and the tools were crude, but the land was freshly cleared out of the forest, so it was fresh and fertile.

There were many men who made their living in the woods by hunting, trapping, and trading with the Indians or by poling boats. They had a clothing style of their own featuring long hunting shirts of homespun or deerskin, buckskin leggings, moccasins, and topped off with a cap of raccoon skin or some other animal fur. These men were the forerunners of the famous "mountain men" who roamed the Rocky Mountains a century later, of whom author Washington Irving wrote:

> It is a matter of vanity and ambition with them to discard everything that may bear the stamp of civilized life, and to adopt the manners, gestures, and even the walk of the Indian. You cannot pay a freetrapper a greater compliment than to persuade him you have mistaken him for an Indian brave.[94]

Of the nearly four million people living in the United States in 1790, about one in seven was a slave of African descent. They lived in every state except Massachusetts. Of the northern states, New York had the greatest number of slaves, about 20,000. By far, most of the slaves lived in Maryland, Virginia, and the Carolinas. There they worked making crops of indigo, rice, and tobacco.

In these middle and southern Atlantic states, life still held some of the traits of aristocracy as in Europe. Some of the wealthy planters lived a life similar to English nobles. They were often involved in the management of community affairs, and from this class sprang a number of the leading statesmen in the years following the War of Independence. The families of these community leaders were usually well educated and skilled in manners.

The poorer people of the south had little chance for an education, and were usually untaught in the things of book learning and fine manners. There were not many towns in the states of the south, and very little manufacturing. The great factories and the shipbuilding that would soon make New England wealthy were unheard of there. Still, during the presidency of George Washington most of the wealth was located in the south because of the favorable conditions for farming. The land was still rich and fertile and the growing season was longer. And, though there was little social life in the few towns, there was much getting together with neighbors in the plantation houses.

Up and down the Atlantic coast, there was fashion to be considered even in this early day. Gentlemen wore their hair long and made it white with powder. Ladies piled their hair into high towers. Both ladies and gentlemen wore rich fabrics and bright colors. The fashionable balls that were held from time to time presented a happy and colorful spectacle.

WASHINGTON'S PRESIDENCY

In the year 1791, the nation's capital was moved from New York to Philadelphia. There it would remain until it found a permanent home on the Potomac River in what is now the District of Columbia. Both the president and the Congress made their homes in Philadelphia for a time.

Washington's popularity had made him president with a unanimous vote of the electors. When he ran for his second term, he had no opponent. The entire nation loved him, for the most part, and he tried not to identify with any particular group or party. But parties will form whether we like them or not, and Washington's belief in a strong central government naturally made him more attractive to the Federalists than to the Anti-Federalists.

The Federalists had taken their name during the time when the states were discussing the ratification of the Constitution. The Federalists were in favor of the Constitution and a strong federal

Washington meeting citizens on the way to his inauguration.

313

Alexander Hamilton

government. They also, in the old English style, liked to see some ceremony and grandeur in the conduct of government affairs. This party largely consisted of people who lived in the cities and tended to be above average in income. They still retained some of their English ways, and when England and France were at war, their sympathies leaned toward the English.

The party that opposed the Federalists was the Anti-Federalist party. As time went by, its name would be changed to the Republican party, then to the Democratic-Republican party, then to the Democratic party. The concern of this party was that the federal government would gain too much power and possibly one day take away some of the freedom of the citizens. They wanted the individual state governments to have more power, and the federal government less power. Their highest ideals were liberty and equality. They were suspicious of aristocracy, as they had seen how it worked in England. They wanted a government of strong citizens and simple ceremonies.

There were great men in both the Federalist and the Republican parties. A strong voice in the Federalists was Alexander Hamilton, who worked with all his might to strengthen the federal government.

Thomas Jefferson was the leader of the Republicans. He was serving as secretary of state in Washington's cabinet while Hamilton served as secretary of the treasury.

During the administration of Washington, the nation was plagued with trouble with the Indian tribes. Some of these problems would not be resolved for another century. Part of the trouble was the fault of the British. Although the Treaty of Paris demanded that they abandon the forts they still held in the Ohio country, the British refused to do so. In addition, they encouraged the Indians to keep on attacking American settlers. This led to a fierce war between the Indians living north of the Ohio River and the white settlers in Kentucky to the south. In seven years' time, over 1,500 Kentucky settlers were killed, with many more carried away into cruel captivity. The vicious slaughter of men, women, and children led to Kentucky being called "the Dark and Bloody Ground," as was noted earlier.

In 1790, an American force under General Harmer was sent against the Indians, but he was careless and his men were poorly disciplined. The force was cut to pieces in a battle with a chief called Little Turtle and his braves. The next year, General St. Clair was sent against the same Indians. He, too, fled before Little Turtle's savages, and the wounded he left on the field were cruelly butchered.

Washington's kind heart grieved over these losses. Who was the general who could go up against the Indians and prevail? Who could end this slaughter? Mad Anthony Wayne was called for.

Wayne was a very brave man and fought like a wolf, but he was as careful as he was courageous. At first, he tried to make peace with the Indians. When this failed, he resorted to violent attacks, driving the Indians ahead of him with bayonet charges. The battle he fought in 1794 on the banks of the Maumee River brought peace to the region. The peace would not last, but for a time it was a wonderful rest from the constant warfare of past years.

At about this time, an event took place in western Pennsylvania that has come to be known as the "Whiskey Rebellion." The people of this region raised large crops of Indian corn. However, their success in raising it was greater than their success in getting the corn to market. The roads over the mountains were rough, so getting their corn to the towns for sale was a challenge. The people began making their corn into whiskey, which was valuable and much easier to carry. But there was a new tax on whiskey and the farmers did not like it. They rose up and resisted the officers sent to collect the tax. Washington sent troops to enforce the law, and the ringleaders of the rebellion took to their heels. After that, the rest of the farmers paid the tax.

As Washington's second term drew to a close, many Americans urged him to run for a third. This was legal then, as it was before the Constitution had been amended to limit presidents to two terms. Washington chose to limit himself. Two terms were enough for any one man to be in power, he said. So in September 1796, he issued his famous "Farewell Address" to America. The address was so full of wise and godly advice that it was studied by American school children for many decades afterward. In March of 1797 he retired to Mount Vernon where he spent the remainder of his years in peaceful home life, cultivating his farm and enjoying his family and friends. He died on December 14, 1799.

Of the many great men of the 18th century, Washington stands in a class by himself. For courage, integrity, godly character, and wisdom, his nation still remembers him today as a special instrument of God in gaining and establishing American independence. It is no wonder that we call him "The Father of Our Country."

—— " ——

Of all the dispositions and habits which lead to political prosperity, religion and morality are indispensable supports. In vain would that man claim the tribute of patriotism who should labor to subvert these great pillars of human happiness — these firmest props of the duties of men and citizenss (emphasis added)

George Washington's Farewell Address

—— " ——

Note to students: If you want to read his whole Farewell Address, it's in the appendix of this book.

315

Signing of
Declaration
of Independence

CHAPTER 33

WHO WERE THE SIGNERS OF THE DECLARATION OF INDEPENDENCE?

We have learned about the Continental Congress and the Declaration of Independence. As Americans, we need to know something about the men who pledged their lives, their fortunes, and their sacred honor for the freedom we enjoy today, over 200 years later. In this chapter, we will learn some important facts about each of the 56 members of the Continental Congress who signed the Declaration.

MASSACHUSETTS

Samuel Adams

Like most American colonists, Adams was in favor of a peaceful resolution to the problems between England and her American colonies. When that proved impossible, he was among the most strident voices for armed resistance to oppression. He encouraged his fellow colonists by saying, "Numerous have been the manifestations of God's providence in sustaining us. In the gloomy period of adversity, we have our 'cloud by day and pillar by night.' "[95] Like most founding fathers, Adams was a man of the Bible. He said,

> "I rely on the merits of Jesus Christ for a pardon for my sins."[96]

Individual images of the signers of the Declaration of Independence are by Ole Erekson, Engraver, c1876, Library of Congress.

The signers all demonstrated many character qualities, but steadfastness characterized the lives of all of them. They knew when they signed their names to the Declaration of Independence that they were risking their lives, their fortunes, and their sacred honor. King George issued orders to find and capture them. Many lost their homes, their possessions, their wealth, family members, and even their own lives for the cause of freedom. They all remained steadfast in purpose. Steadfastness is unwavering resolve. The freedom that you enjoy today is a result of the sacrifice of these brave men. First Corinthians 15:58 says, " Therefore, my beloved brethren, be ye stedfast, unmoveable, always abounding in the work of the Lord, forasmuch as ye know that your labor is not in vain in the Lord."

John Hancock

At the time of the signing, John Hancock was one of the wealthiest men in the 13 colonies and one of the two colonial leaders whom King George wanted to hang. He, too, pledged all that he had for independence, and signed his name so boldly that, even today, a signature is referred to as a "John Hancock."

John Adams

John served in the Continental Congress from 1774–1777. One of the hardest-working congressmen, he awoke at 4:00 each morning and kept going until 10:00 at night. By 1775, he believed that America must become independent.

> "The die is now cast. Sink or swim, live or die, survive or perish with my country is my unalterable determination," he declared.[97]

John wrote to his wife, Abigail,

> "We have appointed a continental fast. Millions will be upon their knees at once before the great Creator, imploring his forgiveness and blessing; He smiles on American councils and arms."[98]

Elbridge Gerry

Gerry was such a slight, thin man that one of his fellow signers is said to have joked to him that if all the signers were hanged by the British he would be the unluckiest because he was "so light that he would kick the longest." He considered signing the Declaration to be the crowning achievement of his life.

Robert Treat Paine

Paine said,

> "I am constrained to express my adoration of . . . the Author of my existence, in full belief of . . . His forgiving mercy revealed to the world in Jesus Christ, for there is salvation in no other."[99]

William Paca

This patriot poured thousands of dollars of his own personal fortune into clothing the American soldiers. He worked to establish Maryland's state government and served as governor from 1782 to 1785.

Charles Carroll

Carroll wrote,

"On the mercy of my Redeemer, I rely for salvation and on His merits; not on the works I have done in obedience to his precepts."[100]

Samuel Chase

Chase was a spiritual patriot whose campaign against the British helped inspire the state of Maryland to support the Declaration of Independence. Chase rode 150 miles in two days to sign the document.

Thomas Stone

Stone hoped for reconciliation with Great Britain, but finally came to the conclusion that a Declaration of Independence was necessary. He said:

"It seems essential to our very existence as a free people, and without it we may soon be constrained to bid adieu to independence, to liberty, and safety — blessings, which from the justice of our cause, and favour of our Almighty Creator, visibly manifested in our protection, we have reason to expect, if in an humble dependence on his divine providence, we strenuously exert the means which are placed in our power."

Josiah Bartlett

His staunch support of the cause of the patriots led to his dismissal from the post of justice of the peace by the royal governor and to the burning of his house.

Matthew Thornton

"Dr. Thornton's character as a Christian, a father, a husband, and a friend was bright and unblemished. He had a habit of prudence and diligence in discharging the various duties of public and private life."

William Whipple

Once independence was declared, Whipple wanted to fight — even though he was starting to suffer from a heart condition that caused him to faint at times. Whipple was one of 16 signers who served as soldiers during the war.

DELAWARE

Thomas McKean

McKean recalled to John Adams that he was hunted like a fox during the revolution and at one time was compelled to move his family five times in a few months. Later, while serving as Chief Justice of the Supreme Court of Pennsylvania, he presided over a case in which a man named John Roberts was sentenced to death after being found guilty of treason. Justice McKean delivered his sentence and then preached to him an exhortation to accept Jesus Christ as his Savior right away, before his death, so he could spend eternity in heaven rather than hell — right in the courtroom!

Caesar Rodney

Rodney chose to stay in America and fight for freedom rather than go to England to seek a cure for his skin cancer. He was absent from Congress when the resolution for independence was being voted on. Returning home at night from helping to put down a Loyalist uprising, he received a message from Thomas McKean: Rodney was needed to cast the deciding vote for independence. He jumped on his horse without even taking time to change clothes and rode 80 miles through a driving thunderstorm, stopping only to change horses. As John Hancock rose to open the session, the sound of hooves on the cobblestone pavement was heard and in came Rodney, wet, muddy, and bedraggled. He sank into his seat and then, with the help of other members, stood to cast his vote for independence.

George Read

In attempting to move his family safely across the Delaware River, he looked for a place to cross, as the river was almost covered with ships of the enemy. The tide was low and the Reads' boat became grounded. The British dispatched an armed barge in their pursuit. Mr. Read presented himself as a country gentleman, returning to his home. The Royal Navy, with good humor, actually assisted him. The sailors offered to carry their baggage, his wife, children, and mother up the bank. It wasn't until months later they discovered they had let one of the most hunted Americans in the Middle Colonies slip through their fingers.

New Jersey

Abraham Clark

Clark served in Congress throughout the war. He had two sons in the Continental army, both of whom received harsh treatment at the hands of the British after they were captured. One of them would have starved had it not been for a fellow prisoner who pushed bread crumbs to him through the key hole.

Richard Stockton

Stockton rushed home to Princeton, New Jersey, in 1776 to rescue his family from approaching British troops. He was captured and thrown into prison, where was repeatedly beaten and kept near starvation. The British also destroyed his home and burned his papers. As a result of his mistreatment, he became an invalid and died in 1781.

John Hart

Known as "Honest John," Hart was the father of 13 children and had a wife with a debilitating disease. Though a man of little schooling, Hart educated himself well enough to serve in his county's governing board and be chosen as a judge in the Court of Common Pleas. During the Revolutionary era he served on the Committee of Safety and the Committee of Correspondence. When the British overran much of New Jersey in the winter of 1776, Hart fled to the woods for some weeks, hiding like a hunted animal because of his signature on the Declaration and his position in the New Jersey Assembly. Seldom sleeping in the same place two nights in a row, Hart took refuge in caves and hollows. One bitter cold night a stray dog joined him and kept him from freezing to death. After the patriot victory at the battle of Trenton on December 25, 1776, Hart was able to return to his home but found it partially destroyed by the British.

Francis Hopkinson

Hopkinson's home was twice ransacked, but his enthusiasm for the war effort never wavered. He was a church musician and set the entire Book of Psalms to music.

John Witherspoon

He was a minister of the gospel and president of Princeton University in its very early days. He trained many of the Founding Fathers. He published books of gospel sermons. He always wore his clerical robes to remind people that God was on America's side. Even when prospects seemed bleak, he remained a beacon of hope. He said,

"I entreat you in the most earnest manner to believe in Jesus Christ, for there is salvation in no other."[102]

John Witherspoon and Richard Stockton both arrived early at the Continental Congress in June of 1776. They arrived in time to hear the debate over independence between John Adams and John Dickenson. When Dickenson remarked that the colonies were "not yet ripe for a declaration of independence," Witherspoon said, "In my judgment sir, we are not only ripe, but rotting."[103]

NEW YORK

William Floyd

The Floyd's home in New York was overrun and ruined by the British. Although he could not return to his home during the seven years of the war, he gallantly served his country in the New York Senate as a representative from New York in the first Continental Congress.

Lewis Morris

His Westchester, New York, estate was ransacked by the British and nearly 1,000 acres were burned. His home was destroyed, his cattle butchered, and his family driven from home.

Phillip Livingston

Even though his 150,000-acre estate was seized by the British, he continued to contribute his dwindling fortune to Congress for the war effort.

Francis Lewis

In early September of 1776, the British burned the home of Francis Lewis of New York and seized his wife. Held in a prison with no bed and no change of clothes, with only a slop bucket for furniture, she was finally released after two years of suffering. Her health was gone, and she died soon after her release. Heartbroken, her husband continued to serve in the Continental Congress until 1779.

Connecticut

Roger Sherman

Sherman said,

"I believe that there is only one living and true God, existing in three persons, the Father, the Son, and the Holy Ghost . . . and that at the end of the world, there will be a judgment of all mankind, when the righteous shall be publically acquitted before Christ the Judge, and be admitted to everlasting life and glory, and the wicked be sentenced to everlasting punishment."[105]

Samuel Huntington

"Governor Huntington lived the life of the irreproachable and sincere Christian. Hence, as a devoted Christian and a true patriot, he never swayed from duty, or looked back after he had placed his hand to the work. One of his leading traits was that of the love of justice; this principle was so deeply and indelibly impressed upon his heart, that in whatever situation of life he was placed, he was steadfastly and strenuously it's advocate and promoter."[106]

William Williams

This Founding Father sacrificed his fortune for the cause, financing a number of enterprises, including the Ticonderoga offensive.

Oliver Wolcott

This Connecticut signer was present when the statue of King George was pulled down at the reading of the Declaration of Independence in New York. He took the broken pieces of the headless statue home to Connecticut, where his wife, daughter, son, and neighbor ladies melted it down, making over 42,000 bullets, which he later used to fight the British at the Battle of Saratoga.

GEORGIA

George Walton

As a colonel in the Georgia militia, Walton was wounded and captured in the fall of Savanah to the British. After being released in a prisoner exchange, he served as governor and chief justice of Georgia and as a US senator.

Lyman Hall

Hall's rice plantation was destroyed by the British, but his family escaped to the north.

Button Gwinnett

Converted from Tory principles by Lyman Hall, Button Gwinnett entered the fight for freedom with all his energy and determination. In doing so, he made political enemies. In May of 1777, he was challenged to a duel, was fatally wounded, and died 12 days later. He was the second signer of the Declaration to die.

It was July 4, 1776. The Declaration of Independence lay on the table before the Continental Congress. John Witherspoon, preacher of the gospel, intellectual, proponent of liberty, president of the College of New Jersey (later Princeton University), stood and spoke:

"There is a tide in the affairs of men, a nick of time. We perceive it now before us. To hesitate is to consent to our own slavery. That noble instrument upon your table, which ensures immortality to its author, should be subscribed this very morning by every pen in this house. He that will not respond to its accents and strain every nerve to carry into effect its provisions is unworthy the name of freeman. For my own part, of property I have some, of reputation more. That reputation is staked, that property is pledged, on the issue of this contest; and although these gray hairs must soon descend into the sepulchre, I would infinitely rather that they descend thither by the hand of the executioner than desert at this crisis the sacred cause of my country."[104] He would soon feel the effect of his decision.

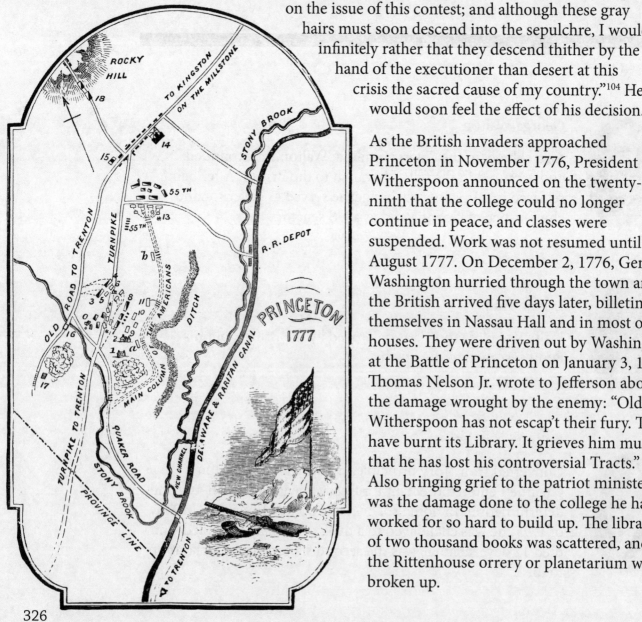

As the British invaders approached Princeton in November 1776, President Witherspoon announced on the twenty-ninth that the college could no longer continue in peace, and classes were suspended. Work was not resumed until August 1777. On December 2, 1776, General Washington hurried through the town and the British arrived five days later, billeting themselves in Nassau Hall and in most of the houses. They were driven out by Washington at the Battle of Princeton on January 3, 1777. Thomas Nelson Jr. wrote to Jefferson about the damage wrought by the enemy: "Old Witherspoon has not escap't their fury. They have burnt its Library. It grieves him much that he has lost his controversial Tracts." Also bringing grief to the patriot minister was the damage done to the college he had worked for so hard to build up. The library of two thousand books was scattered, and the Rittenhouse orrery or planetarium was broken up.

Joseph Hewes

Hewes was assigned as head of the Navy committee, which in effect made him the first Secretary of the Navy. Hewes was a good friend of John Paul Jones, whom he outfitted with a ship that Jones used to harass the British navy. Ill health made him resign from Congress in 1779, and he died shortly thereafter.

William Hooper

Hooper's signature on the Declaration won him the attention of the British. They took delight in hounding him and his family. Once a British captain went out of his way to sail up the Cape Fear River to a point about 3 miles from Wilmington, just to shell a house belonging to Hooper. They burned his home and lands.

John Penn

Penn formed a band of patriots that used guerilla tactics to harass Cornwallis on his drive northward.

PENNSYLVANIA

George Clymer

Clymer's home in Chester, Pennsylvania, was taken over by the British. Although he lost more than 100 of his ships during the Revolution, he dedicated himself to raising money for the war effort, working closely with his friend, Robert Morris.

Benjamin Franklin

As governor of Pennsylvania, Ben Franklin not only drafted a statewide prayer proclamation for his own state, he also recommended Christianity in the state's public schools and encouraged church attendance in the state. He also desired to start a colony in Ohio with the Reverend George Whitefield to

> "facilitate the introduction of pure religion among the [Indians]. . . ." He enthused, "in such an enterprise, I could spend the remainder of my life with pleasure, and I firmly believe God would bless us with success."[105]

Robert Morris

In 1781, Robert Morris issued over a million dollars of personal credit to finance the war effort, and raised $200,000 from friends to defeat the British at Yorktown. In 1798, his personal finances collapsed. Never reimbursed by this country, he spent three years in debtor's prison.

John Morton

Morton was criticized bitterly by many of his Pennsylvania neighbors for breaking the tie vote of the Pennsylvania delegation in favor of independence. The criticism depressed him greatly. Early in 1777, he became ill and died. Among his last words were these (speaking of his signature on the Declaration):

> "Tell them that they shall acknowledge it to have been the most glorious service that I have ever rendered to my country."[106]

George Ross

Lawyer George Ross served his country without monetary reward. He considered it

> "a duty of every man to contribute, by every means within his power, to the welfare of his country, without expecting pecuniary rewards."

Benjamin Rush

Rush was the founder of the first Sunday school movement in America and helped start the first Bible society. He wanted to be able to put a Bible in the hands of every American. He was strong on early training of children in the Scriptures. The early influence of his home was felt throughout his life. As he himself noted, his loving mother had paid strict attention to the morals and religious principles of her children. He proclaimed,

> "My only hope of salvation is in the infinite, transcendent love of God manifested to the world by the death of His son upon the Cross. Nothing but his blood will wash away my sins."[107]

James Smith

Smith was a witty speaker and was most entertaining in his speeches to Congress where, he would joke about almost everything, including the loss of his business and large fortune to the war. There were only two things he would not joke about — one was religion and the other was George Washington, whom he loved and admired.

George Taylor

Taylor began his life in America as a bond servant. Through his diligence, he rose to become one of the wealthiest of the delegates to the Constitutional Convention. Due to his commitment to tending to the duties of running the new country, he was away from managing his iron works business a great deal and suffered significant financial loss as a result.

James Wilson

Wilson was a dynamic speaker with a powerful voice, and was one of the first to declare that Britain had no authority to rule over the colonies.

SOUTH CAROLINA

Thomas Heyward Jr.

He served in the army and was taken prisoner. The British raided his plantation while he was in prison and burned his buildings. His wife became ill and died before he was released.

Arthur Middleton

Middleton was captured and imprisoned after the British ravaged his plantation. Later, he served in Congress.

Edward Rutledge

When the British seized Charleston in May 1780, Rutledge was among the first captives. He was imprisoned at St. Augustine, Florida, where "dangerous" rebels were held. He was released about a year later on prisoner exchange. He learned that his mother had also been held captive. South Carolina then elected him to the state legislature, where he served many years.

Thomas Lynch

Thomas Lynch served as captain in the 1st South Carolina Regiment during the war and there contracted a serious illness that left him a partial invalid. Shortly after signing the Declaration, his doctors suggested he sail for the West Indies to hopefully improve his health. His ship disappeared, and he and his wife and all aboard were lost at sea.

RHODE ISLAND

William Ellery

Ellery sought a spot where he could witness the signature of each of the signers during the signing of the Declaration.

> "I was determined to see how they all looked as they signed what might be their death warrants," he said. "Undaunted resolution was displayed on every countenance."[108]

His Newport home was burned during the invasion of Rhode Island. He nevertheless continued to serve his country.

Stephen Hopkins

This patriot's signature on the Declaration appears very shaky. This is because he had had a recent stroke. He still made the trip to vote and affix his name to the Declaration. As he signed, he had to use his left hand to steady his right hand. He remarked his signature was shaky, but not his resolve.

Carter Braxton

Wealthy before the war, Braxton saw virtually every merchant ship he owned sunk or captured by the British. Although he lost his wealth and was forced to sell his land, he continued to serve in the Virginia legislature.

Thomas Nelson Jr.

Nelson served as the governor of Virginia and distributed large sums of his money to the families of the soldiers. At the Battle of Yorktown, he led 3,000 militiamen against the British. Although the British took refuge in homes belonging to Virginians, Nelson's troops shelled them anyway. During the engagement, Nelson turned one cannon on his own home and lit the fuse, killing two British officers inside. In so doing he destroyed nearly all his earthly possessions.

Richard Henry Lee

It was said of Lee, "In the vigour of his mind, amid the honours of the world and it's enjoyments, he had declared his belief in Jesus Christ as the Savior of men."[109]

George Wythe

During the revolution, Mr. Wythe suffered greatly in respect to his property. His devotion to public service left him little opportunity to attend to his private affairs. He, however, lived a life of sacrifice for the public welfare. He was poisoned by a nephew who suspected he would leave his fortune to a slave whom he treated as a son.

Francis Lightfoot Lee

"Possessed of ample wealth, he used it like a philosopher and Christian in dispensing its blessing, for the benefit of his country and his fellow men."[110]

Benjamin Harrison

He served in Congress and as speaker of the house in the Virginia legislature. During this period, the British raided and plundered their way through Virginia, and the legislature, with Harrison at its head, was forced to flee from town to town to keep from being captured. He came very close to being captured near the end of the war.

Thomas Jefferson

Jefferson said,

> "I have sworn upon the altar of God, eternal hostility against every form of tyranny over the mind of men."[111]

While the Virginia legislature was meeting at Charlottesville, British officer Tartleton was rapidly approaching in order to capture them. Jefferson and his family barely had time to make arrangements to arrange their escape before the enemy was seen ascending the hill. Mr. Jefferson mounted his horse and narrowly escaped through a course in the woods. While president, he negotiated a federal treaty with the Kaskakia Indians in which he included direct federal funding to pay for Christian ministers to work with the Indians and for the building of a church in which Indians could worship.

The Constitutional Conventio

CHAPTER 34
★ ★ ★

WHO WERE THE SIGNERS OF THE CONSTITUTION?

DELAWARE

John Dickinson

Born into a wealthy Quaker family, John Dickinson was trained to practice law, but he discovered while still young that he had a passion for politics. He served in both the Delaware and Pennsylvania colonial legislatures. After independence, he served as governor of both states. He worked to end slavery and educate poor children.

George Read

Known as "the honest lawyer," Read was a champion of the rights of the small states in the Convention. He was the only man to sign the Constitution twice, signing once for himself and once for fellow Delawarean John Dickinson, who had left the convention because of illness.

Gunning Bedford Jr.

Bedford was a lawyer but served briefly as an aide to Washington during the war. His family owned a pair of pistols they said were given to Bedford by the general when sending him on a dangerous secret mission. Later in life, Bedford was a federal judge. In his private hours, he worked to promote education and abolish slavery.

Signer of the Constitution

Rendering thanks to my Creator for my existence and station among His works, for my birth in a country enlightened by the Gospel and enjoying freedom, and for all His other kindnesses, to Him I resign myself, humbly confiding in His goodness and in His mercy through Jesus Christ for the events of eternity.

— Will of John Dickinson (left)

Jacob Broom

Though shy about speaking in public, Jacob Broom may have saved the Constitutional Convention. Amid wrangling about the rights of large states versus small states, some of the delegates grew angry and threatened to walk out of the convention. Broom rose to his feet and declared that it would be wrong to part in anger without producing a constitution. The other delegates heeded his words, and the convention continued to a successful conclusion. When he died in 1810, Broom left a large amount of money to help a school for black children and several other benevolent causes.

This is the text of Jacob Broom's letter with certain words in parenthesis to explain the text:

Wilmington Feb. 24, 1794

Dear James,

I recd.[received] your favor of the 27th ulti [last] & am well pleased at the sentiments expressed – whilst you go on, having your own approbation you have nothing to fear – I flatter myself you will be what I wish but don't be so much flattered as to relax of your application – don't forget to be a Christian, I have said much to you on this head [topic of discourse] & I hope an indelible impression is made –

Tell Mr. Harrison that I shall attend to his request, very soon – I am & have been very much engaged for some time past; being about to establish a Cotton Manufactory at this place – it is an arduous undertaking for an individual; but I hope to accomplish it – I have bought a valuable plantation on B. Wine and have secured a Mill seat [site] where I intend building (the ensuing summer) a Cotton Mill to spin part of the stuff

Your mamma, sisters & brothers are well & so is J.S. Littler – they join with me in love to you –

I expected sir now to receive another letter from you – I have sold my Mercht.[Merchant] Mill & Plantations in Kent for 25,000 I am improving my other seat there – all this is nothing without economy, industry & the blessing of Heaven – I am building another Mill there –

I am, in haste yours affectionately

Jacob Broom

Richard Bassett

Richard Bassett's father abandoned the family when Richard was a child. Unable to care for him, his mother sent him to live with a relative who trained him to be a lawyer like himself. Bassett served as a captain of cavalry under Washington, then was elected to the Delaware legislature. After the Constitution was ratified, Bassett was elected one of Delaware's first two US senators.

PENNSYLVANIA

Benjamin Franklin

Also a signer of the Declaration of Independence, Ben Franklin is one of our most remarkable Founding Fathers. He was a statesman, inventor, author, printer, and a diplomat, and wore many other hats as well. He was a personal friend of George Whitefield and contributed money to Whitefield's ministry.

James Wilson

Born in Scotland, James Wilson came to America at the age of 23 and studied to be a lawyer. In the Continental Congress he was a signer of the Declaration of Independence. In the Constitutional Convention, Wilson spoke 168 times, more than any other delegate except Governor Morris. He was a great advocate for the power of the citizen. He declared, "No government can long subsist without the confidence of the people."

Gouvernour Morris

As a college student, Morris accidentally scalded his right arm so badly that he had to take a year off from his studies. As an adult, he was injured so badly in a carriage accident that his right leg had to be amputated. But none of that stopped him from public service. In the Convention, he railed against slavery, saying it was evil for "the inhabitant of Georgia or South Carolina to go to the coast of Africa and tear away his fellow creatures from their dearest connections and damn them to the most cruel bondages."

Robert Morris

Also a signer of the Declaration of Independence, Robert Morris was one of the wealthiest men in America when the Revolutionary War started. At the Constitutional Convention he was rather quiet, not speaking often. George Washington stayed at his home while the Convention was going on. The two often went fishing together during breaks. Morris later served as a U.S. senator from Pennsylvania. He had contributed around one million dollars of his personal funds to the nation during the war.

George Clymer

Clymer served in the Continental Congress and was one of six men who signed both the Declaration of Independence and the Constitution. He lived in Philadelphia but moved his family 25 miles out of town for fear of the British. It is said that he was so dedicated to his wife and children that he galloped all the way home from the Convention every afternoon to be with them and then rode back in the morning. Later, he served as a U.S. congressman. At Washington's request, he traveled 1,000 miles to George to make a treaty with the Creek Indians.

Thomas Mifflin

Mifflin won election to Pennsylvania's colonial legislature at the age of 28, and spent the rest of his life in public service. He was then wealthy, but was known as a man who enjoyed the company of poor working people as much as that of rich businessmen. He served in the Continental Congress and was a special military assistant to General Washington. In 1783, he was president of Congress when the peace treaty with Britain was ratified. After independence he was elected governor of Pennsylvania for three terms.

Jared Ingersoll

Entering college at only 12 years old, Jared Ingersoll was at Yale when the Stamp Act was passed. His father was a collector for the stamp tax, but was forced to quit by an armed mob. Young Jared shared his father's loyalist opinions until he traveled to Europe. In Paris, he met Benjamin Franklin, who may have influenced his views. When he returned to America, he changed sides and took up a patriot position. Excelling as an attorney, he was elected to the Continental Congress in 1780. He later served for many years as Pennsylvania's attorney general.

Thomas Fitzsimmons

Born in Ireland, Fitzsimmons became a wealthy merchant after moving to America. He represented Pennsylvania in both the Continental Congress and the Constitutional Convention. Later, he represented his state as a US congressman. He supported education with his own funds. Too kindhearted to say no to needy friends, Fitzsimmons loaned and gave away so much of his fortune that he ended up bankrupt at 64 years of age.

New Jersey

William Livingston

Livingston was born in New York and practiced law in both New York and New Jersey, entering politics in the 1750s. He was well off financially, and in the early 1770s moved his family to New Jersey, where he lived in semi-retirement. One day, a homeless boy appeared at his door with letters of introduction. Livingston took the young man under his wing, paid for his schooling, and often invited him to his home. The young man was Alexander Hamilton, who would become one of America's most important patriots.

William Paterson

The city of Paterson, New Jersey, is named after this patriot. He attended Princeton College starting at age 13. Later, he studied law under Richard Stockton. He said he hoped to live a quiet life, but politics called him away from that when he was elected to New Jersey's revolutionary legislature. He helped create the state's first constitution in 1776. Sent by his state to the Constitutional Convention, he was a champion for the rights of the small states. It was his influence that led to a U.S. Senate in which each state had two senators, regardless of its size or population.

David Brearly

Brearly was a devoted patriot, though his home state was about half Loyalist in sentiment. Arrested for treason before the war, Brearly was rescued by a mob of his patriot friends before he could be tried and possibly hung. He fathered seven children by two wives. He served ten years as New Jersey's chief justice.

Jonathan Dayton

Jonathan Dayton graduated from Princeton in 1776 at 15, and immediately joined the Continental army. He rose to the rank of captain and saw service in many battles, including the final great battle at Yorktown. The youngest delegate at the Constitutional Convention, Dayton was only 26 when he signed the great document.

GEORGIA

Abraham Baldwin

This Georgian served as a chaplain in Washington's army and suffered through the terrible winter of 1777–1778 with them. Baldwin had been one of 12 children, whose blacksmith father had sacrificed greatly to educate Abraham and his siblings. The father died in 1787, the year his son signed the Constitution. Abraham Baldwin then paid off his father's debts and finished paying for his siblings' education out of his own pocket.

William Few

Born near Baltimore, Maryland, in 1748, William moved with his family to North Carolina when he was ten years old. The Fews became involved with the Regulator movement, and early resistance against tyranny in the colony. The Few farm was destroyed by the British and one of William's brothers was hung for his part in the resistance. This made William decidedly anti-British. The family moved to Georgia and William joined the militia. He served in the Continental Congress and signed the Constitution, making Georgia the fourth state.

CONNECTICUT

Roger Sherman

Roger Sherman was a farmer, shoemaker, and the father of 15 children. He also studied law on his own and became a lawyer. He was elected to several positions in New Milford and later to the colonial legislature. He also served as a judge. When Connecticut sent him to the Continental Congress, Sherman began a 20-year career in national politics. At the Constitutional Convention, he was the second oldest signer at age 66.

William Samuel Johnson

Young "Sammy" Johnson was educated at home by his minister father until he was almost 13 years old, when he entered Yale College. He graduated at 16. Feeling that he could not take sides against England in the Revolutionary War, he also could not take arms against his own country. Some of his patriot neighbors were enraged at him, and in 1779 he was arrested and nearly imprisoned. He then took an oath of loyalty to Connecticut and was released. As time went by, people came to admire him because he did what he felt was right regardless of the consequences. He became so popular that at the end of the war he was elected to the Continental Congress. Three years later he was chosen to represent his state at the Constitutional Convention.

MASSACHUSETTS

Nathaniel Gorham

Gorham impressed his colleagues in the Constitutional Convention as a natural leader and a man of good reputation and sense. He suggested a last-minute change just before the Constitution was signed. The document said that there would be a member of the House of Representatives "for every forty thousand inhabitants." Gorham suggested that the number be changed to thirty thousand, so that there would be more representatives in Congress. Offering an opinion for the only time at the convention, George Washington spoke up and agreed with him. The vote passed unanimously.

Rufus King

At the age of 32, King was one of the youngest delegates to the Convention. His impassioned stand against slavery led to the ban on the importation of slaves years later. Later, in the US Senate, he held the position that slavery violated the principles of American independence.

MARYLAND

James McHenry

Irish-born James McHenry was a doctor, a legislator, and an amateur poet. He served as an army surgeon and an aide to both Washington and Lafayette. After signing the Constitution, he served in the Maryland legislature, where he fiercely opposed slavery. He later served as Secretary of War.

JAMES MCHENRY'S INFLUENCE

James McHenry was born in Northern Ireland in 1753. While attending an academy in Dublin, he made himself sick by studying too much. Consequently, in 1771 his family sent him to America to recuperate. He was 17 years old. His family arranged for him to live with a baker in Philadelphia. This baker had a nine-year-old stepdaughter named Peggy who James taught to read.

James loved America and persuaded his family to join him. They opened a store in Baltimore and soon became wealthy. At about the time his parents arrived, James began attending Newark Academy. There he discovered his love for poetry. He wrote hundreds of poems during his lifetime.

When James returned to Baltimore, he studied medicine under Benjamin Rush, signer of the Declaration of Independence. As he finished up his training, the War of Independence broke out. He served as an army surgeon during the war and as an aide to Gen. Washington and Marquis de Layfayette as well.

At the war's end he returned to Baltimore and married Peggy Caldwell, whom he had taught to read when he first arrived in this country. James and Peggy had five children.

After the war, James became interested in politics, and in 1781 was elected to the Maryland senate. Two years later he was sent to represent Maryland in the Continental Congress.

Although he spoke little, he took extensive notes that have provided us with much insight as to the proceedings that took place. He concluded, "Comparing the inconveniences and the evils which we labor under from the present confederation with the probable benefits promised us by the new system, I am clear that I ought to give it all the support in my power."

He worked for years for the gradual freeing of slaves. In January of 1796, George Washington wrote to him, "It would give me sincere pleasure if you will fill the office of Secretary of War."

James accepted the position and held it for four years, at which time he retired to spend time with his family and write poems. He died at this home on May 3, 1816, at age 62. Baltimore's Fort McHenry, where the flag flew that inspired Francis Scott Key to write "The Star Spangled Banner" was named in his honor.

Daniel St. Thomas Jenifer

The man with the strange name became a leader in Maryland's revolutionary government during the War of Independence. He was not selected originally as a delegate to the Constitutional Convention, but was sent in the place of a delegate who could not go. He ordered in his will that his slaves were to be freed after his death.

Daniel Carroll

Charles Carroll of Carrollton, a signer of the Declaration of Independence, was selected to represent Maryland at the Constitutional Convention. However, he decided not to go and his cousin Daniel was sent in his place. Daniel voted for the Constitution, signed it, and then wrote many letters to newspapers encouraging its ratification.

SOUTH CAROLINA

John Rutledge

Rutledge was governor of the state of South Carolina in 1776 when Fort Moultrie was successfully defended against the British. He also served in the Continental Congress and as a judge. He was the head of South Carolina's four-man delegation to the Convention.

Pierce Butler

Butler was born in Ireland and joined the British army when he was only 11. At 22, he was sent to America. He married Mary Middleton, resigned from the army, and became a planter. He was a frequent speaker at the Constitutional Convention, and it was his suggestion that the proceedings be kept secret so that delegates would not be pressured to vote one way or the other.

Charles Cotesworth Pinckney

Pinckney served in the Continental army and fought in several different states during the war. He was captured by the British and held for two years. The British tried to induce him to join their side, but he replied, "My heart is altogether American." Pinckney was responsible for a religious freedom clause in Article VI of the Constitution.

Charles Pinckney

Charles was a cousin of Charles Cotesworth Pinckney. Though one of the youngest of the delegates to the Convention, he spoke over 100 times and presented a plan to the delegates that, while it was not adopted as a whole, contributed around 30 provisions to the finished Constitution.

New Hampshire

John Langdon

Langdon was a successful merchant. He served New Hampshire in the state legislature and the Continental Congress. After signing the Constitution, he was a U.S. senator from New Hampshire and later the governor of the state. He remained in political office until the age of 71.

Nicholas Gilman

Gilman's greatest service to his country was his work in getting New Hampshire to ratify the Constitution after he had signed it. He spent the second half of his life in the US Congress, the state legislature, and the US senate.

Virginia

James Madison

Madison is called "The Father of the Constitution." He spoke over 150 times in the Convention and kept detailed notes that provide today's best record of the proceedings. Madison, along with Alexander Hamilton and John Jay, wrote 85 articles urging the states to ratify the Constitution. These articles came to be known as The Federalist Papers. They are still considered the best explanation of the principles of the Constitution.

—— 66 ——

In the name of God, Amen. I, Daniel of Saint Thomas Jenifer . . . of disposing mind and memory, commend my soul to my blessed Redeemer. . . .

Will of Daniel St. Thomas Jenifer

—— 66 ——

George Washington

The general said little during the Convention, but his presence lent importance to the proceedings. Washington was pleased with the document that the delegates produced. He called it "the best Constitution that can be obtained." His signature on the document helped to win ratification for it in all 13 states. No one was surprised when he was elected America's first president under the new Constitution.

John Blair

Blair was a red-haired lawyer who earned a reputation as a fair and honest judge. That reputation won him a place as a delegate from Virginia to the Constitutional Convention. He served on no committees and made no speeches, but his influence was felt strongly enough that George Washington, after being elected president, nominated him to a seat on the first US Supreme Court.

New York

Alexander Hamilton

War hero Alexander Hamilton had little effect on the Constitutional Convention because New York's other two delegates, Lansing and Yates, had different views than Hamilton and so could sway the New York vote away from his position. Ironically, both Lansing and Yates left the convention early, so that Hamilton was the only New Yorker to sign the document. His great contribution to the Constitution was his writing of 51 of the articles that came to be called The Federalist Papers and so impacted the ratification of the document.

———— 〝 ————

I believe that there is one only living and true God, existing in three persons, the Father, the Son, and the Holy Ghost. . . . that the Scriptures of the Old and New Testaments are a revelation from God. . . . that God did send His own Son to become man, die in the room and stead of sinners, and thus to lay a foundation for the offer of pardon and salvation to all mankind so as all may be saved who are willing to accept the Gospel offer.

Roger Sherman

———— 〝 ————

Hugh Williamson

Like his friend Benjamin Franklin, Hugh Williamson was a wearer of many hats. He was at various times in his life a preacher, a scientist, a doctor, an astronomer, and a politician. He served as a medical doctor to North Carolina troops during the War of Independence. After the war he was elected to the North Carolina legislature. Then he was sent to the Continental Congress. In 1787, Williamson was elected to represent North Carolina at the Constitutional Convention. There, he was a member of five committees and offered many suggestions in the debates. It was his idea that U.S. senators' terms be six years in duration. He served as a US congressman from North Carolina for two terms before moving with his family to New York City. He spent his last years writing and working for charitable causes.

Richard Dobbs Spaight

Chosen by North Carolina to represent her at the Constitutional Convention, faithful Richard Spaight attended every single session of the meeting. After signing the Constitution, Spaight went home to fight for its ratification. That was not an easy job, in fact, for North Carolina took longer than any other state except Rhode Island to ratify. He was killed in a pistol duel with a rival politician at the age of 44. His son would later become a governor of North Carolina.

William Blount

It is a shame to end these brief character sketches with the tale of a scoundrel, but such is the legacy of this North Carolina delegate. Blount had a long career in land speculation, and after the Convention he entered into a conspiracy to support land prices in the western regions where he had bought much land that he hoped to sell to settlers. The plot called for cooperating with England in getting control of Florida and Louisiana for the British in exchange for free access to New Orleans and the Mississippi River to American merchants. Blount was by this time a US senator from North Carolina. His maneuverings in this plot led to his being the first man ever expelled from the Senate.

———— 66 ————

To the eternal, immutable, and only true God be all honor and glory, now and forever, Amen!

Will of Charles Cotesworth Pinckney

———— 66 ————

IN CONGRESS, JULY 4, 1776.

The unanimous Declaration of the thirteen united States of America.

When in the Course of human events, it becomes necessary for one people to dissolve the political bands which have connected them with another, and to assume among the powers of the earth, the separate and equal station to which the Laws of Nature and of Nature's God entitle them, a decent respect to the opinions of mankind requires that they should declare the causes which impel them to the separation. — We hold these truths to be self-evident, that all men are created equal, that they are endowed by their Creator with certain unalienable Rights, that among these are Life, Liberty and the pursuit of Happiness. — That to secure these rights, Governments are instituted among Men, deriving their just powers from the consent of the governed, — That whenever any Form of Government becomes destructive of these ends, it is the Right of the People to alter or to abolish it, and to institute new Government, laying its foundation on such principles and organizing its powers in such form, as to them shall seem most likely to effect their Safety and Happiness. Prudence, indeed, will dictate that Governments long established should not be changed for light and transient causes; and accordingly all experience hath shewn, that mankind are more disposed to suffer, while evils are sufferable, than to right themselves by abolishing the forms to which they are accustomed. But when a long train of abuses and usurpations, pursuing invariably the same Object evinces a design to reduce them under absolute Despotism, it is their right, it is their duty, to throw off such Government, and to provide new Guards for their future security. — Such has been the patient sufferance of these Colonies; and such is now the necessity which constrains them to alter their former Systems of Government. The history of the present King of Great Britain is a history of repeated injuries and usurpations, all having in direct object the establishment of an absolute Tyranny over these States. To prove this, let Facts be submitted to a candid world. — He has refused his Assent to Laws, the most wholesome and necessary for the public good. — He has forbidden his Governors to pass Laws of immediate and pressing importance, unless suspended in their operation till his Assent should be obtained; and when so suspended, he has utterly neglected to attend to them. — He has refused to pass other Laws for the accommodation of large districts of people, unless those people would relinquish the right of Representation in the Legislature, a right inestimable to them and formidable to tyrants only. — He has called together legislative bodies at places unusual, uncomfortable, and distant from the depository of their Public Records, for the sole purpose of fatiguing them into compliance with his measures. — He has dissolved Representative Houses repeatedly, for opposing with manly firmness his invasions on the rights of the people. — He has refused for a long time, after such dissolutions, to cause others to be elected; whereby the Legislative powers, incapable of Annihilation, have returned to the People at large for their exercise; the State remaining in the mean time exposed to all the dangers of invasion from without, and convulsions within. — He has endeavoured to prevent the population of these States; for that purpose obstructing the Laws for Naturalization of Foreigners; refusing to pass others to encourage their migrations hither, and raising the conditions of new Appropriations of Lands. — He has obstructed the Administration of Justice, by refusing his Assent to Laws for establishing Judiciary powers. — He has made Judges dependent on his Will alone, for the tenure of their offices, and the amount and payment of their salaries. — He has erected a multitude of New Offices, and sent hither swarms of Officers to harass our people, and eat out their substance. — He has kept among us, in times of peace, Standing Armies without the Consent of our legislatures. — He has affected to render the Military independent of and superior to the Civil power. — He has combined with others to subject us to a jurisdiction foreign to our constitution, and unacknowledged by our laws; giving his Assent to their Acts of pretended Legislation: — For Quartering large bodies of armed troops among us: — For protecting them, by a mock Trial, from punishment for any Murders which they should commit on the Inhabitants of these States: — For cutting off our Trade with all parts of the world: — For imposing Taxes on us without our Consent: — For depriving us in many cases, of the benefits of Trial by jury: — For transporting us beyond Seas to be tried for pretended offences: — For abolishing the free System of English Laws in a neighbouring Province, establishing therein an Arbitrary government, and enlarging its Boundaries so as to render it at once an example and fit instrument for introducing the same absolute rule into these Colonies: — For taking away our Charters, abolishing our most valuable Laws, and altering fundamentally the Forms of our Governments: — For suspending our own Legislatures, and declaring themselves invested with power to legislate for us in all cases whatsoever. — He has abdicated Government here, by declaring us out of his Protection and waging War against us. — He has plundered our seas, ravaged our Coasts, burnt our towns, and destroyed the lives of our people. — He is at this time transporting large Armies of foreign Mercenaries to compleat the works of death, desolation and tyranny, already begun with circumstances of Cruelty & perfidy scarcely paralleled in the most barbarous ages, and totally unworthy the Head of a civilized nation. — He has constrained our fellow Citizens taken Captive on the high Seas to bear Arms against their country, to become the executioners of their friends and Brethren, or to fall themselves by their Hands. — He has excited domestic insurrections amongst us, and has endeavoured to bring on the inhabitants of our frontiers, the merciless Indian Savages, whose known rule of warfare, is an undistinguished destruction of all ages, sexes and conditions. In every stage of these Oppressions We have Petitioned for Redress in the most humble terms: Our repeated Petitions have been answered only by repeated injury. A Prince, whose character is thus marked by every act which may define a Tyrant, is unfit to be the ruler of a free people. Nor have We been wanting in attentions to our Brittish brethren. We have warned them from time to time of attempts by their legislature to extend an unwarrantable jurisdiction over us. We have reminded them of the circumstances of our emigration and settlement here. We have appealed to their native justice and magnanimity, and we have conjured them by the ties of our common kindred to disavow these usurpations, which, would inevitably interrupt our connections and correspondence. They too have been deaf to the voice of justice and of consanguinity. We must, therefore, acquiesce in the necessity, which denounces our Separation, and hold them, as we hold the rest of mankind, Enemies in War, in Peace Friends. —

We, therefore, the Representatives of the united States of America, in General Congress, Assembled, appealing to the Supreme Judge of the world for the rectitude of our intentions, do, in the Name, and by Authority of the good People of these Colonies, solemnly publish and declare, That these United Colonies are, and of Right ought to be Free and Independent States; that they are Absolved from all Allegiance to the British Crown, and that all political connection between them and the State of Great Britain, is and ought to be totally dissolved; and that as Free and Independent States, they have full Power to levy War, conclude Peace, contract Alliances, establish Commerce, and to do all other Acts and Things which Independent States may of right do. — And for the support of this Declaration, with a firm reliance on the Protection of divine Providence, we mutually pledge to each other our Lives, our Fortunes and our sacred Honor.

John Hancock

Button Gwinnett
Lyman Hall
Geo Walton.

Wm Hooper
Joseph Hewes,
John Penn

Edward Rutledge.

Thos Heyward Junr.
Thomas Lynch Junr.
Arthur Middleton

Samuel Chase
Wm Paca
Thos Stone
Charles Carroll of Carrollton

George Wythe
Richard Henry Lee
Th Jefferson
Benja Harrison
Thos Nelson jr.
Francis Lightfoot Lee
Carter Braxton

Robt Morris
Benjamin Rush
Benja Franklin
John Morton
Geo Clymer
Jas. Smith
Geo. Taylor
James Wilson
Geo. Ross
Caesar Rodney
Geo Read
Thos M:Kean

Wm Floyd
Phil. Livingston
Frans Lewis
Lewis Morris

Richd Stockton
Jno Witherspoon
Fras Hopkinson
John Hart
Abra Clark

Josiah Bartlett
Wm Whipple
Saml Adams
John Adams
Robt Treat Paine
Elbridge Gerry
Step Hopkins
William Ellery
Roger Sherman
Sam el Huntington
Wm Williams
Oliver Wolcott
Matthew Thornton

W.J. STONE SC. WASHn

Appendix I

The Declaration of Independence

IN CONGRESS, July 4, 1776.

The unanimous Declaration of the thirteen united States of America,

When in the Course of human events, it becomes necessary for one people to dissolve the political bands which have connected them with another, and to assume among the powers of the earth, the separate and equal station to which the Laws of Nature and of Nature's God entitle them, a decent respect to the opinions of mankind requires that they should declare the causes which impel them to the separation.

We hold these truths to be self-evident, that all men are created equal, that they are endowed by their Creator with certain unalienable Rights, that among these are Life, Liberty and the pursuit of Happiness. — That to secure these rights, Governments are instituted among Men, deriving their just powers from the consent of the governed, — That whenever any Form of Government becomes destructive of these ends, it is the Right of the People to alter or to abolish it, and to institute new Government, laying its foundation on such principles and organizing its powers in such form, as to them shall seem most likely to effect their Safety and Happiness. Prudence, indeed, will dictate that Governments long established should not be changed for light and transient causes; and accordingly all experience hath shewn, that mankind are more disposed to suffer, while evils are sufferable, than to right themselves by abolishing the forms to which they are accustomed. But when a long train of abuses and usurpations, pursuing invariably the same Object evinces a design to reduce them under absolute Despotism, it is their right, it is their duty, to throw off such Government, and to provide new Guards for their future security. — Such has been the patient sufferance of these Colonies; and such is now the necessity which constrains them to alter their former Systems of Government. The history of the present King of Great Britain is a history of repeated injuries and usurpations, all having in direct object the establishment of an absolute Tyranny over these States. To prove this, let Facts be submitted to a candid world.

He has refused his Assent to Laws, the most wholesome and necessary for the public good. He has forbidden his Governors to pass Laws of immediate and pressing importance, unless suspended in their operation till his Assent should be obtained; and when so suspended, he has utterly neglected to attend to them.

He has refused to pass other Laws for the accommodation of large districts of people, unless those people would relinquish the right of Representation in the Legislature, a right inestimable to them and formidable to tyrants only.

He has called together legislative bodies at places unusual, uncomfortable, and distant from the depository of their public Records, for the sole purpose of fatiguing them into compliance with his measures.

He has dissolved Representative Houses repeatedly, for opposing with manly firmness his invasions on the rights of the people.

He has refused for a long time, after such dissolutions, to cause others to be elected; whereby the Legislative powers, incapable of Annihilation, have returned to the People at large for their exercise; the State remaining in the mean time exposed to all the dangers of invasion from without, and convulsions within.

He has endeavoured to prevent the population of these States; for that purpose obstructing the Laws for Naturalization of Foreigners; refusing to pass others to encourage their migrations hither, and raising the conditions of new Appropriations of Lands.

He has obstructed the Administration of Justice, by refusing his Assent to Laws for establishing Judiciary powers.

He has made Judges dependent on his Will alone, for the tenure of their offices, and the amount and payment of their salaries.

He has erected a multitude of New Offices, and sent hither swarms of Officers to harrass our people, and eat out their substance.

He has kept among us, in times of peace, Standing Armies without the Consent of our legislatures.

He has affected to render the Military independent of and superior to the Civil power.

He has combined with others to subject us to a jurisdiction foreign to our constitution, and unacknowledged by our laws; giving his Assent to their Acts of pretended Legislation:

For Quartering large bodies of armed troops among us:

For protecting them, by a mock Trial, from punishment for any Murders which they should commit on the Inhabitants of these States:

For cutting off our Trade with all parts of the world:

For imposing Taxes on us without our Consent:

For depriving us in many cases, of the benefits of Trial by Jury:

For transporting us beyond Seas to be tried for pretended offences

For abolishing the free System of English Laws in a neighbouring Province, establishing therein an Arbitrary government, and enlarging its Boundaries so as to render it at once an example and fit instrument for introducing the same absolute rule into these Colonies:

For taking away our Charters, abolishing our most valuable Laws, and altering fundamentally the Forms of our Governments:

For suspending our own Legislatures, and declaring themselves invested with power to legislate for us in all cases whatsoever.

He has abdicated Government here, by declaring us out of his Protection and waging War against us.

He has plundered our seas, ravaged our Coasts, burnt our towns, and destroyed the lives of our people.

He is at this time transporting large Armies of foreign Mercenaries to compleat the works of death, desolation and tyranny, already begun with circumstances of Cruelty & perfidy scarcely paralleled in the most barbarous ages, and totally unworthy the Head of a civilized nation.

He has constrained our fellow Citizens taken Captive on the high Seas to bear Arms against their Country, to become the executioners of their friends and Brethren, or to fall themselves by their Hands.

He has excited domestic insurrections amongst us, and has endeavoured to bring on the inhabitants of our frontiers, the merciless Indian Savages, whose known rule of warfare, is an undistinguished destruction of all ages, sexes and conditions.

In every stage of these Oppressions We have Petitioned for Redress in the most humble terms: Our repeated Petitions have been answered only by repeated injury. A Prince whose character is thus marked by every act which may define a Tyrant, is unfit to be the ruler of a free people.

Nor have We been wanting in attentions to our Brittish brethren. We have warned them from time to time of attempts by their legislature to extend an unwarrantable jurisdiction over us. We have reminded them of the circumstances of our emigration and settlement here. We have appealed to their native justice and magnanimity, and we have conjured them by the ties of our common kindred to disavow these usurpations, which, would inevitably interrupt our connections and correspondence. They too have been deaf to the voice of justice and of consanguinity. We must, therefore, acquiesce in the necessity, which denounces our Separation, and hold them, as we hold the rest of mankind, Enemies in War, in Peace Friends.

We, therefore, the Representatives of the united States of America, in General Congress, Assembled, appealing to the Supreme Judge of the world for the rectitude of our intentions, do, in the Name, and by Authority of the good People of these Colonies, solemnly publish and declare, That these United Colonies are, and of Right ought to be Free and Independent States; that they are Absolved from all Allegiance to the British Crown, and that all political connection between them and the State of Great Britain, is and ought to be totally dissolved; and that as Free and Independent States, they have full Power to levy War, conclude Peace, contract Alliances, establish Commerce, and to do all other Acts and Things which Independent States may of right do. And for the support of this Declaration, with a firm reliance on the protection of divine Providence, we mutually pledge to each other our Lives, our Fortunes and our sacred Honor.

The 56 signatures on the Declaration appear in the positions indicated here:

Column 1

Georgia:

Button Gwinnett

Lyman Hall

George Walton

Column 2

North Carolina:

William Hooper

Joseph Hewes

John Penn

South Carolina:

Edward Rutledge

Thomas Heyward, Jr.

Thomas Lynch, Jr.

Arthur Middleton

Column 3

Massachusetts:

John Hancock

Maryland:

Samuel Chase

William Paca

Thomas Stone

Charles Carroll of Carrollton

Virginia:

George Wythe

Richard Henry Lee

Thomas Jefferson

Benjamin Harrison

Thomas Nelson, Jr.

Francis Lightfoot Lee

Carter Braxton

Column 4

Pennsylvania:

Robert Morris

Benjamin Rush

Benjamin Franklin

John Morton

George Clymer

James Smith

George Taylor

James Wilson

George Ross

Delaware:

Caesar Rodney

George Read

Thomas McKean

Column 5

New York:

William Floyd

Philip Livingston

Francis Lewis

Lewis Morris

New Jersey:

Richard Stockton

John Witherspoon

Francis Hopkinson

John Hart

Abraham Clark

Column 6

New Hampshire:

Josiah Bartlett

William Whipple

Massachusetts:

Samuel Adams

John Adams

Robert Treat Paine

Elbridge Gerry

Rhode Island:

Stephen Hopkins

William Ellery

Connecticut:

Roger Sherman

Samuel Huntington

William Williams

Oliver Wolcott

New Hampshire:

Matthew Thornton

Congress OF THE United States,

begun and held at the City of New-York, on

Wednesday the fourth of March, one thousand seven hundred and eighty-nine.

THE Conventions of a number of the States, having at the time of their adopting the Constitution, expressed a desire, in order to prevent misconstruction or abuse of its powers, that further declaratory and restrictive clauses should be added: And as extending the ground of public confidence in the Government, will best ensure the beneficent ends of its institution.

RESOLVED by the Senate and House of Representatives of the United States of America, in Congress assembled, two thirds of both Houses concurring, that the following Articles be proposed to the Legislatures of the several States, as amendments to the Constitution of the United States, all, or any of which Articles, when ratified by three fourths of the said Legislatures, to be valid to all intents and purposes, as part of the said Constitution; viz.

ARTICLES in addition to, and Amendment of the Constitution of the United States of America, proposed by Congress, and ratified by the Legislatures of the several States, pursuant to the fifth Article of the original Constitution.

Article the first... After the first enumeration required by the first Article of the Constitution, there shall be one Representative for every thirty thousand, until the number shall amount to one hundred, after which the proportion shall be so regulated by Congress, that there shall be not less than one hundred Representatives, nor less than one Representative for every forty thousand persons, until the number of Representatives shall amount to two hundred, after which the proportion shall be so regulated by Congress, that there shall not be less than two hundred Representatives, nor more than one Representative for every fifty thousand persons.

Article the second... No law, varying the compensation for the services of the Senators and Representatives, shall take effect, until an election of Representatives shall have intervened.

Article the third... Congress shall make no law respecting an establishment of religion, or prohibiting the free exercise thereof; or abridging the freedom of speech, or of the press; or the right of the people peaceably to assemble, and to petition the Government for a redress of grievances.

Article the fourth... A well regulated Militia, being necessary to the security of a free State, the right of the people to keep and bear Arms, shall not be infringed.

Article the fifth... No Soldier shall, in time of peace be quartered in any house, without the consent of the Owner, nor in time of war, but in a manner to be prescribed by law.

Article the sixth... The right of the people to be secure in their persons, houses, papers, and effects, against unreasonable searches and seizures, shall not be violated, and no Warrants shall issue, but upon probable cause, supported by Oath or affirmation, and particularly describing the place to be searched, and the persons or things to be seized.

Article the seventh... No person shall be held to answer for a capital, or otherwise infamous crime, unless on a presentment or indictment of a Grand Jury, except in cases arising in the land or naval forces, or in the Militia, when in actual service in time of War or public danger; nor shall any person be subject for the same offence to be twice put in jeopardy of life or limb; nor shall be compelled in any criminal case to be a witness against himself, nor be deprived of life, liberty, or property, without due process of law; nor shall private property be taken for public use, without just compensation.

Article the eighth... In all criminal prosecutions, the accused shall enjoy the right to a speedy and public trial, by an impartial jury of the State and district wherein the crime shall have been committed, which district shall have been previously ascertained by law, and to be informed of the nature and cause of the accusation; to be confronted with the witnesses against him; to have compulsory process for obtaining witnesses in his favor, and to have the Assistance of Counsel for his defence.

Article the ninth... In suits at common law, where the value in controversy shall exceed twenty dollars, the right of trial by jury shall be preserved, and no fact tried by a jury, shall be otherwise re-examined in any Court of the United States, than according to the rules of the common law.

Article the tenth... Excessive bail shall not be required, nor excessive fines imposed, nor cruel and unusual punishments inflicted.

Article the eleventh... The enumeration in the Constitution, of certain rights, shall not be construed to deny or disparage others retained by the people.

Article the twelfth... The powers not delegated to the United States by the Constitution, nor prohibited by it to the States, are reserved to the States respectively, or to the people.

ATTEST,

Frederick Augustus Muhlenberg, Speaker of the House of Representatives.

John Adams, Vice-President of the United States, and President of the Senate.

John Beckley, Clerk of the House of Representatives.

Sam. A. Otis, Secretary of the Senate.

APPENDIX 2

THE BILL OF RIGHTS

Amendment I

Congress shall make no law respecting an establishment of religion, or prohibiting the free exercise thereof; or abridging the freedom of speech, or of the press; or the right of the people peaceably to assemble, and to petition the government for a redress of grievances.

Amendment II

A well regulated militia, being necessary to the security of a free state, the right of the people to keep and bear arms, shall not be infringed.

Amendment III

No soldier shall, in time of peace be quartered in any house, without the consent of the owner, nor in time of war, but in a manner to be prescribed by law.

Amendment IV

The right of the people to be secure in their persons, houses, papers, and effects, against unreasonable searches and seizures, shall not be violated, and no warrants shall issue, but upon probable cause, supported by oath or affirmation, and particularly describing the place to be searched, and the persons or things to be seized.

Amendment V

No person shall be held to answer for a capital, or otherwise infamous crime, unless on a presentment or indictment of a grand jury, except in cases arising in the land or naval forces, or in the militia, when in actual service in time of war or public danger; nor shall any person be subject for the same offense to be twice put in jeopardy of life or limb; nor shall be compelled in any criminal case to be a witness against himself, nor be deprived of life, liberty, or property, without due process of law; nor shall private property be taken for public use, without just compensation.

Amendment VI

In all criminal prosecutions, the accused shall enjoy the right to a speedy and public trial, by an impartial jury of the state and district wherein the crime shall have been committed, which district shall have been previously ascertained by law, and to be informed of the nature and cause of the accusation; to be confronted with the witnesses against him; to have compulsory process for obtaining witnesses in his favor, and to have the assistance of counsel for his defense.

Amendment VII

In suits at common law, where the value in controversy shall exceed twenty dollars, the right of trial by jury shall be preserved, and no fact tried by a jury, shall be otherwise reexamined in any court of the United States, than according to the rules of the common law.

Amendment VIII

Excessive bail shall not be required, nor excessive fines imposed, nor cruel and unusual punishments inflicted.

Amendment IX

The enumeration in the Constitution, of certain rights, shall not be construed to deny or disparage others retained by the people.

Amendment X

The powers not delegated to the United States by the Constitution, nor prohibited by it to the states, are reserved to the states respectively, or to the people.

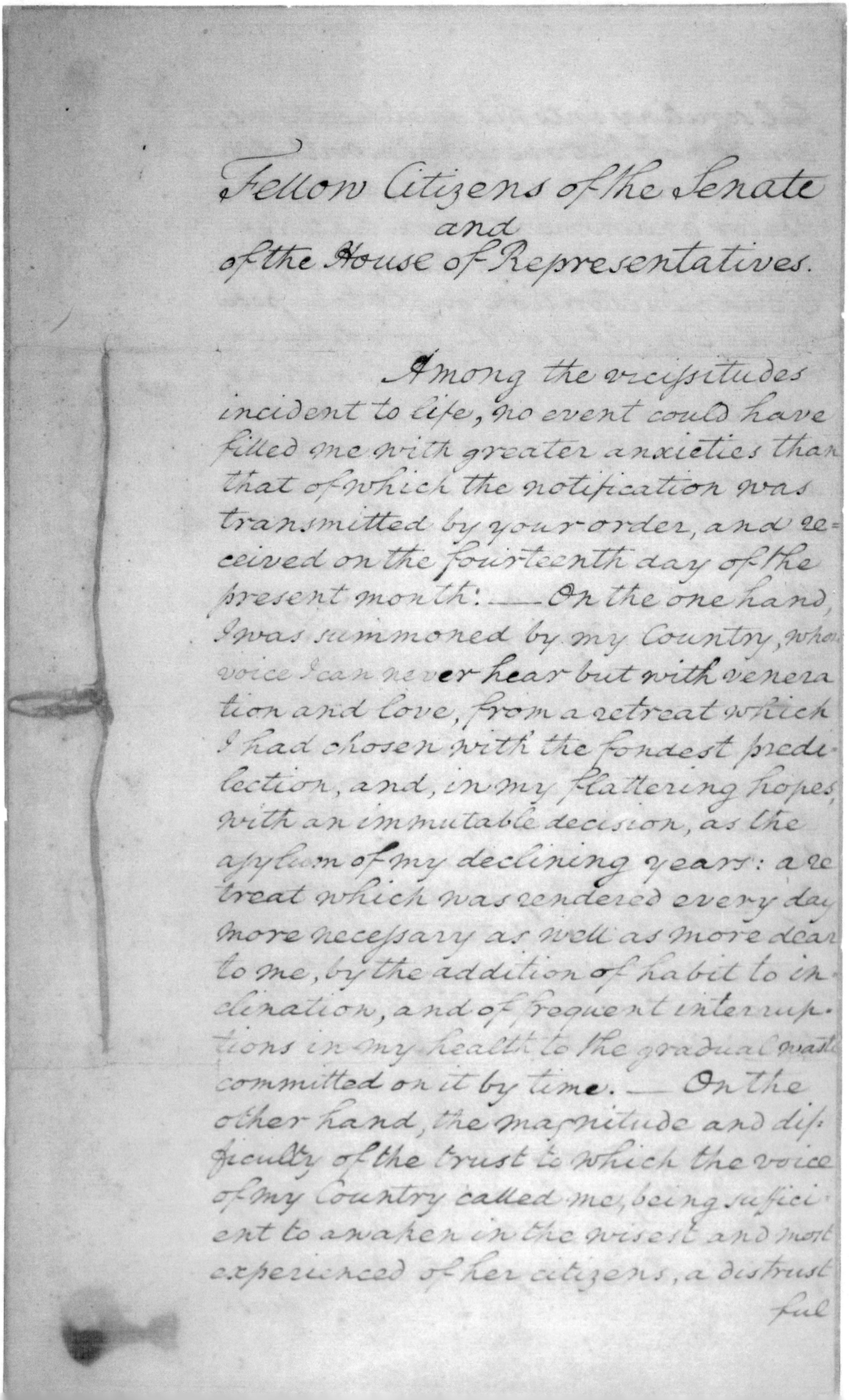

Fellow Citizens of the Senate
and
of the House of Representatives.

Among the vicissitudes incident to life, no event could have filled me with greater anxieties than that of which the notification was transmitted by your order, and received on the fourteenth day of the present month: ___ On the one hand, I was summoned by my Country, whose voice I can never hear but with veneration and love, from a retreat which I had chosen with the fondest predilection, and, in my flattering hopes, with an immutable decision, as the asylum of my declining years: a retreat which was rendered every day more necessary as well as more dear to me, by the addition of habit to inclination, and of frequent interruptions in my health to the gradual waste committed on it by time. ___ On the other hand, the magnitude and difficulty of the trust to which the voice of my Country called me, being sufficient to awaken in the wisest and most experienced of her citizens, a distrustful

George
Washington's
First Inaugural
Address
(page 1)

APPENDIX 3

Washington's Inaugural Address of 1789

A Transcription

[April 30, 1789]

Fellow Citizens of the Senate and the House of Representatives.

Among the vicissitudes incident to life, no event could have filled me with greater anxieties than that of which the notification was transmitted by your order, and received on the fourteenth day of the present month. On the one hand, I was summoned by my Country, whose voice I can never hear but with veneration and love, from a retreat which I had chosen with the fondest predilection, and, in my flattering hopes, with an immutable decision, as the asylum of my declining years: a retreat which was rendered every day more necessary as well as more dear to me, by the addition of habit to inclination, and of frequent interruptions in my health to the gradual waste committed on it by time. On the other hand, the magnitude and difficulty of the trust to which the voice of my Country called me, being sufficient to awaken in the wisest and most experienced of her citizens, a distrustful scrutiny into his qualifications, could not but overwhelm with dispondence, one, who, inheriting inferior endowments from nature and unpractised in the duties of civil administration, ought to be peculiarly conscious of his own deficiencies. In this conflict of emotions, all I dare aver, is, that it has been my faithful study to collect my duty from a just appreciation of every circumstance, by which it might be affected. All I dare hope, is, that, if in executing this task I have been too much swayed by a grateful remembrance of former instances, or by an affectionate sensibility to this transcendent proof, of the confidence of my fellow-citizens; and have thence too little consulted my incapacity as well as disinclination for the weighty and untried cares before me; my error will be palliated by

Inauguration of Washington

the motives which misled me, and its consequences be judged by my Country, with some share of the partiality in which they originated.

Such being the impressions under which I have, in obedience to the public summons, repaired to the present station; it would be peculiarly improper to omit in this first official Act, my fervent supplications to that Almighty Being who rules over the Universe, who presides in the Councils of Nations, and whose providential aids can supply every human defect, that his benediction may consecrate to the liberties and happiness of the People of the United States, a Government instituted by themselves for these essential purposes: and may enable every instrument employed in its administration to execute with success, the functions allotted to his charge. In tendering this homage to the Great Author of every public and private good I assure myself that it expresses your sentiments not less than my own; nor those of my fellow-citizens at large, less than either. No People can be bound to acknowledge and adore the invisible hand, which conducts the Affairs of men more than the People of the United States. Every step, by which they have advanced to the character of an independent nation, seems to have been distinguished by some token of providential agency. And in the important revolution just accomplished in the system of their United Government, the tranquil deliberations and voluntary consent of so many distinct communities, from which the event has resulted, cannot be compared with the means by which most Governments have been established, without some return of pious gratitude along with an humble anticipation of the future blessings which the past seem to presage. These reflections, arising out of the present crisis, have forced themselves too strongly on my mind to be suppressed. You will join with me I trust in thinking, that there are none under the influence of which, the proceedings of a new and free Government can more auspiciously commence.

By the article establishing the Executive Department, it is made the duty of the President "to recommend to your consideration, such measures as he shall judge necessary and expedient." The circumstances under which I now meet you, will acquit me from entering into that subject, farther than to refer to the Great Constitutional Charter under which you are assembled; and which, in defining your powers, designates the objects to which your attention is to be given. It will be more consistent with those circumstances, and far more congenial with the feelings which actuate me, to substitute, in place of a recommendation of particular measures, the tribute that is due to the talents, the rectitude, and the patriotism which adorn the characters selected to devise and adopt them. In these honorable qualifications, I behold the surest pledges, that as on one side, no local prejudices, or attachments; no seperate views, nor party animosities, will misdirect the comprehensive and equal eye which ought to watch over this great assemblage of communities and interests: so, on another, that the foundations of our National policy will be laid in the pure and immutable principles of private morality; and the pre-eminence of a free Government, be exemplified by all the attributes which can win the affections of its Citizens, and command the respect of the world.

I dwell on this prospect with every satisfaction which an ardent love for my Country can inspire: since there is no truth more thoroughly established, than that there exists in the economy and course of nature, an indissoluble union between virtue and happiness, between duty and advantage, between the genuine maxims of an honest and magnanimous policy, and the solid rewards of public prosperity and felicity: Since we ought to be no less persuaded that the propitious smiles of Heaven, can never be expected on a nation that disregards the eternal rules of order and right, which Heaven itself has ordained: And since the preservation of the sacred fire of liberty, and the destiny of the Republican model of Government, are justly considered as deeply, perhaps as finally staked, on the experiment entrusted to the hands of the American people.

Besides the ordinary objects submitted to your care, it will remain with your judgment to decide, how far an exercise of the occasional power delegated by the Fifth article of the Constitution is rendered expedient at the present juncture by the nature of objections which have been urged against the System, or by the degree of inquietude which has given birth to them. Instead of undertaking particular recommendations on this subject, in which I could be guided by no lights derived from official opportunities, I shall again give way to my entire confidence in your discernment and pursuit of the public good: For I assure myself that whilst you carefully avoid every alteration which might endanger the benefits of an United and effective Government, or which ought to await the future lessons of experience; a reverence for the characteristic rights of freemen, and a regard for the public harmony, will sufficiently influence your deliberations on the question how far the former can be more impregnably fortified, or the latter be safely and advantageously promoted.

Inauguration of Washington

To the preceeding observations I have one to add, which will be most properly addressed to the House of Representatives. It concerns myself, and will therefore be as brief as possible. When I was first honoured with a call into the Service of my Country, then on the eve of an arduous struggle for its liberties, the light in which I contemplated my duty required that I should renounce every pecuniary compensation. From this resolution I have in no instance departed. And being still under the impressions which produced it, I must decline as inapplicable to myself, any share in the personal emoluments, which may be indispensably included in a permanent provision for the Executive Department; and must accordingly pray that the pecuniary estimates for the Station in which I am placed, may, during my continuance in it, be limited to such actual expenditures as the public good may be thought to require.

Having thus imported to you my sentiments, as they have been awakened by the occasion which brings us together, I shall take my present leave; but not without resorting once more to the benign parent of the human race, in humble supplication that since he has been pleased to favour the American people, with opportunities for deliberating in perfect tranquility, and dispositions for deciding with unparellelled unanimity on a form of Government, for the security of their Union, and the advancement of their happiness; so his divine blessing may be equally conspicuous in the enlarged views, the temperate consultations, and the wise measures on which the success of this Government must depend.

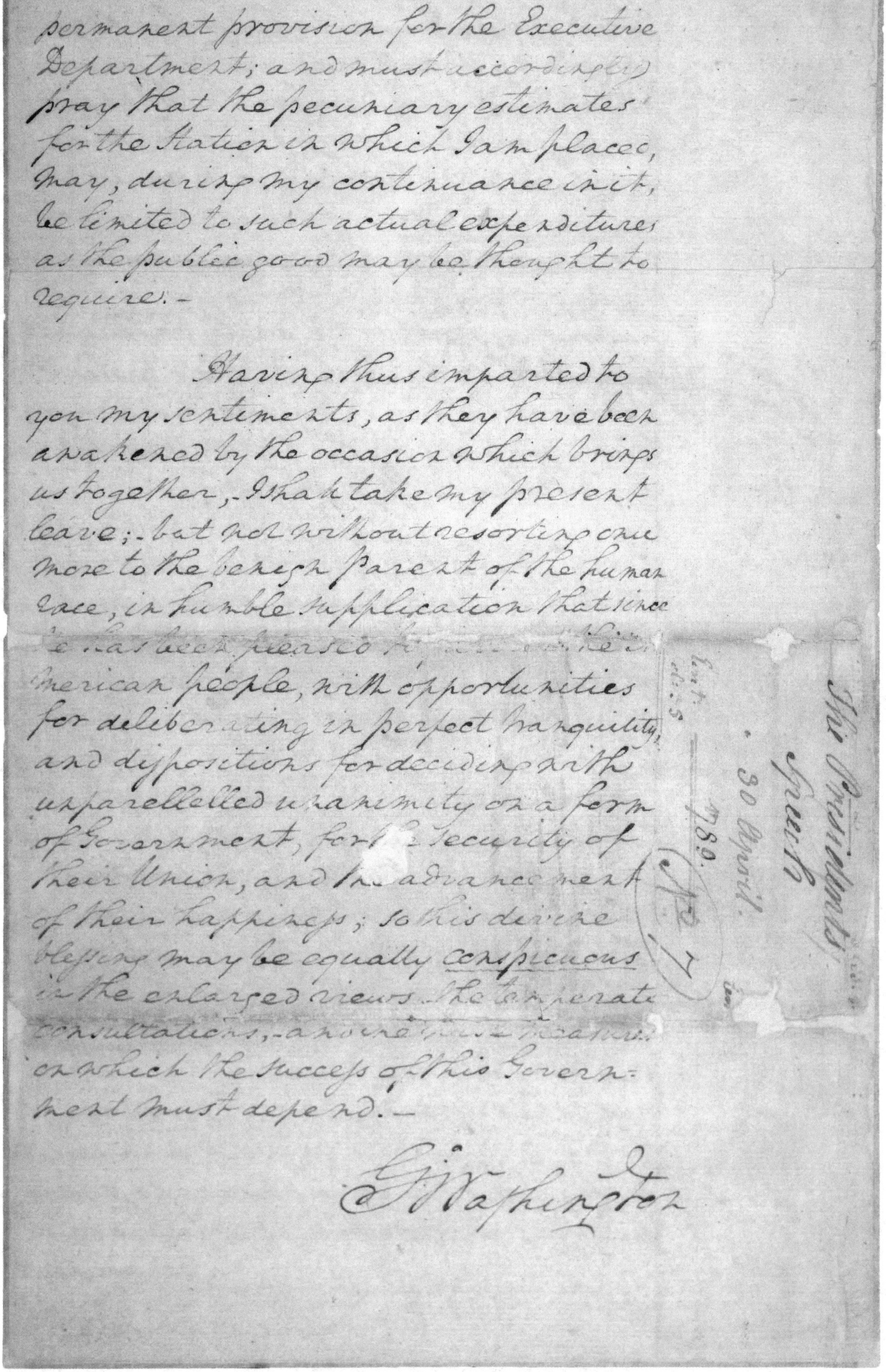

permanent provision for the Executive Department; and must accordingly pray that the pecuniary estimates for the station in which I am placed, may, during my continuance in it, be limited to such actual expenditures as the public good may be thought to require. –

Having thus imparted to you my sentiments, as they have been awakened by the occasion which brings us together, I shall take my present leave; - but not without resorting once more to the benign parent of the human race, in humble supplication that since he has been pleased to favour the American people, with opportunities for deliberating in perfect tranquility, and dispositions for deciding with unparellelled unanimity on a form of Government, for the security of their Union, and the advancement of their happiness; so his divine blessing may be equally conspicuous in the enlarged views, the temperate consultations, and the wise measures on which the success of this Government must depend. –

G Washington

George
Washington's
First Inaugural
Address
(last page)

APPENDIX 4

(There is an outline and a select dictionary at the end of this address.)[112]

Friends and Fellow-Citizens:

The period for a new election of a citizen, to administer the Executive Government of the United States being not far distant, and the time actually arrived, when your thoughts must be employed in designating the person, who is to be clothed with that important trust, it appears to me proper, especially as it may conduce to a more distinct expression of the public voice, that I should now apprise you of the resolution I have formed to decline being considered among the number of those out of whom a choice is to be made.

I beg you at the same time to do me the justice to be assured, that this resolution has not been taken, without a strict regard to all the considerations appertaining to the relation which binds a dutiful citizen to his country; and that in withdrawing the tender of service, which silence in my situation might imply, I am influenced by no diminution of zeal for your future interest, no deficiency of grateful respect for your past kindness, but am supported by a full conviction that the step is compatible with both.

The acceptance of, and continuance hitherto in the office to which your suffrages have twice called me have been a uniform sacrifice of inclination to the opinion of duty and to a deference for what appeared to be your desire. I constantly hoped that it would have been much earlier in my power, consistently with motives which I was not at liberty to disregard, to return to that retirement from which I had been reluctantly drawn. The strength of my inclination to do this previous to the last election had even led to the preparation of an address to declare it to you; but mature reflection on the then perplexed and critical posture of our affairs with foreign nations, and the unanimous advice of persons entitled to my confidence impelled me to abandon the idea. I rejoice, that the state of your concerns, external as well as internal, no longer renders the pursuit of inclination incompatible with the sentiment of duty, or propriety, and am persuaded, whatever partiality may be retained for my services, that in the present circumstances of our country, you will not disapprove my determination to retire.

The impressions with which I first undertook the arduous trust were explained on the proper occasion. In the discharge of this trust, I will only say that I have, with good intentions, contributed towards the organization and administration of the government the best exertions of which a very fallible judgment was capable. Not unconscious in the outset of the inferiority of my qualifications, experience in my own eyes, perhaps still more in the eyes of others, has strengthened the motives to diffidence of myself; and every day the increasing weight of years admonishes me more and more that the shade of retirement is as necessary to me as it will be welcome. Satisfied that if any circumstances have given peculiar value to my services they were temporary, I have the consolation to believe that, while choice and prudence invite me to quit the political scene, patriotism does not forbid it.

In looking forward to the moment which is intended to terminate the career of my public life my feelings do not permit me to suspend the deep acknowledgment of that debt of gratitude, which I owe to my beloved country for the many honors it has conferred upon me; still more for the steadfast confidence with which it has supported me, and for the opportunities I have thence enjoyed of manifesting my inviolable attachment by services faithful and persevering, though in usefulness unequal to my zeal. If benefits have resulted to our country from these services, let it always be remembered to your praise and as an instructive example in our annals, that under circumstances in which the passions, agitated in every direction, were liable to mislead; amidst appearances sometimes dubious; vicissitudes of fortune often discouraging; in situations in which not unfrequently want of success has countenanced the spirit of criticism, the constancy of your support was the essential prop of the efforts and a guarantee of the plans by which they were effected. Profoundly penetrated with this idea, I shall carry it with me to my grave as a strong incitement to unceasing vows that Heaven may continue to you the choicest tokens of its beneficence that your union and brotherly affection may be perpetual; that the free Constitution which is the work of your hands may be sacredly maintained; that its administration in every department may be stamped with wisdom and virtue; that, in fine, the happiness of the people of these States, under the auspices of liberty, may be made complete by so careful a preservation and so prudent a use of this blessing as will acquire to them the glory of recommending it to the

applause, the affection, and adoption of every nation which is yet a stranger to it.

Here, perhaps, I ought to stop. But a solicitude for your welfare which cannot end but with my life, and the apprehension of danger natural to that solicitude, urge me on an occasion like the present to offer to your solemn contemplation and to recommend to your frequent review some sentiments which are the result of much reflection, of no inconsiderable observation, and which appear to me all important to the permanency of your felicity as a people. These will be offered to you with the more freedom as you can only see in them the disinterested warnings of a parting friend, who can possibly have no personal motive to bias his counsel. Nor can I forget as an encouragement to it your indulgent reception of my sentiments on a former and not dissimilar occasion.

Interwoven as is the love of liberty with every ligament of your hearts, no recommendation of mine is necessary to fortify or confirm the attachment.

The unity of government which constitutes you one people is also now dear to you. It is justly so, for it is a main pillar in the edifice of your real independence, the support of your tranquillity at home, your peace abroad, of your safety, of your prosperity, of that very liberty which you so highly prize. But as it is easy to foresee that from different causes and from different quarters much pains will be taken, many artifices employed, to weaken in your minds the conviction of this truth, as this is the point in your political fortress against which the batteries of internal and external enemies will be most constantly and actively (though often covertly and insidiously) directed, it is of infinite moment, that you should properly estimate the immense value of your national union to your collective and individual happiness; that you should cherish a cordial, habitual, and immovable attachment to it; accustoming yourselves to think and speak of it as of the palladium of your political safety and prosperity; watching for its preservation with jealous anxiety; discountenancing whatever may suggest even a suspicion that it can in any event be abandoned, and indignantly frowning upon the first dawning of every attempt to alienate any portion of our country from the rest, or to enfeeble the sacred ties which now link together the various parts.

For this you have every inducement of sympathy and interest. Citizens by birth or choice of a common country, that country has a right to concentrate your affections. The name of American, which belongs to you in your national capacity, must always exalt the just pride of patriotism more than any appellation derived from local discriminations. With slight shades of difference, you have the same religion, manners, habits, and political principles. You have in a common cause fought and triumphed together. The independence and liberty you possess are the work of joint counsels, and joint efforts, of common dangers, sufferings, and successes.

But these considerations, however powerfully they address themselves to your sensibility, are greatly outweighed by those which apply more immediately to your interest. Here every portion of our country finds the most commanding motives for carefully guarding and preserving the union of the whole.

The North, in an unrestrained intercourse with the South, protected by the equal laws of a common government, finds in the productions of the latter great additional resources of maritime and commercial enterprise and precious materials of manufacturing industry. The South, in the same intercourse, benefiting by the same agency of the North, sees its agriculture grow and its commerce expand. Turning partly into its own channels the seamen of the North, it finds its particular navigation invigorated; and while it contributes in different ways to nourish and increase the general mass of the national navigation, it looks forward to the protection of a maritime

strength to which itself is unequally adapted. The East, in a like intercourse with the West, already finds, and in the progressive improvement of interior communications by land and water will more and more find, a valuable vent for the commodities which it brings from abroad or manufactures at home. The West derives from the East supplies requisite to its growth and comfort, and what is perhaps of still greater consequence, it must of necessity owe the secure enjoyment of indispensable outlets for its own productions to the weight, influence, and the future maritime strength of the Atlantic side of the Union, directed by an indissoluble community of interest as one nation. Any other tenure by which the West can hold this essential advantage, whether derived from its own separate strength, or from an apostate and unnatural connection with any foreign power, must be intrinsically precarious.

While, then, every part of our country thus feels an immediate and particular interest in union, all the parts combined in the united mass of means and efforts cannot fail to find greater strength, greater resource, proportionately greater security from external danger, a less frequent interruption of their peace by foreign nations, and what is of inestimable value, they must derive from Union an exemption from those broils and wars between themselves which so frequently afflict neighboring countries not tied together by the same governments, which their own rivalries alone would be sufficient to produce, but which opposite foreign alliances, attachments, and intrigues would stimulate and embitter. Hence, likewise, they will avoid the necessity of those overgrown military establishments which, under any form of government, are inauspicious to liberty, and which are to be regarded as particularly hostile to republican liberty. In this sense it is, that your union ought to be considered as a main prop of your liberty, and that the love of the one ought to endear to you the preservation of the other.

These considerations speak a persuasive language to every reflecting and virtuous mind, and exhibit the continuance of the union as a primary object of patriotic desire. Is there a doubt whether a common government can embrace so large a sphere? Let experience solve it. To listen to mere speculation in such a case were criminal. We are authorized to hope that a proper organization of the whole, with the auxiliary agency of governments for the respective subdivisions, will afford a happy issue to the experiment. It is well worth a fair and full experiment. With such powerful and obvious motives to union affecting all parts of our country, while experience shall not have demonstrated its impracticability, there will always be reason to distrust the patriotism of those who in any quarter may endeavour to weaken its bands.

In contemplating the causes which may disturb our union it occurs as matter of serious concern that any ground should have been furnished for characterizing parties by geographical discriminations — Northern and Southern, Atlantic and Western — whence designing men may endeavor to excite a belief that there is a real difference of local interests and views. One of the expedients of party to acquire influence within particular districts is to misrepresent the opinions and aims of other districts. You cannot shield yourselves too much against the jealousies and heart burnings which spring from these misrepresentations; they tend to render alien to each other those who ought to be bound together by fraternal affection. The inhabitants of our Western country have lately had a useful lesson on this head. They have seen in the negotiation by the Executive and in the unanimous ratification by the Senate of the treaty with Spain, and in the universal satisfaction at that event throughout the United States, a decisive proof how unfounded were the suspicions propagated among them of a policy in the General Government and in the Atlantic States unfriendly to their interests in regard to the Mississippi. They have been witnesses to the

formation of two treaties — that with Great Britain and that with Spain — which secure to them everything they could desire in respect to our foreign relations towards confirming their prosperity. Will it not be their wisdom to rely for the preservation of these advantages on the union by which they were procured? Will they not henceforth be deaf to those advisers, if such there are, who would sever them from their brethren and connect them with aliens?

To the efficacy and permanency of your union a government for the whole is indispensable. No alliances, however strict, between the parts can be an adequate substitute. They must inevitably experience the infractions and interruptions which all alliances in all times have experienced. Sensible of this momentous truth, you have improved upon your first essay by the adoption of a Constitution of Government better calculated than your former for an intimate union and for the efficacious management of your common concerns. This Government, the offspring of our own choice, uninfluenced and unawed, adopted upon full investigation and mature deliberation, completely free in its principles, in the distribution of its powers, uniting security with energy, and containing within itself a provision for its own amendment, has a just claim to your confidence and your support. Respect for its authority, compliance with its laws, acquiescence in its measures, are duties enjoined by the fundamental maxims of true liberty. The basis of our political systems is the right of the people to make and to alter their constitutions of government. But the constitution which at any time exists till changed by an explicit and authentic act of the whole people is sacredly obligatory upon all. The very idea of the power and the right of the people to establish government presupposes the duty of every individual to obey the established government.

All obstructions to the execution of the laws, all combinations and associations, under whatever plausible character, with the real design to direct, control, counteract, or awe the regular deliberation and action of the constituted authorities, are destructive of this fundamental principle and of fatal tendency. They serve to organize faction; to give it an artificial and extraordinary force; to put in the place of the delegated will of the nation the will of a party, often a small but artful and enterprising minority of the community, and, according to the alternate triumphs of different parties, to make the public administration the mirror of the ill-concerted and incongruous projects of faction rather than the organ of consistent and wholesome plans, digested by common councils and modified by mutual interests.

However combinations or associations of the above description may now and then answer popular ends, they are likely in the course of time and things to become potent engines by which cunning, ambitious, and unprincipled men will be enabled to subvert the power of the people, and to usurp for themselves the reins of government, destroying afterwards the very engines which have lifted them to unjust dominion.

Toward the preservation of your Government and the permanency of your present happy state, it is requisite not only that you steadily discountenance irregular oppositions to its acknowledged authority, but also that you resist with care the spirit of innovation upon its principles, however specious the pretexts. One method of assault may be to effect in the forms of the Constitution alterations which will impair the energy of the system, and thus to undermine what cannot be directly overthrown. In all the changes to which you may be invited remember that time and habit are at least as necessary to fix the true character of governments as of other human institutions; that experience is the surest standard by which to test the real tendency of the existing constitution of a country; that facility in changes upon the credit of mere hypothesis and opinion exposes to perpetual change, from the endless variety of hypothesis and opinion;

and remember especially that for the efficient management of your common interests in a country so extensive as ours a Government of as much vigor as is consistent with the perfect security of liberty is indispensable. Liberty itself will find in such a government, with powers properly distributed and adjusted, its surest Guardian. It is, indeed, little else than a name where the Government is too feeble to withstand the enterprises of faction, to confine each member of the society within the limits prescribed by the laws, and to maintain all in the secure and tranquil enjoyment of the rights of person and property.

I have already intimated to you the danger of parties in the State, with particular reference to the founding of them on geographical discriminations. Let me now take a more comprehensive view, and warn you in the most solemn manner against the baneful effects of the spirit of party generally.

This Spirit, unfortunately, is inseparable from our nature, having its root in the strongest passions of the human mind. It exists under different shapes in all governments, more or less stifled, controlled, or repressed; but in those of the popular form it is seen in its greatest rankness and is truly their worst enemy.

The alternate domination of one faction over another, sharpened by the spirit of revenge natural to party dissension, which in different ages and countries has perpetrated the most horrid enormities, is itself a frightful despotism. But this leads at length to a more formal and permanent despotism. The disorders and miseries which result gradually incline the minds of men to seek security and repose in the absolute power of an individual, and sooner or later the chief of some prevailing faction, more able or more fortunate than his competitors, turns this disposition to the purposes of his own elevation on the ruins of public liberty.

Without looking forward to an extremity of this kind (which nevertheless ought not to be entirely out of sight), the common and continual mischiefs of the spirit of party are sufficient to make it the interest and duty of a wise people to discourage and restrain it.

It serves always to distract the public councils, and enfeeble the public administration. It agitates the community with ill-founded jealousies and false alarms; kindles the animosity of one part against another; foments occasionally riot and insurrection. It opens the door to foreign influence and corruption, which find a facilitated access to the government itself through the channels of party passion. Thus the policy and the will of one country are subjected to the policy and will of another.

There is an opinion that parties in free countries are useful checks upon the administration of the government, and serve to keep alive the spirit of liberty. This within certain limits is probably true and in governments of a monarchical cast patriotism may look with indulgence, if not with favor, upon the spirit of party. But in those of the popular character, in governments purely elective, it is a spirit not to be encouraged. From their natural tendency it is certain there will always be enough of that spirit for every salutary purpose; and there being constant danger of excess, the effort ought to be by force of public opinion to mitigate and assuage it. A fire not to be quenched, it demands a uniform vigilance to prevent its bursting into a flame, lest, instead of warming, it should consume.

It is important, likewise, that the habits of thinking in a free country should inspire caution in those entrusted with its administration to confine themselves within their respective constitutional spheres, avoiding in the exercise of the powers of one department to encroach upon another. The spirit of encroachment tends to consolidate the powers of all the departments in one, and thus to create, whatever the form of government, a real despotism. A just estimate of that love of power and proneness to abuse it which predominates in the human heart is sufficient to satisfy us of the truth of this position. The necessity of reciprocal checks in the exercise of political power, by dividing and distributing it into different depositories, and constituting each the guardian of the public weal against invasions by the others, has been evinced by experiments ancient and modern, some of them in our country and under our own eyes. To preserve them must be as necessary as to institute them. If, in the opinion of the people, the distribution or modification of the constitutional powers be in any particular wrong, let it be corrected by an amendment in the way which the Constitution designates. But let there be no change by usurpation; for though this in one instance may be the instrument of good, it is the customary weapon by which free governments are destroyed. The precedent must always greatly overbalance in permanent evil any partial or transient benefit which the use can at any time yield.

Of all the dispositions and habits which lead to political prosperity, religion and morality are indispensable supports. In vain would that man claim the tribute of patriotism who should labor to subvert these great pillars of human happiness – these firmest props of the duties of men and citizens. The mere politician, equally with the pious man, ought to respect and to cherish them. A volume could not trace all their connections with private and public felicity. Let it simply be asked, "where is the security for property, for reputation, for life, if the sense of religious obligation desert the oaths which are the instruments of investigation in courts of justice?" And let us with caution indulge the supposition that morality can be maintained without religion. Whatever may be conceded to the influence of refined education on minds of peculiar structure, reason and experience both forbid us to expect that national morality can prevail in exclusion of religious principle.

It is substantially true that virtue or morality is a necessary spring of popular government. The rule indeed extends with more or less force to every species of free government. Who that is a sincere friend to it can look with indifference upon attempts to shake the foundation of the fabric?

Promote, then, as an object of primary importance, institutions for the general diffusion of knowledge. In proportion as the structure of a government gives force to public opinion, it is essential that public opinion should be enlightened.

As a very important source of strength and security, cherish public credit. One method of preserving it is to use it as sparingly as possible, avoiding occasions of expense by cultivating peace, but remembering also that timely disbursements to prepare for danger frequently prevent much greater disbursements to repel it; avoiding likewise the accumulation of debt, not only by shunning occasions of expense, but by vigorous exertions in times of peace to discharge the debts which unavoidable wars have occasioned, not ungenerously throwing upon posterity the burden which we ourselves ought to bear. The execution of these maxims belongs to your representatives; but it is necessary that public opinion should cooperate. To facilitate to them the performance of their duty it is essential that you should practically bear in mind that towards the payment of debts there must be revenue; that to have revenue there must be taxes; that no taxes can be devised which are not more or less inconvenient and unpleasant; that the intrinsic embarrassment inseparable from the selection of the proper objects (which is always a choice of difficulties), ought to be a decisive motive for a candid construction of the conduct of the Government in making it, and for a spirit of acquiescence in the measures for obtaining revenue which the public exigencies may at any time dictate.

Observe good faith and justice towards all nations. Cultivate peace and harmony with all. Religion and morality enjoin this conduct. And can it be that good policy does not equally enjoin it? It will be worthy of a free, enlightened, and at no distant period a great nation to give to mankind the magnanimous and too novel example of a people always guided by an exalted justice and benevolence. Who can doubt that in the course of time and things the fruits of such a plan would richly repay any temporary advantages which might be lost by a steady adherence to it? Can it be that Providence has not connected the permanent felicity of a nation with its virtue? The experiment, at least, is recommended by every sentiment which ennobles human nature. Alas! is it rendered impossible by its vices?

In the execution of such a plan nothing is more essential than that permanent, inveterate antipathies against particular nations and passionate attachments for others should be excluded, and that in place of them just and amicable feelings towards all should be cultivated. The nation which indulges towards another an habitual hatred or an habitual fondness is in some degree a slave. It is a slave to its animosity or to its affection, either of which is sufficient to lead it astray from its duty and its interest. Antipathy in one nation against another disposes each more readily to offer insult and injury, to lay hold of slight causes of umbrage, and to be haughty and intractable when accidental or trifling occasions of dispute occur. Hence frequent collisions, obstinate, envenomed, and bloody contests. The nation prompted by ill-will and resentment sometimes impels to war the government contrary to the best calculations of policy. The government sometimes participates in the national propensity, and adopts through passion what reason would reject. At other times it makes the animosity of the nation subservient to projects of hostility, instigated by pride, ambition, and other sinister and pernicious motives. The peace often, sometimes perhaps the liberty, of nations has been the victim.

So, likewise, a passionate attachment of one nation for another produces a variety of evils. Sympathy for the favorite nation, facilitating the illusion of an imaginary common interest in cases where no real common interest exists, and infusing into one the enmities of the other, betrays the former into a participation in the quarrels and wars of the latter without adequate inducement or justification. It leads also to concessions to the favorite nation of privileges denied to others, which is apt doubly to injure the nation making the concessions by unnecessarily parting with what ought to have been retained, and by exciting jealousy, ill-will, and a disposition to retaliate in the parties from whom equal privileges are withheld; and it gives to ambitious, corrupted, or deluded citizens (who devote themselves to the favorite nation) facility to betray or sacrifice the interests of their own country without odium, sometimes even with popularity, gilding with the appearances of a virtuous sense of obligation, a commendable deference for public opinion, or a laudable zeal for public good the base or foolish compliances of ambition, corruption, or infatuation.

As avenues to foreign influence in innumerable ways, such attachments are particularly alarming to the truly enlightened and independent patriot. How many opportunities do they afford to tamper with domestic factions, to practise the arts of seduction, to mislead public opinion, to influence or awe the public councils! Such an attachment of a small or weak toward a great and powerful nation dooms the former to be the satellite of the latter. Against the insidious wiles of foreign influence (I conjure you to believe me, fellow-citizens), the jealousy of a free people ought to be constantly awake, since history and experience prove that foreign influence is one of the most baneful foes of republican government. But that jealousy, to be useful, must be impartial, else it becomes the instrument of the very influence to be avoided, instead of a defense against it. Excessive partiality for one foreign nation and

excessive dislike of another cause those whom they actuate to see danger only on one side, and serve to veil and even second the arts of influence on the other. Real patriots who may resist the intrigues of the favorite are liable to become suspected and odious, while its tools and dupes usurp the applause and confidence of the people to surrender their interests.

The great rule of conduct for us, in regard to foreign nations, is, in extending our commercial relations to have with them as little political connection as possible. So far as we have already formed engagements, let them be fulfilled with perfect good faith. Here let us stop.

Europe has a set of primary interests which to us have none or a very remote relation. Hence she must be engaged in frequent controversies, the causes of which are essentially foreign to our concerns. Hence, therefore, it must be unwise in us to implicate ourselves by artificial ties in the ordinary vicissitudes of her politics or the ordinary combinations and collisions of her friendships or enmities.

Our detached and distant situation invites and enables us to pursue a different course. If we remain one people, under an efficient government, the period is not far off when we may defy material injury from external annoyance; when we may take such an attitude as will cause the neutrality we may at any time resolve upon to be scrupulously respected; when belligerent nations, under the impossibility of making acquisitions upon us, will not lightly hazard the giving us provocation; when we may choose peace or war, as our interest, guided by our justice, shall counsel.

Why forgo the advantages of so peculiar a situation? Why quit our own to stand upon foreign ground? Why, by interweaving our destiny with that of any part of Europe, entangle our peace and prosperity in the toils of European ambition, rivalship, interest, humor, or caprice?

It is our true policy to steer clear of permanent alliances with any portion of the foreign world, so far, I mean, as we are now at liberty to do it; for let me not be understood as capable of patronizing infidelity to existing engagements. I hold the maxim no less applicable to public than to private affairs that honesty is always the best policy. I repeat, therefore, let those engagements be observed in their genuine sense. But in my opinion it is unnecessary and would be unwise to extend them.

Taking care always to keep ourselves by suitable establishments on a respectable defensive posture, we may safely trust to temporary alliances for extraordinary emergencies.

Harmony, liberal intercourse with all nations are recommended by policy, humanity, and interest. But even our commercial policy should hold an equal and impartial hand, neither seeking nor granting exclusive favors or preferences; consulting the natural course of things; diffusing and diversifying by gentle means the streams of commerce, but forcing nothing; establishing with powers so disposed, in order to give trade a stable course, to define the rights of our merchants, and to enable the Government to support them, conventional rules of intercourse, the best that present circumstances and mutual opinion will permit, but temporary and liable to be from time to time abandoned or varied as experience and circumstances shall dictate; constantly keeping in view that it is folly in one nation to look for disinterested favors from another; that it must pay with a portion of its independence for whatever it may accept under that character; that by such acceptance it may place itself in the condition of having given equivalents for nominal favors, and yet of being reproached with ingratitude for not giving more. There can be no greater error than to expect or calculate upon real favors from nation to nation. It is an illusion which experience must cure, which a just pride ought to discard.

In offering to you, my countrymen, these counsels of an old and affectionate friend I dare not hope they will make the strong and lasting impression I could wish — that they will control the usual current of the passions or prevent our nation from running the course which has hitherto marked the destiny of nations. But if I may even flatter myself that they may be productive of some partial benefit, some occasional good — that they may now and then recur to moderate the fury of party spirit, to warn against the mischiefs of foreign intrigue, to guard against the impostures of pretended patriotism — this hope will be a full recompense for the solicitude for your welfare by which they have been dictated.

How far in the discharge of my official duties I have been guided by the principles which have been delineated the public records and other evidences of my conduct must witness to you and to the world. To myself, the assurance of my own conscience is that I have at least believed myself to be guided by them.

In relation to the still subsisting war in Europe my proclamation of the 22d of April, 1793, is the index to my plan. Sanctioned by your approving voice and by that of your representatives in both Houses of Congress, the spirit of that measure has continually governed me, uninfluenced by any attempts to deter or divert me from it.

After deliberate examination, with the aid of the best lights I could obtain, I was well satisfied that our country, under all the circumstances of the case, had a right to take, and was bound in duty and interest to take, a neutral position. Having taken it, I determined as far as should depend upon me to maintain it with moderation, perseverance, and firmness.

The considerations which respect the right to hold this conduct it is not necessary on this occasion to detail. I will only observe, that, according to my understanding of the matter, that right, so far from being denied by any of the belligerent powers, has been virtually admitted by all.

The duty of holding a neutral conduct may be inferred, without any thing more, from the obligation which justice and humanity impose on every nation, in cases in which it is free to act, to maintain inviolate the relations of peace and amity towards other nations.

The inducements of interest for observing that conduct will best be referred to your own reflections and experience. With me a predominant motive has been to endeavor to gain time to our country to settle and mature its yet recent institutions, and to progress without interruption to that degree of strength and consistency which is necessary to give it, humanly speaking, the command of its own fortunes.

Though, in reviewing the incidents of my Administration, I am unconscious of intentional error, I am nevertheless too sensible of my defects not to think it probable that I may have committed many errors. Whatever they may be, I fervently beseech the Almighty to avert or mitigate the evils to which they may tend. I shall also carry with me the hope that my country will never cease to view them with indulgence, and that, after forty-five years of my life dedicated to its service with an upright zeal, the faults of incompetent abilities will be consigned to oblivion, as myself must soon be to the mansions of rest.

Relying on its kindness in this as in other things, and actuated by that fervent love toward it which is so natural to a man who views in it the native soil of himself and his progenitors for several generations, I anticipate with pleasing expectation that retreat in which I promise myself to realize without alloy the sweet enjoyment of partaking in the midst of my fellow citizens the benign influence of good laws under a free government – the ever-favorite object of my heart, and the happy reward, as I trust, of our mutual cares, labors, and dangers.

—George Washington

OUTLINE

I. Retirement from office.

   A. He realizes people must be thinking about his replacement, therefore he declines re-election.

   B. He has thought it through, and feels like it is in everyone's best interest.

   C. He wanted to retire earlier, but foreign affairs and advice from those he respected caused him to "abandon the idea."

   D. Now that everything is calm, he is persuaded that the people will not disapprove of this "determination to retire."

   E. He is convinced his age forces retirement, and he welcomes the opportunity.

   F. He offers gratitude for the people's support.

   G. He offers a blessing "that Heaven may continue to you the choicest tokens of its beneficence. . . ."

II. Scope of the Address.

   A. His sentiments are for the people's "frequent review," he wanted us to read and re-read the Address.

   B. His only motive was as a friend.

   C. He felt no need to recommend a love of liberty — it was already there.

III. Unity of Government.

   A. Unity is a "main pillar" of "real independence":

374

1. for the support of "tranquility at home"

2. for "your peace abroad"

3. for "your safety"

4. for "your prosperity"

5. for "that very liberty which you so highly prize."

B. Common attributes of unity:

1. same religion

2. manners

3. habits

4. political principles.

C. The most commanding motive is to preserve the "union of the whole."

D. The North, South, East, and West all depend on each other.

E. Unity leads to greater strength, resources, and security.

F. Unity will help "avoid the necessity of . . . overgrown military establishments" and will be the main "prop of your liberty."

G. He questions the patriotism of anyone who tries to "weaken its bands."

H. It was unity that brought two valuable treaties:

1. with Great Britain

2. with Spain.

I. Government for the whole — via the Constitution — is indispensable; not just alliances between sections.

1. the adoption of the Constitution was an improvement on the former "essay."

2. respect for its authority, compliance with its laws, and acquiescence in its

measures are fundamental maxims of true liberty.

3. the people's right to alter constitutions is the basis of our political system.

IV. Spirit of Party.

A. Parties are "potent engines" that men will use to take over the "reins of government."

B. Washington warns against parties' "baneful effects":

1. leads to the absolute power of an individual

2. "discourage and restrain" the spirit of party

3. leads to "jealousies and false alarms"

4. "animosity of one part against another"

5. can lead to "riot and insurrection"

6. opens "door to foreign influence and corruption"

7. "it is a spirit not to be encouraged."

V. Spirit of Encroachment.

A. Leads to "a real despotism."

B. There is a necessity of "reciprocal checks in the exercise of political power."

C. If a problem arises, correct it by an amendment, not by "usurpation."

VI. Religion and Morality.

A. Are "indispensable supports" for "political prosperity."

B. Are the "firmest props of the duties of Men and Country."

C. The oaths in our courts would be useless without "the sense of religious obligation."

D. "And let us with caution indulge the supposition, that morality can be maintained without religion."

E. "Reason and experience both forbid us to expect, that national morality can prevail in exclusion of religious principle."

F. "Promote, then, as an object of primary importance, institutions for the general diffusion of knowledge."

VII. Debt.

A. "Avoid occasions of expense by cultivating peace. . . ."

B. "Timely disbursements to prepare for danger" are better than "greater disbursements to repel it."

C. Avoid debt: in time of peace, pay off debts..

D. Public opinion should "cooperate" with their representatives to pay off debt.

E. Some taxes are necessary even though "inconvenient and unpleasant."

VIII. Foreign Policy.

A. We should exercise "good faith and justice towards all nations."

1. "religion and morality enjoin this conduct"

2. we should be guided by "an exalted justice and benevolence."

B. Replace "inveterate antipathies" (hatred) and passionate attachments with "just and amicable feelings."

1. "passionate attachments" produce a variety of evils

2. these attachments will lead you into "quarrels and wars"

3. they will also lead to favoritism, conceding "privileges denied to others."

C. Foreign "attachments" are "alarming" because they open the door to foreigners who might:

1. "tamper with domestic factions"

2. "practise the arts of seduction"

3. "mislead public opinion"

4. influence "Public Councils."

D. "Foreign influence is one of the most baneful foes of Republican Government."

E. "The great rule of conduct for us": "as little political connection as possible."

1. we should fulfill obligations, then stop

2. we should not get involved in Europe's affairs.

F. Our "detached and distant situation . . . enables . . . a different course."

G. "Steer clear of permanent alliances with any portion of the foreign world."

H. However, we may have "temporary alliances, for extraordinary emergencies."

I. Maintain "a liberal intercourse with all nations."

IX. Conclusion.

A. Washington hopes his counsel will:

1. "help moderate the fury of party spirit"

2. "warn against the mischiefs of foreign intrigue"

3. "guard against the impostures of pretended patriotism."

B. He believes himself to be guided by the "principles which have been delineated" above.

C. A "neutral position" is the best course to take regarding the "subsisting war in Europe."

1. that neutrality is the right course has been "admitted by all."

2. our "motive has been to endeavor to gain time for our country to settle and mature" until America has "command of its own fortunes."

D. Washington asks "the Almighty" to correct any unintentional errors or defects from his administration.

E. He looks forward to retiring and enjoying "good laws under a free government."

F. Closing words.

VOCABULARY

acquiescence — agreement without protest; consent

actuate — put into motion; motivate

admonish — to counsel against; caution

alienate — to cause to become unfriendly; exclude

alliance — a formal pact between nations; partnership

animosity — bitter hostility; hatred

antipathies — strong feelings of hatred or opposition; aversions

apostate — abandoning one's principles; defective or traitorous

appellation — a name or title

appertaining — relating to

apprise — to give notice; to inform; notify

arduous — demanding great care, effort, or labor; difficult

artifices — subtle but base deceptions; tricks

assuage — make less burdensome or painful; relieve

auspice — protection or support; authority

auxiliary — giving assistance or support; supplementary

avert — to turn away; prevent

baneful — causing death, destruction, or ruin; harmful

belligerent — inclined or eager to fight; hostile

beneficence — a charitable act or gift; kindness

benevolence — an inclination to do kind or charitable acts; goodness

benign — tending to promote well-being; beneficial

beseech — to call upon earnestly; request

bias — to cause to have a prejudice view; distort

conceded — acknowledged as true, just, or proper; given

conjure — to call upon or entreat solemnly; call upon

consigned — turned over to another's charge; delivered

consolation — the comforting in time of grief, defeat, or trouble; comfort

contemplation — thoughtful observation; meditation

countenanced — to give or express approval to; approved

covertly — concealed, hidden, or secret

cultivate — promote the growth of; develop

deference — yielding to the wishes of another; consideration

deliberate — planned in advance; intentional

delineated — depicted in words or gestures; outlined

despotisms — political system with one man in absolute power; oppression

diffidence — the quality of lacking self-confidence; humility

diffusing — causing to spread freely; spreading

diffusion — the process of diffusing; spreading

diminution — reduction; decrease

disbursements — money paid out; expenditures

discriminations — acts based on prejudice; prejudices

dispositions — an habitual tendency or inclination; tendencies

diversifying — giving variety to; varying

dubious — causing doubt or uncertainty; uncertain

edifice — a building of imposing appearance or size; structure

efficacy — power to produce a desired effect; effectiveness

encroach — to advance beyond proper limits; intrude

enmities — deep-seated mutual hatred; hostilities

ennobles — raises in rank; elevates

envenomed — poisoned or embittered; poisoned

evinced — to show clearly or convincingly; demonstrated

exemption — a freedom from obligation or duty; freedom

exigencies — situations needing immediate attention; necessities

expedients — something adopted to meet an urgent need; schemes

facilitating — making something easier; assisting

fallible — capable of making an error; imperfect

felicity — great happiness or bliss; happiness

fervently — having great emotion or warmth; earnestly

hypothesis — something considered to be true; assumption

impostures — deceptions through false identities; deceptions

inauspicious — unfavorable

incongruous — not consistent with what is logical, customary, or correct; disagreeable

indispensable — not able to be done away with; essential

indissoluble — impossible to break or undo; indestructible

inducement — something that leads to action; influence

indulgent — granted as a favor or privilege; agreeable

inferred — figured out from evidence; understood

infidelity — lack of loyalty; disloyalty

insidiously — spreading harm in a subtle way; dishonestly

instigated — stirred up or urged on; aroused

intercourse — communication between persons or groups; business

intimated — to announce or proclaim; spoken

intractable — hard to manage or govern; stubborn

intrigue — secret schemes or plots; affairs

intrinsic — having to do with the very nature of a thing; natural inveterate — firmly established and deeply rooted; established

inviolate — not violated or changed; unchanged

invigorated — given strength and vitality; energized

inviolable — not able to be violated; unchanging

laudable — deserving approval; praiseworthy

magnanimous — noble of mind and heart; idealistic

maxim — fundamental principle or rule of conduct; principle

mitigate — to make less severe or intense; weaken

monarchy — a state ruled by an absolute ruler, such as a king or emperor

obligatory — legally or morally binding; required

oblivion — the condition of being completely forgotten; nonexistence

obstinate — hard to manage, control, or subdue; uncontrollable

odium — a strong dislike for something; disfavor

pernicious — causing great harm and destruction; destructive

perpetrated — to be guilty of bringing something about; committed

perpetual — lasting for eternity; unending

plausible — appearing to be valid, likely, or acceptable; believable

posterity — future generations

precarious — lacking in security and stability; uncertain

precedent — an act used as an example in future situations

predominant — having great importance, influence, or authority; important

procured — obtained or acquired

progenitors — a direct ancestor; ancestors

propensity — a tendency to do something; tendency

propagated – cause to multiply; spread

provocation — a reason to take action

prudence — good judgment and common sense; wisdom

recompense — payment for something done; repayment

requisite — essential or required

scrupulously — to do something with ethical considerations; conscientiously

seduction — the act of leading away from proper conduct; misleading

solicitude — the state of being concerned or eager; concern

specious — appearing to be true, but being false; deceptive

subservient — under the control of something; subject

subvert — to undermine the character, morals, or allegiance of; overthrow

suffrages — votes

supposition — the idea that something is true; idea

tenure — the terms under which something is held; terms

tranquility — the state of being free from disturbance; peace

transient — passing away with time; temporary

umbrage — offense; resentment

usurpation — the seizing of power by force and without legal right; overthrow

vicissitudes — changes or variations; changes

vigilance — alert watchfulness; watchfulness

virtuous — morally excellent and righteous; pure

weal — the welfare of the community; welfare

Bibliography

Amstel, Marsha. *Sybil Ludington's Midnight Ride*. Minneapolis, MN: Millbrook Press, 2000.

Barton, David. *Original Intent*. Aledo, TX: Wallbuilders Press, 1996.

Blaisdell, Albert F., and Francis K. Ball. *Hero Stories from American History*. Boston, MA: Ball, Ginn and Co, 1903.

Boyer, Marilyn. *For You They Signed*. Green Forest, AR: Master Books, 2010.

Boyer, Marilyn, and Grace Tumas. *Portraits of Integrity*. Rustburg, VA: Learning Parent, 2012.

——— *Profiles of Valor: Character Studies from the War of Independence*. Rustburg, VA: Learning Parent, 2013.

Brooks, Elbridge S. *The Story of the United States*. Boston, MA: D. Lothrop and Co., 1891.

——— *The True Story of the United States of America: Told for Young People*. Boston, MA: Lothrop Publishing Co., 1891.

Eggleston, Edward. *A History of Our United States and Its People*. New York: American Book Co., 1888.

Federer, William. *American Minute: Notable Events of American Significance Remembered on the Date they Occurred*. St. Louis, MO: Amerisearch, Inc., 2003.

Fradin, Dennis Brindell. The Founders: *The 39 Stories Behind the U.S. Constitution*. New York: Walker and Co., 2005.

Kirkpatrick, Katherine. *Redcoats and Petticoats*. New York: Holiday House, 1999.

Mace, William H. *Mace's Beginner's History*. Chicago, IL: Rand McNally and Co., 1909.

——— *Mace's Primary History: Stories of Heroism*. Chicago, IL: Rand MCNally and Co., 1909.

——— *Mace's School History of the United States*. Chicago, IL: Rand, McNalley and Co., 1904.

Montgomery, D.H. *The Beginners American History*. Boston, MA: Ginn and Co., 1892.

——— *The Leading Facts of American History*. New York: Chautauqua Press, 1892.

Moore, Frank, and C.T. Evans. *Patriot Preachers of the American Revolution*. New York: Charles T. Evans, 1862.

Stevenson, Burton Egbert. *Poems of American History*. Boston and New York: Houghton Mifflin and Co., 1908.

Tomlinson, E.T. *Young Folks History of the Revolution*. New York: Grosset and Dunlap, 1901.

Wallbuilders.com resources.

White, Henry Alexander. *Beginners History of the United States: Stories of the Men Who Made Our Country*. New York: American Book Company, 1906.

ENDNOTES

1. Jacob Duche, *The Duty of Standing Fast in our Spiritual and Temporal Liberties, A Sermon Preached in Christ Church, July 7, 1775*. Before the First Battalion of the City and Liberties of Philadelphia (Philadelphia, PA: James Humphreys Jr., 1775), p. 13–14; http://www.wallbuilders.com/libissuesarticles.asp?id=24548.

2. John Witherspoon, *The Works of John Witherspoon* (Edinburgh: J. Ogle, 1815), Vol. IX, p. 250, "The Druid," Number III.

3. http://www.wallbuilders.com/LIBissuesArticles.asp?id=24548

4. Samuel Adams, *The Life and Public Services of Samuel Adams*, William V. Wells, editor (Boston, MA: Little, Brown, and Company, 1865), Vol. I, p. 504; http://www.wallbuilders.com/LIBissuesArticles.asp?id=24548.

5. Everett Titsworth Tomlinson, *A Short History of the American Revolution* (New York: Doubleday, Page & Co., 1901), p. 6; https://books.google.com/books?id=Bhw-TAAAAYAAJ&pg.

6. John Roy Musick, *John Hancock: A Character Sketch* (Chicago, IL: The University Association, 1898), p. 95; https://books.google.com/books?id=UU6cOeOx9HMC.

7. http://www.foundingfatherquotes.com/quote/583.

8. http://www.wallbuilders.com/LIBissuesArticles.asp?id=24548.

9. http://www.patrickhenrycenter.com/Speeches.aspx#LIBERTY.

10. http://www.greatseal.com/committees/firstcomm/reverse.html.

11. http://www.greatseal.com/committees/firstcomm/.

12. http://www.wallbuilders.com/libissuesarticles.asp?id=158412, from *The Oration of Henry Armitt Brown on the 100th Anniversary of the Meeting of Congress in Carpenter's Hall*.

13. The Rev. Peter Powers, *Jesus Christ the true King and Head of Government; A Sermon Preached before the General Assembly of the State of Vermont, on the Day of Their First Election, March 12, 1778 at Windsor* (Newbury-Port: printed by John Michael, 1778), p. 18.

14. Everett Titsworth Tomlinson, *Young People's History of the American Revolution* (New York: D. Appleton and Co., 1921), p, 46.

15. Ibid., p. 46.

16. Ibid., p. 47.

17. Ibid., p. 47.

18. Everett Tomlinson, *Young Folks History of the Revolution* (New York: Grosset and Dunlap, 1901), p. 49.

19. http://captainjamesdavis.net/2013/04/06/the-rising-1776-by-thomas-buchanan-read-1822-1872/.

20. "Ethan Allen Captures Fort Ticonderoga, 1775," EyeWitness to History, www.eyewitnesstohistory.com (2010).

21. Ibid.

22. *Young Folks History of the Revolution*, Everett Tomlinson, p. 55   also in "Ethan Allen Captures Fort Ticonderoga, 1775," EyeWitness to History, www.eyewitnesstohistory.com (2010).

23. The Journals of Each Provincial Congress of Massachusetts, 1838, p. 706.

24. *Young Folks History of the Revolution*, Everett Tomlinson, Grosset and Dunlap, NY, 1901 p. 59

25. *Profiles of Valor*, Marilyn Boyer, The Learning Parent, 2013 p. 228

26. http://compmast.tripod.com/putnam/breeds.html.

27. General Order (July 9, 1776), George Washington Papers at the Library of Congress, 1741–1799: Series 3g Varick Transcripts.

28. General Orders (May 2, 1778); published in *Writings of George Washington* (1932), Vol.XI, pp. 342–343.

29. George Washington, July 4, 1775, General Orders, The George Washington Papers at the Library of Congress, 1741–1799.

30. Washington Irving, *The Life and Times of George Washington* (G.P. Putnam & Sons, 1876), p. 169.

31. Horace Kephart, "The Birth of the American Army," *Harper's New Monthly Magazine*, vol. 98, 1899, p. 965.

32. Prescott, William. 1774, in writing to the citizens on the occasion of the British blockade. George Bancroft, *History of the United States of America*, 6 vols. (Boston: Charles C. Little & James Brown, Third Edition, 1838), Vol. VII, p. 99.

33. William J. Federer, *American Minute* (Amerisearch, Inc., 2003), p. 73.

34. Thomas Pownall, *The Remembrancer, or Impartial Repository of Public Events*, Vol. 1 (London: J. Almon, 1775).

35. Noah Brooks, *Henry Knox, a Soldier of the Revolution: Major-general in the Continental Army, Washington's Chief of Artillery, First Secretary of War Under the Constitution, Founder of the Society of the Cincinnati; 1750–1806* (New York: G.P. Putnam's Sons, 1900).

36. Richard Frothingham, *History of the Siege of Boston, and of the Battles of Lexington, Concord, and Bunker Hill: Also*

an *Account of the Bunker Hill Monument* (Boston, MA: Little, Brown. 1903).

37. John C. Fitzpatrick, ed., *The Writings of George Washington from the Original Manuscript Sources*, 1745–1799, 39 vols. (Washington, DC: Government Printing Office, 1931–44).

38. Tomlinson, *Young Folks History of the Revolution*, p. 90.

39. Wayne Whipple, *The Story-life of Washington: A Life-History in Five Hundred True Stories, Selected from Original Sources and Fitted Together in Order* (Philadelphia, PA: The John C. Winston Co., c1911).

40. Everett Titsworth Tomlinson, *Young People's History of the American Revolution* (New York: London, D. Appleton and Company, 1921).

41. Abigail Adams, The Book of Abigail and John: Selected Letters of the Adams Family, 1762–1784 (Cambridge, MA: Harvard University Press, 1975), p. 142.

42. Frank Moore, *The Diary of the Revolution* (Hartford, CN: J.B. Burr Publishing Co. 1876), p. 255.

43. American Archives, editor Peter Force, entered according to an Act of Congress in the year 1848, Clerk's Office, District Court, District of Columbia.

44. http://www.ministers-best-friend.com/George-Washington-Prays-God-sends-Supernatural-Fog-to-Allow-Escape.html.

45. Frank Moore, *Songs and Ballads of the American Revolution,* 1856, https://archive.org/details/mooresongsball00franrich.

46. Moore, *The Diary of the Revolution*, p. 353.

47. Collected and edited by Burton Egbert Stevenson. Poems of the American People (Houghton Mifflin Company: Boston. Cambridge Press. USA), p. 188.

48. William Leete Stone, *Life of Joseph Brant-Thayendanegea: Including the Border Wars of the American Revolution, and Sketches of the Indian Campaigns of Generals Harmar, St. Clair, and Wayne*, Volume 1 (New York: G. Dearboran and Co., 1838), p. 210.

49. William Leete Stone, *Memoir of the Centennial Celebration of Burgoyne's Surrender,* Vol. 2 (Albany, NY: Joel Munsell, 1878), p. 41.

50. Samuel Adams Drake, *Burgoyne's Invasion of 1777* (Boston, MA: Lee and Shepard Publishers, 1889).

51. http://www.u-s-history.com/pages/h1302.html.

52. http://www.britishbattles.com/battle-freemans-farm.htm.

53. E.T. Tomlinson, *A Short History of the American Revolution* (New York: Doubleday & Page, 1901), p. 208.

54. Elizabeth F. Ellet, *The Women of the Revolution* (Philadelphia, PA: George W. Jacobs & Co., 1900).

55. Ibid.

56. Burton Egbert Stevenson, ed., Poems of American History (Boston, MA; New York: Houghton Mifflin Co.), p. 213.

57. *The American Historical Register*, Vol. II, published by The American Historical Register Publishing Co., 1895, p. 1319.

58. http://thefederalist.com/2014/12/19/would-general-george-washington-approve-of-todays-torture-policies/.

59. Lewis Stevens, *The History of Cape May County, New Jersey* (Cape May City, NJ: Lewis T. Stevens, 1897), p. 210.

60. Everett Tomlinson, *Young Folks History of the American Revolution* (New York: Grosset & Dunlap, 1901), p. 282.

61. Abbie Sage Richardson, *The History of Our Country* (Cambridge, MA: H.O. Houghton & Co. 1875), p. 259.

62. http://www.goodreads.com/quotes/182542-war-is-sometimes-described-as-long-periods-of-boredom-punctuated.

63. B.J. Lossing, *Pictorial Book of the Revolution* (New York: Harper & Brothers, 1860), p. 312.

64. http://www.earlyamerica.com/early-america-review/volume-6/pows-during-the-american-revolution/.

65. http://www.annasmithstrongchapter-nsdar.org/.

66. Katherine Kirkpatrick, *Redcoats and Petticoats* (New York: Holiday House, 1999); http://longislandgenealogy.com/LIWoman.html.

67. Burton Egbert Stevenson, ed., *Poems of American History* (New York: Houghton Mifflin, 1908), p. 247–248.

68. Harry Alonzo Cushing, editor, *The Writings of Samuel Adams* (New York: G.P. Putnam's Sons, 1904), Vol. IV, p. 38, to the Earl of Carlisle and Others on July 16, 1778.

69. Donald N. Moran, "The Diary of Comte Clemont-Creveceur" as quoted in *The Washington-Rochambeau Trail*, from the *Liberty Tree and Valley Compatriot Newsletter*, Nov. 2000.

70. Joseph Plumb Martin, *A Narrative of Some of the Adventures, Dangers, and Sufferings of a Revolutionary Soldier: Interspersed with Anecdotes of Incidents That Occurred within His Own Observation* (Hallowed, ME: Glazier, Masters, and Co., 1830), p. 165–75.

71. Tomlinson, *Young Folks History of the Revolution,* p. 380.

72. Washington's diary, quoted in http://www.thehistoryreader.com/modern-history/british-surrender-george-washingtons-diary-articles-capitulation/.

73. http://www.christianitytoday.com/gleanings/2013/july/missionaries-countries-sent-received-csgc-gordon-conwell.html.

74. Benjamin Tallmadge, *Memoir of Col Benjamin Tallmadge*, Society of Sons of the Revolution in the State of New York, 1904, p. 73.

75. Ibid., p. 73.

76. Frank Landon Humphreys, *Life and Times of David Humphreys* (New York: G.P. Putnams Sons, 1917), p. 287.

77. Charles Morris, *Decisive Events in the Story of the Great Republic* (Philadelphia, PA: J.B. Lippincott Co., 1892), p. 145.

78. Arthur E. Palumbo, *The Authentic Constitution: An Originalist View of America's Legacy* (New York: Algoro Publishing, 2009), p. 11.

79. Noah Webster, *History of the United States* (New Haven, CT: Durrie & Peck, 1832), p. 6.

80. David Ramsay, *The Life of George Washington* (Baltimore, MD: Joseph Jewett and Cushing & Sons, 1832), p. 13.

81. See http://www.wallbuilders.com/LIBissuesArticles. asp?id=111.

82. Rufus King, *The Life and Correspondence of Rufus King*, Charles R. King, editor (New York: G.P. Putnam's Sons, 1900), Vol. VI, p. 276, to C. Gore on February 17, 1820.

83. From the Journals of Congress, http://memory.loc. gov/cgi-bin/query/r?ammem/hlaw:@field(DOCID+@ lit(jc00237)).

84. http://avalon.law.yale.edu/18th_century/fed85.asp.

85. Elbridge S. Brooks, *The Story of the United States of America, Told for Young People* (Boston, MA: Lothrop Pub. Co., 1898), p. 121.

86. John Fiske, *Civil Government in the United States* (Boston and New York: Houghton, Mifflin and Co., 1892), p. 209.

87. http://www.ushistory.org/more/sun.htm.

88. http://www.archives.gov/exhibits/american_originals/ inaugtxt.html.

89. http://blog.constitutioncenter.org/2015/04/it-was-225-years-ago-today-america-gets-its-first-president/.

90. http://pabook.libraries.psu.edu/palitmap/bios/Muhlenberg__Frederick_Augustus_Conrad.html.

91. http://www.learntheconstitution.com/Constitution_Overview.html, used with permission from Linda Hackett.

92. Benjamin Pierce, *A History of Harvard University* (Cambridge, MA: Brown, Shattuck and Co., 1833), p. 5.

93. More information about this can be obtained in *For You They Signed,* by Marilyn Boyer (Green Forest, AR: Master Books, 2009), p. 326–328.

94. Washington Irving, *Adventures of Captain Bonneville* (London: Richard Bentley, 1837), p. 141.

95. http://www.christianitytoday.com/ch/booksandresources/reviews/indispensablesamueladams.html.

96. From the Last Will & Testament of Samuel Adams, attested December 29, 1790; see also Samuel Adams, *Life & Public Services of Samuel Adams*, William V. Wells, editor (Boston, MA: Little, Brown & Co., 1865), Vol. III, p. 379, Last Will and Testament of Samuel Adams.

97. Samuel Arthur Bent, *Familiar Short Sayings of Great Men: With Historical and Explanatory Short Notes* (Boston, MA: Ticknor and Co., 1882), p. 1.

98. John Adams, Letters, Vol. 1, p. 46, to Abigail Adams on June 17, 1775.

99. Robert Treat Paine, *The Papers of Robert Treat Paine*, Stephen Riley and Edward Hanson, eds. (Boston, MA: Massachusetts Historical Society, 1992), Vol. I, p. 48, March/April, 1749.

100. From an autographed letter in our possession written by Charles Carroll to Charles W. Wharton, Esq., on September 27, 1825, from Doughoragen, Maryland.

101. Boyer, *For You They Signed,* p. 135.

102. John Witherspoon, *The Works of John Witherspoon* (Edinburgh: J. Ogle, 1815), Vol. V, p. 276, 278, The Absolute Necessity of Salvation Through Christ, January 2, 1758.

103. William Sapphire, ed., *Lend Me Your Ears: Great Speeches in History* (New York: Norton and Co., 2004), p. 480.

104. Thomas Miller, ed., *The Selected Writings of John Witherspoon* (Carbondale and Edwardsville, IL: Southern Illinois Univ. Press, 1990), p. 31.

105. Lewis Henry Boutell, *The Life of Roger Sherman* (Chicago, IL: A.C. McClurg and Company, 1896), p. 272–273.

106. B.J. Lossing, *Biographical Sketches of the Signers of the Declaration of Independence* (New York: Derby and Jackson, 1856), p. 55.

107. David Barton, Benjamin Rush (Aledo, TX: Wallbuilders Press, 1999), p. 32–33, from Rush, Autobiography, p. 162–163

108. 108-Merle Sinclair and Annabel Douglas MacArthur, They Signed for Us (New York: Duell and Sloan and Pearce, 1957), p. 30.

109. B.J. Lossing, *Biographical Sketches of the Signers of the Declaration of Independence* (New York: Derby and Jackson, 1856), p. 167.

110. Ibid., p. 96.

111. David C. Whitney, *Founders of Freedom in America: Lives of the Men Who Signed the Declaration of Independence* (Chicago, IL: JG Ferguson Publ. Co., 1964), p. 126.

112. http://www.wallbuilders.com/LIBissuesArticles. asp?id=62.